A COMMUNITY AT WAR

The Civil War in Bath
and North Somerset
1642 - 1650

JOHN WROUGHTON

THE LANSDOWN PRESS
1992

First published in Great Britain in 1992 by
The Lansdown Press, 6 Ormonde House, Sion Hill, Bath BA1 2UN

ISBN 0 9520249 0 X

Produced by R. Milsom & Associates (0454) 312879

CONTENTS

Acknowledgements

I should like to express my sincere thanks to the following people who have contributed in various ways to the production of this book:

Dr Ronald Hutton, my Tutor, for his encouragement and inspiration during the completion of my doctorate at Bristol University; Dr John Morrill and Professor John Guy, my examiners, for their helpful suggestions and advice; Mr Stephen Beck for his excellent line-drawing in the text; Mrs Marta Inskip and Miss Elizabeth Holland, my fellow researchers into the history of seventeenth century Bath, for placing at my disposal their considerable expertise and the fruits of their scholarly work on the period; Mr Mike Chapman for his three superb maps; Mr Stephen Bird, of Bath City Council Museums Service, for his constant support and practical assistance in bringing this book to publication; the staff of the British Library and the Public Record Office in London, the Bodleian Library in Oxford, the County Record Offices in Taunton and Trowbridge, the National Portrait Gallery Archive, the Bath Reference Library, the Bristol Record Office, the Cambridge University Library and the Bath Record Office for all their patience, courtesy and advice; the Governors of King Edward's School, Bath for granting me leave of absence during a sabbatical term at Pembroke College, Oxford, where much of the additional research for this book was undertaken; Mrs June Hodgson for her accurate and painstaking typing of the text; Mr John Glen for the compilation of the index.

Illustration Acknowledgements

Photographs and illustrations on the following pages are reproduced by courtesy and permission of the following:

Ashmolean Museum, Oxford 70, 71, 89, 98, 105, 109, 111, 114, 121; Bath Archaeological Trust 35; Bath Record Office, Bath City Council 119, 154, 195; Mr Stephen Beck 12, 17, 20, 74, 90, 106, 107, 108, 123, 125, 134, 140, 144, 146, 159, 166, 185; The British Library 35, 46, 99, 103, 130, 180; Mr Mike Chapman 33, 101, 104; Mrs Marta Inskip 51; The Lord Bishop of Bath and Wells 58 and cover (from a photograph provided by the Paul Mellon Centre for Studies in British Art); The Lord Oxford and Asquith 44 (from a photograph provided by the Radstock, Midsomer Norton and District Museum Society); The Lord Saye and Sele 94; Methuin Collection, Corsham Court, Wiltshire 31 and cover (from a photograph provided by the Courtauld Institute of Art); National Portrait Gallery 60, 73, 92, 96, 117, 127, 167; Miss Elizabeth Holland 33; Plymouth City Museum and Art Gallery: Clarendon Loan Collection 126; The Rector, Bath Abbey 152; Somerset Archive and Record Service 26; Victoria Art Gallery, Bath 10, 13, 15, 18, 22 (bottom), 24; Sir David Seton Wills, former owner of Littlecote House 42, 76 (items now in the Royal Armouries Collection); York City Art Gallery 122.

The following were taken from the author's own collection (copyright reserved) 6, 8, 9, 11, 14, 16, 22 (top), 36, 37, 48, 100, 102, 110, 112 (by permission of Mrs Caroline Davey), 164; with these photographs taken on his behalf by Mr Hugh Bungay 42, 45, 76, 128, 152.

1.
The Community on the Eve of War

The five Hundreds, which formed the north-eastern corner of Somerset, in many ways shared a similar outlook and a similar economy. Hemmed in by the Mendip Hills to the south, the river Avon to the north and the Selwood Forest to the east, they had a character and an identity which marked them off from the rest of the county.

In the first place, the inhabitants were far more part of the mainstream of life than were their neighbours in other areas of Somerset, who were somewhat isolated by the steep hills and impossible roads over the Mendip barrier. For the merchants and traders who lived in the north-eastern sector, however, access to the markets of London was comparatively easy. Regular visits to the capital inevitably exposed them to the fierce political and religious debates of the 1630s, thus creating in them an awareness of current issues which was somewhat unusual in countrymen of that time. They therefore became much more radical, independent and self-sufficient than their more conservative colleagues in the south of the county - qualities which not only characterised their conduct throughout the war, but also ensured that they played a major role in it.[1]

Secondly, the community which made up the Hundreds of Bathforum, Keynsham, Wellow, Frome and Kilmersdon (see map) enjoyed a fairly prosperous standard of living. In spite of periods of severe recession and pockets of noticeable poverty within the area, there was sufficient in-built affluence for most of its inhabitants to survive major disasters such as civil war. Its economy was well-diversified and was largely based on a recently-revived cloth industry, a mixed farming operation and a highly lucrative health trade in the City of Bath. The proximity of Bristol, a thriving port, increased its market opportunities. On the other hand, these advantages also ensured that North-East Somerset became a main artery for the armies of both King and parliament as they wrestled for control of Bristol and competed to quarter in 'as fruitful parts as are in England'.[2]

(i) Population, Wealth and Poverty

A close examination of Somerset Hearth Tax Assessments for 1664-65 uncover the detail of parish structure, population, affluence and poverty at the end of our period after the Civil War and Interregnum had done their worst to the local economy (see below). The returns are complete or almost complete for the City of Bath and the Hundreds of Bathforum, Wellow and Keynsham; they are something like half complete for the Hundreds of Frome and Kilmersdon. [3]

There is little doubt that the affluence of the area was based to a large extent on the City of Bath. In general terms, it is true to say that people living nearer to the city were more affluent and that those living further away were more subject to poverty. The reasons for this marked feature will be fully analysed later, but they chiefly centre around the diversification of the economy which enabled the city and its surrounding area to survive the harsh realities of both the pre-war depression and the wartime atrocities - diversification of agriculture, diversification of industry and diversification within the cloth trade. Bathforum was therefore the most affluent Hundred in North-East Somerset, closely followed by Keynsham. Although 55.5 per cent of Bathforum's population lived

NORTH·EAST SOMERSET IN THE 17TH CENTURY

BRISTOL
R. Avon
GLOUCESTER
Brislington
WILTS

KEYNSHAM

BATHFORUM
Langridge
North Stoke
Woolley
Swainswick
Whitchurch
Queen
Charlton
Saltford
Kelston
Charlcombe
Batheaston
KEYNSHAM
Weston
Bathampton
Dundrey
Burnett
Newton
St. Loe
Twerton
BATH
Claverton
Compton
Dando
Publoe
Stanton
Prior
Englishcombe
CHEW
Hunstrete
Markesbury
South
Stoke
Combe
Chelwood
Priston
BRADFORD
Clutton
Farmborough
Combe
Hay
Freshford
Timsbury
Dunkerton
Hinton
Charterhouse
Wellow
Paulton
Camerton
WELLOW
Farleigh
Hungerford
Norton
St. Philip
Tellisford
CHEWTON
Foxcote
Radstock
Writhlington
Woolverton
Hemington
Laverton
Rode
Kilmersdon
Lullington
Beckington
Babington
Stratton
Binegar
Holcombe
Mells
Elme
Berkley
Ashwick
KILMERSDON
FROME
Leigh-upon-
Mendip
Whatley
FROME
Stokeland
Nunney
Shepton
Mallet
Cloford
Marston
Bigot
East Cranmore

THE MENDIP HILLS
Selwood Forest
R. Frome
Wanstrow
Witham
Friary
WILTS

0 1 2 3 4 5 miles

The five hundreds of North-East Somerset in 1642

J.P.W.

in houses with fewer than three hearths (normally taken to denote a fair degree of poverty) [4], this figure rose to 56.1 per cent for Keynsham, 63.2 per cent for Wellow, 67.9 per cent for Frome and 71.7 per cent for Kilmersdon. On the other hand, whereas 37.6 per cent of Bathforum's inhabitants (mainly craftsmen, small merchants and farmers) lived in comfortable homes with between three and five hearths, the figure dropped to 31.5 per cent in Wellow, 26.4 per cent in Frome and 26.3 per cent in Kilmersdon, but rising to 38.1 per cent in Keynsham. Similarly, homes of between six and nine hearths, usually reflecting the fairly high standard of prosperous living enjoyed by the larger merchants and farmers, were occupied by 5.2 per cent of the residents in Bathforum, 4.5 per cent in Keynsham, 4.0 per cent in Wellow, 3.5 per cent in Frome and 1.2 per cent in Kilmersdon.

The poorest parish within Bathforum was Walcot which, curiously enough, was right on the very outskirts of Bath. No fewer than 89 per cent of its population of about 190 were distinctly poor, living in accommodation with only one or two hearths. Indeed, fifteen out of the thirty-seven houses were so dilapidated that they were exempt from paying the tax. 'The house is voyd and almost fallen downe'; 'not rated to Church nor poore by reason of his povertie'; 'very poore noe distress' - are typical comments from the Walcot returns. Even so, this figure of 40.5 per cent tax exemption for the poorest parish on the outskirts of the city and 11.4 per cent for the city itself is distinctly favourable when compared with returns from elsewhere. For example, 62 per cent of the householders were exempt in Norwich, 52 per cent in Colchester, 50 per cent in Tonbridge and Ashford, 41 per cent in Newcastle, 39 per cent in Exeter, 27 per cent in Leicester and 20 per cent in York [5]. As far as Walcot was concerned, the truth of the matter was that this run-down area had become something of a temporary refuge for the unemployed who swarmed on Bath like bees round a honeypot. The genuine inhabitants had complained to the Quarter Sessions in 1638, for instance, that

> 'one Robert Meslin of the said parishe liveinge in a cottage there hath taken into the said cottage three severall families that are chargeable to the said parishe of Walcott.'

Meslin, who was 50, lived with his wife and daughter in a rented cottage with a small garden but no land. [6] Although this situation was almost unique in Bathforum, there was a much more general problem of extreme poverty elsewhere. Even in the Hundred of Wellow which also benefited from its proximity to Bath, there was a noticeable pocket of deprivation in the extreme south-west corner where it bordered onto Wiltshire. The parishes of Norton St Philip (with 74.6 per cent of the houses with less than three hearths), Hinton Charterhouse (74.1 per cent) and Farleigh and Tellisford (70 per cent) were all extremely vulnerable to economic fluctuations, but even their plight was not as severe as that experienced by a cluster of villages at the southern tip of the Frome Hundred. No fewer than 95 per cent of the inhabitants of Wanstrow (with a population of just over two hundred) lived in poor accommodation - indeed the whole population only averaged 1.4 hearths per household. The situation, which was little better in East Cranmore (83.3 per cent) and Whatley (77.8 per cent), was largely attributable to the deafforestation of Selwood Forest and the decline in the Frome cloth industry (see below). The poverty in the Kilmersdon Hundred, however, was much more general with villagers endeavouring to eke out a meagre living from farming through gradual involvement in coalmining. Writhlington (with 90 per cent of the people living in poverty), Hemington (84.4 per cent) and Holcombe (81.2 per cent) could average little more than 1.5 hearths per household. It is perhaps significant that the poorest parish in the Keynsham Hundred was also becoming involved with coalmining. Compton Dando, with an average of 1.4 hearths per household, had 85.7 per cent of its inhabitants living in sub-standard accommodation.

Mr Ford's Lodging House in Staul Street, near the Baths, from Gilmore's map of 1694.

Nevertheless, each Hundred could also boast areas of real affluence within its boundaries, often associated with the residency of wealthy gentry. Individuals who dominated the local scene and were to play an important part in the Civil War not only possessed fine houses themselves, but in many cases managed to transform their parishes into what we would call 'high class residential areas!'. This was certainly true of the 'clothing villages' of Freshford (with an average of 3.7 hearths per household), Lullington (3.4) and Beckington (3.0), which were largely under the influence of those great families of clothiers, the Ashes and the Brewers. To a lesser extent it was true of Mells, where Sir John Horner was rated for twenty-six hearths and where an average of 2.4 hearths per household was something of a luxury in that impoverished Hundred of Kilmersdon. The village of Corston was the most affluent one in Wellow with as many as 3.9 hearths per household, although John Harington's secondary residence with nine hearths (his main one being at Kelston) was modest by comparison with that of Sir Edward Hungerford who boasted 45 hearths at Farleigh Castle. Sir William Bassett (18 hearths) at Claverton, Sir George Horner (17 hearths) at Coleford, Sir Thomas Bridges (17 hearths) at Keynsham and Sir Ralph Hopton (49 hearths) at Witham Friary completed the scene.

Taking the area of North-East Somerset as a whole, there was an average over the five Hundreds of 2.5 hearths per household, indicating a standard of living which was certainly above the breadline. Bathforum led the way with an average of 2.8 hearths, followed by Keynsham with 2.5, Wellow 2.5, Frome 2.3 and Kilmersdon 2.1. Set against these figures is the fact that the City of Bath itself enjoyed an average of 3.9 hearths per household throughout its three parishes, an indication of the prosperity that it still possessed by the middle of the seventeenth century. It denotes a far greater degree of affluence than was found in the cities of Newcastle (2.06 hearths), Exeter (2.59), Leicester (2.4) and York (3.2) [7] although its average was certainly inflated by the large number of inns and lodging houses which dominated the city. All the streets within the area of Bath's medieval walls contained comfortable stone houses with little sign of squalor, many of them reflecting the prosperity of local Tudor clothiers and depicted on Gilmore's map of 1694. [8] Binbury (i.e. the south-western corner) was the most affluent sector with an average of 7.3 hearths, followed by Westgate Street (4.8), Stall Street (4.5), Cheap Street (4.3) and

Mr More's Lodging House in the Abbey Churchyard from Gilmore's map of 1694.

Northgate Street (3.5). Poverty was most acute in the overspill areas outside the two main gates. It was worst in Southgate Street (1.9), while the returns available for Broad Street and Walcot Street indicate an average of 2.8 (see Gilmore's map below).

It is normally assumed that at this time each household would contain on average five occupants, plus a further allowance of fifteen per cent to cover domestic servants and apprentices. Using this calculation, we find that the 45 parishes outside Bath for which records survive would each average 29.1 households producing a total of 167.3 persons per parish. On the same basis, the population for Bathforum (306 houses) would be 1759, Wellow (372 houses) 2139 and Keynsham (556 houses) 3197. If

The Hart Lodging House in Staul Street, rear the Baths, from Gilmore's map of 1694.

Kilmersdon's recorded figures are doubled (half the returns are missing), it would give a rough working total of 524 houses with a population of 3012. Although assessments are only available for six parishes within the Frome Hundred and are missing from Frome itself, Hardington, Woolverton, Nunney and Babbington, the population for the area was assessed at 6,506 inhabitants by the Somerset magistrates in 1631. [9] It was certainly the most heavily populated part of the region, a factor which contributed greatly to its prolonged distress (see below). The population of Bath itself can be estimated not only from the Hearth Tax Assessments, but also from the 1641 survey of the city [10] and John Speed's Detailed Map of Bath (1611 edition). When allowance has been made for the inmates of the Hospitals and the unusually large number of servants who would be required to cater for the visitors, a population figure in the region of 2,000 residents becomes realistic, (i.e. using the same formula as above based on the number of households). [11] This number would be considerably increased by the seasonal influx of people seeking cures at the baths. There is also some evidence that the population of the city had been growing steadily. A study of the baptism and burial registers for the three parishes revealed that, between 1569 and 1625, christenings averaged 47 per annum compared with deaths which averaged 44. The total population had probably increased therefore by some 240 during the period in question. [12] Taking all these estimates into account, it seems likely that the population of the North-East Somerset by the middle of the century was roughly in the region of 18,600 people.

Mr Pocock's Lodging House in Westgate Street from Gilmore's map of 1694.

Bath was one of some seven hundred towns in England by 1603. Up to six hundred of these were small market towns and decaying boroughs with populations of less than 2,000. Then there were the centres of regional administration, like Salisbury (7000), Worcester (7000), Coventry (6500), Leicester (3500) and Warwick (3000), and finally the large provincial capitals consisting of London (200,000), York (11,000), Norwich (15,000),

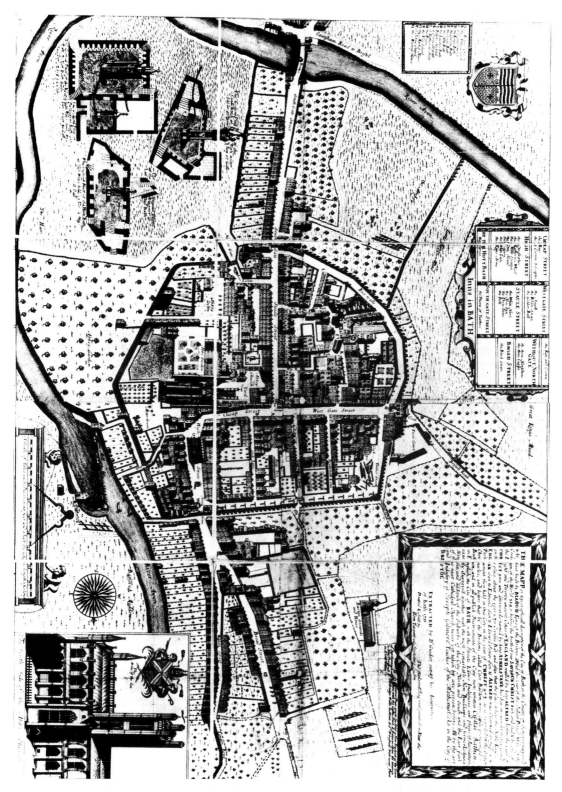

The City of Bath drawn by Joseph Gilmore in 1694.

Bristol (12,000), Exeter (9,000) and Newcastle (13,000). In spite of its age, Bath was regarded as one of the 'new' towns - a rising spa, like Tunbridge Wells, with just as specialised an economic function as the new dockyard and industrial towns (Portsmouth, Chatham, Halifax and Manchester). [13]

(ii) The City of Bath

In order to understand the dominant role played by the City of Bath during the war and its economic importance to the area of which it was part, it is necessary to examine its government and institutions, as well as the atmosphere created by its inhabitants in 1642. Thomas Venner, writing in 1628, commented: 'Bath ... is a little well compacted city,

A small surviving section of the battlements on the northern wall of the city, not far from the site of Gascoyn's Tower.

and beautified with fair and goodly buildings for the receipt of strangers'. [14] In 1642 Bath's outward form was still medieval. Most of its 'fair and goodly buildings', however, belonged to the Tudor age when the city had reached a peak of prosperity. Because the community had remained comparatively small, there had been little physical expansion over the years. The old town wall still contained the vast majority of the houses. It is true that the Walcot suburbs were already beginning to straggle out through the north gate along Broad Street and Walcot Street. It is also evident from contemporary maps that Southgate Street and Holloway were comfortably populated to the south. But these were not more than ribbon developments. On every side green fields and orchards ran right up to the very foot of the walls. Leland, visiting the city in 1530, described his approach:

> 'Or ever I came to the bridge of Bath that is over the Avon, I came down by a rokky hill, fulle or fair springes of water; and on this rokky hill is settle a longe streate as a suburbe to the Cyte of Bath ... Betwixt the bridge and the south gate of Bath I markid fair medowes on eche hand, but especially on the lift hand, and they ly by south west on the toune.' [15]

The busy North Gate standing next to the dis-used Church of St. Mary, which by 1642 housed King Edward's School in the nave and the city prison in the tower.

Bath, like Chester, Lincoln and other county towns of the period, still retained its old medieval wall as a distinctive and prominent feature.[16] The 'noble ancient wall', built of 'a time-defying stone', measured under a mile around its whole course.[17] An extension had been built from the south-west angle to the river bank to provide additional cover for the southern part of the city, already protected by the loop of the Avon. The wall and its flanking ditch had clearly been kept in good repair. Leland in 1530 remarked that 'it standith allmost alle, lakking but a peace about Gascoyn's tower'. Some years previously, Gascoyne - a local citizen - had himself built the tower in the north-west corner to repair 'a little peace of the walle that was in decay, as for a fine for a fight that he had committed in the cyte'.

The City Council continued to treat the walls with respect and, in a state of nervous tension created by parliament's rumours of catholic 'plots', had already launched a feverish programme of renovations some months before the war actually broke out. As early as 1641 it had spent the considerable sum of £36 on 'stone digginge, carryinge lyme and for makeing upp of the Towne Wall by the Prison'. Further payments were made shortly afterwards for carrying away 'rubbell from the Burrowalls', 'repairing the North and South Gates', 'scoringe of the ditch under Gascoines tower', 'stone, lyme, hurdells used at Gascoines' and 'a barr for the East-gate.'[18] Their labour was well rewarded. The walls were to survive the war. Pepys, at least, was able to spend some time in 1668 'walking round the walls of the city, which are good, and the battlements all whole'.[19]

The gateways into the city were strong and well-fortified. The North or Town Gate, 'over which stood a grotesque figure of King Bladud, was ten feet wide and fifteen feet high'. The statue would certainly be much in evidence by the outbreak of the war, reforms because Thomas Quilly had been paid six shillings as recently as 1637 'for payntinge King Bladud.'[20] This main entrance to the town, leading out onto the London Road, had a smaller postern gate of each side. The East Gate, giving access only to the mill and the river, was by comparison quite small. It was a mere nine feet high and seven feet wide. The West Gate, which looked out across the common and meadows to Bristol, was described as 'a very large, clumsy pile of buildings' and was finally pulled down in 1776. Over the gate, apparently, were 'some handsome apartments, occasionally used by divers of the Royal family and other persons of distinction in their visits to the city'. The South Gate, which had been rebuilt in 1362, had fine statues of Edward III, Bishop Ralph and Prior John in a niche over the arch. Not far way was the Ham Gate which gave direct access into the Abbey ground. The South Gate took the traveller out across the bridge up Holloway and Beechen Cliff on to the Fosse Way. The bridge itself, supported by five 'fair stone arches' had a separate gate at the far end flanked on one side by a bear and on the other by a lion, each carved in stone.[21] It also carried at least one shop, owned by Nicholas Long, who paid the Council a nominal rent of 3s. 4d.[22]

Even by 1642, the atmosphere of the medieval, walled town was still very real in Bath. 'The streets are most of the narrowest size', wrote Chapman, 'especially that nearest the centre, called the Cheap street, the greatest eye-sore to its beauty.'[23] These rather cramped conditions, brought about by the smallness of the defended area, were unhealthy to say the least. Foul-smelling rubbish accumulated on every footpath to rot away slowly in the still and humid air of Bath. Although the city's revised charter of 1590 had given the Corporation powers to make by-laws over such matters as street cleaning, it was not until 1646 that these were taken up. The evidence is that previously the streets were only cleaned at very irregular intervals. Payments were made occasionally by the Chamberlain for 'shovlinge upp the Durte in Westgate Street', 'cleansing ye way by the Bridge', or 'cleansing the way by the Burrowalls'[24] but little systematic was attempted until the

An engraving of 1845, showing the East Gate with part of the city wall.

in 1646. Even as late as 1654, John Evelyn described the streets as 'narrow, uneven, and unpleasant'. Samuel Pepys, however, writing in 1668, referred to the town as being 'most of stone, and clean, though the streets generally narrow'.

The streets, nevertheless, were certainly well cobbled and kept in reasonable repair. Sometimes it was only a matter of employing workmen 'for mending the highways at Holway' or for 'pitching at Southgate'. But occasionally whole stretches of road were completely re-made. In 1648, for instance, the Council re-surfaced 268 yards of Westgate Street and 'under ye gate', a task which required thirty-four loads of stone. Fourteen loads of 'rubbish stone' were carted away by the workers who spent in all a week on the job. (25)

The sanitary arrangements were probably no better and no worse than in most cities at this time. Judging by references in the 1646 regulations, earth closets were almost certainly in use in the houses. Payments made in 1634 'for cleansing the hame privye' would seem to suggest that at least one public convenience had been situated near the Ham Gate. Whether this was abused by vandals or merely over-used by visitors is difficult to tell, but in 1636 the Chamberlain sealed its fate by paying money for 'walling upp the privie door and 2 sacks of lime'. It was usual practice at this time for dung from domestic closets to be dumped outside the city or flung into the river. However, in 1613 such behaviour had been banned by the Council, who appointed a scavenger to collect the refuse and ordered the citizen to 'send his dust to be brought to the scavenger's cart ... in some vessel to be emptied into the said cart'. Water-borne diseases, like typhoid, thrived when rivers were carelessly polluted.

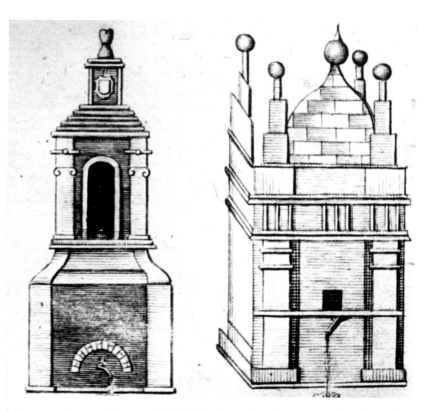

Two of the stone water conduits or public drinking fountains, the one on the left situated outside the North Gate and the one of the right in the centre of the High Street. Drawings are taken from Joseph Gilmore's map of Bath, 1694.

Bath, however, had one vital asset which helped to protect its citizens from these terrible hazards to health - an abundant supply of fresh water. As early as 1530 Leland had noticed that Bath

> 'is environed on every side with great hills, out of the which come many springs of pure water, that be conveyed by divers ways to serve the city. Insomuch that lead being made there at hand, many houses in the town have pipes of lead to convey water from place to place'.[26]

This remarkable situation meant that Bath was never obliged to rely on the polluted waters of the Avon and thus was able to maintain its reputation as a healthy place (unlike Bristol, for instance, where plague from the rat-infested port frequently swept through its densely packed population).

The water was carried down into the city by a variety of underground lead pipes and stone watercourses. Even wooden pipes seem to have been used in Walcot Lane. Needless to say, all these required regular attention and repair from the Council, which had seemingly made itself generally responsible for the system. Frequent references are thus made in the Bath Chamberlain's Accounts to 'mending water course at Becknall', 'mendinge the pipes at Walcott', 'opening the grounde in Blinde Lane to mend the pipes' etc... The expense involved in this was considerable. From 1647, therefore, the Council paid Thomas Burford £2 a year to look after the important watercourse from Beechen Cliff to Southgate.

A drawing of the west front of Bath Abbey by Daniel King, published in 1655.

People who could not afford the luxury of their own piped supply were able to obtain fresh water from several conduits erected at points around the city. These were often lavishly decorated with elegant stone work. St Mary's conduit stood in the middle of the street just inside the North Gate -

> 'a handsome quadrangular reservoir of water, built in the Dorick Style, with a cymatium roof terminating in a point, and decorated with pinnacles at the angles'.

Not far away, near the Market hall, was the High Cross Conduit actually built in the form of a cross. Stall's Conduit was placed on the Bear Corner at the junction of Cheap Street with Stall Street. At the end of this street, just outside the South Gate, was St James's Conduit. St Michael's Conduit, 'a handsome lofty structure, composed of four Ionick pilasters, standing upon a pedastal' was situated outside the North Gate - not far from the Broad Street Conduit and the Carnwell Conduit in Walcot Street.[27] With all these facilities and a well into the bargain at the North Gate (which safeguarded the city's supply during time of siege), Bath was spared the anxieties and problems over health which affected most cities at this time.

In Worcester, for instance, the Corporation had not only failed to give proper attention to the City's water supply, but had also failed to appoint scavengers after the example of Bath, Chester and Norwich. Although a private scheme for piped water had been launched in 1614, this did not become the responsibility of the Council, as was the case in Bath. Health hazards in Worcester were alarming with the river constantly polluted from the dyers' vats and outbreaks of the plague frequent. The bubonic plague was in fact the scourge of most towns. Norwich suffered six epidemics between 1579 and 1666; Bristol lost a sixth of its population on three occasions between 1565 and 1603; Newcastle witnessed a mortality rate of a third during the epidemic of 1646-7; and Chester lost over two thousand during the attack of 1647. Bath, by comparison, remained largely immune, except for one small-scale outbreak in 1625 (see below).[28]

St James's Church near the South Gate from Gilmore's map of 1694.

Several important buildings dominated the Bath Street scene. The Abbey Church of St Peter and St Paul, with its gardens and churchyard, monopolised the south-east corner of the city. This fine building had been started by Bishop Oliver King in 1499 as a new church for the old Abbey, halted before completion by the dissolution of the monasteries in 1539 and only finished in 1616 at the instigation of Queen Elizabeth on an earlier visit to the city. By 1572 the Corporation had bought up the advowsons of all the city churches, which were soon consolidated into one rectory. The Abbey inevitably became the city parish church, taking over this role from St Mary de Stalls, which fell into dis-use together with the churches of St Mary's (by the North Gate) and St Michael's (by the West Gate). By 1640, therefore, only two other churches had survived - St James's Church, just inside the South Gate, which according to Collinson, was 'ancient and curious, consisting of a nave, chancel, and north aisle, with an embattled tower at the west end'; and St Michaels' Church, just outside the North Gate - 'a small venerable structure of one pace or aisle, with a chancel on the east and a lofty quadrangular tower at the west end'.

The medieval church of St. Michael, Bath, which was demolished in 1731, as depicted in a lithograph of 1835 by Joseph Hollway.

When Samuel Pepys visited the city in 1668, he saw a 'pretty good market place, and many good streets, and very fair stone houses'.[29] The Town Hall and Market House, built in 1625 after a plan of Inigo Jones and demolished in 1777, stood in the middle of the High Street. Just outside were the city pillory, originally erected in 1612, and the city stocks. Both of these are clearly shown on Speed's earlier map and were still very much in use in 1642 for the punishment of local offenders. In 1634, for instance, money was found by the Chamberlain 'for mending the stocks'. More hardened criminals were committed to the town prison which, in 1642, consisted of the tower of St Mary's, a dis-used church

16

The Schoolroom inside the dis-used Church of St. Mary by the North Gate.

inside the North Gate. The Free School, founded by King Edward VI, occupied the nave of the same church (before it moved into Broad Street in 1752). A good deal of money was spent by the Council on both the schoolmaster's stipend (£20) and the upkeep of the buildings. In 1640 the tiled roof had been repaired and money spent on 'white lineinge the school house' and 'nails and plasteringe used there'.[30]

The government of the city was conferred, by the revised Charter of 1590, on a 'body corporate' consisting of a Mayor (who in 1640 carried a stipend of £50), between four and ten aldermen and up to twenty Common Councillors. This Corporation could elect new members onto the Council for life from amongst the ranks of the freemen of the city. Freedom could be gained in Bath either by servitude (i.e. serving a seven year apprenticeship under a resident freeman of the city) or by purchase (i.e. paying a sum not less than £5 into the coffers of the Corporation). The Corporation, which had the power to return two Burgesses to parliament, was assisted by various officials - a Chamberlain (who in 1640 was paid a stipend of £8), A Recorder (£2), a Town Clerk (£2), two Constables, two Justices, two Bailiffs and two Sergeants-at-Mace. Apart from the Recorder and Town Clerk, these officers were normally drawn from the members of the Council on the basis of one year's spell of duty. Refusal to take office could mean a fine or even imprisonment.

Bath's Corporation was somewhat smaller in size than that of many other towns in seventeenth century England. Aldermen and Common Councillors sat together as a self-perpetuating oligarchy in one body with no great discrimination between them but with the freemen excluded from all say in elections and government. This was also the case at Gloucester, where the governing body was a forty-six strong council, which included

The Guildhall and Market House as depicted in Edward Eyre's watercolour of the High Street of c.1776.

twelve Aldermen.[31] Elsewhere, the situation was different. At Worcester, there were two distinct grades within the governing body, the Companies of the Twenty-Four and the Forty-Eight. Although these met as a unit in Common Council, chief officers were only elected from within the 24, whose leading members also formed the magisterial bench and the Court of Record. At Windsor, there were three grades - the Aldermen, the Benchers and the Brethren.[32] Small, powerful groups of wealthy merchants and businessmen therefore tended to monopolise power in many of the towns, including Chester, where the 40 Common Councillors were always subservient to the Aldermanic bench of 24;[33] Bristol, where the 12 Aldermen, though part of a single Council of 43, met separately to discuss business before joining the Common Councillors and were largely key members of the Society of Merchant Venturers;[34] Newcastle, where the 10 Aldermen were selected for life, whereas the Twenty-Four others who made up the Council were selected annually, and where an inner ring of mercers and coal-traders emerged as a governing clique;[35] Exeter, where a small, closed obligarchy of 24 (the total size of the Council) filled all the offices between them; York where effective power lay with an inner elite of Aldermen; and Norwich, where the 24 Aldermen (the Norwich Court) took decisions which the 60 Common Councillors merely ratified. Norwich was also the borough in which freemen were most politically active. Whereas in other places, members of the Corporation usually had the sole right under the terms of their Charter to fill any vacancies which occurred and to appoint their officers, in Norwich the freemen nominated and elected all the Aldermen and Common Councillors as well as nominating the two candidates for mayor. In Exeter, Bristol, Newcastle and York, on the other hand, the power of the freemen was limited to the election of mayor from two candidates nominated by the inner clique[36] This was also the case in Bedford from 1649, although there at least the freemen had 13 representatives on a governing body of 70.[37]

The Corporation owned the vast majority of the property in Bath and were very much responsible for maintaining law and order. The Mayor, the Recorder and the two Justices had the power not only to apprehend felons, thieves and malefactors, but also to enforce local laws by the imposition of fines. Civil disputes concerning trespass and debts were heard every Monday at the Court of Record by the Mayor, the Recorder, two Aldermen and the Town Clerk. The Mayor, in addition, was both the Coroner and the Clerk-of-the Market, which was held twice a week on Wednesday and Saturdays. Finally, the Court of Piepowder met under a bailiff to try offenders during times of the ancient city fairs.[38]

Before the days of professional police forces and fire services, the Corporation was also directly responsible for the security of the City, its buildings and its inhabitants. In Bath, during peacetime, the gates were locked at night and the streets patrolled by a bellman and two watchmen.[39] A new bell had been purchased in 1636 for the bellman, [40] who was required by the council to call out the time and to raise the alarm on sight of fire or felon:

'Ordered that John Davis shall be the Bellman of this Cittie for one yere next coming to walk the street of the Cittie every night from the houres of ten of the clock at night till three in the morning in summer and the hour of nine of the clock at night till five in the morning in winter and to have for his paines 10 li per annum to be paid quarterly by a general rate made throughout the Cittie.'[41]

The watchmen, who accompanied him, were sworn not to enter any house until their tour of duty was over, on pain of imprisonment. They were sometimes rewarded with gifts of beer by the Council[42] and were always responsible for dealing with suspicious characters. This was not easy in dark, unlit streets. Some light at least was given by the new lantern bought in 1642 for six shillings and erected on the front of the Town Hall - although it was frequently in a state of disrepair.[43] Fires were even more worrying than intruders in the days when some buildings were still made of wood and many were still thatched with straw. The Council attempted to reduce the risk by making it a condition of lease

'that every person that hath thatched house shall not mend his house with thatch or newe thatche his house, but shall repair it with tyle or slate'.

In 1641 the Corporation, ever conscious of this hazard, bought twenty buckets for four pounds, which were hung on hooks outside the Town Hall.[44] At the same time, 'towne ladders' were purchased, partly for use on the walls and partly for use during fires.

News of imminent danger, as well as imminent taxation and other disasters, was broadcast locally by the Town Cryer. For this he was paid a stipend of ten shillings and provided with a special 'coate and buttons' freshly made in 1638.[45] The City was well equipped to deal with any physical danger his news might threaten. Even before the outbreak of war in 1642, Bath maintained a useful armoury inside the Town Hall. There is no doubt that this was kept in good condition: weapons were repaired regularly and replaced where necessary. In 1640 John Gray was paid £2 for 'scourringe the armor'; while in 1636 further money was spent on 'mending faults in the armourie - 2 new rests, 5 more scowerers' and 'a board to set the armour on'. Three years later a good deal of additional stock was bought - bandoliers, three musket stocks, a new musket for 16s. 6d, 200lb of powder for £16 3s 4d, ' a Spanish picke' for 6s 8d, a rest and 'tuch boxes' for 1s 3d, and 'reade cloth for the pickes'.[46]

Nor were these weapons merely there for show. From 1573 Elizabeth had based the country's defences largely on the 'trained bands' of citizens within each county. This system, financed by a 'trained-soldier's rate', had survived into the Stuart times. Deputy-Lieutenants were responsible for calling periodic musters to see that the men of this

Trained Bands on exercise.

militia were in fact adequately trained. By 1638 the local force in Somerset numbered 4,000 foot and 300 horse. The infantry was organised into five regiments each based on a particular part of the county. Sir Robert Phelps commanded the Bath Regiment of 800 pikes and muskets drawn not only from the city itself, but also from the whole surrounding area of North-East Somerset. Within the regiment, the seven companies were each recruited from a group of neighbouring parishes, which helped to produce something of a local spirit. [47] Bath would probably contribute between twenty and thirty men, whose arms were provided by the city and stored, as we have seen, in the Town Hall.

However, we do know from a muster roll, dated in Bath on 22nd May 1639, that Sir Ralph Hopton commanded a company of two hundred foot soldiers within the Bath Regiment. The structure and organisation are clearly indicated. Hopton was assisted by eleven officers (a lieutenant, a quartermaster, an ensign, four sergeants, a clerk and two drums) who together were responsible for pikemen and musketeers in fairly equal numbers. Almost half the company's strength was drawn from the Keynsham Hundred, with larger towns like Keynsham providing a quota of eight men and smaller ones like Stanton Drew just three. A few villages only from within the Hundreds of Bathforum, Frome and Wellow contributed the remainder, although there is no doubt that the company was chiefly associated with the Keynsham area. Bath itself was not represented in this part of the regiment. [48] Bristol, as one would expect, had a much larger detachment of Trained Bands. According to one visitor during the 1630's, the local Captains frequently drilled the three foot companies in the Marsh, where the river 'causeth a sweet and pleasant echo of their martiall musicke, drums, fifes and volleys of shot.' There was in addition a volunteer company 'of gentile, proper, martiall, disciplined men, who have their armes lodged in a handsome artillery house, newly built up in the Castle Yard, where once a yeere, they invite and entertain both Earles and Lords, and a great many knights and Gentleman of rank and quality, at their military feast; and this yard affords them a spacious and a large place to drill and to exercise in.' [49]

Although Bath was a fairly affluent city, not all its inhabitants were prosperous. Indeed, the problem of poverty, which was just as real there as elsewhere, became a source of increasing anxiety to the Corporation. The Poor Law Act of 1601, as a counter to the growing number of vagabonds, had enabled local authorities to establish Houses of Correction (or Bridewells) so that the jobless poor could be set to work in rather harsh surroundings. The Somerset magistrates had decided as early as 1624, when poverty and unemployment were reaching a peak (see below), to establish three Houses of Correction to serve the county at Taunton, Ivelchester and Shepton Mallet, funded by rates charged on local residents. The five hundreds, which formed the north-eastern sector, were provided for by the one at Shepton Mallet. [50] Bath Corporation, however, did not take action until 1630 - the year of the Midford Hill riots (see Chapter 2) - when the Chamberlain received the first three voluntary subscriptions of £5 each (from Mr Robert Hyde, Dr Mountayne and the Bishop of London) 'towards the building of a House of Correction'.[51] Although Bath was always able to survive a period of acute hardship, poverty in the city was frequently aggravated by the seasonal presence of wealthy visitors who attracted beggars like bees round a honeypot:

> Many beggars in that place, some natives there, others repairing thither from all parts of the land, the poor for alms, the pained for ease; whither should flock in an hard frost, but to the barn door? Hence all the two seasons the general confluence of this gentry. Indeed, laws are daily made to restrain beggars, and daily broke by the connivance of those who make them; it being impossible, when the hungry belly barks and the bowles sound, to keep the tongue silent. And although oil of whip be the proper plaster for the cramp of laziness, yet some pity is due to impotent person. [52]

By 1630, the city councillors had decided, in the face of a threatening situation, to implement their work ethic and to apply the 'whip' on 'the cramp of laziness'. Two years later, as subscriptions continued to trickle in, they finally resolved 'to sett the poore of this cittie to work'. Suitable premises were finally found in the north-western corner of the city (in what later became known as Bridewell Lane) when Mr Chambers as paid £5 'to quit the possession of a barne stable and backside which is to be converted into House of Correction...for the setting of poore people on worke.' A committee was formed to receive and list further contributions which were then to be applied to necessary alterations of existing fabric. The work was considered to be of such urgency that, as contributions began to dry up towards the end of 1634, the council resolved to charge a general rate on the whole town 'towards the finishinge of the House of Correction'. Although little is known of its conditions, small clues appear in payments made for 'window bars' and 'wooden barrs' (denoting its prison-like atmosphere); 'hookes and twists' from Goody Smith (suggesting employment); and the loan of a rope Goody Parker 'to digge the well at the house of correction'. [53]

The city's ruling elite had earlier reacted swiftly to another apparent threat to civil order. Their growing anxiety over the problem of widespread unemployment and poverty was nothing compared with the panic that swept through the area in 1625 in connection with plague. The 'contageious sickness did so much affright' the inhabitants of Widcombe 'that they were fearful to come on in others company'. Alarming news also spread from Frome of a man called Phillips who had returned from London with his wife and child, having been exposed to the 'infeccon of the plague'. The authorities ordered them to be locked up in a house outside the town and placed under strong guard at the door, which remained until the family eventually died. [54] In Bath, the Corporation also isolated those who were sick of the plague by building three special houses 'for the sicke folkes' on the Common, but saw that they were well catered for by spending £13 1s 8d on their succour in the following year. [55]

In one sense, this isolation of the poor and the sick helped to bring about a polarisation of society within the community of Bath. There is, however, no evidence to suggest that the behaviour of the local elite during the 1620's and 1630's was characterised by undue harshness. Indeed, the picture we gain from the Chamberlain's Accounts and the Minute

Books is one of a society which continued care deeply for those less fortunate. The Act of 1601 had also allowed parish officers to use the poor rate to provide assistance for the aged or sick either by supporting them in a poor house or by granting them doles of money, food or clothing. That Bath was quick to provide this form of 'pity' to 'impotent persons' is abundantly clear, through its maintenance of four almshouses for elderly people (see below). The charity of the Corporation was also expressed in the form of annual gifts to those in need; 'To the poor in bread at Lent - £5 2s.', 'to the poor in coal at Michaelmas '£2 8s.', 'to the poor in wood - £3 4s.'

St John's Hospital, from Gilmore's map of 1694.

Occasionally, special additional payments were made to deal with particular circumstances; 'for provisions for the poore people out in the field - 15s 0d.', 'more for wood given to the poore of the cittie', 'for warme feed for the sicke folkes - 4d.'

It was further shown in a regular sequence of small acts of kindness to individuals in distress. Thus money was devoted to 'mendinge Joan Emonds chimly' and 'widdow Tysocks windowe'; 'for a pair of shoes for Comings boy'; 'for 4 shirts for 2 boys of the widdow Uggins'; 'a shroud for Walter Werrett's child'; 'for making the grave and ringing the bell for goody Uggins'; 'a shroude for a poor man that was drownd and for a grave'; 'to two and thirty poore widowes - £1 12s 0d.'; 'for 3 ells of hambrow and threed to make blind man a shroude'. Apart from these gifts for clothing, funeral expenses and fabric repairs, the Council sometimes provided money for the upkeep of pauper children who had been orphaned. Twelve shillings, for instance was paid to John Bush for 'the keeping of goody Uggens youngest sonn'. [56] The result of Bath's twin policy of 'whip' and 'pity' was that poverty in the city never seriously got out of hand - 'for such care is taken' wrote Henry Chapman, 'that the wealthier sort eat their morsels free from such importunate clamours and outcries as are too frequently seen in other places that have a higher celebration for riches, this principally arising (without doubt) from Magistratical care, at every Quarter Sale day wherein the poorer sort are not only kindly used (beyond comparison) but are also so tyed up, that they cannot squander away their good bargains, but are reserved in case of necessity to their needy families'. The poor rate collected from the three city parishes amounted to under £30 per annum [57] and, although Chapman's words imply a certain degree of polarisation, the city was nevertheless compassionate in its approach.

In addition to granting these spasmodic doles, Bath Corporation also heavily involved itself in the maintenance of the four almshouses (or hospitals) which catered for some of the city's aged and sick. St Johns' hospital, situated near the Cross Bath, had been directly under the Council's control since 1578. Founded originally in 1180 'for the succour of such

Bellot's Hospital as it appeared in an engraving of 1845.

sick poor as came hither for the benefit of the water',[58] by 1640 it maintained four poor men and four poor women each with a weekly allowance of 4s 2d. These were clothed in blue gowns, with white cotton linings and clasps.[59] They attended prayers twice daily in the Hospital's own chapel and were under the care of three paid officials - the Master, the Reader and the Washer.

Not far away in Binbury Lane, near the South Gate, stood St Catherine's Hospital or the Black Alms House. Rebuilt by the Corporation in 1553, it was ' a mean structure, two stories high and contains fourteen tenements for as many poor persons of either sex, ten of whom only have the allowance of three shillings and sixpence each weekly, and a black coat once in two years'.[60] The Council frequently concerned itself with repairs to the fabric, gifts or money to the occupants and donations of wood and coal. Ten new black gowns with red linings were made in 1643.[61]

Just round the corner from Binbury Lane was Bellot's Hospital, founded originally in Elizabeth's reign. According to Collinson, 'It is a small low building and contains fourteen apartments, the entrance into which is from the court within.' Twelve poor men and women were given free lodging, free baths and 2s 10d per week for six months of the year. [62] Finally, just outside the city, there was the Alms House belonging to the Chapel of St Mary Magdalene on Holloway. This received at least the occasional Christmas gift from the Council in the form of money.[63]

Nevertheless, life was hard and luxuries rare for most of Bath's working population in 1642. Wages for manual workers varied from one shilling a day for assistant plumbers and road repairers to 9d a day for 'Oulde Frye' whose job consisted of 'casting rubish abroade'.[64] The lowest paid worker would therefore average about 5 shillings a week and would doubtless rely heavily on the supplementary earnings of the rest of the family. When it is realised that the poor people of St John's Hospital were allowed 4s 2d a week for maintenance, it soon becomes clear that ordinary workers outside - with rent to pay and families to support - would find 5 shillings scarcely adequate.

More skilful workers, like the pump maker employed at the Bridewell could earn 3 shillings per day. Professional people were slightly better off and certainly more secure. Mr Mynn the Schoolmaster, for instance, was paid a salary of £20 per annum, plus board and lodging. Although the exact cost of living is difficult to assess, prices of certain items are recorded in the Bath Chamberlain's Accounts. Small bread loaves and cakes cost a penny each; rabbits sixpence each; a sack of coal eightpence; boys' shoes 2s 4d a pair; stockings 1s 4d a pair; shirts 3s 1 1/2d each; a pint of sack eightpence.[65] It was extremely difficult, therefore, for most working families to provide more than the basic food, heat and rent. Clothes were made to last.

In addition to the security of the walled area, the Council was also responsible for much of the land outside. Bath Common, on the north-west side of the city, was controlled by the Mayor and Corporation on behalf of the freemen who shared equally in its use and profits. A hayward and two or three overseers of the common were appointed annually to execute orders which the Council issued from time to time:

'Ordered that the Comon Groundes belonging to this Cittie shall from henceforth by hayned only for hay and no cattle shall be put therein till the hay be out and carried and the hay thereof shall be sold to the best advantage and the rent and other necessary charges being deducted, the overplus shall be equally divided amonst all the freemen of this Cittie. And that after the hay of the said ground shall be carried, the overseers of the same shall take in cattle for the rest of this year...[66]

The overseers were responsible for keeping a careful check that the number of cattle and sheep allowed to each freeman on the common was not exceeded and that each animal was 'marked with a piched marke'. A pound was certainly still in use for straying cattle

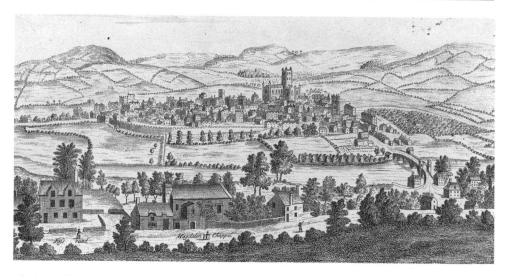

A view of Bath from the south engraved from a drawing by William Stukeley in 1723. The medieval fortifications are still clearly visible.

and a lock was provided for its door in 1646.[67] The common was also extensively used for quarrying stone for road repairs inside the city.[68]

The City of Bath, then, was an affluent, vigorous and well-administered city with many assets as it faced up to the challenge of the Civil War. It dominated the area both politically and economically, sharing a common interest in both trade and agriculture.

(iii) THE LOCAL ECONOMY
(a) Agriculture:

One feature of North-East Somerset in the early seventeenth century was a growing interest in the idea of producing goods for the market, as well as for personal use.

This commitment to the market economy was increasingly witnessed in the operation of agriculture throughout the region. It was not uncommon for townsmen in the seventeenth century to supplement their urban trades with agricultural activities. The smell of the countryside was still strong, even within the confines of a walled city like Oxford, where animals were regularly kept. Leicester, like Bath, enjoyed its orchards and gardens within the walls, whereas Barnstable could even boast some arable land.[69] Many of the wealthier citizens of Bath, for instance, were quick to exploit the opportunities provided by the fields and pastures that still surrounded their ancient city walls. The demand for food in local markets created by a rapidly rising population and the growing numbers of a landless workforce offered lucrative bait even to those whose prime interests lay within the city. Councillor Henry Chapman, inn-keeper of The Sun in Northgate Street,[70] also rented a five-acre close in the neighbouring parish of Widcombe where he raised geese, hens and turkeys and grew apples, pears, cherries and other fruit for the market.[71] Alderman Robert Fisher, a mercer by trade, not only rented a property in Stall Street near the South Gate, but also operated the Corporation's 'cole workes' at Timsbury (see below)[72] In addition to all this, however, he was the tenant of three orchards and other land in Widcombe which, according to witnesses, was highly profitable in 1653. His market gardening operation enabled him to keep four cows and four calves and to produce one hundred bushels of apples at 12d per bushel; £10 worth of garden fruit (including forty quarters of strawberries at 5d per quarter and plums, cherries, gooseberries, raspberries, cabbage, carrots and peas); a small quantity of hops and £12 worth of teazles from his two-acre crop. [73] Councillor John Atwood, a baker with property in Stall Street and adjacent to the Shambles off Northgate Street, also rented an orchard and three plots of pasture ground in the northern suburbs of the city. [74] Similarly, Councillor Samuel Wintle, innkeeper of The George in Lower Borough Walls was the tenant of a fourteen-acre close in Widcombe which he used to rear geese, horses and cattle. His near-neighbour there, John Biggs, who did not apparently possess property in the city, nevertheless used his thirty acres of meadow, pasture and orchards in Widcombe to create produce for the market. It was estimated that he harvested in 1652 between thirty and forty bushels of apples and about fifty-seven loads of hay worth twenty shillings a load. [75]

To add to this picture of the involvement of Bath citizens in agricultural activity, a clear impression of the general nature and extent of farming in North-East Somerset is gained from two contemporary surveys: The Manor Survey of Farmborough (1630) and the Survey of Walcot (1638-41). [76] Four distinct features emerge. It is apparent, first of all, that some enclosure of open fields and common pasture had already taken place throughout the region; secondly, that the open field system was nevertheless still a reality; thirdly, that agriculture on the whole was a 'mixed' operation, not totally dependent on dairy farming as in some areas; and fourthly, that there was a surprising absence of large-scale capitalist farmers.

The village of Farmborough in 1630 typified most of these features. It was a village of twenty-nine households, indicating a total population of no more than 165 (i.e. using the formula stated earlier in this section). There were approximately 1188 acres of land, with a yearly value of £387 5s, rented out by the Lord of the Manor (Sir Francis Popham) to twenty-seven copyholders and two leaseholders for a mere £33 14s 9d. The Manor Court functioned strongly, implementing a list of manor customs based on local land law and outlined in an appendix to the Survey (e.g. the imposition of the 'herriot' tax on death, the payment of chickens to supplement the small annual rents and the application of large fines when new names were added to the agreement). Agriculture in the village was, in every sense, mixed. There were four main open fields (the North, South, East and West Fields), containing 557 acres in 274 separate strips (averaging 2 acres each). Changes to traditional methods, however, were well under way with 500 additional acres already enclosed for arable (22 closes) and pasture/meadow (154 closes). Ten of these closes were specifically noted in the Survey as being 'newly enclosed', including two on the edges of the open fields. Although the farming was a mixture of arable, dairying and cattle grazing, arable still dominated the scene claiming 642 acres against 414 acres for meadow and pasture. The common provided further grazing for 72 beasts. Holdings tended to be fairly modest; five families possessed only a garden alongside their cottages; two worked a mere 5 acres each; eight rented between 13 and 25 acres; a further eleven operated between 37 and 69 acres; two larger tenants farmed 100 acres each; and the most substantial one of all had a total of 260 acres.

England by this time was suffering from the general population crisis which was affecting the whole of Europe. By 1650, it was estimated that the figure had reached 5.5 millions, compared with a total of 2 millions in 1500. This population explosion in the country at large was quickening both the process of enclosure and the creation of larger units by wealthy gentlemen and yeomen farmers who wished to capitalise on the lucrative profits now possible from rising rents and rising prices. It was with these incentives that they devoted their attention increasingly to the market, seeking to increase their land-holding at the same time. Unfortunately for them, the system of land tenure in North-East Somerset slowed down the process and greatly inhibited the creation of large-scale capitalist enterprises in this region. Local land law was based on the granting of land in small units on long leases normally for three lives. These lifehold tenancies provided the landlord with income not so much from annual rents, which tended to be minimal, but from sizeable 'fines' which was paid when a new ii lives James Smyth claymeth by Coppy of Court Roll bearringe date the One and Twentieth day of October in the Sixth yeare of the late Kinge James his Raigne over Englande of the demise of John Addams and Thomasine his Wief. One Tenemt wth thapp(er)tinance in ffarme burraw late in the tenure of Agnes Allyn Widoe To have and to hold to the said James and Richard Smyth his sonn for terme of their lives successively accordinge to the Custone of the Mannoe under the yearly Rent of xxvi x And two Capons At Michaelmas yearly And all Customes and service therefore due and right accustomed.

The house backside orchard and garden adioyninge about the house xiiii acres

The grounde called the Woode lyinge in three p(ar)cells adioyninge cont xx acres

One Close of pasture called Kingwell cont one acre

Seaven p(er)ocke and Closes lyinge neare adioyninge against the home grounde cont xx acres

At Kingwell enclosed of arrable iii acres

At Smallbrooke newly enclosed of arrable vi acres

A Close devided at

In the West feild

At Stiblande viii acres in one peece

At Bremlande one acre

In the North feild

One peece tawarde Pensford tenn acres

By Pensfforde Way devided two acres

At ffarmehams stile one acre

At Swarge acre one acre

At Blackwell one acre

And neare there adioyninge halfe an acre

In the North side of the Way at Blackwell ii acres

And Six Beaste lease

valet p(er) ann(um) xxx li

Suma of the acres lxxxxiiii acr & halfe

But by estimacon C acres

Extract from the Farmborough Manor Survey, 1630

life was added to the lease. In view of the fact that the arrangements were normally protected by manor custom, the lifeholder was in a favourable position on his small holding, whereas the landlord found it virtually impossible to raise the rent to its true market value.

William Snygges, Lord of the Manor of Walcot, was in many ways typical of the local would-be capitalist farmer, who was increasingly frustrated by his inability to consolidate his lands by amalgamation or to maximise his income by charging realistic rents. The annual survey he took of his property in the Walcot Lordship and the Barton Farm, which became something of an obsession between 1638 and 1641, revealed that the vast majority of the 610 acres in his possession was let out on lifehold tenancies, mostly in holdings of 12 acres or less (each subdivided into fields of a mere two or three acres). In his somewhat frenzied jottings, he estimated that whereas the real market value of the Walcot Lordship (329 acres) was £343 per annum, it was actually producing a pitiful £10 3s 10d. He tried to draw up a scheme for buying out his tenants, but was ultimately thwarted in his ambition by the exactness of manor custom and the complexity of individual leases.[77]

The inability of some of the wealthier farmers to create a large-scale commercial operation, aimed at producing a good surplus for the local markets, contributed to the hardship experienced by many inhabitants of North-East Somerset in the years prior to the outbreak of the Civil War in 1642. There were several contributory factors to the general state of poverty within the area as a whole, but more particularly within the bounds of the Frome Hundred on the Wiltshire border. An ever-increasing mass of landless labourers, often living in rough cottages on the edge of the forest, had been created in part by the rapid rise in the population, in part by the buying out in some areas of small holders by capitalist farmers, in part by the attraction of a booming cloth industry in the previous century. The precarious existence of these landless labourers was seriously threatened during the first part of the seventeenth century by a general depression which hit the west country broadcloth industry, thus making thousands unemployed; by frequent corn shortages, caused both by low production and by harvest failure, which ensured that bread prices remained high; and by the deafforestation of the Frome Selwood Forest (see below).[78]

In many respects, the problem of poverty was a general problem that affected the whole area. The magistrates, meeting in Quarter Sessions, responded as best they could to a growing cry for help from all corners of the five Hundreds - or, more frequently, simply referred their plight to the Council in London. Bath itself was reported to be 'a verie little poore cittie' in 1622 'and clothing much decayed', while its neighbour, Widcombe, also pleaded two years later 'that the parish is very poor'. The inhabitants of Saltford petitioned in 1616 for help in providing accommodation for 'the many poor that want houses', because they were 'much more burdened with poor people than they were formerly'. Perhaps the overall situation was best summarised by the Justices of Somerset in their communication to Council in May 1622:

'There is great want of money; the breed of cattle is decayed by the import of Irish cattle; wools and cloth are grown almost valueless: the people are desperate for want of work, and the harvest prospects are bad'.[79]

But if the situation in general was distressing, it was particularly acute in the area around Frome. As early as August 1622 the vicar, Anthony Methuin, and the inhabitants petitioned the county magistrates with their desperate plight. They explained that the parish had in recent years deeply depended upon the cloth trade for survival and that many people had 'planted themselves there in the forest attracted in by the prospect of work in weaving, fulling and spinning'. But now, with the decay of that trade and the collapse of subsidiary trades 'languishing in the decaye of this one', 'the crye of the poore people is grown very great and the burden upon the inhabitants unsupportable'. A special survey on the parish had revealed that the 'multitude of the poore' amounted to five hundred men, women and children. [80]

The magistrates did what they could to alleviate this distress by granting additional money for the relief of the poor. Nevertheless, this merciful action soon proved itself to be totally insufficient to stem the tide of distress that was engulfing the Frome community. Misery brought about by shortage of work was quickly compounded by shortage of food. The problem became particularly acute in the early 1630's when a series of bad harvests seriously affected the situation. In February 1631, the local magistrates (John Horner, Robert Hopton and John Harington) sent a letter to the Council giving an 'estimate as neere as we can of all the corne' in the Hundreds of Frome, Kilmersdon, Bathforum and Wellow. The Hundred of Frome, they said, which contains 'a greate and popular markett Towne and fifteen parishes, is a very poor hundred wherein are six thousand five hundred and six inhabitants consisting most of clothiers, weavers and spinners and other trades, full of cottages both in and neere the markett Towne and the forest of Frome Selwood'. The 200 quarters of wheat and rye, the sum of all that was currently available, would feed the inhabitants for less than a fortnight, while the 241 remaining quarters of barley, oats, beans and peas would scarcely sow a third of land that had been earmarked for next year's crop. [81] Later in the year, (December 1691) Hopton and Horner reported to the Council that there was very little or no corn left in North-East Somerset. Although 'God in his mercie' had sent 'a plentiful harvest', there was 'not sufficient to serve the inhabitants one quarter of the yeare'. They were really suffering from the cumulative effect of a harvest failure in 1629 which had prevented the building up of reserves of corn in the following year. But the fundamental problem was that the Frome area was 'noe great corne county' being mostly inhabited by clothiers, weavers and spinners who were always 'buyers' not producers of corn. This almost total dependence on the market for food was a desperately worrying feature of life for the majority of the cottagers living around Frome. [82]

Their plight had already been further aggravated by a scheme for the deafforestation of Frome Selwood Forest, which had been launched in July 1627 by Charles I, anxious to raise money for his foreign policy. As a result of a lengthy process conducted by local commissioners, the King gave up his right of forest in return for third share of the land which was subsequently sold and enclosed. At the same time, the position of free holders and copy holders claiming rights of common in the forest was respected, enabling further enclosure to take place. The folk who suffered most in this operation were the cottagers living on waste at the edge of the forest. [83] These people, who had often been attracted to the area by the prospect of work in the cloth industry usually had no other land to their credit than a small garden next to the cottage. They therefore tended to rely on supplementing their livelihood, especially during times of unemployment or food shortage, by capitalising on the freely-available benefits of the royal forest - firewood, timber for building, grazing for pigs and cattle, and game for the table. The enclosure, which resulted from the deafforestation scheme for the forest of Frome Selwood, put an end to those unofficial benefits, because the law simply did not recognise that the cottagers had any rights at all. Such was the plight of the cottagers of Frome. [84]

It was desperation of this kind that provoked food riots in the locality in November 1630. For several years, Somerset magistrates had expressed fears that 'the multitudes of poor spinners, weavers, etc. in the county, now without work, tend to mutiny' and that they were 'sensible of the calamities' in Germany. [85] When their worst fears were realised near Midford, just outside Bath, the investigation was led by the Custos Rotulorum himself (Henry Ley, 2nd Earl of Marlborough). This was the only occasion on which he became involved in Petty Sessional work, an indication of the significance that both he and the council attached to these disorders. There were at least three separate incidents involving attacks on licensed corn carriers. William Lansdown of Keynsham was poorer travelling up Midford Hill on his way between Warminster and Bristol with five horseloads of wheat when he was 'sett upon by a greate number of men and women to the number of 100 persons' who pulled down his sacks, making off with four of them. Furthermore, they issued threats of physical violence and warned him that 'within 10 dayes none should travail on the way with corne'. On the same day, Thomas Wickham of Hinton Grange managed to rescue, first, William Harris who was attacked by over thirty men as he was carrying a sack of corn in Hinton Field, and, later, one Hawkings of Rode whose horse convoy was intercepted in Midford 'by a great number of people'. The ruffians withdrew, after pulling down some of the sacks, urging others 'to follow their colours'. When various suspects were cross-examined at the subsequent investigation held in Bath, Agnes Hodson perhaps best typified the plight of local people. Denying her involvement in the raid, she admitted that she had carried away under half a peck of corn, which she had scraped 'up from the ground'.[86] Although history does not record what punishments were meted out on this occasion, the 'twelve or thirteen poor ragged women, many of them very aged', who were involved in a similar incident near Newbury a month later, were dealt with severely. Seven of them were sent to a House of Correction and five were whipped.[87]

Food riots were not uncommon in England at this time. They were most prevalent in the depressed areas of the clothmaking industry and in ports or market towns through which large quantities of grain were shipped. The purchase of substantial amounts in the markets by dealers intent on transporting the stock outside the area often caused local shortages with resultant high prices. Riots therefore ensued as the poor and unemployed attempted to prevent the movement of grain. The river Severn, a route for shipments between the West Midlands and Bristol, was a frequent target for attacks - as were the market towns of Warminster, Reading, Hertford, Canterbury and Wye.[88]

(b) The Cloth Industry

No industry suffered more from fluctuations of the economy than the cloth industry which had dominated the employment scene in North-East Somerset for many generations. During its golden period, in the first half of the sixteenth century, it had brought real prosperity to the area which was clearly evident to the traveller, John Leland. On the road between Bath and Frome he had noticed 'certain good clothiers having fair houses and tucking mills'[89] The fine stone buildings in the city of Bath, depicted on Gilmore's map of 1694, bear further testimony of the affluence which had been generated by this trading activity. The local industry had specialised in the manufacture of broadcloth, each piece normally between 54 and 63 inches in width and requiring two weavers to handle it on the loom. It was made from short-staple English wool which had been carded (not combed) to provide, after fulling and finishing, a fine heavy cloth with a smooth surface. Most of the cloths produced in this way in North-East Somerset were exported as 'white' or undyed cloth to Holland and Germany where the final processes took place. The area was highly suited to the needs of the industry. The Avon and its tributaries provided both power for the fulling mills and clear water for scouring the cloths after fulling; there was a plentiful supply of fuller's earth; the soil around Keynsham proved itself to be ideal for the growing of woad and that around Bath for the growing of teasels; access to the markets was reasonable by road to London and possible by water to Bristol. By 1600, therefore, clothiers were already well established along the river valleys, which bordered the county, in such places as Frome, Beckington, Lullington, Rode, Freshford, Bath and Keynsham. They were a mixture of small independent weavers and large-scale capitalist clothiers who utilised the domestic or 'putting out' system, employing hundreds of local families in the work of carding, spinning, weaving and finishing.

Trade in this white broadcloth had already suffered a number of acute depressions during the second half of the sixteenth century. In 1586 the Privy Council had shown considerable concern for the way in which large clothiers were quick to lay off work 'the sorte of the people inhabiting about the cittie of Bathe and other townes on the easterlie partes of the countie of Somerset' when times were bad. The justices were therefore ordered to call before them all 'clothiers and other men of trade' and to ensure that those with stocks of wool or with an 'ability to employ' immediately set to work as many of the poor as possible.[90] In spite of a revival in the broadcloth industry during the first decade or so of the seventeenth century, the situation deteriorated rapidly from 1614 onwards and remained grave until the outbreak of the Civil War. By 1640 exports had been halved, but as early as 1622 the Mayor had informed the Privy Council that Bath had become 'a verie little poore cittie, our clothmen much decayed and many of their workmen amongst us relieved by the Cittie'. The Council ordered merchants and dealers to help ordinary spinners and weavers by buying up surplus cloth and selling raw wool at fair prices.[91] This did not, however, halt the decline which had been caused by a range of complex factors outside the control of local people.

The prosperity of this flourishing export trade had been badly hit by the Cokayne Project of 1614 which had caused James I to ban the export of undyed cloth in an attempt to foster native skills in dyeing and finishing; by the disruption of markets during the Thirty Years' War; by the debasement of currencies in Germany and Poland, which reduced profitability; by strong competition from developing industries in France, Germany and Holland (where technical skills were often much higher); by the outbreak of plague in 1625, which scattered the London merchants; by the wars against Spain and France which broke out in 1629, blocking outlets to the Mediterranean; and by repeated quarrels between the Merchant Adventurers and the Dutch Government which often ended with the seizure of stocks of English cloth. At the same time, the 'New Draperies' or worsteds (which, though coarser, were both lighter and cheaper) brought fierce competition to the home market, taking a further toll on the region's sales of heavy woollen cloth. To make matters worse, the absence of parliament during the 'personal rule' of the 1630's meant that protective legislation was impossible, in spite of a commission set up by the government in 1638 to investigate the decay of the cloth industry.[92] The acute distress caused locally by the collapse of the trade has already been illustrated above in the plight of the cottagers around Frome.

The general decline of the western cloth industry, however, was successfully reversed from the mid-1620's by a group of individual clothiers operating in North-East Somerset. Their enterprise and vigour brought welcome relief to the hard-pressed economy of the area, particularly in the area around Bath. As early as 1583, a clothier named Benedict Webb of Taunton had invented a new type of cloth which became known as Spanish medley, which he later produced also at Kingswood, near Wotton-under-Edge. The process involved striking an abb of soft, fine-guage Spanish (or, sometimes, English) wool on a warp of stronger, coarser home-produced yarn. These 'dyed in the wool' medleys were woven from previously dyed wool of two or more colours which had been blended and scribbled after carding. Their chief attraction lay in the fact that the cloths were lighter (weighing 16 ounces per square year, as opposed to 19 ounces for ordinary west country cloth), came in an appealing range of new colours and were smoother to the touch. They quickly began to cater for the more fashionable and expensive end of the market.

In 1625, John Ashe, the son of James Ashe the clothier from Westcombe, settled with his family in the village of Freshford, near Bath. Over the next five years, he steadily bought up a large amount of property in both Freshford and Hinton Charterhouse from his father-in-law Henry Davison, who was also a clothier. This included a corn mill, a fulling mill, a fishery, over two hundred acres of meadow, pasture and arable, not to mention numerous cottage, orchards and gardens.[93] From this new base he set about the task of introducing Spanish medleys into the neighbourhood, eventually employing a large work-force. His success, which was both immediate and dramatic, created a great fortune for himself and a measure of prosperity for the area. By 1639 the new cloth generally was in such demand in the markets of Spain, Portugal, the Levant and the

John Ashe (1597 - 1659), clothier of freshford. Portrait attributed to William Dobson (1610 - 1646).

Somerset slowly began to resume their dominant role, making a number of vital contributions to the course of events. The families which had led the local rebellion in 1642 now became champions of the policies of moderation, which were eventually to lead to the Restoration of Charles II. Although several key figures were to die before that event took place (Sir Edward Hungerford in 1648, John Harington in 1654, Sir John Horner in 1659 and John Ashe in 1659), their sons carried on their work.

The family-run firm of Ashe in London was a highly organised operation, which provided an outlet for cloth manufactured not only by John Ashe himself, but for other members of his family. His brother Jonathan, for instance, who was also based in Freshford, sent up 454 cloths between November 1640 and December 1642, valued at £7721; his mother-in-law, Anne Davison in conjunction with John Curle of Freshford, delivered cloths worth £4449 between April 1640 and February 1643 - not to mention the 785 pieces sent by his father, James, from Westcombe during the same period.[96] The firm's aggressive marketing policies by-passed both the factors of Blackwell Hall in London, where all cloth was officially traded, and the Merchant Adventurers' Company which had lost its export monopoly of cloths (other than undyed woollens) in 1621. The Ashe organisation took care of its own exports, eventually establishing a forward base in Antwerp under the control of John Ashe junior and his brother-in-law, John Shaw. At the same time, they began to specialise in the Paris market. John Ashe's brother, Jonathan, periodically went over to France on behalf of the firm to deal directly with leading Parisian drapers such as Jacques le Couteaux, Madam Moulart and John Con. Between January and May in 1642, for instance, these three dealers bought £5872 worth of goods out of the firm's total sales during that period of £7396.[97]

The Ashe family quickly grew rich on the profits of this large-scale enterprise. James Ashe was estimated to have a personal estate worth £15,000 in 1637,[98] whereas John himself was reputed to enjoy an annual income of £3000 by 1656 with personal assets of £60,000.[99] John Aubrey later confirmed the general opinion that 'Mr John Ashe of Freshford in Somersetshire was the second that made medleys, who improved the art, and gott a great estate by it *tempore caroli primi*. He was the greatest cloathier in his time.'[100] One particular way in which he 'improved the art' and thus made his product even more attractive, was to perfect the technique of manufacturing a wholly Spanish cloth. To do this he brought over to Freshford in about 1650 a number of Dutch clothiers who had mastered the difficult skill of using Spanish wool to make the warp. From the outset, he was also determined to maintain his own 'quality control' to ensure that high standards were always reached. In 1637, for instance he strongly petitioned the Privy Council against the soap monopoly, emphasising 'that for making fine West Country cloths we of necessity must have Castile and Venice soap'. If they were compelled by restriction to use 'the usual West Country hard soap', it would end in the ruination of their trade.[101]

By that time, the ruination of their trade would have had disastrous consequences for the large workforce employed by the whole Ashe family. John Ashe clearly directed his own operation in person and regarded himself as being completely indispensable to is success. When in 1637 he was summoned to make a number of appearances before the Privy Council, he pleaded to be released so that he could return to his employment in the country, upon which depended 'the livelyhoods and welfare of thousands of poore people, his workfolks, which by reason of his sudden coming up and during his absence' was 'much districted and out of order'.[102] The nerve centre of the business was at Freshford, where regular income from his dairy farming and landed estates in the neighbourhood provided capital and stability for the business. Ashe 'put out' his wool to hundreds of families for carding, dyeing, spinning and weaving before bringing the cloth back to Freshford for fulling in his own mill by Edward Twynne the Younger and, later, finishing. His own house contained many 'utensells for trade' which were later bequeathed to his wife. There is clear evidence that some of his employees in Freshford rented

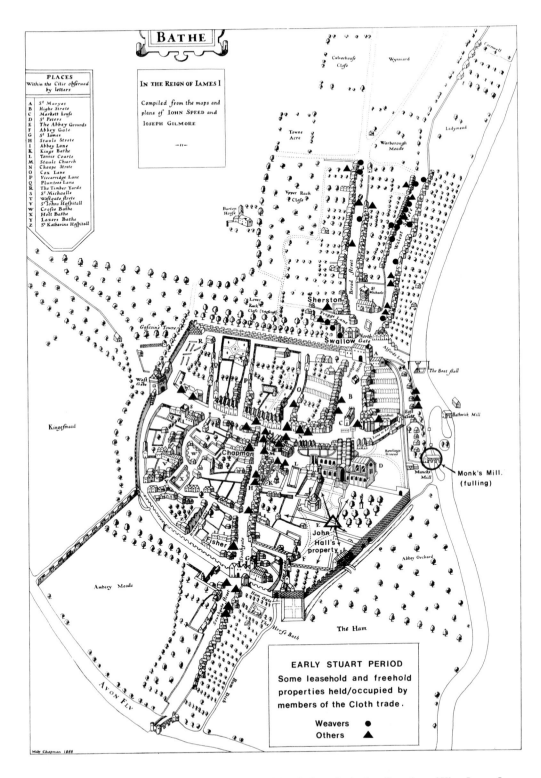

A map showing the location in Bath of members of the cloth trade during the reign of King James I. Reproduced from Citizens of Bath *by courtesy of Elizabeth Holland and Mike Chapman.*

cottages and land from him, like Thomas Fisher, weaver (a tenement, garden and orchard), William Harte, clothworker (four acres) and Walter Pittman, drawer (a cottage, garden and one acre of arable). It is also perhaps significant that other local clothiers brought or rented land in Freshford from either John Ashe or Henry Davison, including Paul Methuin of Bradford (Ashe's son-in-law), John Curle of Freshford, John Taylor of Trowbridge and Thomas Shute of Monkton Combe. [103] The clothing industry in the Freshford area, was still based to some extent on the solid rock of land occupation which gave the clothiers and weavers 'the power to wait for a market'. [104] John Ashe therefore brought far greater security, optimism and prosperity to the cloth industry in the Bathforum Hundred than was the case elsewhere in North-East Somerset. Although other clothiers became involved in the manufacture of Spanish medleys both in Somerset and Wiltshire, no-one quite managed to emulate the success of John Ashe in the pre-war period.

In addition to this large-scale operation in the villages outside, the cloth trade also continued quite vigorously within the city of Bath itself, even though the golden days of the sixteenth century had largely gone for ever. The main hub of activity was just outside the North Gate, as it had always been. There, in the large open space out St Michael's Church, weekly markets were held flanked on the east side by two bustling inns, The Horse Shoe and The Boat. During the period 1630 to 1660, with occasional movement and change of personnel, a number of clothiers, weavers and woollen drapers operated their workshops and businesses in this area. In Broad Street (named after the traditional broadcloths associated with that district) were clothiers William Sherstone, Arthur Sherstone, William Baker (whose son, George, was a clothworker) and woollen draper Edward Parker; in Walcot Street, clothier William Swallow, weaver John Dangerfield and silkweaver William Marden; and in Northgate Street, clothier and woollen draper John Parker. [105] According to John Wood, even as late as 1660 'the cloathing trade flourished so exceedingly, that in the Parish of St Michael's without the North Gate there were no less than 60 broad looms'. [106] The clothiers were able to use the services of Bridget Cutt's 'tucking or fulling mill' (known as Monks Mill) outside the East Gate for the scouring and fulling of their white broadcloths. These were then stretched out to dry on large cloth racks erected in the fields which had been named, appropriately, Over Rack Close and Rackham. Joseph Gilmore's map of 1694 clearly shows these large wooden frames on which the cloth was secured by stitching to prevent it from shrinking unevenly as it dried. [107]

The independent clothiers and weavers of Bath operated on a much smaller scale than John Ashe. There is no evidence that they had abandoned the production of white broadcloth in favour of Spanish medleys, nor do their names appear as suppliers in the cloth books of the Ashe firm in London. [108] It is also probable that, as comparatively small producers, they did not have the incentive to make regular journeys to the capital to take advantage of the trading facilities in Blackwell Hall. It is more likely that they were content to sell their cloth locally at the weekly markets in Bath and Bristol and at occasional fairs throughout the year. Most of them were too small and too much lacking in capital to organise the sort of 'putting out' system favoured by large-scale businessmen such as Ashe. They relied instead on buying their spun yarn from market spinners who could also supply the material ready dyed if required. The local justices, anxious to maintain quality control, were concerned in January 1635 that certain abuses had been creeping into the system. 'The maintenance of the poore spinners of wooll in these places', they reported to Council 'doth at this tyme much relie upon the tradeing of the markett spinners and also many clothiers'. They therefore drew up a set of rules for controlling the way wool was treated and used - to avoid confusion, poor spinners could in future only handle wool from one customer at a time; clothiers and market spinners must only deal in one type of wool and types must not be mixed; market spinners were to label each batch of yarn offered for sale, stating the type of card used in carding and 'the name of him that made the same wool into yarne and the place of his dwelling'. At a meeting in Bath called by the magistrates, the clothiers and market spinners of North-East Somerset endorsed these rules 'with general consent'. Anxious to protect the good name of their product, they furthermore requested stiff punishments for any poor spinner that should 'purloine, corrupt or spill any wooll or yarne delivered to them by any market spinner'. In the absence, therefore, of guild regulations to control their trade, local dealers showed a considerable degree of unity and co-operation. [109]

Small clothiers and independent weavers could operate on a comparatively small amount of capital. Provided they had the resources or credit to purchase wool from the market spinner and to survive until cloth had been sold, they could maintain their business. The Bath clothiers were fortunate in the close proximity of both a fulling mill and weekly market. Nevertheless, their ultimate well-being often depended upon the possession of land or other economic assets to supplement their income and to provide a greater degree of security. At least several of the people already mentioned had sufficient means to enable them to hold stock for a period when trade was bad or even to survive a major disruption. William and Arthur Sherstone were members of a wealthy propertied family which had previously owned Barton Farm. John Parker, with substantial property in Northgate Street, not only ran a draper's shop there but also rented 21 acres of land in Barton Farm just outside the north-west corner of the city. Mark Dallimore, diversified in another way by owning two inns in Southgate Street, The Cock and The Pied Bull. William Marden, the silkweaver with a shop in Walcot Street, added to his income through his work as a button mould maker. [110]

(c) The Health Trade

The comparative strength of the economy of the City of Bath and the Hundred of Bathforum was based in part on its diversity, which ensured that local inhabitants did not

The King's Bath in 1672. This drawing by Thomas Johnson gives a good picture of the fine sixteenth and seventeenth century lodging houses which surrounded the baths.

rely solely on one occupation for survival, and in part on the enterprise of men like John Ashe, who ensured that creeping stagnation of the type experienced in Frome was not allowed to stifle its affluence. Further diversity of employment had also been provided by the enterprise and business acumen of the City Council through their revival of Bath as a major health resort. The turning point came in 1554 when the Baths, previously owned by the Priory, became the responsibility of the Corporation after a legal wrangle. From that moment, they worked vigorously to improve the facilities and to promote the healing qualities of the waters.

By 1640, there were five public baths, all of which owed something to the improving zeal of the Corporation. The Cross Bath was 'a dainty bath for young, weak and tender bodies' and was therefore recommended 'in contractions of any member, in obstructions of the breast, spleen, liver, kidneys'. [111] It had twelve stone seats around the edge and previously had a cross standing upright in the centre. The King's Bath was the largest, 'walled also round about and fitted with 32 seats of arched worke; wherein men and women may sit apart, who when they enter in put upon their bodies linnen garments and have their guides'. [112] The King's Bath had been embellished through the provision of an elaborate structure over the central spring (1578) and a balustrade for spectators (1624). Its neighbour was the much smaller Queen's Bath, opened in 1576 and named after Queen Anne of Denmark (wife of James I) who visited the city in 1613 and 1615. The Hot Bath was 'convenient for cold and moist diseases', although it was enlarged and the temperature lowered towards the close of sixteenth century. The Leper's Bath, also built in 1576, had been designed to cater specifically for the poor and diseased inhabitants, thus removing them from the other baths which now tended to be the reserve of the more affluent and elegant visitors. The bustle and liveliness of the social life, which now became a major feature of the baths, is vividly illustrated in Thomas Johnson's drawing of The King's and The Queen's Baths at Bath in 1672.

The Corporation paid great attention to the task of cleaning, maintaining and improving the facilities to make them attractive to visitors, appointing a Sergeant to supervise the arrangements. By 1642, they were regularly paying two guides, Mary Ady

A drawing from Gilmore's map of 1694, which shows the Abbey House where royalty and other famous visitors stayed during their time in Bath.

The Three Tunns near the King's Bath, from Gilmore's map of 1694.

and Eleanar Singers, an annual sum of £2 10s 'for makeinge cleane about the Bathes and for helpinge of the poore from the bath'. Items for minor repairs at the various baths feature frequently in the Bath Chamberlain's Accounts, including the purchase of 'six hundred blue tiles from Bristol' in 1647. 'The Poore fokes Bath' had already been re-tiled in 1641. Regulations for the use of these unique facilities were periodically made in Council, as in 1645 when it was decided that all baths should be 'drained at fower of the clock in the afternoon and the doores to be shutt and the Bathes to be stopped againe at seaven that it may be full in convenient time the next morning'.[113]

In the meantime great publicity had been given to the benefits to be derived from a visit to the city's baths. Dr William Turner in 1557, John Jones in 1572 and Peter Holland in 1637 all testified to that effect, although it was probably left to Dr Thomas Venner, a physician at the baths, to write with the authority of personal experience in 1628:

> 'They be of excellent efficacy against all diseases of the head and sinews, proceeding from a cold and moist cause, as rheums, palsies, epilepsies, lethargies, apoplexia, cramps, deafness, forgetfulness, trembling or weakness of any member, aches, and swellings of joints'.[114]

He also invited 'those that fear obesity, this is, would not wax gross ... to come to our baths'. People did come - in great numbers. This was in part due to the fact that the continental treatment centres were being badly disrupted by war, but more particularly to the excellence of what Bath had to provide. Royalty and other distinguished guests stayed in Abbey House. Other visitors were welcomed into its many inns. The Survey of Bath, taken by the Corporation of its property in 1641, recorded the following, although others appeared shortly afterwards: The Rose and The Black Horse in Westgate Street; The Bear, The Swan, The Lower Swan and The Raven in Cheap Street; The Catherine Wheel, The Christopher, The Horse's Head and The Sun in Northgate Street: The Horse Shoe, The Boat and The Black Swan in Broad Street; The White Hart, The Three Tuns, The Golden Lyon and The Cross Bow in Stall Street: The Bell at the end of Binbury Lane; and The George in Lower Borough Walls. [115] Bath also welcomed them into its many lodging houses. Indeed, most professional and businessmen were willing to offer accommodation to the 'yearly concourse in the spring and fall, of people of all sorts and from all parts of this Kingdom'.

In the absence of any regulations governing lodging houses, this apparently developed into something of a racket. According to Dr Thomas Venner, writing in 1637, the keepers of such houses sent out their agents 'in every corner of the streets' to locate the newly arrived health visitors and persuade them 'to take their lodging at such and such an house, neere to such and such a bath, extolling the baths neere which they dwell above the rest ... And when they have gotten you into their houses, they will be ready to fit you with a physician; perhaps a doctor of their own creating: as some empiric, upstart apothecary, or the like (magnifying him for the best physician in the towne) that will not crosse them in removing you to another bath, though the bath neere which you are placed be altogether contrary to your infirmities or state of body'.[116]

By fair means or foul, many local inhabitants therefore found employment through the seasonal influx of visitors to Bath in search of a health cure. The city quickly adapted to serve the needs of an increasingly affluent consumer society. Between 1640 and 1660, a growing number of mercers (far more than the size of the city would warrant) ran businesses which sold a wide range of products, including cloth, clothing, sugar, gunpowder, musket bullets, bandoliers, belts, and metal goods - Richard Biggs, John Pearce, John Fisher and Richard Abbott in Cheap Street; Thomas Cole, Robert Fisher and Walter Chapman in Stall Street; Matthew Clift in Broad Street; John Bush in High Street; John Reed in Northgate Street and Robert Penney in Cox Lane. [117]

The Corporation, anxious to cater for the new clientele, issued a certificate in May 1632, authorising no fewer than sixteen shopkeepers to sell tobacco, including '6 grossers and 4 Apothercaries', a book-seller, a buttonmaker and a shoemaker'. [118] The 1641 Survey also mentions, at the luxury end of the market, two glovers (one in Cheap Street and one in Stall Street), an organ maker (in Westgate Street), a vineyard (off Broad Street) and a tannery, owned by William Browning, just outside the North Gate. [119] The popularity of cattle-grazing in the area created a ready supply of raw materials for the leather industry which, in turn, fulfilled the fashionable requirements of the wealthier inhabitants and visitors.

For the year 1625, a total of 16 shoe makers and 12 glovers have been identified. These were served by two tanners (who worked from tanneries situated by the river) and two curriers (who dressed the skins). The glovers were dominated by the Chapman family, prominent among whom was Thomas Chapman whose property was on the corner of Westgate Street and Stall Street. The inventory, which accompanied his will, suggest a comfortable standard of living typical of that enjoyed by most local traders. His house had a cellar, a hall, a shop, a room over the shop and a loft. There were a number of bedsteads with bedding such as a red coverlet and a feather pillow, sheets, bolsters and blankets. He had pewter dishes, several candlesticks, two chamber pots, three kettles, a skillet, a frying pan, a green carpet and three cushions. That house was assessed for 3 hearths in 1664 (against the city average of 3.9). Bath's consumer society was also served by those specialising in catering (3 vintners, 2 coopers, 5 bakers, 2 millers and 10 butchers) and the construction industry (7 tilers and plasterers, 24 masons and paviours, 4 stone merchants, 21 carpenters, 3 glaziers, 3 painters, 4 plumbers and 1 thatcher).[120]

The rise of Bath as a Spa Town in the seventeenth century was all part of a national trend. Although health-bearing hot water springs had been known and utilised since Roman times, the 'Spa Town' as such did not come onto the scene until after 1600. The wealthy gentry, who had previously relied on the fashionable spas in Germany and the Low Countries, found themselves frustrated by the intrusions of the Thirty Years' War. To satisfy, therefore, the growing demand for similar centres in England, spas sprang up in place like Buxton, Epsom, Scarborough, Tunbridge Wells and Bath. Their fame quickly spread, partly through the patronage of royalty and partly through the dissemination of publicity leaflets. Unlike some spas, such Tunbridge Wells which centred almost exclusively on the tourist trade, Bath was able to diversify its economic base through its markets and other activities, including the cloth trade.[121]

(d) Coal Mining

The citizens of Bath were also interested - and to some extent actively involved - in one other industry which was growing in importance within the area. In the face of an acute national shortage of timber, the demand for coal was rapidly increasing from both domestic and industrial consumers. By the seventeenth century, therefore, it was being used not only by private householders, but also by soap-boilers, starch-makers, chandlers, dyers, brewers and salt-petre manufacturers - in fact, in every type of operation which required boiling or heating. Locally, the market was provided by the fairly affluent residents of Bath, by the clothiers (who required both soap and dyes) and by small-scale industrialists such as John Gifford, who was given licence in 1634 to set up a furnace in Bath to make salt-petre (in addition to the one he already owned in Bristol). [122] 'A private furnace' also existed in Weston and three forges in Keynsham, possibly for use in cottage nail-making concerns. [123] Alexander Popham certainly used '54 sacke of cole' from his own mines in 1649 for the 'lyme kiln' on his estates at Hunstrete. [124]

The main centre for coalmining in North-East Somerset lay within the Hundred of Kilmersdon, although it also extended northwards into the Hundred of Keynsham. 'Mendip coal' as it was known, was mined in the forest of Mendip in the manors of Ashwick, Kilmersdon, Holcombe, Mells, Babington, Luckington and Stratton. Further north it was to be found in Brislington, Paulton, Timsbury, Clutton, Chelwood and Compton Dando. An interesting account has survived in mining activity at Timsbury in a Surveyor's Report of 1610:

> 'There now be three pits near widow Blackers house, the highest about 4 fathoms, the middle six fathoms, the lowest 8 fathoms deep. At these depths they cut out their lanes about 4 feet high and broad. They need no great store of timberwork for support. The lane we entered was a good quoits cast in length... They now work in two pits at once, and have below two or three men and four or five boys, and also three men to wind up the coals. At the end of every lane a man worketh, and there maketh his bench, as they call it... The wages allowed to men is to him that hath most 4 shillings the week, and to the boys 1s 6d. Adding for candles, increase of wages for work by night, ropes, sharpening of tools, baskets, etc., the whole week's charge may arise to £3. Reckoning £7 10s the week, and the net gain is £4. 10s, of which one-fourth for the tenant, and the rest remaineth for the lord. It is said the works at Timsbury are near worn out, and all smiths use the coal of Clutton and none of Timsbury'. [125]

Coalmining at Stratton had been taking place since the fifteenth century, although the mines had originally been confined to common and waste land. It was not until the seventeenth century that enclosed ground was broken into after a licence had been granted by the lord of the manor. Disputes inevitably arose once copyhold and leasehold properties became the centre of mining activity. The mines at Stratton, which suffered from flooding 'by reason that the springes are soe superfuente', were held by tenants on payment of £300 fine to the lord of the manor and yearly rent of 18s.2½d. The cost of these leases varied a great deal. In 1649, William Allen, husbandman, signed a twenty-one year agreement to pay his landlord each Saturday night 'the tenth shilling of all the cole' taken from his mine at Timsbury. In return, he was given the sole right to mine within the manor of Timsbury, to set up all 'necessary and fitt workes' for the mining operation and to bring in 'such carriages as they please' with free access. Alexander Popham, on the other hand, granted a seven-year lease in 1656 to George James of Publoe for £30 a year, allowing him to mine for coal on the Popham estate in Compton Dando, excluding any coal found 'in or under any houses, gardens or orchards' of the owner! Two years later, a consortium of Thomas Hippersley, gent., of Camerley, Richard Chaloner, gent., of Clutton, John Day, yeoman, of Camerley and Thomas Nash, coalminer, of Clutton agreed to pay a yearly rent of 3s 4d for a mine at Chelwood. [126] Both capital and practical expertise were required for success in this sphere.

The Bath Corporation was also quick to exploit its opportunity, as trustees of the lands owned by St John's Hospital, by granting a lease in 1640 for 'all that coleworkes, colemynes, vaynes of cole belonginge to a messuage or tenement lyeinge in Timborowe and Littlton and now in the occupacon of Bridgett Chilton, widdowe'. Councillor Robert Fisher paid a fine 'for the colinge' of £10 10s in 1640, followed by a yearly rent of 6s 8d.

In addition to this mine at Timsbury, the city apparently also owned a mine at Paulton, judging by the visit of Mayor Masters in 1658 'to see our coale worke' there.[127] Coalmining, needless to say, brought with it a fair share of problems as well as a certain degree of prosperity. As early as 1634, local magistrates received a petition from the inhabitants of Brislington complaining the 'the high wayes within the parish are of late yeares becoming very founderous and in decaye by means of the greate resorte of colliers with their horses to certaine cole pitts there of late yeares found out'. [128] The cost of repairing those roads fell as always on the community of Brislington.

* * * * *

The 18,000 or so people, who therefore made up the community of North-East Somerset in 1642, shared and suffered much in common. Their compact geographical situation, which had made them somewhat independent of their countrymen to the south, had also provided them with natural access to the political and economic life of the capital. Although they had suffered terribly at times during the 1620's and 1630's from poverty, food-shortage and unemployment, there had been scant evidence of violence or riot apart from isolated incidents on Midford Hill. There is little doubt that the area as a whole was affluent enough to stand the strain of harvest failure and economic fluctuation, in spite of the real misery suffered by some in the process. An average of 2.5 hearths per household in the country with 3.19 within the City of Bath indicates a general standard of living some way in excess of the bread-line.

The prosperity of Bath dominated the local scene. A city well-fortified and well-administered in a healthy environment, it became the major centre for trade and political activity within the northern part of the country. Its economic strength rested on its rich inheritance of Priory lands which created funds to mount any crisis; on the diversity of local agriculture which ensured that corn was usually available even in times of acute shortage elsewhere; on John Ashe's revival of the cloth trade, which salvaged the livelihood of many local families; on the rise of the city as a major health resort, which generated additional employment in the leisure and service industries; and on the continuing importance of land possession, which provided the rock on which all other economic activity was based. This affluence and the confidence it inspired spread out from the city in ripples across the neighbouring countryside, benefiting especially the Hundreds of Bathforum, Keynsham and Wellow. As the ripples weakened towards the southern part of the area, so poverty became greater and the economy less secure in the Hundreds of Kilmersdon and Frome - districts with little arable farming, but with hordes of landless cottagers locked into a declining cloth industry and deprived of their 'rights' of free forest.

This, then, was the community that faced up to civil war in 1642 - a community which had already proved its capacity to withstand the pressure of more than one crisis. But was its economy strong enough to endure the severe impact about to be made by the ceaseless demands of hungry soldiers? Were its members about to lose what quality of life they had previously enjoyed - and were they adaptable enough to survive?

2.
Leadership and the Seeds of War

(i) Leadership in North-East Somerset

The community of North-East Somerset was therefore both resilient and potentially affluent, in spite of the disasters that occurred from time to time. Leadership was centred almost entirely on the gentry. In the whole of Somerset there were only two noble families - Sir Henry Ley, Earl of Marlborough and John Poulett, Baron Poulett of Hinton St George - and, although the former held property in Beckington, he spent most of his time on his Wiltshire estates. As Thomas Barnes has pointed out, county government was therefore largely influenced by about twenty-five gentry families, whose powerful position was mainly based on the acquisition of monastery land from the profits of royal service in previous reigns. These 'magnates' or 'greater gentry', of immense social standing and considerable wealth, dominated the Quarter Sessions in their capacity as justices and the county society in their role as deputy lieutenants. Below them were the so-called 'middle gentry', some seventy-five or so families who formed what Barnes described as the 'magisterial class'. These men were usually justices of considerable local status, but who exercised less power and influence either in Somerset itself or in parliament. At a lower level still, were the many families that could boast an 'Esquire' or 'gent' at their head. These formed the 'lesser gentry', who nevertheless played an important part in local government.[1]

In North-East Somerset, there were four men in 1642 who were clearly of the magnate or greater gentry class - Alexander Popham of Hunstrete, John Harington of Kelston, Sir John Horner of Mells and Sir Ralph Hopton of Witham. Alexander Popham came from one of the wealthiest families in the county. His grandfather, Chief Justice Sir John Popham, had made an enormous fortune through law and by royal service to the Tudors. With it he had acquired substantial estates in Somerset, Wiltshire and Devon; with it he had also been able to marry his four daughters into four established county families (the Mallets, Rogers, Horners and Warres). His son, Sir Francis Popham (1573-1644) father of Alexander, had therefore inherited a position of extreme comfort and local esteem. One of the most affluent residents in Somerset, his estate was reckoned by John Aubrey to have been worth £10,000 a year. He, too, had maintained his family's connections with the court by marrying his younger daughter, Frances, to Lord Conway, son of the Secretary of State, and his connections with the county by marrying his eldest daughter to Thomas Luttrell. Furthermore, he had been knighted by Essex for his part in the expedition to Cadiz in 1596. Sir Francis had also been heavily involved in both local and national affairs. He had sat in every parliament between 1597 and 1644 (with the exception of the Short Parliament), had been deputy lieutenant for Wiltshire and justice of the peace for both Somerset and Wiltshire. In 1640, he was elected as member for Minehead in the Long Parliament (where he served alongside Alexander until his death in 1644) and offered security for £1,000 for the loan of November in that year.[2]

Alexander Popham (1605-1669) therefore inherited from his father not only wealth and connection, but a vast fund of political experience. Educated at Balliol College, Oxford and the Middle Temple in London (where he kept his chamber between 1622 and 1628), he could look forward to inheriting the enormous fortune based on the family seat

COLL ALEXANDER POPHAM

Alexander Popham (1605 - 1669) of Littlecote House. Member of Parliament for Bath and Commander of the Bath Regiment of Trained Bands in 1642. Portrait by an unknown artist.

at Littlecote in Wiltshire (his elder brother, John, had died in 1638). He was later to further his own connections in 1644 by marrying the daughter of William Carre, groom of the Chamber to James I. By 1640, he had already set out on his military and political career by campaigning with the army in the north in 1639 and by securing election as member for Bath in both the Short and Long Parliaments (as his brother, John, had done before him in 1627). Earlier in 1640, he had identified with the puritan faction by standing in the county election for Somerset, where he was nicknamed 'Robin Hood' in a popular appeal to the voters. Although unsuccessful, the list of substantial gentry and 'Little Robins' who supported him included many future adherents of parliament - Sir John Horner, John Ashe, William Prynne, Sir Francis Popham, William Strode, etc. As hostilities drew near, the Popham family could reflect that, in material terms at least, they had little to gain and much to lose from rebellion. Their decision to align themselves with parliament from the outset was one of principal. Their legal minds objected to the extension of royal power. Sir Francis apparently revelled in bringing lawsuits against individuals, which he conducted 'in a vexatious manner'. The war became, in effect, their lawsuit against the King. But religion also played its part. Sir Francis had not only taken a keen interest in the establishment of the puritan colonies in Virginia and New England, but had also quarrelled violently with Bishop Piers in 1637 over the patronage of a rectory in Somerset. Both father and son were keen presbyterians.[3]

A man of almost equal wealth, status and influence was John Harington (1590-1654). His father, Sir John, was Queen Elizabeth's godson and devoted courtier, who was knighted after his participation in Essex's Irish expedition. He bequeathed to his son in 1612 vast estates (mostly of monastic origin) in Dorset, Cornwall, Wiltshire and Somerset, including those adjacent to the City of Bath at Kelston, Batheaston, Corston and St Catherine's. John Harington, after education at Oxford and Lincoln's Inn, became a barrister in 1615 and a bencher in 1633. Thereafter, he supplemented his considerable inherited wealth with lucrative profits from his flourishing law practice. Most distinguished and active in his profession, he was to become treasurer of Lincoln's Inn in 1651. The extent of his wealth can be assessed from the size of the dowries allocated to his two daughters - £1200 to Mary in 1651 and £1500 to Phoebe in 1654. Although well-connected with the courts in his own right through his marriage to the daughter of the Earl of Marlborough, Harington much preferred to live a quiet existence at Kelston as a country gentleman. Nevertheless, from that base he became one of the most respected and influential leaders of county society. A justice of the peace from 1625 to the end of his life, he became Chairman of the Quarter Sessions in his capacity as deputy custodes rotulorum in 1626. Reluctant to become involved in politics or to join factions, he exercised his familiar role as independent peacemaker when the county became divided during the 1630's in a feud between two rival families, the Pouletts and the Phelips. Harington commanded the admiration and loyalty of his fellow magistrates because of the integrity and supreme intellect which set him apart from the other gentry. Totally familiar with a whole range of foreign languages (Latin, Greek, Hebrew, Arabic and Welsh), geometry, medicine, law and theology, he combined culture with godliness, frequently urging his colleagues on the bench to serve God in all their work. A devoted puritan and author of various pamphlets in support of the presbyterian doctrines, he had developed an intense hatred of catholics, who he regarded as 'thorns in our sides and pricks in our eyes.' Although, politically, he was cautious by nature and extremely hesitant to become embroiled in rebellion, his commitment to the puritan cause eventually forced him to regard Charles I as the greatest enemy to the Elizabethan brand of protestantism - just as his legal mind eventually forced him to regard the King as the greatest danger to the constitution and the laws of the land. Nevertheless, John Harington, in spite of real disagreement and mistrust, served his sovereign with a remarkable loyalty which is evident in his speeches even as late as 1642. He, more than any man, emerged as the reluctant revolutionary.[4]

Sir John Horner (1580-1659), like Popham and Harington, was also a man of considerable wealth, who could afford a dowry of £2500 for his daughter Anne's marriage in 1653. His father, Sir Thomas, had gained influence at court through his marriage to Sir John Popham's daughter, Jane, although the Horners - like the Haringtons - had gradually drifted away from court. Nevertheless, they wielded great power and influence in the county, thanks to their undeniable 'magnate' status. Sir John, a staunch puritan who was educated at Oxford and Lincoln's Inn, was knighted in 1614, became Sheriff of Somerset in the same year and also joined the bench as a magistrate. His growing disaffection towards the court was noted at a meeting of the Privy Council in 1639, which expressed concern about 'ill-chosen' sheriffs in recent years. Sir John was described as 'refractory'.[5]

Sir John Horner.

The fourth local member of the magnate class, Sir Ralph Hopton (1596-1652), could more than match the other three in status, connection and political experience. The son of Sir Arthur Hopton, Ralph inherited estates spread over six counties which had been accumulated, largely out of monastic property, by his grandfather (who had been Marshal of the Household to Henry VIII, Edward VI, Mary and Elizabeth I). Born at Witham Friary, Ralph had been educated at Lincoln College, Oxford and the Middle Temple before commencing his career as a professional soldier in the service of the Elector Palatine at the start of the Thirty Years' War. After escorting Queen Elizabeth of Bohemia on her flight from Prague in 1620, he served as a Lieutenant-Colonel in Mansfeld's expedition to the continent before declining to take part in the expedition of Cadiz. The coronation of King Charles I saw him made a Knight of the Bath.

In the meantime, his political career had also commenced. He represented Shaftesbury in parliament in 1621, Bath in 1625, Wells in 1628, Somerset in the Short Parliament of 1640 and Wells again in the Long Parliament. Locally, after his retirement from the military scene, he threw himself wholeheartedly into public service from 1628 as a magistrate and from 1629 as a deputy lieutenant. He was appointed treasurer of the hospitals of the eastern division of the county, although much of his time was devoted to the training of the trained bands. Like Harington, he scrupulously avoided getting embroiled in the fractious rivalry which split county society during the 1630's. As a magistrate, he shared much in common with his puritan colleagues, supporting them in the Church Ales controversy and their campaign for the suppression of ale-houses. Although he served as captain of the royal bodyguard against the Scots in the northern campaign of 1639, he was reluctant to fight co-religionists. A supporter of the Established Church, he was willing to tolerate protestant dissenters far more readily than to show indulgence to catholics. It was in fact Hopton who moved, in December 1640, that 'some course might be taken to suppress the growth of poperie.'[6]

In spite of the fact that Hopton showed no real interest in politics as such and in spite of his reluctance to become involved with any political clique, when the Short Parliament was called in 1640 he quickly found himself caught up in matters of principle. At first he

Effigy of Sir Edward Hungerford (1596 - 1648) in the chapel of Farleigh Castle.

sided with the grievances and attitudes of the King's chief critics. He was an active member of committees which considered the privileges of the House and the reformation of abuses in ecclesiastical courts; referred to frequently in debates as 'that ancient parliament man', he defended the King's prerogative and the Established Church, while at the same time demanding the reform of abuses; he moved that 'the Finches be sent for as deliquents'; he spoke in favour of Strafford's attainder (1641) and was appointed spokesman of the committee named to present the Grand Remonstrance to the King in the December of the same year. Increasingly, however, Hopton became uneasy at the drift of events. By the spring of 1642, he had become one of the King's most outspoken advocates in the Commons. He defended bishops, excused the King's attempted arrest of the Five Members, opposed the militia ordinance and protested so vociferously against one manifesto that he was imprisoned the Tower for ten days. By July, he had been disabled from sitting and was sent for as a deliquent. The moderate reformer, faced with a rebellion against lawful authority, had become a royalist.[7]

In addition to these four magnates, three 'middle' gentry emerged as important leaders of local opinion once the hostilities commenced in 1642 - Sir Edward Hungerford of Corsham and Farleigh, Sir William Bassett of Claverton and Sir Thomas Bridges of Keynsham. Sir Edward Hungerford (1596-1648) enjoyed considerable landed wealth as the heir to both his father and his maternal uncle, and as the husband of Margaret Halliday, co-heiress of the Lord Mayor of London in 1620. He owned estates in Berkshire, Somerset and Wiltshire together with town houses in both London and Bath. A man of unquestionable local prominence and prestige, he sat as member for Chippenham in every parliament from 1614, except in 1626, when he had no seat and in 1625, when he represented Bath. He served his local community as justice of the peace, deputy-lieutenant (from 1624) and sheriff (1632). Educated at Oxford and the Middle Temple,

Claverton Manor, built in 1580 and home of Sir William Bassett (1602 - 1656). This drawing by S.H. Grimm in 1790 was made before its demolition in 1823, after John Vivian had built a new mansion above the village (now the American Museum). The pierced wall, balustrading and stone steps of the Elizabethan Manor House are still visible today.

he developed a particular interest in religion. His father, Sir Anthony, had been brought up as a catholic by Edward's grandmother, who was a devout adherent of that faith. Sir Anthony, however, was eventually converted to protestantism in 1588 and later wrote a memorial to his children acknowledging 'God's great mercy in bringing him to the profession of the true religion at this present established in the Church of England'. This was published by Sir Edward in 1639, who had previously appeared before Archbishop Laud in the Court of Star Chamber (1638) over a dispute regarding the salary of a curate of whom he was patron. By this time, Hungerford had become a committed puritan in doctrine and it is significant that, during the early debates in 1640 and 1641, he should take a somewhat militant stance on the question of reforming the abuses of the church and that he should also emerge as one of the leaders in proposing that Laud should be charged with treason. His partisanship was fast becoming clear. In spite of the fact that he had refused the King's request for a loan in 1639, he readily offered security for £1000 to parliament for the loan they requested in 1640 and offered a further £2000 in 1642. Although there was little doubt, therefore, about his own allegiance on the outbreak of rebellion, his two half-brothers (Anthony and John) both fought actively on the side of the King.[8]

Sir William Bassett (1602-1656) had far greater difficulty over the question of allegiance. His background was, in many ways, very similar to that of the gentry already discussed. He and his wife owned large estates in both Somerset and Cornwall; he had been trained in law at Lincoln's Inn; he had married into a most respectable county family, when he took his second wife, the stepdaughter of Sir John Stawell; and he played a prominent part in the affairs of the local community. Treasurer for the hospitals of the eastern division (with Hopton), he served as justice of the peace from 1631 and sheriff in 1636-7. A neighbour of that vociferous puritan, Humphrey Chambers, Rector of Claverton, Sir William identified himself with puritan sentiment among his colleagues on the bench by expressing alarm at the growing contempt in 1633 for authority within the county. His appointment as sheriff swept him into the bitter conflict over ship money, which proved at times almost impossible to collect. In spite of a personal loan of £800, he was summoned to appear before the Council in 1637 to explain the arrears. Unpopular with his neighbours over the collection of the tax, Bassett's enthusiasm for royal service quickly dwindled and he refused to advance a loan in 1639. When, in 1640, he was chosen to represent Bath in the Short and Long Parliaments, he at first aligned with his colleague, Alexander Popham, in attacking the government. Although he was not often named to membership of committees, his sympathy lay with the popular party until the summer of 1642, when he emerged as a genuine neutral.[9]

Sir Thomas Bridges (1616-1706) had perhaps even more pedigree and natural status than Bassett, although not as much local influence and even less national standing. His great-grandfather, Thomas, had purchased monastic lands in Keynsham from Edward VI in 1552, including the rectory and church, and had enjoyed service at court under three successive sovereigns. His brother, Sir John, had become Lord Chandos of Sudley Castle in 1554. But Sir Thomas could also boast illustrious heirs on his mother's side, because she was descended from the Dukes of Norfolk and Somerset. By the time of the civil war, he was a wealthy man, enjoying demense lands in Keynsham (worth £599 per annum) together with other property in Saltford, Stockwood, Compton Martin and Twerton (valued at £86.18s.1d. per annum).[10]

Two other dominant personalities must be added to the list of gentry who emerged as leaders of the community in 1642. Although lacking the natural status in county society which the others had acquired through birth, marriage or court connections, John Ashe, Esq., of Freshford and William Prynne, Esq., of Swainswick had other assets which were to give them prominence during the period under review. John Ashe (1597-1659), the son of prosperous clothier James Ashe of Westcombe in Batcombe, had made an outstanding success of his cloth industry based on Freshford (see above). Backed by the considerable fortune acquired in this way, he purchased numerous estates in both Somerset and

Wiltshire, before inheriting his father's property in 1642. Ashe quickly proved himself to be a leader of resistance to the policies and attitudes of the government. Although he failed to achieve any local or national office of great significance until 1640, as collector of the 1627 loan he defaulted on his own contribution and was reported accordingly. In 1637, he strongly protested against the soap monopoly. In a petition to the Privy Council with four other clothiers, he insisted 'that for making fine west country cloths we of necessity must have Castile and Venice Soap'. Two years later, he voiced his objection to the assessments for ship money in the Bathforum Hundred - just as his father had earlier led local opposition to its collection. But it was over matters of religion that he felt the government's policy most keenly. An ardent puritan of the presbyterian persuasion, he gave active help to the parishioners of Beckington in their dispute with Bishop Piers and Archbishop Laud over the positioning of the altar in 1634 (see below). Not only did he meet John Boyle in London, helping him to deliver personally to Laud a petition against his excommunication, he also gave moral support at the Assizes to those Beckington men charged with riot. 'I was present and saw and heard the whole matter, these poor men came to the next Assizes when they could not gett any Councell that dared to plead for them.' Later to give evidence at Laud's trial in 1643, Ashe had also been summoned before the Star Chamber in 1637 on charges of distributing in Somerset the libellous writings of Prynne, Bastwick and Burton, in which they attacked the abuses of the church. Although he was eventually released without punishment - partly because of his plea that thousands of local spinners and weavers were totally dependent on him for livelihood - his hatred of Laud's policies and his commitment to the puritan cause turned him into one of parliament's most active members. Elected as member for Westbury in both the Short and Long Parliaments of 1640, 'he did then in ye House publickly engage to pay £10 per week for ye maintenance of ye army'.[11]

William Prynne (1600 - 1669) of Swainswick, Recorder and Member of Parliament for Bath. Engraving by Benoist.

There is little doubt that the most famous of the local leaders on the national scene was William Prynne (1600-1669). His father had rented the manor of Swainswick from Oriel College, Oxford and had dominated the community as local squire and warden of the parish church. His grandfather, William Sherston, had further enhanced the family reputation in Bath by being its Mayor on eight occasions and its member of parliament on five. Sherston, who rented sizeable estates just outside the city composed of old priory land, shaped William's beliefs profoundly in matters of puritan doctrine. Prynne was educated at the Bath Free School (later styled King Edward's School, Bath) before proceeding to Oriel College, Oxford in 1618. He came under considerable Calvinist influence from his teachers both there and at Lincoln's Inn, where he was eventually called to the bar in 1628. Interested almost equally in his study of both law and theology, he soon launched a series of pamphlets which vigorously attacked the abuses in church and state. His legal mind and presbyterian beliefs could tolerate neither the unconstitutional powers seized by the King nor the tyrannical methods used by the bishops. His attack on stage plays in *Histromastix* (1632) was interpreted as a direct insult on the Queen, who had herself been recently engaged in performances at court. For this he was fined £5000, imprisoned for life and sentenced to the loss of both his ears. Prynne's courage was undeterred. From prison he launched a new assault on bishops in general and Laud in particular. Again he was hauled before the Star Chamber in 1637, this time in company with Henry Burton and John Bastwick. Again he was fined, imprisoned, deprived of the rest of his ears and branded with the letters 'S.L.' (seditious libeller). He was not finally released until the Long Parliament assembled in 1640, when he wrote *A New Discovery of the Prelates' Tyranny,* a vigorous attack on episcopacy and defence of parliament. By this time, he had also inherited his father's property in Swainswick (worth probably in the region of £200 a year). This fact was not without its local significance because, from that date he was a regular visitor to the locality and was able to make his own views felt when important decisions were being made over matters of allegiance. Whereas Prynne lacked the wealth, social status, family connections and court influence enjoyed by the other leading gentry, he was above all the local lad made good - a man with a national reputation, a brilliant mind, a rebellious nature and a family who had made their mark in the city of Bath. [12]

Perhaps the most remarkable factor to emerge from these biographical sketches is that in 1642 these nine members of the gentry, who were to dominate the local scene throughout the ensuing years, had much in common - whatever differing shades of political or religious opinion were to appear later. Averaging 46 years of age, they all enjoyed landed estates; with the exception of Prynne, they could all claim to be wealthy; no fewer than seven of them had studied at the bar in London, six of them having previously attended the university of Oxford; five of them had already sat in parliament by 1640 (and three more were to do so later); four of them had actually represented the City of Bath (Sir Edward Hungerford, Sir Ralph Hopton, Sir William Bassett and Alexander Popham); five of them had served the county community as justices of the peace; and all of them were held locally in the highest respect and esteem. Several other features are apparent concerning their beliefs and attitudes during the 1630's. Six clearly regarded religion as a prime issue in the controversy (Popham, Harington, Hopton, Prynne, Hungerford, and Ashe), of who the first four also saw the constitutional situation in strict legal terms. Yet, in spite of differences that were to show as the national crisis deepened, it is true to say that before 1641 there was remarkable harmony among the local leadership. Those who sat as justices (Francis Popham, John Horner, John Harington, Ralph Hopton and William Bassett), even though later they followed their separate ways, nevertheless took a similar pro-puritan attitude before 1642 over both the 'Crisis of Order' and the church ales dispute (see below). [13] When parliament re-convened in 1640, those who sat as members all took up a critical stance against the government's recent policies in church and state. Furthermore, although Hungerford, Prynne, Ashe, Popham and Horner had no hesitation in declaring for parliament in 1642, it is interesting to note how much in common they shared with Harington, Hopton and Bassett. In spite of the fact that Harington, somewhat reluctantly, eventually sided with parliament and his two colleagues with the King, all three displayed the same sense of moderation, the same independence of thought, the same desire to serve their local community and the same aversion to political factions.

(ii) Leadership in the City of Bath

The membership of Bath Corporation had undergone something of a transformation in the years between 1638 and 1642. No fewer than fourteen members had retired (George Clift, Richard Child, Peter Cray, George Elkington, John Griffith, John Hull, Anthony Kingstone, Jacob Langley, George Mounton, Thomas Power, Samuel Price, Matthew Rendall, Arthur Sherston and Jacob Smith). But fresh blood had been introduced at the same time with nine newcomers joining the ranks between 1640 and 1642 (John Boyce, Henry Chapman, Thomas Cole, Richard Druce, John Haywood, Richard Martin, John Pearce, Robert Penney and Robert Sheppard). However, although this inevitably reduced the average age of the Council (Henry Chapman, for instance, was only 32 in 1642), there is no evidence to suggest that the sudden turnover in membership made the body more radical in its policies. [14]

Nevertheless, over the next twenty years, three distinct political groupings were to emerge which, by the end of the period under review, had become involved in a series of bitter disputes. At the one extreme were members of Matthew Clift's faction, consisting of ardent puritans who most actively supported the parliamentary cause during the war, were illegally arrested by Henry Chapman in an attempt to exclude them from council business in 1661 and/or were later ejected from the Council in 1662 under the terms of the Corporation Act[15] (see Chapter 8). Alderman Matthew Clift himself, aged 46 in 1642, was a mercer and draper occupying two properties in Broad Street.[16] He often did business with the Council, supplying 'cloth for to make the poor folkes gownes' in 1640 and providing a metal worker in 1643 for 'keyes and mendinge the lockes of the cittie gates.'[17] Styled 'gent' in the 1641 Subsidy list,[18] he had followed the example of his father by becoming Mayor in 1629 and again in 1640. Alderman John Atwood, gent., (or Wood, as he later became known), aged 52, was a baker who sold cakes to the Council (1642), provided bread for the poor (1643) and supplied fagots for 'bonfiers' (1640).[19] He, too, held various properties in Northgate Street, Stall Street and next to the Abbey, together with orchards, gardens, meadow and pasture in the suburbs of the city.[20] Elected to the Council in 1635, he was to play a prominent part later as Chamberlain during the war years (1643-1646) and Mayor in 1652.[21] Alderman John Biggs, aged 46, was an innkeeper who leased The Unicorn in Northgate Street together with other property in Saw Close and next to the borough walls north of the West Gate.[22] One of the most experienced members of Council, he had already served as Chamberlain in 1635 and Mayor in 1636. A popular figure in the city, his headstone in Bath Abbey reads: 'John Bigge, gent' five times Mayor, who lived pious toward God, charitable to the poor and loving to all.'

Another member of the Clift faction was Alderman John Parker, gent, aged 42, who was a wealthy clothier and woollen draper, leasing several properties in Northgate Street.[23] He also rented some twenty-one acres of meadow, pasture and arable just outside the city in Barton Farm.[24] By 1642, he was already becoming a prominent member of the Corporation, serving as Chamberlain between 1641 and 1643, before being elected to the office of Mayor (1643).[25] His father, Edward Parker, aged 65, served with him on the Council until 1647 and shared his son's political inclinations. A woollen draper, operating his business from just outside the North Gate, he also rented a house in Southgate Street.[26] John Boyce, aged 37, who completed the original membership of this pro-parliament faction in 1642, is a much more obscure figure. His father, Robert, held property in the churchyard of Mary de Stalls next to the tennis court but little is

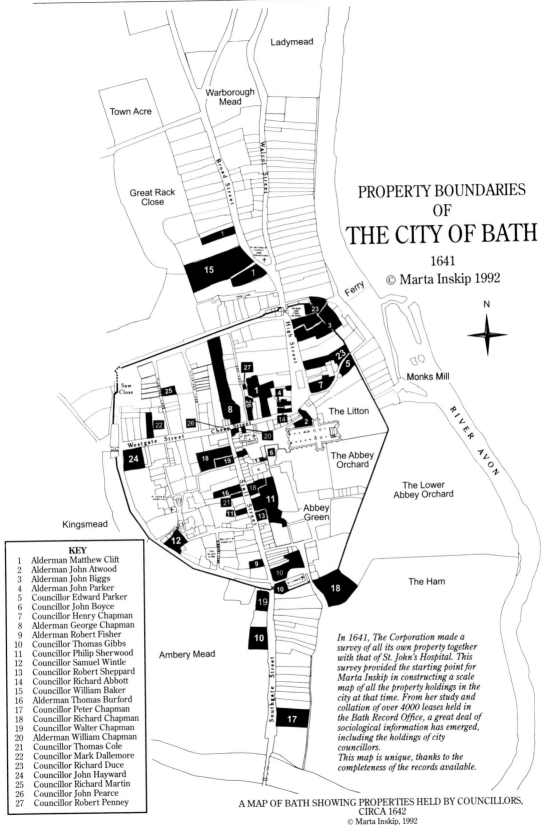

PROPERTY BOUNDARIES
OF
THE CITY OF BATH
1641
© Marta Inskip 1992

Monks Mill

RIVER AVON

The Litton

The Abbey
Orchard

The Lower
Abbey Orchard

The Ham

KEY

1	Alderman Matthew Clift
2	Alderman John Atwood
3	Alderman John Biggs
4	Alderman John Parker
5	Councillor Edward Parker
6	Councillor John Boyce
7	Councillor Henry Chapman
8	Alderman George Chapman
9	Alderman Robert Fisher
10	Councillor Thomas Gibbs
11	Councillor Philip Sherwood
12	Councillor Samuel Wintle
13	Councillor Robert Sheppard
14	Councillor Richard Abbott
15	Councillor William Baker
16	Alderman Thomas Burford
17	Councillor Peter Chapman
18	Councillor Richard Chapman
19	Councillor Walter Chapman
20	Alderman William Chapman
21	Councillor Thomas Cole
22	Councillor Mark Dallemore
23	Councillor Richard Duce
24	Councillor John Hayward
25	Councillor Richard Martin
26	Councillor John Pearce
27	Councillor Robert Penney

*In 1641, The Corporation made a
survey of all its own property together
with that of St. John's Hospital. This
survey provided the starting point for
Marta Inskip in constructing a scale
map of all the property holdings in the
city at that time. From her study and
collation of over 4000 leases held in
the Bath Record Office, a great deal of
sociological information has emerged,
including the holdings of city
councillors.
This map is unique, thanks to the
completeness of the records available.*

A MAP OF BATH SHOWING PROPERTIES HELD BY COUNCILLORS,
CIRCA 1642
© Marta Inskip, 1992

known of John himself. Others who joined the Council at a later date, but who subsequently adhered to this group were Edward Parker, junior, draper (the son of Alderman John Parker), Alderman John Ford (whose occupation is not known), Anthony Colloby, maltster, who owned premises just outside the North Gate, Henry Moore, who joined the Council in 1658 and whose son was an apothecary, and George Reeve, a goldsmith with a shop in the Abbey churchyard, all of whom were arrested by Henry Chapman in 1661 and expelled from the Council in 1662.

At the other extreme, were the members of Henry Chapman's own faction, all of whom identified with the royalist cause during the war, were subsequently excluded from the Council by order of parliament in 1647 and/or appeared before the Committee for Compounding on charges of delinquency. At a later stage, those who had survived the intervening years were also associated with Chapman's protest when he stormed out of the council meeting in 1661 (see Chapter 8). Henry Chapman himself was innkeeper of The Sun in Northgate Street, opposite the Guildhall, a property occupied by his relatives since 1585. The son of Alderman Walter Chapman, he was a member of the most influential and politically experienced family in Bath. Although by no means affluent in 1642, he also rented a close of five acres in the neighbouring village of Widcombe.[27] At thirty-two, he was by far the youngest member of the group he came to dominate. Alongside him for instance, was sixty-five year old Alderman George Chapman, another member of that large family. As innkeeper of The Bear in Cheap Street, he had supplied wine to the Council in 1639 as presents for Sir Charles Berkley, Sir Edward Rodney and The Lord Bishop. A man of undoubted wealth, he rented a house and garden in Stall Street, a stable and garden in Westgate Street, waste ground outside the East Gate for dog kennels, a barn and gardens lying by the borough walls and a further house and garden by the disused St Michael's Church. One of the 'elder statesmen', he had twice been elected Mayor in 1626 and 1635.[28]

Another vastly experienced member of that group was Alderman Robert Fisher who, at the age of sixty-nine, could also look back to his two spells of duty of Mayor in 1628 and 1638. A mercer by trade, he rented a shop in Stall Street, but later acquired additional property at the end of Northgate Street near the bowling green, as well as leasing meadows and orchards in Widcombe. A man of considerable energy and enterprise, he became responsible for the coal-mines at Paulton, frequently selling coal and wood to the Council 'for the chamber use.'[29] Thomas Gibbs, aged fifty-five, was innkeeper of The Golden Lyon by The South Gate. He also occupied tenements, a garden and a stable in Southgate Street and the 'tenysplay' by St James's Church. An experienced councillor, he had been elected Chamberlain in three successive years between 1636 and 1639.[30] Two fellow-innkeepers joined him in this group. Philip Sherwood, at sixty-five, was still innkeeper of The Three Tuns in Stall Street, also renting a tenement immediately opposite. He often supplied goods and services to the Corporation - 'potle of sacke which was brought to the Hall' (1640) or 'lodging, fier and beare' for the Recorder in 1641. Although he had been elected to the Council in 1634, he had not held any office. Nor, indeed, had Samuel Wintle, innkeeper of The George near the Hot Bath. He, too, had frequently supplied the Corporation with wine or horses, as well as accommodating the Recorder from time to time. Just outside the city, he rented a close of 14 acres in the parish of Widcombe.[31] The final member of this original group of seven was Robert Sheppard, aged 31, a baker who started business in 'a shop standinge on the cittie waste', but eventually moved to premises next the The Three Tuns in Stall Street.[32]

Five other men, who joined the Council at a later date, subsequently identified with the political views of Chapman's faction, joining him in the mass walk-out from the Chamber in 1661. These were John Bush, a mercer in High Street with lodgings also at Bear Corner, Robert Child, son of a woollen draper, and his brother, William Child, who rented a small shop in the Abbey Churchyard and married into the Chapman family; John Fisher, son of Robert Fisher and also a mercer by trade; and Walter Gibbs, gent., son of

Thomas Gibbs who, in 1656, bequeathed him a property known as The New House near the South Gate.[33] Walter also acquired through marriage The Bell Inn.

Quite apart from the two emerging factions already mentioned, the Council in 1642 also contained a group of fourteen members who can best be described as moderates. These were men who did not noticeably align with the militants of either extreme, but who tended to sympathise with the parliamentary cause during the war. Although twelve members of this group had left the Council for varying reasons by 1660, the two that remained (John Pearce and Robert Penney) voted against Chapman in the election disputes of 1661 but were nevertheless permitted to retain their seats after the purging of the Corporation in 1662. The moderates consisted of Richard Abbott, a mercer and button maker from Cheap Street, who was licensed to sell tobacco and supplied the Council with bullets, smokers' pipes and plumbers' materials;[34] William Baker, a clothier based in Broad Street, who subsequently became Sergeant-at-Mace:[35] Alderman Thomas Burford, apothecary, who lived in Stall Street, opposite the Hart Lodgings and was in fact Mayor on the outbreak of civil war;[36] Peter Chapman, gent., who rented two adjacent properties in Stall Street near the King's Bath;[37] Richard Chapman, innkeeper of the White Hart and The Hart Lodgings in Stall Street, a man of considerable wealth (with pastures in Barton Farm, Town Acre and Walcot Street) and local stature (having previously been Mayor in 1627 and 1637);[38] Walter Chapman, a mercer with a shop in Stall Street near the former church of Mary de Stalls, who frequently supplied the Council with linen, iron, glass, cloth and shrouds and later succeeded his father as Master of St John's Hospital;[39] his father, Alderman William Chapman, a glover, with premises in Stall Street, who had been Mayor in 1639 and 1641;[40] Thomas Cole, a mercer living in Stall Street;[41] Mark Dallemore, a clothier based in Westgate Street, who later diversified by taking over The Cock and The Pied Bull inns in Stall Street;[42] Richard Druce, a baker with freehold property in Northgate Street, who helped to feed prisoners with bread in 1643;[43] John Haywood, originally a yeoman who later became an organ maker living in Westgate Street;[44] Richard Martin, a shopkeeper living in Culverhouse Lane;[45] John Pearce, a mercer operating in Cheap Street, who supplied the Corporation with canvas, buttons, thread and cloth but who also undertook many special assignments for them (e.g. delivering a petition to parliament about free quarter in 1646, leading a deputation over the navigation of the river Avon in 1654 and supervising the demolition of Stalls Church in 1656)[46] and Robert Penney, a mercer with a shop in Cox Lane, who sold shrouds, sugar tobacco, buttons, silk and gunpowder to the Corporation on various occasions.[47]

The three groups, which gradually formed within the Corporation from 1642, had much in common. All twenty-seven men who have been identified as having seats on the Council in that year were sufficiently prosperous to rent property from the Corporation and all but two of them were listed among the 105 citizens assessed to pay the subsidy in 1641. There was in fact little difference in basic affluence between the members of Clift's faction and those of Chapman's. Clift himself was assessed to pay 16s 0d, as were the other member of his group (apart from newcomer onto the Council, John Boyce, who was not assessed). Although the comparatively youthful Chapman did not himself feature in the list of assessments, his close supporters all paid 16s 0d towards the subsidy, except for Robert Fisher, who paid 21s 4d and Robert Sheppard, who paid 8s 0d. The members of the moderate group were, by comparison, less affluential with as many as half their number paying just 8s.0d. and the remainder paying 15s.0d. - except Richard Chapman, who was assessed for 26s.8d. Furthermore, six of that group were new to the Council, so the two extremist factions tended to monopolise both wealth and political experience among the members of the Corporation. Four of the Aldermen in 1642 (John Biggs, John Parker, John Atwood and Matthew Clift) identified with Clift's Group, two (George Chapman and Robert Fisher) with Chapman's group and two (Thomas Burford and William Chapman) with the moderates.[48]

At first sight, too, there was hardly any difference between them in terms of occupation, the vast majority being drawn from local business. Bakers, woollen drapers, mercers, clothiers and innkeepers, therefore, feature among the adherents both of Clift's group and of the moderates. It is, however, perhaps significant that no fewer than five out of the seven members of Chapman's group were innkeepers (see below). It is also perhaps relevant to note that the average age of the pro-royalist group in 1642 was significantly higher than that of the active parliamentarians (i.e. 52.8 years against 48), almost certainly encouraging a more conservative approach.[49] One other factor must be mentioned as providing a more stabilising influence during periods of conflict - the close inter-relationship brought about by family ties among large sections of the Corporation. Henry Chapman (R) was the son of Alderman William Chapman (M), brother to Walter Chapman (M), cousin to Richard Chapman (M), son-in-law to Alderman Robert Fisher (R) and brother-in-law to Matthew Clift (P), whose mother was a Parker (P). Edward Parker, junior, (P) was son-in-law to Richard Druce (M), while brothers William Child (R) and Robert Child (R) were grandsons of Alderman William Chapman (M) and brothers-in-law to John Pearce (M). Furthermore, Alderman George Chapman (R) was brother to Peter Chapman (M). The fact, therefore, that many members of the Council were not only business neighbours, but also close relatives undoubtedly helped counter any natural tendency for the body to disintegrate during moments of crisis.[50]

Exactly the same domination of the borough oligarchy by closely linked family groups has been noticed in Norwich, Bristol, Exeter, Newcastle and York. In Norwich, as in Bath, prominent families were divided on the outbreak of war.[51]

(iii) The Issues
(a) Taxation

Long before Charles raised his standard at Nottingham in August 1642, the people of Somerset had been seething inwardly - and on occasions outwardly - against his 'unjust' interference with their lives in general and their pockets in particular. The period of the 'personal rule' (1629-40), during which the King dispensed with assistance from troublesome parliaments, inevitably placed a heavy strain on his financial resources. Various methods were tried to raise money for the purposes of government, some with dusty precedents drawn from remote pages of history. When, therefore, in October 1634 the King decided to improve his naval defences, he imposed the notorious 'Ship Money' on coastal areas. In practical terms this meant that the sea-ports of Somerset, together with Bristol, and others in Gloucestershire, were required to raise £6,735 for a fully-equipped vessel of 800 tons. Within a year the money had been collected.[52]

Encouraged by this success, Charles issued a second demand for 'Ship Money' in August 1635. There was, however, one significant difference - the tax was now extended to inland districts as well as coastal areas. Opposition was inevitable. Somerset, assessed for a total of £8,000, paid slowly and reluctantly. Two years later a balance of £1056 was still outstanding. Complaints, mainly about methods of assessment, poured into the Privy Council from places like Bruton, Wellow, Norton St. Philip and the Hundred of Bathforum. Bath itself was forced to find £70 as its own contribution.[53] This seems to have been paid. Certainly the Mayor received expenses in 1635 for 'goeing to Ilchester about the shippinge', presumably to hear details of the assessment from the Sheriff. A year later, Stephen Gettoes (the Town Clerk) received four shillings for likewise 'goeing about the shippinge money', but this time in all probability to pay the tax.[54]

When Charles issued a third writ for ship money in October 1636, the volume of protest in Somerset rose from disgruntled murmuring to an angry roar. The local pattern was set by William Strode, a wealthy and influential resident of Street, who bluntly refused to pay. William Bassett, the Sheriff, and his agents, the local constables, soon found it almost impossible to collect the tax in certain districts. In a letter to the Council he complained of 'factious spirits' which were at work in the hundreds stirring up a great volume of objections. [55] Somerset quickly established itself as one of the worst payers of ship money in the country.

Bath, however, was surprisingly moderate in its opposition. By November 1637 the Council had received '£60 paid by James Galley on behalf of John Bigg, Mayor of Bath, ship money collected in the said city'. [56] In the meantime, Galley (the new Town Clerk) had also delivered a 'petition about the shipp money' [57] to the Sherriff on behalf of the inhabitants of Bath. This demanded that part of their unfair assessment should be borne by the neighbouring areas of Claverton and Bathforum. [58] Bassett was obviously persuaded. Indeed, when the Council wrote to Bath in 1638 demanding the arrears of £10, the Mayor coolly replied that 'William Bassett, then Sheriff of Somerset, willed the than Mayor to make a rate for £60 only and that the £10 residue the hundred of Bathforum would pay, for which cause we paid in but £60'. [59] Bath's protest was therefore not of principle, challenging the King's right to tax, but rather one of detail, questioning the amount of its own contribution.

Whether the city paid anything towards the fourth demand for ship money in 1639 is open to speculation. By then there was such general and open resistance to the levy that local constables had virtually abandoned any attempt to collect it. James Galley, it is true, made his annual pilgrimage in 1640 'about the shipping money' [60] - this time to Bridgwater - but what he did or said is not recorded.

Meanwhile, an additional pressure was being exerted on the pockets of the local people. In 1639 the very policies which had caused discontent in England brought about open rebellion in Scotland in the form of the Bishops' Wars. To counter this threat to the country's security, Charles demanded levies from all the shires: 'The great forces lately raised in Scotland without order from us by the instigation of some factious persons, ill affected to monarchical government, who seek to cloak their too apparent designs under a cloak of religion...has moved us to take care to provide for the safety of Kingdom of England, which is in apparent danger to be invaded.' [61] Somerset was required to send 1,200 fully equipped men from the trained bands to York. Bath itself provided fourteen soldiers 'for the Northerne expedition', paying a total of £6 9s 4d for their upkeep and contributing ten swords into the bargain. [62] The men were eventually collected together at Bruton and Wincanton, where they were given some training and a wage of 8d. per day. Long delays and poor leadership caused mass desertions and the pillaging of local property. [63]

The Scottish problem, however, was not solved quickly. Charles eventually was forced by the lack of funds to summon in 1640 first the Short Parliament and then the Long Parliament. Subsidies granted by the latter in January 1641 to pay for the war against the Scots added further to the financial burden on local people. Although the size of Bath's contribution is not recorded, the Bath Chamberlain's Accounts testify clearly that the subsidy was certainly collected. Fees were paid 'to John Brown for carryinge the certificate for the subside' and 'to Mr Gally for his expences to Beckington about the subsidies and parchment and for ingrossing the Pole money'. [64] On the other hand, we do know that Keynsham paid £19 4s towards the Subsidy of 1641, Englishcombe £6 2s 8d and the Hundred of Wellow a combined sum of £83 1s 4d. Claverton and Bathampton had meanwhile paid the frightening total of £266 1s 6d for the poll tax of the same year. [65]

Discontent steadily grew. Even as early as July 1638, a presentment had been made to the County Assizes at Bath complaining of heavy taxation and high prices. The latter, it claimed, was occasioned not 'so much by scarcity as by other accidents, namely, by the great and heavy taxation by new invented ways, which is so heavy a burden on the farmers as causes them to sell their grain at high rates to support their charge, by which labourers are not able to get sufficient sustenance and is a cause of many thefts and felonies'. [66]

There is, therefore, much evidence to suggest that Somerset festered with complaints and grievances in the years before 1642. Set against a background of food shortages, of rising prices, unemployment and growing poverty in the 1620's and 1630's, the government's taxation policies in particular were distinctly unpopular with both landowners and merchants alike. There is, however, little to suggest that finance developed into more of a major issue in North-East Somerset than elsewhere. Indeed, in some ways local people took their knocks more philosophically than most and avoided any serious confrontation. The real issue for them centred rather on their faith and culture, which seemed to be under sustained attack from the policies of Archbishop Laud. This, more than anything, was a source of increasing anxiety - an anxiety which united the area in its opposition to the government.

(b) The Puritan Revolution

By 1620, North-East Somerset was already firmly under the influence of the puritan religion, thanks to a cultural revolution which had steadily gained forced over the previous fifty years. The actual strength and distribution of puritanism within the area will be considered in detail in Chapter Seven. In summary, however, it should be noted here that puritanism was particularly strong in those parishes closely associated with the clothing industry along the Avon valley and with those districts personally dominated by the puritan gentry. The heartland of puritan activity undoubtedly lay in the Hundreds of Bathforum and Keynsham, where most of the influential puritans resided. Elsewhere, adherence was patchy. Although by 1642 grass root support was very much in evidence at parish level, there is no doubt that the spread of the movement owed much to the steady pressure exerted from above by the puritan elite. Such was the strength of their conviction and the power of their influence that the Pophams, the Horners, the Prynnes, the Haringtons and the Hungerfords - aided by a majority on the Bath City Council and by Ashe's workforce along the Avon valley - were able to mastermind the cultural revolution. They were also supported at a slightly lower level by successful farmers, merchants and businessmen, whose puritan commitment and sense of moral responsibility motivated them to monopolise many important offices within local parishes. Working closely with the gentry, they ensured that puritan doctrines were rapidly disseminated by a succession of ardent preachers and lecturers, foremost among whom was Humphrey Chambers, vicar of Claverton and subsequently a leading member of the Assembly of Divines. Pulpits in all the key centres of population in the area were, by the 1640's, controlled by puritans - Bath, Frome, Kilmersdon, Mells, Saltford and Keynsham - even though it would appear that under a half of the parishes in all were actively and deeply committed to the puritan cause.

Not all beneficed clergy in the locality, however, met with the same approval from the puritan elite. The effect was to increase growing divisions within the community by prompting some to form conventicles of their own and others to attend sermons by visiting lecturers. Officials and residents in several parishes in the area had complained, during the North Somerset visitation of 1615, of the inadequacy of preaching and catechizing. The heartfelt cry uttered by the villagers of Bathwick - 'we have not our sermons as we ought to have according to the canons' - was echoed in Woolley (where no sermons at all had been preached), in Bathampton ('five or six within the year ... and no more') and Langridge ('they have not their monthly sermon ... but six everie year'). Although the parson at St Catherine was presented because 'he doth not cathechise the children every Sunday', he aroused far less disgust in the eyes of his parishioners than the curate of Stanton Drew. This wretched fellow, it was claimed, not only failed to catechize the children, but also left them 'without prayer' on several sabbath days. To make matter worse, he was 'verrie deafe', a user of alehouses and 'a keeper of drunkards companye'.[67] Such was the frustration within the area, that by 1604 conventicles had been formed just over the border in Wiltshire at Bradford-on-Avon, Broughton Gifford and Slaughterford, the latter attended by weavers from Castle Combe. Meanwhile, in 1603, a mason and a weaver from Box had denounced the Prayer Book and the validity non-preaching ministers - further evidence that local puritanism was broadly-based and appealed to a wide section of the population.[68]

The Bath Corporation had been showing similar anxiety over the lack of sermons and had taken a series of appropriate actions. There was some dissatisfaction in 1631, for instance, with the Rector of the Abbey Church of St Peter and St Paul, Dr George Webb, who was clearly enjoying the income from more than one living. At first, they resolved that Dr Webb should 'resign his Parsonage', that no-one should in future 'be presented to the living' if he already had another benefice and that the incumbent should 'always reside in Bath'. Later in the year, however, they relented and decided instead to make it easier for Dr Webb to stay in Bath on their terms by granting a rate to increase his 'wages' to £10 per annum. They had also been building up an endowment fund to encourage the revival of the earlier practice that sermons should be preached in the church on special occasions throughout the year (i.e. Ascension Day, Good Friday, New Year's Day, Ash Wednesday, All Saints' Day and Candlemas Day) - a practice which had long since lapsed. Although, between 1630 (when the sermons re-commenced) and 1639 (when James Masters succeeded) these sermons were normally preached by the Rector himself at a fee ranging from 6s 8d to 10s 0d, several visiting preachers were also invited to take part.[69] In the meantime, Dr George Webb had become Bishop of Limerick in 1634, handing over the living in Bath to Theophilus Webb, his eldest son.

Quite apart from reviving the sermons that were given on special Sundays within the Church's calendar, the Corporation also took the initiative of setting up regular mid-week lectures. The first clues appear in the Chamberlain's Accounts for 1627, when William Chapman received a payment 'towards the lecture charge', and for 1630, when Thomas Power was allocated £6 13s 4d 'towards the chardges of the keepinge of the Ordinary'. The system was explained more fully the Council Minutes of 1645, when lectures were resumed at the end of the royalist occupation. Each Wednesday, a godly minister was invited to visit the city to deliver a lengthy exposition of the sum of £12 a year from the local rates. Aldermen and Common Councillors were expected to take it in turns to hold the Ordinary - i.e. 'to entertain the Minister and his man and their horses for one night if they came overnight and at dinner the lecture day'. Furthermore, the Mayor, together with one Alderman and two Common Councillors chosen on a rota system, were to join the dinner party each week to help in providing hospitality for the guest. They were, however, each required to bear the cost of their meal (one shilling) out of their own pockets. The original decision to take responsibility for the cost of the Ordinary was taken in September 1633 when, after a debate on who should not be invited 'to preach the lecture', it was agreed that the Corporation would 'maintain the ordinary for the preachers if Mr Doctor Webb will provide them'.

Many other cities, of course, had also established lectureships from Queen Elizabeth's reign onwards as urban protestantism became an important force. Early examples included Oxford (1586), Worcester (1589) and Exeter (1600). In Barnstaple, Benjamin Cox undertook in 1625, 'to reade a weekly lecture in the parish church' at a yearly pension of £50 for three years. This stipend compares with those at Exeter (£50 in 1600) and Worcester (£40 in 1631). In Leicester, householders were given a firm instruction by the council to attend the weekly address given by the town lecturer on Wednesdays: 'the Aldermen of everie ward shall cause his Constable to give warninge to everie householder to go or send one or two to the sermon on the weekday'.[70]

Evidence suggests that an active preaching ministry had developed by the late 1620's within many parishes of North-East Somerset and that this was based to a large extent on the system of lectures. A list, for instance, has survived of sixteen holy days which had been assigned 'for ye lecture at Chewton wth ye lecturers'. It is interesting to note that four of the lecturers were drawn from churches in this locality - Humphrey Chambers of Claverton, Samual Tilley of Keynsham, James Aston of Kilmersdon and Mr Jenkins of Stratton.[71] However, all lectures in the county were eventually suppressed by Bishop

William Piers, Bishop of Bath and Wells (1580 - 1670). Portrait by an unknown artist.

William Piers, anxious to impose Archbishop Laud's instructions to that effect issued in 1629. Piers, who had been installed in 1632, was later praised by Laud for bringing about 'a great Reformation' in the diocese 'by his care and diligence'. Margaret Steig suggests that the Laudians used the diocese of Bath and Wells ' as a laboratory to carry out their most cherished policies to a degree not possible in other dioceses with less compliant and less thoroughly convinced bishops'.[72] Their immediate tasks were to eliminate unauthorised theology both inside and outside the church and to ensure that individuals only attended religious gatherings at their own parish church. The Bishop therefore encouraged a number of presentments in an attempt to put a stop to the visiting lecturer system that was operating at Chewton and elsewhere. In September 1638, for instance, the churchwardens of all three Bath parishes, together with the churchwardens of Bathford, were presented 'for permitting their minister to appoint strange preachers to preach'. Although the cases were dismissed because the preachers had in fact been licensed by other bishops, the campaign to silence puritan preachers continued unabated.[73]

Piers tried to enforce conformity by insisting that lecturers should read prayers from the Prayer Book in a surplice and hood before any sermon commenced and that they should preach in a gown rather than a cloak. In June 1640, Robert Bacon, curate of Brislington, was presented for not wearing a surplice, for not reading the Creed or Absolution, for seldom reading a great part of the Common Prayer and for permitting strange preachers to preach. The Bishop regarded both Brislington and Keynsham as 'centres of infection', which attracted crowds of people from Bristol and elsewhere to hear anti-establishment preaching and questionable theology. Although Bacon was subsequently removed from office and excommunicated, he continued to address street gatherings and later established a congregation of Baptists in Gloucestershire.[74] Another local minister to suffer was John Cornish of Dunkerton, who was suspended for failure to comply with a ban on lectures which operated on weekdays and Sunday afternoons. Not only had he preached a funeral sermon in the evening, he had also seized the opportunity to preach against ecclesiastical courts.[75]

Nevertheless, although the Laudians had succeeded in controlling the spread of the lecture system in the short term, the strength of enthusiasm for the puritan cause in the northern parishes ensured a rapid revival once the war had started. The action of the Bath Corporation in 1642, when they restored their own mid-week lectures, was perhaps symptomatic of the general state of feeling. The Chamberlain, who made a payment 'for the stuffe for the lecture gound and all things belonging to it', also significantly made certain of its future security by investing in 'iron shrouds and locks'.[76] The Laudian campaign against lecturers was also experienced in other parts of the country, including Norwich, where Bishop Wren was just as ruthless as Bishop Piers;[77] Worcester, where Dean Potter ordered the lecturer's pulpit to be removed from the cathedral, in spite of the fact that Bishop Thornborough actually supported the corporation;[78] and Gloucester, where a running battle took place between the conservative bishop and the puritan corporation, which was most anxious to retain the service of its distinguished preacher, John Workman.[79]

The general picture provided by this evidence, therefore, is that puritanism had taken firm root in a good proportion of North-East Somerset by the early years of the seventeenth century, a process heightened by the arrival of the preaching ministry in the late 1620's.[80] Judging by the comparative shortage of presentments for unlawful games, sabbath-breaking and tippling, the 'meaner sort' had largely fallen into line in many villages. It is hardly surprising, therefore, that this area failed to become heavily embroiled in the controversy surrounding maypoles and church ales which swept other parts of the county in the 1630's. The tradition of holding 'wakes' to celebrate the foundation of the church had been severely frowned on by puritans as desecration of the sabbath. These revels, which were joined after evening service by members of neighbouring parishes, included maypole dancing and games of various types. Beer flowed freely and rioting sometimes occurred. Local magistrates, throughout the country influenced by puritan pressure, had steadily suppressed such popular festivals from the 1590's. In Somerset, for instance, the justices ordered at the Wells Quarter Sessions in 1608 that all 'churchales, clerkales, woodwardsales, bidales and all kinds of suchlike ales whatsoever be immediately from henceforth throughout the whole countie of Somerset utterly forbidden and suppressed',[81] This order was renewed in March 1632 by Lord Chief Justice Richardson and circulated to every minister in each parish church. Nevertheless, in the following year, a counter attack was staged by Charles I and Archbishop Laud, supported by the Bishop of Bath and Wells, Williams Piers. Anxious

William Laud (1573 - 1645), Archbishop of Canterbury. Portrait after Van Dyke.

to retain these popular festivals in the cause of social and political harmony, the King forced Richardson to withdraw his order and re-issued the Declaration of Sports, which his father had originally published in 1617. This Declaration, which all clergy were required to read from the pulpit, gave approval to 'decent and sober recreation' after the evening service - but not to excess.[82]

There is little evidence that church revels had been held on any large scale in North-East Somerset in the period after 1600, although one clearly took place on a Saturday in 1615 in the neighbourhood of Batheaston. John Humphrey, an ale-house keeper there, was presented for permitting tipling during divine service, when 'his house was full of strangers comeing thither to be merry, it being the morrow after their revell day'.[83] Otherwise, tight puritan control had ensured that such festivities remained firmly suppressed. Maypoles, too, would seem to have disappeared from the scene, although one was belatedly taken down in Bristol in April 1628, when the council spent six pence on the operation.[84] It was hardly surprising, therefore, that Humphrey Chambers, vicar of Claverton, refused to read the Declaration of Sports from his pulpit in 1633 and that he was subsequently suspended and imprisoned for two years.[85]

His reaction probably typified that of many clergy in the area, including Symon Cotton, curate of Dundry in the Keynsham Hundred. In 1634, Cotton and his vicar, Mr Fabian of Chew Magna, were upset that a group of villagers had erected a maypole in the 'church hay', a field next to the church, which they regarded as part of the churchyard. From the evidence presented to the church court which reviewed the case, it seems likely that the villagers had seized the opportunity presented by the Declaration of Sports to revive their local pastimes. Several elderly witnesses looked back to their youth, to 'those daies wherein recreations, sportes and playes of severall sortes were used as setting upp of maypoles and summer luggs, dancing, sporting, kissing, bulbayting, coyting, bowling, shootinge att butts, cudgleplaying, tennis playing and divers other sportes'. They had taken part in these activities themselves and had seen 'heades broken att cudgells and fightings in the plott of ground called the Churchaie of Dundrie'. Although these recreations had continued over a period of living memory, the implication was that they had then died out (presumably under puritan pressure) until their revival in 1634. The curate of Dundry, typifying the reaction of many within the area, thought 'it not seemly to have a maypole soe neere placed unto the church' and grieved, as he saw them leaping and dancing, 'that they should so unreverentilie demeasne themselves'.[86] Nevertheless, this isolated case is sufficient to underline the fact that not everyone in North-East Somerset was entirely happy with the puritan regime and that some ordinary villagers at least looked back to the good old days of parish revels with a warm sense of nostalgia.

There is further evidence from inside the area of a spasmodic revival of the old festive culture, which seems to have bubbled away just beneath the surface. In August 1656, for instance, John Templar of Timsbury was accused of selling a 'a wain load of beer' at the 'revel feast'. A 'great concourse of people' of between three and four hundred 'strangers', who had come to see the 'cudgell match' committed various disorders, chiefly 'by the sale of the said beer'. On Boxing Day in December 1657, Matthew Eyres and his brother from Frome Selwood were assaulted and beaten by certain persons 'who were high in drink, having been drinking, playing cards and fiddling all day in disguised habits'. In April 1656, the petty constable of Pensford presented certain people for 'riotous behaviour ... the day after the fair there at the George Inn and afterwards in the street', thus repeating an earlier incident in 1652 when Colonel Pyne of the Somerset Committee was informed of 'a public disturbance made at the fair' at Norton St Philip. There is even a suspicion that animal baiting continued in Bath - quite apart from incident in 1648 when Henry Chapman and his friends set up bear-baiting outside the city walls (see below). In 1634, George Chapman was given a grant of waste ground outside the East Gate 'to make dog kennells'. The Churchwardens of Publoe appeared before the consistory court in 1639 accused of conspiring to keep a bull and a bear to raise money 'at their Church Ale for the use and maintenance of their Church of Publoe'.[87]

Nevertheless, the strength of puritanism within the area is further underlined by the reaction of local congregations to Archbishop Laud's policy of conformity over altars. In 1634, Bishop Piers had ruled that all communion tables should be taken out of the nave and railed off as altars in the chancel. This resulted in vehement protests and strong resistance from the parishioners of Mells, Stratton and Beckington, who saw the altar as a popish symbol to threaten their protestant tradition. 'We know noe vice in the ancient standing of the table', stated James Wheeler and John Fry the churchwardens of Beckington, 'nor vertue in the innovatinge it to a high altar',[88] Their refusal to comply resulted in their excommunication and subsequent imprisonment. Wheeler and Fry were only released from prison when they agreed to acknowledge publicly that they had 'grievously offended the Divine Majesty of Almighty God' by their conduct. Their humiliation took place in the churches at Beckington, Frome and Bath.[89]

Nevertheless, the whole episode was remarkable in that it demonstrated a unanimity of feeling for the puritan cause in opposition to suspect innovations carried out at the behest of Archbishop Laud. Not only were the Churchwardens backed by John Ashe, son of the lord of the manor, and George Long, gent., a petition appealing against excommunication was signed by one thousand local people and a large sum of money raised to enable them to appeal to the Court of Arches. In giving testimony later at the trial of Laud in 1643, John Ashe emphasised the unity of the village which eventually forced the bishop to order the rector, Alexander Huish, to ensure personally that the communion table was moved. Although Huish hired workmen to do the job, the new Churchwardens brought sixteen local men into the church to persuade the labourers to stop because 'what they did was against the good likeing of the parishioners'. As Margaret Stieg has pointed out, the rector found himself isolated against a community which was fully involved and totally supportive of the churchwardens. 'The men of Beckington were not yokels, but theologically thoughtful, reasonably articulate and politically astute. They fought back in the courts ... they presented a reasoned, cogent argument.' Two of the most typically anti-Laudian gestures which laymen had at their disposal - the recruitment of 'strange preachers' and the refusal to move the communion table - are particularly evident in North-East Somerset. In this area, therefore, where there was no lasting reformation of the diocese, Laudian success was superficial, thanks to the comparative solidarity of grass-roots opinion.[90]

(c) The Reformation of Morals

One further consequence of the puritan revolution within North-East Somerset was the general tightening of moral standards, a fact already illustrated by the concern shown over maypoles and church ales. The traditional culture of the poorer sort, including their revels, games, processions and festivals, had been the source of frequent attacks from clergy and magistrates throughout the country since the time of the Reformation. Puritan preachers increasingly expressed their disapproval of Saints' Days and mystery plays, which smacked of 'popery and suspicion'; all forms of revelling, which not only undermined parental authority, but also caused young people to neglect their work and religion; and dancing, which gave women a dangerous amount of sexual freedom. Festivals of any kind merely encouraged the formation of disorderly crowds, while alehouses were seen as a 'threat to household order', attracting both idlers and vagrants. Similarly, an Act of 1541, summarised the ban on tennis, dice, cards, bowls and other 'unlawful games'. With the rapid extension of poverty and unemployment towards the end of sixteenth century, local leaders became more and more concerned about the state of public order and the need for firm control over all popular activities which had an undermining effect on discipline. This concern for order, however, was symptomatic of the widening gulf between the puritan elite and the disorderly poor. The campaign against popular entertainments, in an attempt to control the turbulent recreations of their poorer neighbours, 'was almost invariably divisive'.[91]

Somerset Justices had demonstrated their anxiety over the growing number of alehouses within the county by issuing a series of orders from 1594 aimed at their control. In 1618, local Justices were instructed to carry out a survey of all alehouses within their district, listing those that were disorderly and needed to be suppressed.[92] Five years later, the Mayor of Bath reported to the Council in London that he had suppressed all unnecessary alehouses and, furthermore, had regulated the strength of all beer brewed within the city.[93] The problem, however, proved intractable. In 1630, the Court of Quarter Sessions noted that 'notwithstanding the care taken both for lessening the number of alehouses and for punishing those who kept ill order therein, the number increased and the disorders multiplied'. They therefore decided to require substantial sureties from all those who were licensees, permitting no man 'to keepe a tiplinge house but such are capable thereof'.

In the following year, a complaint reached the Sessions (which included Sir John Horner, John Harington and Sir Francis Popham as sitting magistrates) that there were many unnecessary alehouses in the Eastern Division in places, like Keynsham, where there were ample inns to receive visitors. They immediately ordered the suppression of such alehouses and promised to take further action if necessary. Later at the same Sessions, in a moment of exasperation, they ordered the suppression of all alehouses in the county, except for those that provided necessary relief for travellers along 'a great thoroughfare' at a distance of at least five miles apart. In towns, a maximum of two or three would be permitted, if there were not sufficient inns 'to give entertainment to passengers'.[94] The underlying reason for the concern, which led Justices to conduct this running battle against ale-houses, is emphasised in the case of Richard Bourne which was brought to their attention in 1637. The parishioners of Paulton complained that Bourne, who was licensed to sell ale, kept a disorderly house by entertaining his neighbours' servants and children, encouraging them 'to continue tiplinge in his house all night' and thus neglect their duties to their parents and masters.[95] The Justices were determined to do what they could to halt the collapse of family discipline.

Similar concern was shown for breaches of sexual morality, which again tended to pose 'a threat to household order'. Throughout the country there was an increasing anxiety, shown in local courts, to control the activities of unruly women who defied their husbands, became involved in unseemly brawls or were unfaithful in marriage. Local communities tended to shame such people by subjecting them to the humiliation of a ducking in the local pond by means of the cucking stool. Such a device was certainly in operation in Bath by 1582, when the Chamberlain paid a bill for 'cuttynge the Cookygestoole shorter'. Its frequency of use thereafter is testified by entries which occur in the Accounts for its repair in 1617 and 1624 and 'for cordes to haule the Cucking stoole' in 1628. Women who offended sexual or social standards could arouse the anger of the whole community, especially if their actions were likely to prove a costly burden. John Crooke was therefore paid three shillings in 1618 ' for followinge a wench with the hue and cry that fledd and left her bastard behinde her'.[96] Sexual morality was also under consideration in the regulation of the city's hot water baths. Although the Mayor wrote to the Council in London seeking their approval in 1621 for the proposed separation of the sexes in all the baths, 'which', he confessed 'ought to have been effected long ago', their action clearly did not go far enough to satisfy local opinion. Four years later, the Council called on Bath Corporation 'to remedy the great disorders committed in the Common use of the baths by men and women together'. This practice not only drew together 'a great concourse of wicked persons', but compelled 'grave and sober people to forbear the place'. The Baths continued to be a source of anxiety to a Corporation intent on maintaining sobriety. In 1634 they again took action, this time dismissing Widow Broade as a 'Bath guide' because 'she miscarried herself through drinking and so caused the Maior to have several checks from the L. Chief Justice'.[97]

Enforcement of the new moral code, which regulated every aspect of human behaviour, depended partly on the willingness of the puritan elite to prosecute offences and partly on the willingness of ordinary people to inform on their neighbours. This process tended to increase divisiveness and to erode even further the harmony and sociability that had existed previously. At the Wells Quarter Sessions in 1630, William Hackett 'exhibited several informations' against John Draper, a weaver from Frome, and Phillip Allen, a husbandman, 'for playing att unlawful games'.[98] Two years earlier, the same constable had produced similar evidence against individuals from Frome, Marston Bigot and Nunney for playing unlawful games. In Bath, Richard Druce handed over £6 2s 6d to the churchwardens when he completed his term of office in 1649, money which he had extracted 'of such as sold ale and beere by small measures and of such as were

This type of person was certainly encouraged by the members of Bath's Council. In 1632, for instance, they had resolved that those residents who swept the dirt from the street in front of their houses into the public water course should be fined twelve pence for each offence - half going to the Bailiff and half to the informer. Sometimes damning information on an individual's conduct could have much more serious consequences. The Council were therefore moved in 1635 to impose a ban on Sarah Dill who, it was decided, 'shall not be admitted into the Almeshouse, because she is a comon beggar, swearer and curser'.[100]

Informants also made their presence felt during the North Somerset Visitations of 1615, another indication that puritanism had gained a strong grip on parish life in general. Particular concern was shown toward those guilty of sabbath-breaking. John Humphrey of Batheaston, Edward Brewer of Freshford and John Tucker of Bath were all presented for opening their alehouses for 'tiplinge and drinkinge...at the time of divine service on Sonday'. Similarly, Eleonara Gibbins of Widcombe gave offence by working on the sabbath, causing ' her myll to grynd on Sunday mornings'. Even worse, however, were those who idled away their time by playing unlawful games. Thomas Clement and four friends were accused at Keynsham, for instance, of bowlinge in the churchyard on the sabbath day', while Richard Day and three other Saltford men were presented 'for playing at cards in the time of the divine service'. The puritan's insistence on order, discipline and respect also demanded that any unseemly behaviour in or near the church should not go unpunished. Evidence was therefore given against Thomas Phelps of Walcot 'for rayling in the Churchyard against Walter Symons'; Walter Symons himself for abusing the minister by suggesting that he came 'out of a cole pitt'; Peter Perman, gent, of Bath 'for not cominge orderlie to Church'; William Mulford and Thomas Tebbitt of Saltford ' for abusing each other in the Churchyard'; and Thomas Cumming of Swainswick for abusive language in the church when he called the Churchwardens 'baggidge knaves'. Nevertheless, in spite of these isolated examples of sabbath-breaking in the parishes of North-East Somerset, the general picture is one of conformity to the puritan ideal. Indeed, the surprising feature of the visitation records is that there were so few presentments in such a large area. The community as a whole, it seems, was both law abiding and meticulous in its Sunday observance.[101]

Towns in general were particularly watchful for any signs of breakdown in law and order, especially in view of the large numbers of poor people that tended to congregate in places like Bath. The ruling puritan elite were therefore opposed in principal to all activities which prompted the formation of large, unruly crowds - such as animal baiting, fairs and performances by travelling players - particularly in view of the fact that these occasions also encouraged idleness and drunkenness. In Bath, 'a proclamacon for prohibitting of the fayers' had been read as early as 1603[102] while the County magistrates, meeting in Quarter Sessions at Wells in 1608, had ordered 'that all Bulbaytings, Bearebaytings ... be immediately from henceforth throughout the whole countie of Somst utterly forbidden and suppressed'.[103] Their failure to eliminate these activities in the county as a whole is underlined partly by the reissue of this order in 1612 and 1624 and partly by a petition of the Grand Jury to the Assizes meeting at Bath in 1638. The scarcity of corn, which resulted in high prices, was blamed to some extent on 'a late practice of gathering great companies of unruly people at bull-baitings', thus causing excessive quantities of ale to be brewed. The poor were thus encouraged to spend more than they could afford, so that 'many thefts' were committed after their departure'.[104] In Bath itself, entries in the Chamberlain's Accounts indicate that occasional bear-baitings took place during the latter part of the sixteenth century. Payments were made to Lord Warwick's bearward in 1576, Lord Dudley's in 1594 and the Queen's in 1602. In addition to these visits by travelling troupes, local people had arranged their own entertainment on at least one occasion in 1577, when a sum of twelve pence was given 'to the bayting of John Chapmans beare'. There is no evidence that such practices were permitted to continue in the City after 1602. Indeed there is every indication that Bath's Corporation and such as swore by prophane oaths' - presumably on the evidence of informers.[99] steadily eliminated this type of crowd-pulling entertainment.[105]

The same was certainly true of travelling players and other entertainers, who had been a regular feature of the social calendar in Bath throughout the Elizabethan period until about 1618, when all such visits ceased. Previous amusements had included a 'bage pype player' (1569), acrobats (1578, 1589), school plays (1583, 1601), a blind organ player (1616) and the fencers and musicians who celebrated the proclamation of James I in 1603. Among groups of theatrical players to perform in Bath, the most regular by far were The Queen's Players who attended almost annually between 1583 and 1607. Others included The Lord Admiral's, The Lord of Derby's, The Lord of Worcester's, The Lord Chamberlain's, The Lord of Pembroke's, the Earl of Hertford's, the Lord of Leicester's, the Lord of Oxford's and many more - including troupe belonging to the Master of the Revels. Although in some years as many as six different companies had visited the city, each receiving payments from the Chamberlain for their services, this practice suddenly ended in 1612 when the final payment was made. Nevertheless, the Queen's Players returned to the city for the last time six years later when they were permitted to hire the Town Hall for 3s 4d, even though the Corporation clearly withheld its usual fee.[106]

Much of the traditional colour of popular entertainment had therefore passed from the local scene by 1620, just as traditional festivals (the crowning of the Autumn King, processions at Pentecost and Rogationtide, the Crowning of the King of Bath at Whitsuntide and the Midsummer Eve festival) had largely disappeared by the second half of the previous century.[107] But although the puritan elite saw such popular gatherings as a danger to both order and morality, they were nevertheless keen to retain some elements of civic ritual as a means of emphasising lessons in authority and obedience. In Bath, therefore, formal processions were still maintained at the coming of the Assizes; trumpeters were engaged to herald royal visits; bonfires were lit to celebrate the birth of royal princes in 1630 and 1634; beer and cakes were regularly offered to the freemen of the city at Whitsuntide, and a splendid banquet was arranged for officers and deputy lieutenants at the annual muster of the Trained Bands. Colour and ritual, therefore, did not entirely disappear, but the focus of attention was hence forth centred on the symbols of authority (judges, councillors, army officers and visiting dignitaries) with the crowd as passive observers on the outside. Gradually, too, the puritans added special celebrations of their own to emphasise their religious and political benefits, especially during the years of royalist occupation when they wanted to make political points to their oppressors. Gunpowder Treason Day (5th November) replaced Hollowe'en as a later autumn celebration, followed a few days later by Crown Nation Day (17th November), commemorating the anniversary of Queen Elizabeth's accession. These occasions, which enabled them to express not only their longing for a return to the Elizabethan 'system' but also their hatred of 'popery', gave local citizens the chance to celebrate through bonfires, fireworks and the ringing of church bells. It is perhaps significant that neither Gunpowder Treason Day nor Crown Nation Day was mentioned in the accounts of the Bath Chamberlain until the occupation of the city by royalist forces between 1643 and 1645, when the celebrations became an annual occurrence.[108]

(iv) The Seeds of War

Three main conclusions emerge from this discussion. Firstly, by 1642, North-East Somerset had become something of a hot-bed of puritanism. This was due to some extent to the role of the Mendips, which effectively isolated the area from the more conservative influences to the south of the county; but to a greater extent to the natural lines of communication which made contact simple with London and Bristol. Travelling preachers were thus given ease of access to spread the word along the Avon valley; cloth merchants, like John Ashe and William Brewer, were able to make regular, weekly visits via the London Road to the markets of the capital, where latest ideas were disseminated. The influence of London cannot be overstated. According to William Prynne, one of William Laud's officials observed that opposition to the railing off of altars was most vociferous in the great clothing towns 'because they see no such thing, as they say, in the churches of London'.[109] It is significant that puritanism was far less strong in the mining areas to the south of the hundred of Frome and Kilmersdon, where there was far less opportunity for trading contact with the capital.

At the same time, there is little doubt that puritanism was largely promoted and inspired from above, although it was not necessarily imposed on a totally unwilling multitude in the clothing districts. The puritan gentry elite - the Pophams, the Horners, the Haringtons, the Ashes and William Prynne -wielded a mighty and popular influence over the area in general, but over the hundreds of Keynsham and Bathforum in particular. There, in the clothing districts along the Avon valley - where the nature of the out-working system gave ample opportunity for the spread of ideas through Ashe's agents - puritan activity was at its greatest. Nor should we underestimate the personal influence of William Prynne, who, on his release from prison in 1641, brought back to the area a passionate commitment to the cause based on personal conflict and personal suffering. By the 1640's, puritan control had been established in all major centres of population and a system of lectureships established. Nevertheless, there is also evidence that the growth of puritanism met with support at the grass roots levels. The opposition encountered by the rector of Beckington to his attempt to rail off the communion table was characterised by the support it received throughout the strata of village society. The one thousand local people who signed the petition and raised money for the appeal, together with the sixteen parishioners who argued to persuade the workmen in church to lay down their tools, are indicative of religious conviction at social levels much lower than the elite. 'The men of Beckington were not yokels', as Margaret Stieg has commented, 'but theologically thoughtful, reasonably cultured and politically astute'.[110] This rather undermines the theory of the 'better sort' imposing their will on the 'multitude' of 'ignorant folk'.

Secondly, as a result of the work of the puritan elite, a distinctive culture had been established within the area by 1642. They had successfully instituted a policy of 'moral reformation', partly out of a sense of religious duty and partly out of a sense of fear caused by the 'crisis of order' in the 1620's and 1630's. In an attempt to strengthen family discipline, improve the state of public order, develop the work ethic and protect the sabbath, they had successfully launched a series of attacks on the traditional culture of the region, including revels, games festivals, alehouses, plays, bullbaiting and maypoles. Their work had largely been completed by the early 1630's.

Thirdly, North-East Somerset was to witness a clash of allegiance based on differing cultures when war broke out in 1642. On the one hand, as David Underdown has pointed out, the majority in the area were to favour parliament 'not only because of the authority of gentlemen such as Popham over their tenants, of great clothiers like the Ashes over their work people; not only because of the influence of the godly middling sort in the cloth-making and dairying parishes, but also because this region too had its own distinctive culture' - a culture that was being threatened by Charles I and Archbishop Laud. On the other hand, there is real evidence to suggest that a traditionalist faction existed within the same area, which bitterly resented the cultural revolution and the domination of local affairs by the puritan elite.[111]

There is certainly clear evidence that this traditional faction sided actively with the King's cause throughout the Civil War in opposition to the puritan majority which, as we have seen, remained unswerving in its loyalty to parliament. The faction included the royalist group on Bath City Council (Henry Chapman, George Chapman, Philip Sherwood, Samuel Wintle, Robert Sheppard, Robert Fisher, Thomas Gibbs and Robert Hyde, the Recorder) in alliance with Sir Thomas Bridges of Keynsham who had been Governor of the city during its occupation by royalist forces. Together they seem to have been motivated by religion, coupled with an intense dislike of William Prynne. Centring their activities on the inns and alehouses of the city, they commanded a certain degree of popular support as they made a stand for traditional culture and pastimes.

As already indicated above, five of the group were in fact innkeepers - Henry Chapman of The Sun on the east side of Market Place; Philip Sherwood of The Three Tuns in Stall Street; George Chapman of The Bear in Cheap Street; Thomas Gibbs of The Golden Lyon by the South Gate; and Samuel Wintle of The George near the Hot Bath. Both The Sun and The Three Tuns became regular meeting places for royalist soldiers during the war, especially between 1643 and 1645 when Chapman, as Captain of the Bath Trained Bands, and Sherwood, as his Lieutenant, were responsible for mounting nightly guard on behalf of the royalist garrison. Several entries were made by the Chamberlain in his accounts which suggest close involvement of this kind - 'given to Captaynes at severall tymes in Wynn as by Mr Sherwood's bill appear ... £1 2s 2d'; 'given of Captaynes in wynn at the Newe Tavern ... 4s 0'; 'Capt. Chapman for wood, cole and candells for the Guards ... 13s 4d'.[112]

Philip Sherwood had already been involved in a serious dispute with the Bath Corporation as early as 1622, twelve years before he himself was elected as Councillor. The controversy, which directly centred on The Three Tuns, arose just at the time when the local puritan elite had launched their latest campaign to suppress unnecessary or disorderly alehouses (see above). The Mayor and Corporation, in response to instructions given by the county magistrates, had dutifully carried out a survey of all inns and alehouses within their district, listing those that were disorderly and in need of suppression.[113] During the course of this investigation, they discovered that Sherwood had recently attempted to upgrade The Three Tuns from an alehouse to an inn (which would also have enabled him to accommodate guests). According to the Mayor, Thomas Murford, for about ten years or so other had merely been 'a post thrust out of the wall of the house and thereon a little sign of 3 tunns hanging, resembling the sign of an alehouse and the house used but as an alehouse'. More recently, however, he had managed to get a licence for an inn from Sir Giles Mompesson, 'whereupon he set a new fair sign of 3 Tunnes, and fixed to support it 2 great posts in the street being the soil of the Mayor and Commalty, which he could not do without their leave'. On the revocation of Mompesson's patent, the Corporation had acted on the Privy Council's instructions in suppressing ten inns licensed by him and removing all their signs - except that of Philip Sherwood who had refused to co-operate.

A frequent visitor to the Quarter Sessions on charges of 'uttering his beer by smaller measures', he was now indicted there 'by his fellow innkeepers for keeping an Inn without a lawful title and an alehouse without a licence'. In consequence, he was fined £5, his inn ordered to be suppressed and his sign removed. However, when bailiffs arrived to dismantle the sign, they were confronted by Sherwood's son 'with a loaded weapon and a maidservant with gunpowder'. In view of the fact that a crowd of some three hundred had now gathered to witness the dispute, the bailiffs waited to complete their task under the cover of darkness. Next morning, Sherwood contemptuously set up the sign again - but, although he complained to the Privy Council that the Corporation had conspired against him out of 'private and particular respects' (Murford was, for instance, a rival innkeeper of the The Hart), the Privy Council rejected his petition. Anxious to support recent proclamations 'touching inns and alehouses', they accepted the Corporation's outline of the 'sundry disorders' that had been committed in The Three Tuns. This episode undoubtedly embittered Sherwood in his attitude towards the Corporation and the puritan elite, feeling as he did a sense of 'oppression' and victimisation.[114]

It is also worth recalling that Philip Sherwood belonged to a well-known Catholic family. His father, Dr John Sherwood who lived in Abbey House until his death in 1621, was described by Anthony Wood as 'an eminent practitioner ... in the City of Bath ... much resorted to by those of the Roman Catholic religion, he himself being of that profession.'

Dr Sherwood's own father and mother were devout papists; his brother, Thomas, an Elizabethan martyr; and three other brothers Catholic priests. Furthermore, four of his seven sons were all converted to the Catholic faith - Thomas (who joined the Society of Jesus), Robert and William (both of whom entered the Benedictine Order) and John (who was a practising Catholic in Ireland). There is no direct evidence that Philip followed his brothers' example, just as there is no evidence for Catholic recusancy in the Bath area between 1627 and 1660. It is nevertheless unlikely that Sherwood, with his particular family background, would look favourably on the growing domination of puritanism within the local area. There are also suspicions that another member of the Chapman faction had secret Catholic tendencies. In 1683, Thomas Gibbs (a brewer and eldest son of Thomas Gibbs, innkeeper of the Golden Lyon) was one of nine people presented by the Grand Jury in Bath under the terms of the Papists (Removal and Disarming) Bill of 1680. His wife, Margaret Carne, had already been presented as a suspected papist at an Archdeacon's visitation in 1662, which investigated absenteeism from Anglican services. [115]

By 1642, therefore, two factions had already emerged in North-East Somerset, based on two competing cultures. In that sense at least Richard Baxter was probably right when later he commented that the civil war 'had begun in our streets before King and Parliament had any armies'. The clash between these factions, which was to continue with increased bitterness beyond the civil war itself, was not finally resolved until 1662.

3.
For King or Parliament?

(i) The Day of Decision, 1642

Opposition to the King's policies and powers had been mounting in the Long Parliament ever since its first meeting in November 1640. The climax, foreshadowed by their Grand Remonstrance of October 1641, was finally reached on 5th January, 1642 when Charles unsuccessfully attempted to arrest five of his most hostile critics. Shortly afterwards, in desperation as much as in hope, he left his capital for the north, basing himself on York until August when the royal standard was finally raised in Nottingham.

During those months a crucial struggle developed for the control of the militia. In February, parliament had issued an Ordinance placing the trained bands under its own control. Most counties had already accepted this by the time that the King issued his Declaration on 11th June. In this he not only condemned the Ordinance as illegal, but went on to grant to individuals in each county commissions of array with the intention of mastering the trained bands himself. Under these circumstances, it was inevitable that each county would become a battleground of words long before the first drop of local blood was shed.

In Somerset both sides found early encouragement. On 25th February, for instance, Sir Thomas Wroth presented a Somerset petition to the Commons expressing concern at the King's breach of parliamentary privileges, which was 'by the device as we conceive of a malignant party of popish lords and bishops'. It assured parliament of their own affection and willingness to shed their 'purest blood' in the cause.[1] Shortly afterwards, however, Somerset royalists circulated another petition which was eventually signed by two hundred 'knights, gentry and freeholders' and reached parliament on 13th June. This demanded 'that the government of the Church and Liturgy established by law' should be continued; that parliament should end its quarrel with the King and declare against 'tumults and unlawful assemblies, seditious sermons and pamphlets'; that the militia should again be controlled 'as it was in the time of Queen Elizabeth' and that parliament should explain how it had used the 'great sum of money' that had been levied.[2]

Meanwhile, both the King and the parliament had been looking with covetous eyes on the west which was generously populated, numerous in trained bands, favoured with ports and extremely wealthy. Somerset, 'that rich and spacious county',[3] held the key. Charles made the first move. 'I am with all speed to repair unto the west, to put his Commissions of Array in execution, which I make no doubt to perform without any great difficulty', wrote the Marquis of Hertford to the Queen on 11th July.[4] The following day, Hertford 'having his Majesties Commission to bee Lieutenant Generall of the sixe Westerne Counties .... accompanyed with his brother, the Lord Seymour, Sir Ralph Hopton, and some other Gentlemen, attended only by their ordinary retinue' left York.[5] Hopton, a westcountryman greatly experienced with the trained bands, clearly hoped to use his local connections to stir up the well-established gentry and their tenants for the King.

While this party of eminent royalists journeyed south, parliament too was making plans for the seizure of the west. On the day after Hertford's departure from York, the

King Charles I surrounded by his supporters, including Bishop Laud, the Earl of Strafford, Sir Ralph Hopton, the Earl of Carnarvon and Sir Bevil Grenvile.

Commons voted to strengthen their grip on the situation by raising an army in addition to those sections of militia already in their hands. Shortly afterwards, on 20th July, Somerset was directly involved in these plans when parliament ordered that twelve local men of standing (including Sir John Horner, John Harington, Alexander Popham and John Ashe from the north-east of the county) should, with the power of deputy lieutenant, form a committee to raise 'horse, horsemen and arms, for the defence of the King and both Houses of Parliament' and to 'receive the subscriptions, according to the said propositions'.[6]

The scene was therefore set for an immediate clash of interests as both groups prepared to raise local troops according to the instructions they had been given. Bath, as it happened, became the meeting point for the first confrontation and trial of strength. The County Assizes were already in session there when the crisis broke. Large numbers of important people, including the sheriff and constables, had assembled in the city from all parts of the county some for business, some for the social attractions. Inns and lodging houses were full to capacity - as was the prison! The Guildhall had been specially decorated for the occasion - the glass had been taken down and 'new work done about it', while fresh 'hangings and carpette stuffe' had been bought.

William Chapman, the Mayor, accompanied by Aldermen in their scarlet robes and Common Councillors, entertained the Assize Judge, Sir Robert Foster, in lavish style. Gifts of 'turkeyes, chickynes and capons', 'cack and clarrett' were presented during his stay in the special lodgings provided at the city's cost. Dr Curll, the Bishop of Winchester, and the Marquis of Hertford both received similar treatment when they arrived in this rather festive atmosphere. The Bishop, in fact, accepted a gift of 'pasties' made by John Roberts, a local baker.[7] But Hertford was interested in more than pasties. Although he was still the King's Lieutenant of Somerset, his motive in visiting Bath was by no means limited to a courtesy call at the Assizes. It was, therefore, perhaps significant that on the day of his coming (25th July), the Grand Jury of Somerset should lodge with the Assizes a petition to the King, in which they protested that the commission of array was 'illegally issued' for their county and demanded its recall.[8]

William Seymour, 1st Marquis of Hertford (1588 - 1660). A drawing by W.N. Gardiner from a portrait by Van Dyke.

Hertford quickly sensed that his welcome in Bath was not quite as cordial as the odd turkey and chicken might suggest. He therefore decided to move his headquarters away from this puritan stronghold to a more congenial spot. At least, according to Hopton, he had been able to meet at the Assizes in Bath 'a great assembly of gentlemen, the most part of the better sort verie well affected.' He discussed with them the merits of going to either Bristol or Wells. Hoping that the gentry would use their power and influence to persuade the county 'to give an eminent testimony of their fidelity', Wells, which lay in the centre of the county, 'was unhappily chosen.'[9]

The royalists were certainly in need of recruits. When Hertford left Bath at the beginning of August, he took with him three troops of horse, a troop of dragoons and a hundred foot. According to Hopton, 'the Marquesse .... was met by a considerable number of people of all qualities upon Mendip amongst which there were twenty-eight of the principal Gentlemen of that County'.[10] On his departure, he sent orders for all the trained bands in the locality to join him. These instructions were never obeyed because, by that time, the trained bands were firmly under the direction of Alexander Popham.

News filtered through to Hopton that 'the disaffected gentlemen of the Easterne Dyvision of that County (which were principally Sir John Horner and Mr Popham) had sent out their tickets about the country for a generall meeting at Shepton Mallett with their armes upon the Munday following and that they would send severall fatt buckes thither to entertaine them'.[11] His information was correct. Alexander Popham, John Ashe, John Horner, William Strode and the other members of the newly-appointed Somerset Committee had been quietly laying their plans 'for the preservation of the peace of this county'. From Bath, on 29th July, instructions had been issued to all their local supporters to assemble at Shepton Mallet on 1st August - the day of Hertford's arrival in Wells. This would enable them 'to issue warrants to severall hundreds...requiring them not to obey the Commission of Array, but to be ready from time to time to obey the Ordinance of Parliament',[12] In other words, they could discuss a course of action and apply pressure on each individual Hundred to co-operate.

Some inhabitants of Shepton, hearing of the rendezvous of parliamentary leaders in their town, had sent a petition to Hertford which, according to Hopton, earnestly prayed 'protection from the dangerous tumult' but which, according to Ashe, insinuated 'that our meeting here was to fire their houses and make their streets run with blood'. Hopton was therefore sent by the Marquis with a body of horse to investigate. Arriving at Shepton early in the morning and finding about two hundred men in arms, he rode to the market place, 'faced the unruly rabble' and read out the petition. At this point William Strode, a local member of the parliamentary committee, burst in upon the town and ordered Hopton to leave. Hopton, however, for the time being had superior strength and Strode was forced to suffer the indignity of temporary arrest for treason. He was nevertheless able to call out to the assembled crowd to 'obey the King as he was guided and counselled by the parliament, and not as he was guided and counselled by evil counsellors, from whom came this Commission of Array, both illegal and destructive to the Kingdom'.[13] Committee men, even when pressed, never missed an opportunity to spread their propaganda! Hopton's moment of glory was short-lived. Hearing of the approach of Popham and other members of the Committee, he returned to Wells leaving Strode to the mercy of the Shepton Mallet constable - who immediately enrolled for parliament. 'And thus innocentlie beganne this cursed warr in these parts', lamented Hopton.[14]

Before they left Shepton, the Committee took steps to see that their work of 'bowing people's hearts to his service' should continue. Orders were given for the immediate muster of two regiments at Chewton Mendip and requests for additional help were sent to Bristol 'who have shewed their good affection to us already in this service for two field peeces of about 6 pound bullet'.[15] From Monday 1st to Friday 5th August, the parliamentarian forces gradually assembled at Chewton. On the Wednesday there was something of a scare. Inhabitants of Shepton Mallet, alarmed by the return of Hopton's

Sir Ralph Hopton (1596 - 1652) of Witham Friary, field commander of the royalist army in the Battle of Lansdown, 1643. Portrait by an unknown artist.

cavalry, dispatched an urgent warning - 'posts were sent to Sir John Horner, Master Popham and others, certifying that these cavaliers were coming to destroy them, whereupon every man made ready for their coming'.[16]

It turned out to be something of a false alarm. For although Hopton and his men sallied forth onto the foothills of Mendip, they quickly returned to Shepton, where, according to the somewhat colourful account of a parliamentarian newsheet, 'they spent a short time refreshing themselves at the Innes and Taverns, during which time some of their cavaliers marching about the Town found out all the honest men's houses that were there, those houses they brake into, plundered and robbed, especially of all armes and ammunition, and made the owners with their wives and children to forsake their houses, and hide themselves for fear of their lives'. They finally returned to Wells after 'they had ordered the billeting of a hundred of their Troopers there upon them of Shepton'.[17] However exaggerated the description, it was rumours of this nature, deliberately exploited for propaganda purposes, that steadily undermined Hertford's cause.

The net was also gradually closing in on the beleaguered royalists in Wells. Volunteers were flooding down into Chewton Mendip from the north and east of the county in support of Horner and Popham. Meanwhile, on Thursday 4th August, John Pyne was leading a group of 600 men from the west of the county in a move to cut off any possible retreat by Hertford to the south. Quickly spotting this threat of encirclement, Sir John Stawell took the royalist cavalry to intercept Pyne's advance at Marshall's Elm, between Somerton and Street. In the ensuing skirmish, the inexperienced local countrymen were easily routed by the cavalier horse, which was well controlled by the only professional soldier on the field, Henry Lunsford. Seven members of Pyne's force were killed, several others mortally wounded and sixty taken prisoner.[18]

By Friday, 5th August, the parliamentary forces had assembled at Chewton about four miles from Wells. During the previous few days, groups had been arriving from different areas to swell the size to a final total of about 12,000. To the Bath Regiment of Trained Bands were added the tenants and neighbours of Sir John Horner, Alexander Popham, Sir Francis Popham, Sir Edward Hungerford, William Strode, John Ashe, Robert Harbin, Richard Cole and John Hippisley together with volunteers from Wiltshire, Gloucestershire and Bristol. Their spirits were high and they were eager for battle.

Down in Wells, Hertford and Hopton were becoming increasingly gloomy at the lack of support. It is true that they had persuaded the Corporation to hand over the keys of the city armoury, but arms would never compensate for the basic lack of men. The marquis's original order that all local trained bands should appear before him had met with some initial success, but he was now faced with mass desertions. According to John Ashe, 'they had got into Wells by faire meanes and by foule, about 400 of the Trayned bands and Volunteers, but that Friday at night, they all stole away out of the Towne, and some of them came up the hill unto us upon Saturday morning'.[19] Hopton, too, confirms that 'the most part of the trained band soldiers had quitted their guards and their officers in the dark of the night, and had run away.'[20]

In all, he now had something in the region of 900 men to face Popham's force, estimated at between ten and twelve thousand.[21] Under these circumstances, he wisely decided to withdraw to Sherborne in Dorset without a battle. This feeling was quickly confirmed when 'Sir Francis Popham (Alexander's father) caused some shots to be made from Mendip Hill against the Bishop's Palace, which (by reason of the strength thereof) they had made their quarters, it being a place of considerable strength and moted round about'.[22] By the end of September, the royalist forces had disintegrated; Hertford had disappeared into Wales, while Hopton had ridden into Cornwall in the hope of a more successful recruiting campaign.

A field gun in action against the Bishop's Palace in Wells.

Meanwhile, back in Bath, the final seal of approval had been set on the work of Popham and Ashe. On 12th August Robert Bagnall, Constable of Keynsham, presented a petition on behalf of twenty-one High Constables of Somerset to Sir Robert Foster, the Assize Judge. This bluntly attacked the Commission of Array as illegal and reminded Foster that 'the Judges in their charges are ordered by the Houses to declare it to be contrary to the law, to satisfy the people and preserve the Kingdom's peace'. It then went on to ask him 'to direct that the declaration and order of both Houses of Parliament, condemning all Commissions of Array as illegal, may be openly read in Court, that so petitioners and the rest of the county may know the law therein and accordingly shape their obedience'.[23]

Foster, having scrupulously avoided any personal commitment during the early weeks of the Assizes, was now forced to choose and 'being soundly put to it, he concluded it to be illegal'.[24] In open court at the Guildhall in Bath, he formally read out parliament's votes against the Commissions of Array. At the same time Martin Sanford, the County Sheriff, who was in Bath for the Assizes, also declared for parliament, refusing to support Hertford. Instead, he sent the Marquis a copy of the Constables' petition and Foster's answer to it.[25] The rejection of Hertford by the county of Somerset now seemed complete.

Furthermore, the puritan gentry from North-East Somerset had succeeded not only in leading the local community onto the Mendips in the summer of 1642, but also in pressurising their neighbours in Bristol to declare their allegiance for the same cause later that autumn. The Corporation of that city, which had not been officially represented in the skirmishes with Hertford outside Wells, had tried hard to maintain a neutral stance.[26] But then on 24th October, they received a letter, signed by some of the gentry from Somerset, Gloucestershire and Wiltshire, 'desiring a mutual association with this citty for the defence of the Kinge and Kingdom ... against all such force and power as shall be raised or brought into any of the said counties without consent of Parliament'. The Council tentatively agreed to the idea, nominating representatives to meet with the gentry and discuss further details. Shortly afterwards, however, they had a change of heart and decided to revert to their former plan of armed neutrality. On 8th November they therefore agreed to revive the idea of a peace petition to both King and Parliament, declaring themselves 'to be in love and amity one with another' and to desire 'a friendly association together in all mutual accommodation'. Then on the 24th of the month, they agreed to strengthen the defences by building an earthwork 'in all necessarie places round about the cittee'. Meanwhile, the puritan gentry of the newly-formed Association were becoming irritated and frustrated by the prevarication of the Bristol Council. There is no doubt, judging by the brisk correspondence which was then exchanged, that the dominating figures on the gentry side were Alexander Popham, John Ashe, John Horner, Edward Hungerford and William Strode and that Bath had become their operational headquarters.

Popham's next move was to write a letter to Captain Harington, commander of the Bristol trained bands - and the son of John Harington of Kelston, a close friend of Popham, Ashe and Horner - announcing his plan to bring forces into Bristol. The Council, hearing of this letter, wrote an agitated reply to Popham, on 24th November, expressing hurt surprise that he had asked Harington 'to be ready with his trayned bands and volunteers at one houres warning and meantyme to use all secrecie touching this designe.' In asking Popham 'to desist', they concluded: 'We shall be glad, when occasion shall require, to receave all friendly assistance from you, but as we now stand, we consider there is none.' The gentry of the Association now put even further pressure on the Bristol Councillors. Firstly, Popham, sent another invitation from 'us your neighbours and true friends' to a meeting in Bath so that agreement could be reached on a course of action for their common safety. He added, somewhat ominously, 'and we shall know who are for us or against us, and provide accordingly'.

The armour worn by Colonel Alexander Popham (1605 - 1669) when he led the Bath Regiment of Trained Bands in the Civil War both on the Mendips in 1642 and at the battle of Lansdown in 1643.

Secondly, a day later on 26th November, a joint letter from five of the gentry was despatched complaining of the Council's rudeness in not replying to previous correspondence; warning them of the serious consequences of procrastination ('your safetie with ours is alike concerned .... the miscarriage of your cittie may wound us as much as the country round about may endanger you'); and announcing that they had instructed Popham 'to draw together soe many of his regiment as he shall think fitt neere your cittie and within our countie, there to be ready for your assistance and defence as any occasion shall afford.' Popham advanced to Pensford, an action which undoubtedly precipitated the long-awaited meeting which finally took place in Bath on 28th. The Council's slow deliberations on the proposals made were somewhat overtaken by the news that parliament had approved a plan to send 2000 troops under Colonel Essex into Bristol. In a noticeably anxious letter written on 7th December, the Council, alarmed at the news that Essex was now at Thornbury 'with intent to be heere tomorrow', asked Popham 'to do us the favour as to be heere next day in the forenoone' so that together they might 'friendly compose and accommodate the provisions to avoid the effusion of blood which otherwise would undoubtedly happen.' Bristol's armed neutrality was at an end - thanks largely to the determined persistence and crusading zeal of the gentry of North-East Somerset.[27]

(ii) Reasons for Allegiance

The summer and autumn of 1642 witnessed a wave of popular uprisings throughout the country - in Manchester, where the inhabitants rioted when the corporation proposed to make an agreement with the royalists; in Nottingham, where a mob obstructed the corporation's plans to hand over the magazine to Lord Newark; in South Molton, where the ordinary citizens rose in protest at the mayor's action in admitting royalist leaders; in Cirencester, where thousands of local people met Lord Chandos and forced him out before he could read the commission of array; in Middlesex, where crowds rioted against delinquents and papists; and in Colchester and many of the cloth manufacturing villages on the Essex-Suffolk border, where further tumults against royalists took place. Brian Manning has observed that in many places the King's cause collapsed when royalist leaders were attacked by hostile crowds. 'These popular insurrections in many different parts of the country', he argues, 'all seem to have been inspired by a panic fear of imminent attack from some sort of enemies. The enemies were labelled 'papists', 'delinquents', 'malignants', 'cavaliers', etc., and so the risings took place in the name of parliament and in support of parliament.' There was an acute fear of soldiers and so, with groups of armed gentlemen riding round the countryside, parliamentarian propagandists had little difficulty in playing on those fears. Nevertheless, 'the risings and riots .... were fundamentally spontaneous popular movements.'

Many of the manufacturing towns and areas were particular centres of parliamentarian support - London, where thousands volunteered to join Essex's army and to build the earthworks; Coventry and Birmingham, where local iron workers sent 15,000 swords to the Earl of Essex; Manchester and its linenweaving population in the country outside; and the West Riding of Yorkshire, where 20,000 people were engaged in textiles in Halifax, Bradford, Bingley and Keighley. Brian Manning highlights one characteristic shared by these 'firmest and most radical supporters of parliament.' Like their counterparts who worked in the cloth industry in the area round Bath (see above), the clothiers of the West Riding, the linen-weavers of South-East Lancashire and the metal workers of Birmingham, were small-holding farmers as well as manufacturers. Therefore, they were 'not wholly dependent on the gentry, nor wholly dependent on the merchants or larger manufacturers; men not rich, nor yet impoverished, independent in their economic life and in their opinions.' They shared common fear of attacks by papists and royalists; common distress at the disruption of their livelihood by depression and war; and common ideals based on religious and political reform.[28] Let us now consider how far our own area of study fits into this general pattern of popular uprisings.

Why had the people of North-East Somerset, when faced with the choice, risen in such numbers to support Parliament's committee men in opposition to the personal representatives of the King? In doing so, were they expressing their own views or were they merely being manipulated by a few dominant personalties? What part did ordinary people play in influencing the outcome of the political struggle which took place within the area during July and August 1642? Various theories have been advocated, which must now be analysed.

(a) Social Conflict?

There is, first of all, the view that the motivating force behind this upsurge of feeling was social conflict; that the jealousy of the 'middling sort' towards the gentry inspired a class hatred among the lower orders, who were deliberately led to believe that Hertford's commission was an instrument of tyranny. This view of the situation in Somerset was originally advocated by the Earl of Clarendon and subsequently repeated by other historians:

> For though the gentlemen of ancient families and estates in that county were for the most part well affected to the King .... yet there were a people of inferior degree, who, by good husbandry, clothing, and other thriving arts, had gotten very great fortunes, and, by degrees getting themselves into the gentlemen's estates, were angry that they found not themselves in the same esteem and reputation with those whose estates they had; and therefore, with more industry than the other, studies all ways to make themselves considerable. These from the beginning were fast friends to the Parliament.[29]

However, this class interpretation of the division of loyalties does not stand up to close examination within North-East Somerset. Out of the six main leaders of the parliamentary organisation in the 'northern clothing districts', only John Ashe fits Clarendon's description of a man of 'inferior degree' who had gained gentlemen's estates through his success in the clothing industry. The other five, who played a dominant role at Chewton Mendip, were men of substantial means, large estates and genteel birth - Sir John Horner, Sir Francis Popham, Sir Edward Hungerford, Alexander Popham and George Horner. Nor is there any evidence to suggest that Ashe was in any way jealous of the status of these neighbours or 'angry' that he was lacking their esteem. Indeed, his relationships with them were always most harmonious, both working and social, a fact amply supported by the diary of John Harington.[30] Ashe himself stressed in his letter to the Speaker that their supporters who faced Hertford outside Wells were drawn from all sections and classes of society. 'This great company', he wrote, 'was made up of all the Gentry, Yeomondry and lastly youths that inhabited the north-east part of the County.' He repeatedly emphasised that the massive gathering of some 12,000 people contained, what is abundantly obvious, far more than just the 'middling sort'. 'Everyone of Master Smith's tennants', for instance, rubbed shoulders with '300 lusty stout men *of very good ranke and quality* of the City of Bristoll.' In particular, he said, 'they all dwelt within the compasse of one quarter of our shire, and they were *the best and principallest Company* from whom Sir Ralph Hopton, Sir Francis Doddington and M Smith might expect obedience, and over whom they had the greatest power heretofore.' For his part, Hopton admitted by implication that Hertford's attempt to send the sons of Lord Poulet and Lord Stawell to recruit men, horses and arms from 'several houses belonging to their fathers' met with limited success.[31]

There is no doubt that, whatever Hertford's initial impressions, the vast majority of both the leading gentry and the minor gentry in North-East Somerset sided with parliament. Even the Marquis of Hertford later admitted in a letter to the people of Somerset, recalling the incident at Shepton Mallet at the end of July, that it was 'persons of the best quality' who had visited the town 'under the colour of eating venison' to issue tickets for a rendezvous of foot and horse.[32] Inspite of Hopton's claims, repeated by Clarendon, that 'so many of the principal Gentlemen of Somerset appeared so franckly and cordiallie in the business' and that Hertford was greeted upon Mendip by 'twenty-eight of the Principall Gentlemen of that county',[33] there is no evidence that any of these gentry (except Hopton himself) were drawn from the north-eastern sector - if indeed as many as twenty-eight ever gathered there at all. It is perhaps significant that, in the exchange of correspondence between the two sides outside Wells, only sixteen signatures appear on the royalist letter, including Hertford and several of those who had accompanied him from the north - but no-one from the northern parishes. [34]

Apart from Hopton himself, the only member of the gentry with any great influence or standing within the area who supported the royalist cause from start to finish was Sir Thomas Bridges of Keynsham. Lesser figures included Sir Christopher Neville of Newton St Loe, and Richard Prater (a papist) of Nunney Castle [35] but there is no indication that they could even begin to match the reputation of men like Horner, Hungerford and Popham. Nor did these royalist sympathisers have many local allies. Of 303 royalist delinquents later referred to the Committee for Compounding from the County of Somerset, only twenty-one lived within the five Hundreds of North-East Somerset. Although several of these were clearly persons of some quality with reasonable holdings of land (e.g. Valentine Powell, gent., of Frome, Robert Leversage, Esq., of Frome Selwood, Edward Paston, Esq., of Charlcombe Manor, Robert Fisher, gent., of Widcombe, George Chapman, gent., of Bath, etc.) [36], the number also included various men of the 'middling sort' - not to mention John Horsey, husbandman of Compton Dando. Henry Chapman, Philip Sherwood and Thomas Gibbs were all innkeepers with property in Bath, while Maximilian Macie, William Hall and David Macie formed a clutch of royalist yeomen from the village of Weston, who worked closely there with John Shepherd, gent., and his son in offering resistance to parliamentary control. [37] At the celebrations in Bath of Charles II's coronation in April 1661, 'a volunteer company of sixty men out of his Majesty's loyal and much-suffering parish of Weston, commanded by their loyal Captain John Shepherd', was given a special place of honour. [38]

This appearance of royalist yeomen and royalist innkeepers does much to destroy the 'class' theory of the division of loyalties - as does the realisation that James Strode, one of those who opposed the committeemen in Shepton Mallet, petitioned Hertford for assistance and was subsequently arrested as a delinquent by order of parliament, was himself a clothier! [39] Similarly, the parliamentarians could rightly claim to have had a complete cross-section of society within their ranks, as indicated by the occupations of those members of Bath City Council who were known to favour Popham, Ashe and Horner. Whereas several of these styled themselves 'Gent.' (including John Biggs, Walter Chapman, Peter Chapman, Matthew Clift, Mark Dallemoor and Thomas Burford), their supporters also numbered Richard Druce (a baker), Robert Penney (a mercer), John Pearce (a mercer), John Parker (a clothier), John Hayward (an organ-maker), Thomas Cole (a mercer), William Baker (a clothier), Richard Abbott (a button-maker) and John Atwood (a baker). [40]

Professor David Underdown's assertion, therefore, that parliament's strength in the area was 'clearly related to the social structure of the region' is without foundation. Furthermore, his claim that many of the gentry from the northern parishes were 'with Hertford' is, as we have seen, totally untrue. His argument is based on the fact that parliament's committeemen lamented the lack of officers within their army. It is certainly true that Popham and Horner only managed to put the masses assembled on the Mendips into some sort of order 'with much ado, for want of expert soldiers and commanders' and that their men were 'raw, untutored and unexperienced both in the use of their arms and horsemanship.' [41] But it is quite another thing to argue that therefore 'it was the Royalists who had the natural leaders, the gentlemen and their sons.' [42] The parliamentarians, in fact, had by far the majority of the natural leaders within their ranks - but, as in most areas of the country in 1642, these local gentry were not professional soldiers and they were not prepared for war. Alexander Popham's Bath Regiment of Trained Bands, numbering no more than one thousand, would certainly have been familiar with the basic elements of pike and musket drill - but neither they nor their commander had ever previously experienced the rigours of battle or the demands of a military campaign. The remainder of the Mendip army, consisting largely of an enthusiastic rabble, many of whom were equipped with 'pitch forks, dungpicks, and suchlike weapons', made up a total of 12,000 troops - nearly twice the number that fought under Sir William Waller at the Battle of Lansdown one year later!

No wonder John Ashe pleaded with parliament: 'we are lost and spoiled if we have not commanders, for though the countrie people be stout and resolved, yet we are not able to maintaine the cause, and support our courage, without experte men that can leade and advise us.'[43] By this he meant those professional army commanders who had seen service on the continent, men of the calibre of Sir Ralph Hopton and Lieut. Col. Henry Lunsford whose expertise with cavalry had won the skirmish at Marshall's Elm for the royalists. But these two gentlemen had accompanied Hertford from the north and were not typical of local royalist gentry, whose flair for military leadership was no more evident in August 1642 than that of their parliamentarian counterparts. By early September, Ashe's request was answered with the arrival of Colonel Charles Essex, a seasoned continental campaigner, with eight troops of horse. The local gentry, in North Somerset, like Oliver Cromwell in East Anglia, would take longer to learn their new calling. Even as late as 6th June 1643, Captain Henry Archbowl wrote to Colonel Nathaniel Fiennes, Governor of Bristol, requesting to serve under him instead of Sir Edward Hungerford. 'There is none but Capt. Franklin and Capt. Fennes that doth know anie thinge', he lamented, 'and I doe feare if the enemy should come, it would be a desperate cause for want of good soldiers.'[44]

(b) Deference to Leadership?

If, therefore, the 'class' theory is not valid for explaining why the men of the northern clothing parishes rose up against the Marquis of Hertford, how relevant is the second theory of allegiance, namely that of 'deference'? This assumes that the natural leaders of the community had an automatic following from their servants, tenants and workforce, based partly on the traditional respect generated by the paternalist relationship of master and servant and partly on the moral pressure brought about by various systems of land tenure.

Examples of this type of allegiance are not difficult to find in the Civil War. Clive Holmes, in describing the unanimous enthusiasm shown by crowds at musters in Essex for thwarting the 'hellish designs and actings of a malignant party', stresses that this was largely the work of influential leadership. The inhabitants acted more 'through love of the Earl of Warwick' than through genuine commitment to the parliamentarian cause - a fact illustrated by the speed with which his army disbanded in November 1642, when he resigned his commission. He concludes that, 'as in Nottinghamshire, the influential leadership provided by a great peer was the dominant consideration in forming their actions in 1642.'[45] Anthony Fletcher makes a similar point in stressing that the fourteen counties which executed the militia ordinance between late May and mid-June in 1642 - well ahead of the others - were counties in which influential individuals took a decisive lead (the Earl of Warwick in Essex, Lord Brooke in Warwickshire, Lord Willoughby in Lincolnshire, the Earl of Stamford in Leicestershire) or forceful groups of MPs attended the musters (as in Hampshire, Warwickshire, Lincolnshire, Lancashire and Cheshire).[46]

Derek Hirst has given a reminder that certain types of tenant were vulnerable to landlord influence. Sir John Stawell, in raising a force in 1642, was quoted as saying that most of his tenants 'holdeth their lands by rack-rent . . . if they would not obey his command, he might out with them.' However, Hirst also stresses that times were changing . The steady growth in franchise had created 'the larger political nation.' The gentry 'were not always able to control it, and they had to take account of its wishes. ' There was now a 'wavering multitude' and 'popular involvement was not a stream that could be channelled at will by the gentry'[47] J H Plumb, in writing about the growth of the electorate, emphasised that the views of the freeholders of England were 'never ignored' and that the gentry had now become skilled at the art of political persuasion through propaganda leaflets. 'To sway his mind, to persuade him to the hustings, to secure his vote by every art became a vital preoccupation with all who were concerned with government.' It was no longer sufficient to rely on deference alone, because 'the meaner sort were no longer at the disposal of their masters.'[48] Brian Manning goes even further in the argument against deference as the main factor in allegiance. 'What was happening,' he wrote, 'was that the people were choosing between one set of rulers and another - in Somerset they opted for Alexander Popham and Sir John Horner rather than Sir Ralph Hopton and Sir John Stawell, and this meant that power lay with the people, rather than with Popham and Horner, at least for the moment.'[49] How far does this view stand up to analysis?

In the absence of nobility in the area, the gentry had inevitably emerged as the group which exercised most influence and natural authority in North-East Somerset. Professor Underdown, in advocating the 'class' theory and partially explaining the Mendip episode as a middle class rising against royalist gentry who had sided with Hertford, is forced to conclude in consequence that 'the deference hypothosis is a less convincing explanation for the behaviour of regions such as north Somerset...'[50] It is certainly true that the majority of inhabitants failed to respond to a call to arms issued by the few gentry of royalist sympathy within the area. Ashe was quick to point out, for instance, that the committee's army on Mendip included 'all the inhabitants in that quarter where Sir Ralph Hopton liveth unto his very gates' as well as 'every one' of the tenants of Thomas Smyth from Long Ashton - in fact all the most worthy residents from those districts where Hopton, Dodington and Smyth 'might expect obedience, and over whom they had the greatest power heretofore.'[51] It was the same story in Keynsham, where Sir Thomas Bridges, a man of large estates and considerable wealth from a well-established family, might have been expected to rally the townsmen in support of Hertford. He was, however, forced to witness the full extent of his failure, partly through the galling sight of his own Constable (Robert Bagnall) presenting a petition to the Assize Judge on 12th August requesting a formal condemnation of the Commission of Array; and partly through the massive contributions made voluntarily by the people of Keynsham at the start of the war to raise dragoons for the use of Alexander Popham (worth £219).[52]

It is quickly apparent, therefore, that deference alone would not guarantee a gentleman the allegiance of his servants and tenants in the Civil War - an indication, perhaps, that even ordinary people had views and feelings of their own. Underdown rightly points out that 'where the sympathies of the gentry coincided with those of the population .... elite leadership was little impaired by the civil war. But where a landlord was seriously out of step with the general opinion of the neighbourhood war conditions might make it impossible to impose his authority.'[53] Sir Ralph Hopton was a case in point, as John Ashe pointed out in his letter to Parliament: 'Although Sir Ralph Hopton be a Gentleman very well beloved in the whole country, yet so highly are they incensed against him for the last action, that from Evercrutch his owne tenants and servants came against him and cry him downe now, more than ever they extolled him when the Knights of the Shire were chosen.' He added, in a second letter, that Hopton was keeping close to Hertford's side for protection 'for that the whole country doe take Sir Ralph Hopton for no better than a Rebell.'[54] Yet this was the same Hopton who had commanded a company within the Bath Regiment of Trained Bands in 1639 - a company drawn from all the villages of the Keynsham Hundred, together with some from the Hundreds of Frome, Bathforum and Wellow. The influence and loyalty which he had established then apparently counted for nothing just three years later. Five of the men who had served with him as musketeers in that company - John Cox, Jacob Hancock, John Weeks, Richard Gibbins and Pollider Parsons from Farmborough - were all to contribute generously to the parliamentarian cause when the call came.[55] There are no recorded examples of tenants of the local parliamentarian gentry deserting their lords and joining the royalist camp.

However, the natural leaders who *were* in step with general opinion in the neighbourhood were those members of the local gentry, who opposed Hertford's Commission of Array and fought against him at Wells. These, as we have seen, counted for the vast majority of gentry in the northern area. It was therefore not surprising that they continued to exercise their leadership, to influence the local scene and to command the allegiance of their subordinates who were glad of their protection and direction in a period of crisis. The deference factor cannot be ignored in North-East Somerset.

There is clear evidence that the northern members of the committee used their considerable influence to raise forces on behalf of parliament. John Ashe related how, after Hopton's threatening behaviour in Shepton Mallet, 'Sir John Horner called many of his neighbours and tenants together and armed them or caused them to be armed; and so marched unto Master Alexander Popham, to whom reported presently above 1000 armed men ready to spend their lives for the sayd Gentlemens safety.' At the same time, Sir Edward Hungerford had been hard at work among his tenants at Farleigh. He not only lent 'armes of his owne unto 150 or 200 volunteers', but also inspired the service of two or three hundred horsemen 'out of those parts of Wiltshire neare Sir Edward Hungerford's quarter.' Popham's own influence extended far beyond his Hunstrete estates. As Commander of the Bath Regiment of Trained Bands, he ensured that they remained loyal for service even in the face of forceful instructions from the Marquis of Hertford that they should follow him to Wells in compliance with the Commission of Array. Such was Popham's natural authority within the area, however, that the Regiment arrived on Mendip not only 'compleate in number', but 'doubled twice over by means of volunteers.'[56] Furthermore, as Member of Parliament for Bath, he carefully guided the deliberations of the Council who frequently turned to him for advice. When, for instance, a copy of the June petition of Somerset royalists reached the Council for consideration, they immediately sent for him to ask his opinion. He not only warned them against it because 'there were great aspersions laid upon the Parliament in it', but also sought ways with his father 'to nip this in the bud.' The Council rejected the petition and 'no hands' were put to it in Bath.[57]

Nor should we lightly dismiss the Council's own influence on the citizens of Bath. Under the active leadership of much-respected 'gentlemen' such as Matthew Clift, Walter Chapman, Thomas Burford and Mark Dallemoor, the 'deference factor' could be just as vital to the war effort in the city as it was on the estates of Horner and Popham. The Corporation had deeply involved itself already by supporting the material needs of its regiment at Chewton. A sum of £4 18s 4d. had been contributed 'for charges of the soldiers to Wells and for Horsehier', whilst the armoury had been emptied and Thomas Saunders given the task of 'carryinge the Armes to Wells'. At the same time their expert in metal work, John Gray, had been despatched to provide what practical assistance he could. The Town Clerk, James Galley, took their official communications to Colonel Popham and kept them in touch with the latest news. But the Council perhaps best demonstrated its affection for the parliamentary cause by sending out one of its own members, John Biggs, to entertain Popham and the other commanders as they waited on the Mendips. A generous supply of wine was forwarded to add to the food brought by Biggs at a cost of £5 14s. 'for entertayneing the Colonell and Commander at the General Muster'. A tent had also been made at the city's expense - presumably for use by the regiment's officers on occasions like this.[58]

Nevertheless, inspite of the front-line leadership of Horner, Popham, Hungerford and the Bath City Council in influencing the raising of men and materials, there is little doubt that the driving force behind the campaign was John Ashe, the gentleman clothier from Freshford. He was a born organiser, a hyper-active member of the committee, an enthusiastic eye-witness reporter of the whole episode on the Mendips - and a man of enormous personal influence. This influence far exceeded that of Horner, Popham and Hungerford because, in addition to the control he exerted over his tenants as landlord of estates in Freshford and Hinton Charterhouse, he was also by far the greatest employer in the whole of Somerset. We have already examined in Chapter One the extent of his cloth industry along the Avon valley on which depended 'the livelihood and welfare of thousands of poor people'.[59] When an acute depression hit the west country industry during the first part of the seventeenth century, 'the needy multitude' in North-East Somerset consisted not so much of the agricultural labourers and citizens of Bath, but rather of the poor spinners and weavers whose subsistence was threatened. Those living towards Bath rather than Frome found a saviour in John Ashe - not John Ashe the gentleman landlord, but John Ashe the clothier who transformed an ailing industry and brought work to thousands of people within the area. When events eventually turned him into a revolutionary in 1642, he had a ready-made following of grateful people close at hand. The deference factor therefore ensured that the massive gathering on the Mendips in August 1642 included a vast number of cloth workers. It is worth adding that at the start of the war, Ashe 'raised, armed and for many weeks paid a troop of horse, a company of foot and a company of dragoons for ye service of ye west country, before ye contribution was any way settled for ye payment of soldiers in those parts... and paid for powder, match and bullet expended by them all, which cost him above £3,000'.[60] The men of North-East Somerset partly followed Horner, Popham, Hungerford and Ashe, therefore, because these natural local leaders were in step with the general opinion of the neighbourhood.

(c) Localism?

In addition to the 'class' and 'deference' theories of allegiance, three other possibilities need to be considered - first, that the ordinary people rose to defend their community against an outside threat (the theory of 'localism'); second, that their sole aim was to bring about peace (the theory of 'neutralism') and third, that they actually possessed positive views and a natural inclination of their own. These three theories often converge. There is at least on the surface, plenty of evidence to support the theory of localism, which centred on the need to protect one's area from outside attack. Arrangements made in Gloucester, as early as November 1641, for twelve men to keep watch and ward were prompted not through commitment to one party, but 'by reason the tymes are dangerous.' Similar feelings prevailed in August 1642 when a Committee of Defence was established there 'to doo anythinge ... that they, in their discretion, shall conceive may concerne the defence of this city.' So vital was the local cause, that women and children worked on the fortifications and councillors supervised watches in rotation.[61] The same story was true in Nottingham in December 1642 and January 1643, when the Corporation urged 'the gentlemen of the towne and countrie' to join together for the defence of the city as fortifications were strengthened at a common charge.[62] But *local* defence was the first priority. The men who had joined the Earl of Warwick's local army in Essex in 1642, withdrew their support when parliament turned it into 'a running army' or mobile force under experienced Scottish officers. Countrymen showed a possessiveness towards their arms and an unwillingness to cross the county boundary. In Suffolk, the gentry showed little enthusiasm for executing the Militia Ordinance until a wave of violence in the Stour Valley sparked them into mobilising the trained bands - not to demonstrate support for the parliamentarian cause, but to drive out marauders who were a threat to order.[63] Even if outsiders were admitted, they were regarded with suspicion, as Lord Strange indicated in Chester in September 1642. If the Commissioners of Array should 'make any plundering contrary to his request to them, he would joine with the country against them.'[64] Anthony Fletcher has made the point that no fewer than thirty-three towns had raised troops of volunteers in response to parliament's Militia Ordinance between June and September 1642, but that most of those who joined had no vision of a war against the King. Enforcing the ordinance 'made men feel more secure.'[65]

There is no doubt that the inhabitants of the five hundreds in North-East Somerset bitterly resented the high-handed intrusion of 'foreigners' who were cleverly portrayed by Ashe and his committee as disturbers of the peace intent on tyrannising them with an 'illegal' Commission of Array. Countrymen always regarded it as a high priority to protect the fabric of their own society against attack. Their concern was for local custom, ancient law and personal freedom as well as personal property, family livelihood and religious belief. In that sense, 'the 1642 Mendip rising was, among other things, a rising of the 'Country' against outsiders'.[66] Local people, therefore, witnessed with distrust the arrival of Hertford and his followers in Bath on 25th July, lodging a petition with the Assize Judge on the same day against the Commission of Array; witnessed with indignation the treatment meted out to William Strode at Shepton Mallet on 1st August., 'which the country people, seeing with admiration, got up their spirits and so bestirred themselves that in a short time they had treble the Marquesse power'; heard with horror the stories which were circulating about the way in which Hopton's cavalry had terrorised and plundered villages around Shepton on 3rd August, 'the people seeing it could not suffer it, for if they prevaile now they think, they shall be slaves for ever';[67] and witnessed with stunned disbelief the loss of blood at Marshall's Elm on 4th August. Natural instincts of self-preservation caused many countrymen to rally to the flag, which had already been raised by Horner, Popham and Ashe.

Feelings of 'localism' were cleverly exploited by the parliamentarian gentry who used and exaggerated these incidents to good effect in a brilliant propaganda campaign designed to win over any waverers in a great upsurge of emotion. The controversial royalist petition, which had been rejected by Bath Council on Popham's advice in June (see above), was now reprinted and widely distributed with an 'answer' from the committee. In it they referred slightingly to 'this vagrant petition which now travelleth the country' as being the work of 'some few gentlemen, whom you value by the acre, rather than by their powers'. What was more they would quickly bring in 'a malignant party, who of bad guests will soon become worse masters, domineering over your peace, liberties, and estates, and turning your Somersetshire into a field of blood and dead men's bones'. Finally,they posed the question - 'Whether it may not be that these few gentlemen (who have this influence on you) have ambitions, covetous or militious ends of their own?'.[68]

In this way, Ashe, Popham and their confederates gradually sowed doubts and fears in the minds of many - fears of tyranny and fears of papacy. Given the background of Laud and the 'personal rule', this was not difficult. In particular, much was made of the terrors which would result from the Commission of Array, a fact emphasised by Clarendon:

> ...the other party, according to their usual confidence and activity, wrought underhand to persuade the people that the marquis was come down to put the commission of array in execution, by which commission a great part of the estate of every farmer or substantial yeoman should be taken from them; alleging that some lords had said that £20 by the year was enough for any peasant to live by; and so, taking advantage of the commission's being in Latin, translated it into what English they pleased; persuading the substantial yeoman and freeholders that at least two parts of their estates would by that commission be taken from them, and the meaner and poorer sort of people that they were to pay a tax for one day's labour in the week to the King; and that all should be, upon the matter, no better than slaves to the lords, and that there was no way to free and preserve themselves from this insupportable tyranny than by adhering to the Parliament, and submitting to the ordinance for the militia, which was purposely prepared to enable them to resist these horrid invasions of their liberties.[69]

Hopton's excursion played right into his enemy's hands. His high-handed behaviour around Shepton Mallet seemed to confirm all that the Committee had been saying. News of the incident spread so rapidly that the parliamentary leaders apparently had no need to issue formal warrants at their Shepton meeting - 'the country hearing how we were like to be surprised, came in without warrants or any request of ours, with such diligence and affection, both horse and foot, that before noon were above 2,000 horse, though most unarmed, and about 100 foot'. Stories of Hopton's efforts at recruiting were also used to good effect locally by Ashe, Popham, and Horner to strengthen the idea of royalist tyranny - 'our scouts bringing us word very frequently how they (Hopton's cavalry) surprised the countrymen coming to us, laboured to increase their fears, beat and wounded His Majesties subjects, took away their powder, bullets and provision they brought to assist us'. At this stage in the struggle it is interesting to notice that great stress was placed in all this propaganda on the fact that parliament was not resisting *the King* but his evil councillors. This emphasis no doubt made rebellion far easier for local consciences to accept. At any rate, the Committee was able to report back to parliament that it had had 'great experience amongst us already of God's great mercy in bowing people's hearts to his service, and raysing their spirits to most gallant resolutions for the defence of the King and Parliament against all opposers'.[70]

This task of 'bowing people's hearts to his service', the Committee had accomplished with great skill. John Ashe was, after all, highly experienced at marketing his products and therefore approached the challenge with business-like efficiency and a certain lack of scruples. Hopton noted with admiration that 'the Enemy play'd their game shrewdly, endeavouring (which they afterwards in some measure effected) to rayse the country secretly, and in an instant, with intention from East and West to surround the Marquesse att Wells'.[71] There is no doubt that propaganda played a large part in rallying the area for parliament in August 1642 - but this in itself is a clear indication of the importance attached to winning the minds and hearts of ordinary people in the Civil War. Ordinary people were beginning to matter. They could no longer be regarded as mere pawns on a chessboard operated by rival gentry. Hertford, who in a 'gentle way endeavoured to compose the fears and apprehensions of the people',[72] also realised the importance of convincing the local populace of the justice of his cause without ever matching the expertise and flair of his opponents.

He mounted his campaign of counter-propaganda far too late to achieve any lasting effect. Writing 'to the people of the county' on 25th August - long after the episode at Wells had been settled - he attempted to nullify 'the malicious suggestions and deceitful pretences of those men who disturb the peace of the Kingdom and endeavour to bring in great changes in the Church and State against the King's consent and just authority'. He then went on to deny 'all manner of slanders', including the allegation that the Commissioners were 'papists or popishly affected', before switching his attack to the members of the parliamentary committee, accusing them of despising the Common Prayer Book and favouring 'Brownists, Anabaptists and other disturbers of all order and government'. Finally, he went over in detail the sequence of events at Shepton Mallet and elsewhere, giving his own interpretation and justification to counter the 'foul untruths' that had been spread by others.[73] The significance of Hertford's response lies not in its effectiveness at the time, but in the fact that it was addressed 'to the people of the County'. Both sides realised that they could no longer rely on the 'deference' factor alone. The local populace was still willing to follow its natural leaders, but it first needed to be convinced that its own values were being protected and not attacked by those in question. The local community was gradually developing a mind and a will of its own hence the importance of a propaganda campaign which was directed essentially at ordinary people.

(d) Neutralism?

Nevertheless, localism must not be confused with neutrality, whose objective was peace and whose policy was non-involvement. One widespread view of allegiance, as David Underdown has pointed out, is that 'the common people were essentially neutral, moved primarily by the impulse to protect home and community from plundering soldiers and tax gatherers.' They therefore had little sympathy for either side, were 'mere cannon-fodder, targets for plunder, at best deferential pawns' and, in Arthur Haselrig's words, did not care what government they lived under, so long 'as they may plough and go to market.'[74]

There is no doubt that people throughout England struggled with the problem of allegiance when war broke out in 1642. Neutralism was an attractive idea. In many areas, as Clive Holmes has suggested, the 'desire to stave off the fatal choice ... was institutionalised in a local pacification or declaration of neutrality' (as in Essex, where two peace petitions were presented to King and parliament in January 1643); elsewhere (as in Kent and Cornwall), small cliques 'struggled for control of the shire, while the bulk of the inhabitants sat still as neuters, assisting neither.'[75] Many towns took up a stance of 'defensive neutrality' at the start of the war. The corporation at Worcester was at pains to avoid involvement. Not only did it purchase its own stock of arms 'for the generall use and defence of the cittie and not to be imployed but by consent of the chamber', it petitioned vigorously against the royalist troopers 'which daily appear here to the terror of the citizens, the hindrance of our trade and market, and tend to be dividing of the King and Parliament.'[76] At Leicester, the Council requested Lord Grey 'to forbear bringing any forces into this Town lest otherwise he should be the means to cause our prejudice in this Corporation'.[77] In Bristol, the Common Council, as early as 21st May 1642, resolved that petitions in favour of reconciliation should be addressed to both King and parliament. Later, while agreeing to entertain the Marquis of Hertford lest he 'be driven to take up his lodgings at an inn', they nevertheless refused his request to send some cavalry into the city. Furthermore, in an attempt to quell the growth of factions, they made a determined effort to suppress the wearing of colours and badges in the hats of inhabitants.[78] John Corbet was quick to condemn the inhabitants of Tewkesbury for abandoning their principles, accepting peace terms and desiring 'an everlasting neutrality.'[79] Counties as well as towns pursued a search for isolation from war. The Derbyshire gentry, for instance, remained united and held to a neutralist stance until October 1642, while Sir John Potts in Norfolk succeeded in his policy of neutralisation by suspending both the ordinance and the commission until late August. The Staffordshire gentry also gave short shrift to both sides.[80] 'Militant neutralism' took hold in Cheshire, which saw the presentation of a peace petition to King and parliament on 6th June and the publication of a demilitarisation manifesto on 25th August. In Shropshire, 'the efforts of both sets of partisans foundered in a sea of local indifference', emphasised when the Corporation 'outlawed all partisan insignia within the town.' Meanwhile, in Cirencester, the inhabitants barricaded the streets against Lord Chandos, forcing him to disclaim the commission and support local peace instead.[81]

In the light of this evidence from the country at large, how far did the community of North-East Somerset also take up a neutralist stance? How far did the gentry 'close ranks behind county barriers' in an attempt to stave off the fatal choice, or had they already brought about their own division by choice? Did the ordinary people think only of protecting their homes from plunder; were they simply to become victims of the committed activist who 'dragged the reluctant majority into war'?[82] or were they in fact already committed at heart themselves to the parliamentarian cause? Was Bath, like so many towns, pledged to 'defensive neutralism' or was it, like Birmingham, an exception to the rule of 'urban indifference and hostility to war', manifesting in the same way 'a virulent and spontaneous puritanism'?[83] Ronald Hutton has argued that the decisive point in the events came after the Royalist victory at Marshall's Elm when Hertford's cavalry indulged themselves by plundering and terrorising the local people. 'These incidents', he suggests, 'convinced many that the Royalists had to be driven out to restore order producing the demonstration of support for the parliamentarian gentry'.[84] He substantiates his claim by referring to the Grand Jury's petition on 15th August (i.e. after Hertford's force had fled the area) which begged 'for the avoidance of the miseries that befall us by means of contrary commands' and for both King and Parliament to lay down their arms and settle their differences.[85] This interpretation assigns no more than a peace-keeping role to the local community.

The theory that the local people were essentially neutralist in attitude would be more convincing if their allegedly 'defensive' actions had been confined to the period of terror (i.e. between the confrontation on Monday 1st August at Shepton Mallet and the departure of Hertford's men from Wells on Saturday 6th). This was not the case. Parliamentary supporters had commenced the task of raising men, money and weapons on 20th July - five days *before* the arrival of Hertford in Bath with his Commission of Array;[86] they had issued invitations on Friday 29th July for a general rendezvous over a venison barbecue at Shepton Mallet three days *before* the first ugly incident occurred - and many people had already arrived there by the Sunday;[87] and their efforts to support the parliamentary cause by voluntary contributions continued throughout the autumn and winter of 1642 long *after* Hertford's departure. Indeed, the subcommittee's accounts are dominated by the lists from parish officials itemising gifts of money and weapons offered freely by local people towards the setting up of dragoons under Alexander Popham during the early months of the war. The Hundred of Keynsham alone contributed over £610 in this way *before* the element of compulsion was added during the first part of 1643.[88] The end of Hertford's terror, therefore, did not mark the end of their interest and involvement in the local political scene.

It is certainly true that the ingredient of fear, heightened by the propaganda campaign, had removed all traces of complacency and ensured a massive following for the Committeemen in their resistance to Hertford's intrusion. 'The people in general', wrote Ashe on 5th August, 'being apprehensive of and much incensed by the late accidents, occasioned since the bringing of these commissions into this Countie, by seizing of arms, maiming some and murdering others, the report whereof hath spread far and nigh, and hath brought many hither out of their counties to rescue this from their miseries, least the same evills fall upon themselves afterwards'.[89] It is also true that the local community fervently desired peace so that they could concentrate fully again on the problems of everyday survival in the face of harvest failure, unemployment and starvation. The petition of the Grand Jury on 15th August 1642 had a similar ring to the letter written by the Mayor of Bath to Captain Harington in the Spring of 1646 - 'God preserve our Kingdom from these sad troubles much longer!' (see Chapter Six). The people of North-East Somerset were, in fact, perfectly consistent in their attitude throughout the entire war. They preferred peace - but not peace at any price. If war were to come, then they knew clearly which side they were on, which leaders they would follow and which principles they would defend. There was no place for neutralism in North-East Somerset. No-one tried harder to bring about a peaceful compromise than William Bassett of Claverton. Member of Parliament for Bath alongside Alexander Popham, he was also married to the step-daughter of Sir John Stawell, one of Hertford's closest advisers. Bassett therefore willingly accepted the role of mediator when he was summoned to Wells to negotiate a settlement on Hertford's behalf. He not only failed on that occasion, but was to suffer for his neutralism later at the hands of both sides, being imprisoned by the royalists and fined nearly £2,000 by the Committee for Compounding for his alleged delinquency![90]

(e) Religious Commitment?

Why, then, did the community of North-East Somerset enlist so fervently for parliament in July and August, 1642? It was certainly not an expression of class hatred. It was clearly more than an expression of neutralism which merely sought an end to Hertford's rule of terror and a restoration of the status quo, because their commitment to the cause commenced *before* Hertford's worst excesses had occurred and it continued, as we shall see, throughout the remainder of the war. Their commitment, it is true, had been heightenedc2 by fear, which in turn had been inflamed by propaganda but that steady commitment remained, even during royalist occupation, long after the passions aroused on Mendip had subsided. The influence of the local gentry was crucial, but only because they were 'in step with the general opinion in the neighbourhood'. The spirit of localism was also important, but only because it united the majority of local people in a determination not merely to eject an intruder, but to preserve in a positive way the very special attitudes which now prevailed in North-East Somerset. It was no coincidence that almost the entire resistance offered against Hertford was provided, in the words of John Ashe, by those who 'dwelt within the compasse of one quarter of our shire'.[91] Success mattered deeply in that region.

What, then, did the parliamentarian gentry and ordinary people have in common? The first clue is to be found on the slopes of Mendip as their massive army began to assemble. The scene was more reminiscent of a religious convention or pilgrimage than a military parade ground.[92] A wave of emotion and idealism swept across the hills as the local people prepared to fight for their cause. 'You would not imagine', wrote Ashe, 'how confidently and willingly the country take to arms'. He went on to describe how the officers and men together not only 'spent the time in prayers and singing of Psalms' but also willingly endured hardships, almost as a form of penance, lying 'all that night upon the hill, fasting and in the cold'. He was at great pains to stress the unity of the gentry and ordinary people, shown by the fact that the Horners, the Pophams 'with many other young Gentlemen, Captaines and others, lay all that night in their Armes upon Fursbushes in the Open Fields amidst the Camp, the old Knight often saying that his Furs-Bed was the best he lay upon'.

These were not the words and emotions of soldiers merely drawn together to eject an intruder. This religious fervour spread from their camp on Penn Hill outside Wells with such rapidity to the countryside around that by morning a miracle had taken place - the feeding of the twelve thousand! 'But such was the love and affections of all the Country within eight and ten miles distance', wrote Ashe, 'that by the next morning daylight they sent in such provision of all sorts in waynes, carts and on horses, that this great company had sufficient and to spare, both for breakfast and dinner, and would not take a penny for it, nay many did carry home againe their provisions, for want of Company to eate it'.[93] This great upsurge of local feeling is substantiated by occasional references in the subcommittee accounts. In the Keynsham Hundred, for instance, the villagers of Charlton 'sent unto Pen Hill halfe a hundred of cheese for the use of the Parliament', while their neighbours in Belluton 'sent provisions to Penn Hill neere Wells to the value of £3 4s 0d.'[94]

Their real motivation was revealed immediately following the departure of Hertford from Wells. Inspite of an appeal from the Mayor and citizens requesting that the soldiers should refrain from entering the city, 'the Mendip men, who had spent the night in prayer and singing psalms, entered the city with such great expression of joy as is hardly imaginable, gloried in having vanquished 'the Papists', tore down the painted glass in the Cathedral, and visited and sacked the Bishop's Palace'. Organs and pictures were destroyed and one portrait of the Virgin Mary 'was put on a spear and carried about in contempt and derision'.[95] Earlier a correspondent had noted that many villagers from a wide area had joined the throng bringing 'pitchforks, dungpicks and such like weapons', not knowing who they were to fight against, but 'supposing they were Papists'.[96] Fear and hatred of popery was certainly a common theme that united the parliamentarian gentry and the ordinary people. They had bitter memories of the 1630's when Archbishop Laud's High Church policies were implemented locally by Bishop Piers in the county and by James Masters in the City of Bath. In a more positive way, however, the 'Mendip men', including Horner, Popham, Ashe and Hungerford, stood for the puritan brand of religion, personal morality, family discipline and sober pastimes. If we are looking for causes of allegiance, it is worth moving on briefly to 1648, the year of the Second Civil War, when royalist supporters around Bath staged demonstrations in the city against the parliamentarian regime. They selected two symbols for their own cause, which they knew would be anathama to their opponents - the Book of Common Prayer and bull-baiting. Dr Jones, 'a great plunderer and late Chaplain in the King's Army' read Common

The Souldiers in their passage to York turn unto reformers pull down Popish pictures, break down rayles, turn altars into Tables,

A contemporary print which depicts puritan soldiers ransacking a church to destroy pictures, altars and other symbols of 'Papist' religion. This is reminiscent of the attack by Popham's force on Wells Cathedral in 1642.

Prayer several times in a disused church, while Henry Chapman organised weekly bull-baiting sessions just outside the city walls 'to which disaffected people flocked from the adjoyning counties'.[97] (see below)

The Marquis of Hertford was not just a 'foreign' intruder who was found disturbing the peace and security of the county. There were fears that his commission of array would herald a return of the tyranny and high church practices they had experienced in the 1630's and which were still fresh in their minds. Then, their religion had been undermined by the ban on lectures and the railing off of altars; their moral code had been slighted by the re-publication of the Book of Sports; their wealth had been taxed by the dubious application of Ship Money; their livelihood had been threatened by the enclosure of Selwood Forest; and their employment had been disrupted by the restrictions of monopolists and by Ashe's lengthy appearance before the Court of Star Chamber. The cause of ordinary people had been advocated during the 1630's by those self-same gentry who later emerged to lead the Mendip army in 1642. John Ashe had led the fight against the soap monopoly and the trading monopoly of the East India Company; John Horner and Francis Popham had been foremost among the signatories of a petition to the King against Church Ales[98]; John Ashe had not only lent his support and encouragement to the Beckington Churchwardens over the communion table controversy, but had also undertaken the local distribution of Prynne's pamphlets attacking Bishops and immorality at court.[99]

The community of North-East Somerset had therefore become politically aware long before the outbreak of war. Unlike the rest of the county, which was penned in by the Mendip barrier, the northern parishes were part of the mainstream of life with easy access to both London and Bristol. Two men, in particular, were responsible for the education and enlightenment of the locality during these pre-war years - John Ashe, whose personal organisation of his Freshford cloth industry gave him close regular contact with both his own workforce and the 'revolutionary' ideas of the London merchants; and William Prynne, a former pupil of the local grammar school, who lived in Swainswick and whose grandfather had been Mayor of Bath on eight occasions. Prynne was shortly to emerge as a prominent local leader alongside Ashe, Popham and Horner - but, even by 1642, he had become a powerful force. His vigorous attacks on Laud and his subsequent punishment before the Court of Star Chamber in 1637 had turned him into a major national hero. It was therefore not without significance that his release from prison in 1641 brought him back into the area at a crucial time to influence the course of events. He was a popular local figure, with a common touch, who regularly visited Bath and enjoyed close contacts with the other leading gentry.[100]

North-East Somerset was certainly not alone in its response to the outbreak of the war. The strength of puritan commitment proved to be a decisive factor in many towns and rural communities when allegiances were settled. Brian Manning has highlighted a panic fear of papists which caused certain places, as well as North-East Somerset, to take to arms in violent opposition to the royalists - Manchester, the clothing towns of West Riding, South Molton, Essex and Suffolk, where 'the conflict in popular terms took on the character of a religious war'. Elsewhere, 'the godly people' played a key role in causing towns to rise for parliament, particularly in Nottingham, Coventry and Gloucester.[101] Although 'nominal parliamentarianism' had more of an appeal to towns in general, Anthony Fletcher has identified a good deal of 'positive urban parliamentarianism' with 'well-established puritan piety' as its surest foundation. This is particularly noticeable in those places which were totally decisive in their allegiance - Great Yarmouth, King's Lynn, Rye, Poole, Dartmouth, Barnstable, Birmingham and the textile towns of Bradford, Halifax and Leeds. Puritan majorities on city councils were often vital (as in Bath), but towns could also be influenced by ardent puritan leaders from outside the walls, such as John Hutchinson and Henry Ireton at Nottingham and the Earl of Pembroke at Salisbury. Similarly, county communities could be swayed by 'militant puritans' like Sir Thomas Barrington (Essex), Sir William Brereton (Cheshire), Herbert Morley (Sussex) and Sir Anthony Weldon (Kent) - just in the same way that North-East Somerset had been swayed by John Ashe, John Horner and William Prynne.[102] Norwich, in many respects, mirrored the experience of Bath. The puritans there had not been a radical movement but had simply wanted the establishment of a puritan ministry, protection for the sabbath and a godly community. The Corporation, like that in Bath, had established a system of puritan lectures, only to be subjected to the same sort of persecution by Bishop Wren that had been experienced in North-East Somerset at the hands of Bishop Piers in the 1630's. By 1640, therefore, the plight of the puritans in Norwich was urgent and, because bolder steps were needed, 'the puritan religious faction of the 1630's was transformed into the parliamentary-puritan political party of the 1640's.' The backbone of that party 'consisted of men who were animated by religious issues and strongly opposed the church establishment'.[103] The same was true in North-East Somerset.

P.S.W.B.

4.
The Battle of Lansdown and the Fall of Bath, 1643.

By the beginning of 1643 the King had set up his headquarters in Oxford and was planning a major offensive to recapture London. Victory in the west was vital to his ambitions. Much depended upon Sir Ralph Hopton's ability to recruit a new army in Cornwall and his skill in persuading them to fight outside their native county. If he succeeded, he would then be free to seize the vital port of Bristol and to join forces with the King for an assault on the capital. News of his victory at Braddock Down on 19th January seemed to indicate that he was gradually prevailing. Shocked by these ominous signs, parliament took swift action to preserve their grip on the west. Sir William Waller, whose wife lay buried in Bath Abbey, was appointed as Major-General of the Western Forces in Somerset, Wiltshire, Gloucestershire, Worcestershire and Shropshire.

Waller, who had already earned the nickname of William the Conqueror through his military exploits in the south during the early months of the war, brought professional expertise to the parliamentarian cause in the west. Initially, he brought very little else. Marching westward from London through Wiltshire and Dorset, he finally reached Bath and Bristol on 15th March with no more than 2,000 men. At Bristol he was greeted by the Governor, Nathaniel Fiennes, with the garrison force consisting of his own cavalry regiment, three troops of horse, Thomas Essex's foot regiment and Alexander Popham's Bath Regiment (which then numbered 600).[1]

Since Hopton had not yet stirred from his Cornish stronghold, Waller decided that the first priority was to tighten his control on the Severn Valley, threatened on one side by the Welsh and on the other by Prince Rupert's Oxford cavalry. This he did in a lightning campaign, which lasted a month in the early spring in 1643 and which resulted in the capture of Malmesbury, Tewkesbury, Chepstow and Cirencester, as well as the successful defence of Gloucester and Bristol. His military reputation was now without equal on the parliamentarian side.

While Waller had been away, Alexander Popham's Bath Regiment had remained in Bristol with the rest of the garrison to cover any sudden emergencies. Although Somerset, Dorset and Wiltshire were almost completely under parliament's dominion at this stage of the war, two towns with strong royalist factions gave repeated trouble - Sherborne and Malmesbury. Sherborne, under Sir John Strangeway, had acted defiantly until Waller's arrival on his westward journey in March. The royalist leaders had quickly fled, only to return a short time later. Probably because of this, Alexander Popham took two cavalry troops from Bristol on 16th April to investigate the situation. The story is taken up by the parliamentarian newsheet,

> Here came newes this morning from Sherborne of a bloudy fight in the Towne this last night, occasioned through the base treachery of the Townesmen: Colonell Popham, coming for this place, sent a Trumpet to Sherborne to know if he might quarter his men in the Towne that night, answer was returned that he should be welcome; but as soon as the Trumpeter was gone, these perfidious villains made all the preparation they could to have cut off every man of them; so that when the Colonell came with two Troopes into the Towne, they most treacherously fell upon

Sir William Waller (1579 - 1668), commander of parliament's forces at the Battle of Lansdown, 1643. Portrait attributed to E. Bower.

his unawares with all their force, shooting out at the windowes and cutting the horses bellies with sithes in the midst of the streets, but it pleased God to preserve the Colonell himselfe, who retreated with the losse of his Brother Captain Popham, and one other Captain; and divers of his men, besides many wounded ... The Colonell is raising the Countie of Sommerset to be avenged on this bloudy act.[2]

Popham could not easily forgive the inhabitants of Sherborne for the death of his younger brother, Hugh. The revengeful sequel to this incident a few days later is told by the royalist newsheet, *Mercurius Aulicus*. The two passages taken together provide good illustrations of the colourful and biased reporting of the war, which both sides turned to good use as political propaganda:

This day advertisement came from Sherborne in Dorsetshire of the horrible outrages lately committed there by the rebel forces under the command of Colonell Alexander Popham who wasted and spoiled the Towne though the inhabitants laid downe their arms, and then pillaged the Earle of Bristoll's house of all the plate, jewels, money, great store of linnen, bedding and other things to the value of many thousands pounds ... and indeed did pull downe 3 dwelling houses of Master Hugh Hodges, and disposed of the timber to build some houses which Colonell Popham had burned the Saturday night before, pillaged Master Cooth 2000 *1* deep, killing all the fat sheepe and calves, and taking away all the barley and malt in the Towne; and though they convenanted with some houses for a certain summe to be spared, yet (true to their principle) tooke their money and then perfidiously plundered the houses and carried away the poore men prisoners, and at their departure pulled downe the fire bell which was to give notice when any fire or commotion was in the Towne, and then being not able to invent more villany and cruelty to be exercised on their fellow subjects, they left the Towne carrying their pillage along with them.[3]

Certainly the local forces under Alexander Popham were not idle during the spring of 1643. Given this early experience of conflict against their west country neighbours, they had shown themselves to be tough and ruthless. Treachery deserved no mercy or sentiment. These characteristics were also displayed a few days later in Wells. 'On Wednesday 10 May, being Ascension, Mr Alexander Popham's soldiers, he being a Colonel for the Parliament, after dinner rushed into the Church, broke down the windows, organs, fonts, seats in the choir, and the Bishop's seat, besides many other villainies'. The Bath Regiment, inspired partly by religious zeal and partly by memories of royalist sentiment shown by the citizens of Wells in 1642, was becoming loutish in its behaviour. This was partly the fruit of the boredom caused by waiting for the real war to start. Meanwhile these local incidents kept them busy.

Malmesbury was one of the few places in Wiltshire to defy the control of the parliamentarian committee. Waller, therefore, had made the town his first target at the outset of his campaign along the Severn Valley. It surrendered after a short siege on 26th March and was left under the command of Sir Edward Hungerford. The royalists in the area, however, remained troublesome. As a result, 'Sergeant-Major Burghill marched from Bath with one hundred horse to relieve Sir Edward Hungerford's house from plundering, two hundred and fifty horse of the cavaliers being gone thither for that purpose, but before he came were gone, yet he pursued them to Sherestone to their quarters, routed them, killed tenne, tooke five and twenty prisoners, one Captaine, two Lieutenants, one Quarter-master and fifty horses, some with armes, and this performed without the losse of one man'. [4] Nevertheless, in spite of these successes, the Wiltshire royalists quickly recaptured Malmesbury and held it until the end April when the King recalled the garrison to help in the relief of Reading.

When Waller returned to Bristol at the end of April, therefore, the parliamentarian cause in the west seemed at first sight to be strong and healthy. This impression was largely false and Waller knew it. There were basically three problems facing him - the problem of Hopton, the problem of men and equipment and the problem of money. First and foremost was the danger caused by a sudden revival of royalist fortunes in the south west. In spite of his success along the Severn, in spite of his apparent control of Somerset, Dorset and Wiltshire, Waller was now confronted by the dramatic advance of Sir Ralph Hopton out of Cornwall. After his skilful victory over larger parliamentarian forces at Stratton on 16th May, he led his tough, well-disciplined army into Devon. Three days later the King, anxious to consolidate his strength, dispatched a substantial number of troops from Oxford under the command of the Marquis of Hertford to rendezvous with Hopton. This plan constituted a major threat to the security of parliament's position in the west. Waller was hurriedly summoned to London where he was given precise instructions to check the royalist advance and to protect Bristol at all costs.

Hopton, meanwhile, was advancing at speed, covering something like twenty miles a day. By 31st May he had reached Honiton with little resistance. Three days later he pitched camp at Chard in Somerset where, on 4th June, he was joined by Hertford. The two royalist armies together presented a total force of 4,000 foot, 2,000 horse, 300 dragoons and 16 field pieces under the overall command of the Marquis of Hertford with Prince Maurice as commander of the horse and Hopton as marshal of the field. Taunton was the first town to fall before the power of this joint force. The royalists were also able to seize from the garrison a large store of arms and ammunition together with a ransom of £8,000, all of which went a long way to replenishing their stocks. They were now confidently poised for the final thrust northwards.

Waller had no such confidence either in the strength of his army or in the resources available. Alarmed by the news of the royalist approach, he planned a general rendezvous in Bath of all parliamentarian forces towards the end of May. This would mean combining local regiments (which were mainly under the rather possessive grasp of the Governor of Bristol) with Waller's own brigade (which at that moment was based on Gloucester eagerly awaiting its pay). Waller hurried north to draw his Gloucester forces down to Bath,[5] leaving local commanders the task of doing the same with their own units.

The newsheet, *A Perfect Diurnall,* was as optimistic as ever: 'But Sir Wm. Waller is at Bath with a considerable partie daily increasing, having disarmed most of the malignants in some part of Wiltshire and Somerset, to whom also Sir Edward Hungerford, Sir John

Colonel Nathaniel Fiennes (1608 - 1669), Governor of Bristol for parliament in 1643. Portrait by Mirevelt.

Horner, Colonell Stroud and some others are joining their forces to oppose the Marquis of Hartford.'[6] This optimism was certainly not shared by Alexander Popham and other officers in the local parliamentary forces. Repeated requests were sent to Colonel Fiennes at Bristol to release more of the garrison for service in Waller's field army. Thus on 22nd May, Popham asked that the remaining companies of his own regiment should be dispatched to Bath along with a number of Bristol horse and dragoons.[7] Fiennes complied on his occasion, but understandably hesitated to undermine his defences any further when, on 7th June, Anthony Nichole and William Gould wrote to him from Bath requesting an additional force of 500 men.[8] Even as late as 24th June Waller instructed Colonel Edward Cooke to write yet again to Fiennes, begging him to send 500 foot as a matter of urgency.[9]

The real problem facing Nathaniel Fiennes was whether it was right to weaken the garrison at Bristol in order to strengthen Waller's field army. Bristol was vital to the parliamentarian cause both as a port and as a strategic base for operations in Wales, Ireland and the Severn Valley. The Earl of Essex had rightly called it 'the Key of the West of England'. But Bristol's defences were totally inadequate. As early as 20th March Fiennes and Popham had written a letter to Lord Say in London urging him to take up the whole question of settling a 'sufficient garrison' on Bristol.[10] By June a proposal was actually being considered by the Commons for establishing a garrison of 3 foot regiments (including Popham's Bath Regiment), 2 troops of horse and 1 company of dragoons for the defence of Bristol, Bath and the surrounding areas. These would, in addition, be supported by three new regiments of Trained Bands.[11]

The proposal came too late, however, to solve the present crisis. Bristol still lacked a proper, permanent garrison at the time of its fall in late July. Meanwhile, Fiennes continued to be badgered by Waller as he later recalled: 'When Sir Wil. Waller came from Woster, and had his Randevous at Bath, both he and Sir Arthur Haselrig and all the Gentlemen of the county were very earnest with me to afford a good strength of foot to his horse, whereby he might be ... master of the field .. as the onely means to preserve Bristoll and the West of England'. [12] Fiennes resisted these pleas on behalf of the field army until the very last moment. On 1st July, the day before the Lansdown campaign commenced, Waller and Haselrig sent an urgent final request via John Ashe:

> Sure you think we have both a lame and a patient enemy that will be knockt and stay till we be ready to answer his returne. We expected Col. Fines Regiment this day.. What good will this Regiment do Bristoll if we perish... It is said you captains have not yet cast lots who shall come forth; I thought they would have petitioned for the imployment.[13]

Fiennes at last yielded to the pressure and sent a further 1,200 foot (mostly members of his brother's newly-raised regiment, which had been particularly requested in Waller's letter).

These letters all point to a significant weakness in Waller's field army before the arrival of the Bristol reinforcements. He was worried not so much about the overall size of the parliamentarian forces, which probably matched that of the royalists, [14] but at their noticeable lack of infantry. Apart from Popham's Bath Regiment and a Welsh Regiment under Colonel Edward Cooke, there were few foot soldiers available for service. Altogether they numbered no more than 1,500 and were still under 3,000 with the addition of the new regiment from Bristol.

The Cavalry, on the other hand, was extremely strong. Waller had originally brought with him his own regiment of horse and several companies of dragoons. These had later been joined by Sir Arthur Haselrig 'with a verie strong Regiment of extraordinarily armed horse', numbering 1,200 and nicknamed 'Lobsters' by the royalists 'because of the bright iron-shell with which they were all couvered'; [15] by Nathaniel Fiennes' own regiment of

Sir Arthur Haselrig (d 1661), parliamentarian commander of the 'Lobsters' cavalry which fought at Lansdown in 1643. Portrait by Van Dyke.

horse from Bristol; by 1,200 roundhead cavalry from Devon and by various other local troops. Waller and Haselrig in writing to the Speaker of the House on 22nd June could therefore justly boast: 'Wee have a bodie of horse by God's blessing able to doe the kingdome good service' - but they could also fairly state that, under the circumstances, this was of little use. 'The enemie lies still att Wells. That part of the cuntrie is altogether unfitt for horse. It greeves our sules wee dare not attemp what wee desire.'[16] Footsoldiers, not cavalry, were desperately needed to work the narrow lanes between Bath and Wells.

This, however, was not Waller's only problem as he quartered his unbalanced army around his headquarters at Bath. The question of cash, as always, raised its ugly head. Reference has been made earlier to the growing difficulties experienced by John Ashe, the treasurer of the local parliamentary committee, in collecting the weekly assessment. It is true, according to a letter written later by Ashe, that Waller's arrival in the area apparently encouraged 'the several hundreds of the eastern part to bring in money to pay his army, and about £500 to £600 was so brought in; this was shared between Waller's and Colonel Popham's men.'[17] But this was a temporary bonus brought about by sudden impulse and quickly exhausted.

Waller soon realised that the situation was fast becoming desperate. There was a grave danger that large sections of his army would desert through lack of pay. He wrote to the Speaker imploring him send help from London: 'Neither can wee stay heare and starve. Wee have longe and often supplycated for you for money. Find us but a way to live without it, or else wee humblie begge a present supply, if not, *this horse will certeinly disband,* which thought makes our harts to bleed...'[18] The local correspondent of the newsheet, *Speciall Passages,* continued this theme of the importance of ready money of the discipline of an army; '... and these forget that an Army, though consisting of valiant men, and furnished with all warlike abillements, yet is but lame and uselesse, and unable to move itselfe, without money, the sinewes of warre; for pay is the poore souldiers *aqua vita,* but want is such an *aqua fortis,* as it eates though the iron doores of discipline.'[19]

Regular payment of his troops was essential to success as Waller found out to his cost at the end of May. Reaching Gloucester with the intention of taking his own brigade to the rendezvous at Bath, he suddenly changed his mind. Anxious to extend his control along the Severn before the arrival of Hertford from the south, he now made a lightning raid on Worcester (29th May). No sooner had he arrived than he was summoned back to Bath by a series of urgent messages. His army, however, refused to leave Gloucester until they had been paid - 'The want of money hath bred such mutinous dispositions in the soldiers that no arguments will make them stir.'[20] Eventually, after nearly a week's delay, enough weekly assessments were collected around Gloucester to enable the army to march to Bath.

Because of the seriousness of the situation, therefore, Waller used whatever methods he could to raise cash. Begging letters were sent not only to London but also to Bristol - 'We therefore make it our request to you to supply us with five hundred powndes.'[21] 'Let not the west of England be lost for a little monies, neither send your supplies too late!'[22] Captured plate was also put to good use, as related by the newsheet, *A Perfect Diurnall:* 'Sir Wm. Waller hath sent to London and safely arrived here about the beginning of this weeke; 5 trunkes of plate to be coyned here and returned back to him to pay his souldiers, which plate he tooke at the gaining of Hereford.'[23]

Once the army had arrived back at its headquarters in Bath on 8th June, Waller took every advantage of easing the financial strain by exploiting the system of free quarter. Neighbouring villages suffered badly in the three weeks prior to the battle of Lansdown. Because the parliamentarian forces had established a position on Claverton Down, Bathampton Down and Odd Down in anticipation of the royalist advance, people living to the south of the city bore the main brunt of their demands (see Chapter Six.)

While Waller had been facing up to the problems of his army in Gloucester and Bath, the royalists had been consolidating their position in Taunton. In order to check their progress, Waller had finally decided on 26th May to send out some of the local forces under the command of Alexander Popham. The Bristol garrison inevitably suffered: 'Six companies of Colonel Popham's Regiment were drawn forth to joyn with the forces of Somerset',[24] while a troop of horse under Colonel John Fiennes 'went with ye rest of ye regiment into Somersetshire with Colonel Popham.'[25] Once he had arrived in Bath, John Fiennes wrote a letter to his brother, Nathaniel, in Bristol reporting Waller's latest ideas: 'I percieve Sir Will. Wallers designe is something altered, he would have Coll. Popham with your horse and Sir Edw. Hungerford's and the rest of the horse in Somersetshire to march strayt towards Bridgewater togeather with Coll. Popham's foot; and himself will eyther come after or march another way...'[26]

The Bristol cavalry, unconvinced by the wisdom of this plan, agreed to accompany Popham only after they had received an advance payment of '80 li for the troop att Bath' from Sir William Waller and Colonel Popham.[27] By 5th June the parliamentarian forces had reached Glastonbury, some twenty-five miles north of Taunton. But, out of a total of 2,000 cavalry and dragoons who had left Bath, half had already deserted.[28]

Contact with the enemy was finally made on 12th June when parliamentarian horse attacked a small party of royalist dragoons near Somerton. Hertford immediately sent Maurice and Hopton from Taunton with the main royalist force to seek them out. In face of this steady advance, Alexander Popham, realizing that he was heavily outnumbered, gradually withdrew from Glastonbury through Wells and onto the Mendip Hills. Alexander's brother, Colonel Edward Popham, who commanded the cavalry, provided cover to the foot solders and baggage train as they scrambled on to the top of the Mendip plateau. Nevertheless, the royalists pressed so hard 'that they lost two of their waggons going up the hills'.[29] Then, as the whole parliamentarian force struggled its disorderly way home, Prince Maurice, Sir Ralph Hopton and the Earl of Carnarvon gave merciless

The Earl of Carnarvon, who commanded a cavalry regiment under Prince Maurice in the Marquis of Hertford's army.

chase. Ruthlessly they harassed and scattered Popham's retreating army. His own Bath Regiment suffered heavily with both casualties and loss of weapons. At this stage in the fighting Carnarvon's horse, over-excited and heedless of Hopton's sober advice, rushed on madly in pursuit of the enemy for several miles.

Waller, meanwhile, who had finally arrived in Bath with his main forces from Gloucester, quickly sensed the danger and sent out a body of horse and dragoons to cover Popham's retreat over Mendip. A heavy mist enabled them to advance unseen until Carnarvon finally fell headlong into their path. The Earl, whose cavalry by this time were largely exhausted, fled back in considerable panic along the plateau to Chewton Mendip where the rout was only halted by the welcome appearance of Prince Maurice's regiment of horse. Eventually, this parliamentarian relief force - having done its job - was driven off and retired in some disorder back to its headquarters in Bath.

There the long-awaited rendezvous of all roundhead forces was at last made under Sir William Waller, but the cost of recent events to their morale and numerical strength had been considerable. *Mercurius Aulicus* reported: '...such a number of wounded men fled into Bristol, that at the sight of these the people ran about the streets wringing their hands and saying that they were undone..'[30] Even the parliamentarian newsheets admitted the disaster: 'The truth is, they were utterly routed and scattered.'[31]

Both sides now paused to lick their wounds. During this lull Waller took time to write a letter to his old friend and army comrade, Sir Ralph Hopton, at the royalists' new headquarters in Wells. It illustrates vividly the tragic divisions caused by the war:

To my Noble friend Sir Ralphe Hopton at Wells
Sr

The experience I have had of your Worth, and the happinesse I have enjoyed in your friendship are woundinge considerations when I look upon this present distance between us. Certainly my affection to you are so unchangeable, that hostility itselfe cannot violate my friendship in your person, but I must be true to the cause wherein I serve; The ould limitation *usque adaras* holds still, and where my conscience is interested, all other obligations are swallowed up. I should most gladly waite on you according to your desire, but that I looke upon you as you are ingaged in that partie, beyond a possibilitie of retraite and consequentlie uncapable of being wrought upon with any persuasion. And I know the conference could never be so close betweene us, but that it would take wind and receive a construction to my dishonour; That great God, which is the searcher of my heart, knows with what a sad sence I goe upon this service, and with what a perfect hatred I detest this warr without an Enemie, but I looke upon it as *Opus Domini,* which is enough to silence all passion in mee. The God of peace in his good time send us peace, and in the meane time fitt us to receive it: Wee are both upon the stage and must act those parts that are assigned us in this Tragedy: Lett us do it in a way of honor, and without personall animosities, Whatsoever the issue be, I shall never willingly relinquish the dear title of

Your most affectionate friend and faithfull servant
Wm. Waller.[32]

The stalemate was finally broken at the end of June when the royalists advanced on Frome. From there they pushed forward on Sunday, 2nd July to Bradford-on-Avon, a town no more than five miles from Bath. Although Hertford had thoughts of returning to Oxford, Bristol was a rich prize which dangled temptingly before their eyes - and Bath was the gateway to Bristol. It was therefore decided to approach the city along the north side of the Avon and to seek an early opportunity to encounter the enemy.

In the meantime, Waller had assembled the whole of his army on the flat top of Claverton Down with his guns on the ridge. This gave him a magnificent commanding view of the Avon valley beneath and the two roads which led to Bradford (on each side of the river). Just below this strong position he had built a temporary bridge across the river right next to the ford near Claverton House. Having secured this crossing by earthwork defences (traces of which can still be seen in Ham Meadow today), he then sent Colonel Burghill and Sergeant-Major Dowett with 'a great part of his army, both horse, foote and dragoones' under the cover of darkness over the river. These were placed at Monkton Farleigh on the high wooded slopes overlooking the road from Bradford.

Early on the following morning (3rd July) the royalist cavalry advance guard encountered the ambush which had been prepared for them, but managed to survive until the arrival of the rest of the army. ' The Cornish foote in an hower or two beate the Enimy out of the Ambuscado, and then both foote and horse advanced up theire main body on the topp of Munckton-farley hill, where they durst not to stande them, and so they had the chase of them as farr as Bathe-Easton'[33] According to a parliamentarian account, however, common sense not cowardice in the face of much greater numbers caused Dowett 'to call off his men in the best order he could, which was so well performed

Rear view of Claverton manor, home of Sir William Bassett (1602 - 1656), with Claverton Parish Church on the right. This drawing by S.H. Grimm in 1790 shows in the background the hill on the other side of the valley, with the road along which the royalist army advanced to the right. Waller's army, camped on Claverton Down behind the Manor House, would have had a commanding view of this approach.

that he lost onely ten common souldiers, and two hammer-pieces, through the gunners negligence. Wee took of theirs thirteen prisoners, whereof one was a Captain, yet, for all the enemie boasted (as their manner is) of a great defeat'.[34]

As the royalists pursued the parliamentarians, they noticed for the first time Waller's guns glistening on the top of Claverton Down and his bridge across the river beneath. Prince Maurice immediately sent the main body of Cornish foot down to the river to take the bridge, which was achieved 'just as it was night'. The skeletons of four soldiers killed in this action were found in Claverton churchyard when a new grave was being dug in 1764. They were identified by the remains of their military clothing. Seeing that the royalists now commanded the river crossing, 'Sir William Waller in the darke retreated into Bathe'. He could not risk leaving either his army unprotected on Claverton or the city unguarded from within.

Hopton's cavalry had meanwhile chased Burghill's force through Bathford on the north side of the river 'into the fields under Lansdown close by Bathe'. There, at midnight, Carnarvon, Hopton and the other royalist commanders held a council of war to decide whether or not to take up immediately a position on the top of Lansdown. The advantages were obvious - an assault on the city itself could easily be made from such a commanding situation. On the other hand, the Cornish foot - 'being surprised by the night' - had still not rejoined them after the fighting by the bridge. They would be difficult to locate and would probably be in a state of disorder. It was therefore decided to quarter for the night at Batheaston and ' to drawe out the next morning verie early' to seize control of Lansdown.[35]

View of Waller's position across the Avon Valley, gained by Hopton's royalist army, as they advanced through Warleigh on their march from Bradford-on-Avon (3rd July, 1643).

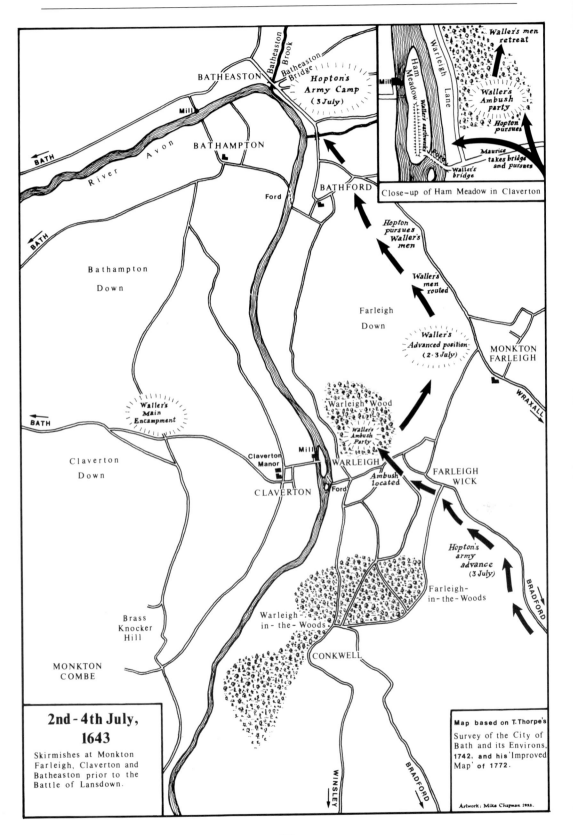

Close-up of Ham Meadow in Claverton

2nd - 4th July, 1643

Skirmishes at Monkton Farleigh, Claverton and Batheaston prior to the Battle of Lansdown.

Map based on T. Thorpe's Survey of the City of Bath and its Environs, 1742, and his 'Improved Map' of 1772.

Artwork: Mike Chapman 1992.

Just before daybreak, the royalist camp was astir. Men, horses, cannon and baggage moved hastily away 'with a little more heate than was altogether expedient' towards the foothills of Lansdown. With some difficulty the carriages and wagons were manoeuvred into a field on the lower slopes when, suddenly, the horrible truth dawned. Waller had beaten them to it! As the royalist commanders looked up to the high ridge above, they could see the parliamentarian army already assembled with their guns in position pointing ominously down the slope. Waller was beginning to show his real craft and generalship. Always renowned for his rapid night marches, his ascent of Lansdown in the early hours of the morning had snatched the initiative dramatically from the royalists' hands. What is more, Hertford had placed his army in an unenviable position. Their heavy guns and baggage carts were now almost inextricably wedged in the small fields at the bottom of Lansdown, 'out of which', as Hopton wrote, 'there were verie inconvenient wayes to retreate, to advance noe possibility, and to stay there least of all, for the Enimyes' cannon played in to them.[36]

For several hours the armies faced each other. Five parliamentarian guns blazed down upon the royalists as the commanders debated their next move. Eventually, 'about one in the afternoone' they decided to withdraw their forces to Marshfield, a village four miles north of their present position and six miles north-east of Bath. From there it would be possible either to approach Lansdown from the other end or to continue their journey to Oxford. Hopton was given the task of ordering the army's retreat.

It turned out to be a difficult and tricky operation. Two narrow lanes with high flanking hedges led to Marshfield, winding their way upwards to the ridge on which the village stood. The cannon and baggage train, sent first under escort, struggled furiously to get clear. Meanwhile Hopton had planted one thousand musketeers in the hedges at the

A view of the lower slopes of Lansdown, which Hopton's royalist army attempted to climb (4th July, 1643).

entrance to these lanes to cover the rest of army as they retreated. He personally remained behind with a strong cavalry rearguard 'with which at last he marched off without any loss, and drew a strong party of the Enimye's horse within the ambuscade of musketeers, which having tasted they quickly retired. And so the Army came that night safe to Marshfield'.[37]

The parliamentarian account of this operation, however, claimed that Hopton's rear guard, when pressed, retreated speedily 'without striking one stroke, and left behind them three hundred waight of bullet, which wee highly prized as a rich mite out of their penurie. Our partie chased them to Marshfield, and that night gave them a sound alarm, but not one of them stirred, although they had bragged to be in Bathe that night; for they wisely considered that after so hot a chase the water in Bathe would have been too hot for them, which might have produced a fatall malignant fever upon them'.[38] But difference in detail, with colourful exaggerations for the sake of propaganda on both sides, cannot disguise the real truth of a skilful withdrawal in which Hopton clearly demonstrated his supreme ability as a field commander.

Early on the morning of Wednesday, 5th July Sir William Waller, anticipating the royalists' next move, took his parliamentarian forces along the flat top of Lansdown and established a new position on the far northern ridge, overlooking the road from Marshfield. 'There upon the verie point of the hill over the high way, suddenly raysed breast works with faggotts and earth.'[39] From here Waller sent out parties of horse to reconnoitre the enemy's position. These successfully 'beate in' the royalist horse guards who sounded the alarm. Shortly afterwards, at about 8 o'clock, the whole army left its Marshfield encampment and marched in the direction of Lansdown. As they drew nearer, they saw to their dismay the enormous strength of the parliamentarian position.

The Monument to Sir Bevil Grenvile (1596 - 1643) on the site of the Battle of Lansdown. This drawing by S.H. Grimm in 1789 illustrates the view from Waller's earthworks, uncluttered by present-day trees, of the royalist advance from Tog Hill (rear) and Freezing Hill (left).

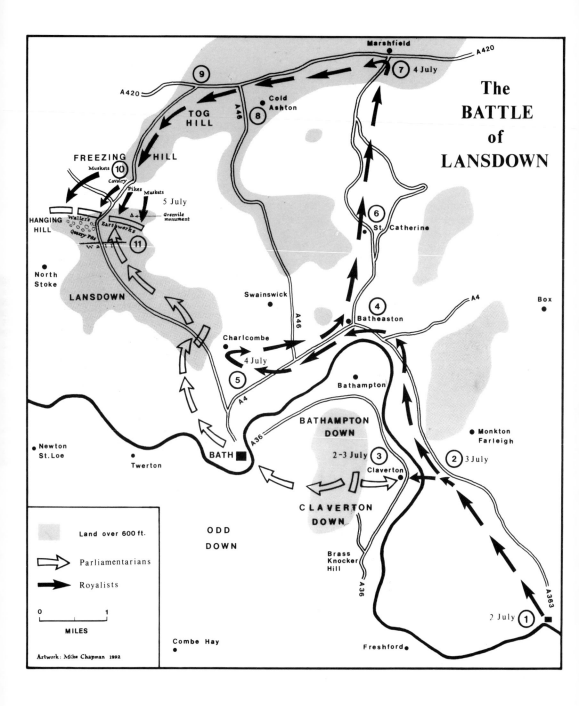

Colonel Slingsby, a royalist commander who praised Waller as 'the best shifter and choser of ground', described their initial impression: '...we could see the Rebells army drawne up upon the top of the hill, he upon a piece of ground almost inaccessible. In the brow of the hill, he had raised brestworke in wch his cannon and greate store of small shott was placed; on either fflanke hee was strengthned with a thicke wood wch stood upon the declining of the hill, in wch hee had putt store of muskeiteires; on his reare hee had a faire plaine where stood rang'd his reserves of horse and ffootte...thus fortyfied stood the foxe gazing at us...'[40]

The royalists had halted in a large corn field on Tog Hill, 'called by the inhabitants thereabout Toug-hill, and very fitly too, at this time, for there we had a fierce and furious touging with our enemies for mastery before wee parted'.[41] As the two armies faced each other on their respective hills, they were separated by a steep valley and over a mile's distance. For something like three or four hours little happened apart from light skirmishing by dragoons in the hedges and small parties of horse on the flanks. Eventually the royalist commanders decided that Waller was unlikely to be drawn down from his favourable position and that this sort of haphazard skirmishing was merely wasting their ammunition, of which there was already a shortage. The order was therefore given to withdraw in an orderly fashion back to Marshfield.

Prince Maurice (1620 - 1652), brother of Prince Rupert and commander of the royalist cavalry in the Marquis of Hertford's army.

The royalist infantry are rallied during the skirmishes in the corn field on Tog Hill (5th July, 1643).

They had scarcely retreated a mile when they looked round to see a large body of Waller's cavalry and dragoons charging at them down the hill. Major Dowett led the first line of 200 horse, closely followed behind by Colonel Carre with a further 200.[42] Waller was clearly anxious to impede any possible advance they might be considering to Oxford. A union of the King's forces there would constitute a major threat on London.

The royalist forces turned about yet again, hurrying to regain their former position in the cornfield 'wch wee gott with much diffultye and hazard, our horse receiving some dangerous foiles; so that had not our ffoote bin excellent wee had certainly suffer'd there'. After initial success in charging the flanks of the rather disordered royalist lines, Waller's cavalry was eventually driven out of the cornfield by a series of well-aimed volleys of musket fire. Their dragoons, too, were finally dislodged from 'the walls and hedges upon the farre end of the field' by a determined advance of the Cornish foot. The roundhead horse now found itself trapped in the confines of the lane which led to Lansdown and 'were observ'd to be in some disorder by reason of the narrow and ill passage'.[43]

Quickly seizing his opportunity, Prince Maurice sent his own cavalry to 'wing' them by firing in through the hedges on both sides of the lane. The situation, however, was partly retrieved when Waller sent down a second wave of reinforcements under Colonel Burghill.[44] Richard Atkyns (Captain of a royalist cavalry troop) admitted that 'this was the boldest thing that I ever saw the enemy do; for a party of less than 1,000 to charge any army of 6,000 horse, foot and cannon, in their own ground, at least a mile and a half from their body'. They fought bravely for two or three hours, before tiredness eventually began to affect the foot soldiers. Although Waller tried hard to relieve them by sending down some of his reserve infantry, they 'being but fresh souldiers, did not make good their ground.'[45] The rawness and inadequacy of his foot was already beginning to hamper the effectiveness of Waller's schemes on the battlefield. Finally, after two or

From Freezing Hill, the royalist army commences its assault on Waller's earthworks situated high on the Lansdown ridge. Sir Bevil Grenvile's Cornish infantry lead the surge.

three hours of stiff fighting, a combined push by the Cornish foot and Carnarvon's horse drove the parliamentarians down Tog Hill 'where in the bottom they were cruelly gall'd by our ffoote'.[46]

Casualties, indeed, had been heavy on both sides. The royalists' cavalry had been badly mauled and had lost 'Major Lower, Major James and many others'. The parliamentarians, too, had suffered. Colonel Burghill, for instance, 'had received a shot through his right arme, just as his sword was even at the throat of the Lord of Carnarvon, who at this terrible conflict was also shot in the legge'. Desertions also had taken their toll 'of at least 500 of our common souldiers who causelessley ran away.'[47] On the other hand, they had managed to re-capture their two small field guns which had been taken during the fighting at Monkton Farleigh on Monday.

Nevertheless, in spite of their casualties and the tiredness brought about by such a gruelling encounter, the royalists suddenly found a new determination. According to Richard Atkyns, this false sense of security had been created quite deliberately by the parliamentarians in an attempt to draw the royalists up onto the steep slopes of Lansdown. Waller's withdrawal from Tog Hill had been made to look like a disorderly flight. ' The enemy to encourage us to persecute this success, gave all the symptoms of a flying army; as blowing up of powder, horse and foot running distractedly upon the edge of the hill, for we could see no further: these signs made Sir Robert Welsh importunately desire the Prince to have a party to follow the chase.' The ploy had worked. Even the rugged Cornish infantry were now thoroughly roused. Their successful thrust to the bottom of Tog Hill had boosted their confidence to such an extent that they believed 'noe men their equals and were so apt to undertake anything' - even the seemingly impossible ascent of Lansdown's steep northern face. 'Lett us fetch those cannon', they cried out[48] It was a murderous decision. The situation was ready-made for fools and heroes. Death could be the only victor in the inevitable blood bath that followed.

Sir Bevil Grenvile is mortally wounded as he leads the attack on Waller's earthworks in the Battle of Lansdown.

The whole royalist army advanced to the foot of Lansdown. Strong parties of musketeers were sent into the woods on each flank to clear out the enemy dragoons and to work their way up gradually to the top of the hill. Even the parliamentarians praised the skill of these 'Cornish excellent firemen at their hedge fight in a little wood there adjacent'.[49] Meanwhile, Sir Bevil Grenvile led forward his regiment of Cornish foot with pikes astride the road in the centre, muskets on the left behind a wall and cavalry on the open ground to the right. Bravely they pushed forward but 'had much to doe, by reason of the disadvantage of the grounde, the enimye's foote and batteryes being under couvert of theire breastworkes, and theire horse ready to charge upon the verie browe of the hill'.[50]

The royalist forces took a heavy pounding from the cannon and muskets in the parliamentarian earthworks. Five times they were charged by the enemy cavalry and driven back from the brow of the hill with considerable losses. Indeed, so effective was Waller's counter-attack that the royalist cavalry was 'soe discomforted' that 1,400 out of a total of 2,000 fled at speed to Oxford leaving 'their foot naked'. Grenvile himself was mortally wounded at the head of the pikes and Sir Nicholas Slannings' horse was 'kild under him with a greate shott'.

Nevertheless, in spite of these setbacks, the Cornish foot refused to be beaten, but slowly inched their way forward and finally 'gain'd with much gallantry the brow of the hill'. When Richard Atkyns, with much difficulty, reached the top of those steep slopes, he saw; 'Sir Bevil Grenvile's stand of pikes, which certainly preserved our army from a total rout, with the loss of his most precious life: they stood as upon the eaves of an house for steepness, but as unmoveable as a rock'. At this point the royalist musketeers on the left fired so fast and effectively that the roundhead cavalry was forced to retreat and 'the rebells ffoote tooke example by theire horse and quitt their brestworks retyring behind a long stone wall that runs acrosse the down',[51] The earthworks were quickly seized by the royalists who then proceeded to draw up their infantry, cannon and remaining horse into a new line on the top of the hill. They took cover not only in Waller's earthworks but also in the small old quarry pits which are still visible today and which gave their musketeers a more forward position.

Sir Arthur Haselrig's standard

Parliamentarian accounts of the struggle for the ridge admitted that the enemy had partly taken it by force, but also claimed that they had largely surrendered it by choice - 'and upon good advice considering our horse exceeded theirs in number, as much as their foot did ours, wee might have sufficient roome to fight with our horse'.[52] The flat open top of Lansdown was much more suited to the cavalry charge than the steep wooded slopes beyond. Once the bulk of the royalist horse had fled, Waller was quite content to draw their weary, bloodstained foot onto the top of the hill. But royalist and roundhead agreed that there had been a 'a very bloudy and terrible fight'.

Acts of bravery abounded on both sides. Sir Arthur Haselrig 'received a wound in the thigh with push of a pike, and after that another in his arme', but he and his 'London-Lads' fought 'like so many invincible Romans .. as long as light would suffer them to distinguish friends from foes ... and wee must doe our enemies right, who fought it out very stoutly too; and indeed the charges were so incessantly hot on both sides, as the like (I believe) was never seene in England, no not at Keynton-battaile, yea some old souldiers did say'.[53]

The wall, behind which Waller's army retreated after the fierce battle for the control of the ridge (5th July, 1643). The monument to Sir Bevil Grenvile, near to the position of Waller's original earthworks, can be seen in the distance.

Richard Atkyns, too, found the battle both hot and furious: '...the air was so darkened by the smoke of the powder, that for a quarter of an hour together (I dare say) there was no light seen, but what the fire of the volleys of shot gave; and 'twas the greatest storm that ever I saw, in which though I knew not whither to go, nor what to do, my horse had two or three musket bullets in him presently, which made him tremble under me at that rate, and I could hardly with spurs keep him from lying down: but he did me the service to carry me off to a led horse, and then died: by that time I came up to the hill again, the heat of the battle was over, and the sun set, but still pelting at one another half musket shot off.'[54]

Waller had now withdrawn to a new position, about a hundred yards from his old earthworks, behind a long stone wall which ran across the down. There he reformed his whole army, lining the wall with musketeers. In several places he broke down the stones to create large openings for his cavalry, if they needed to charge. These breaches meanwhile, were carefully guarded by his cannon and the bodies of pikes. 'Thus stood the two armys taking breath looking upon each other, our cannon on both sides playing without ceasing till it was darke, legs and arms flying apace.'[55] As dusk fell, the repeated explosions could be seen and heard from as far away as Bristol.[56]

The battle had been raging since early morning. Guns on both sides were still blazing away when darkness finally parted the two armies and, according to the parliamentarian John Vicars, 'hindred our totall compleating of the victory'. After nightfall there was an ominous silence for several hours. Then, in the early morning, the royalists heard a great volley of musket fire. This startled their edgy nerves. The general feeling spread through the camp that the enemy intended to launch a night attack to recover their earthworks. Momentarily there was an element of panic 'for wee were then seated like a heavy stone upon the very brow of the hill, wich with one lustye charge might well have bin rowl'd to the bottom'.[57]

Again there was silence. In the darkness it was extremely difficult to pick out anything in the roundhead camp apart from the glow of matches slung over the wall by musketeers and groups of pikes silhouetted against the sky. For an hour the royalist commanders discussed the situation, some of them feeling that the enemy had withdrawn. Finally, a soldier was given a reward for creeping forward to the wall to investigate. He found indeed that the parliamentarians had gone, leaving behind some burning matches and upright pikes to confuse the royalists and to cover their retreat.

Waller had decided on a tactical withdrawal to Bath so that his men and horses could be refreshed - 'our horse being in continual service for three dayes together, and without meat or water for the space of at least twenty-four houres, and our foot much tyred'. He therefore wisely used the resources available to him in the city (as he had also done on the Monday night), again demonstrating his skill as a 'night owl' and a clever 'shifter of ground'. He also hoped to bolster up the numbers of his foot by some overnight recruiting. But of course he had no intention of staying in Bath. He realised full well that the royalists, with heavy casualties sustained by the infantry and large desertions suffered by the cavalry, were in no position to besiege Bath:...

> wee very well knowing wee could easily recover the hill again, and so fall upon the enemy to prosecute the victory the next morning. Our retreat was so orderly and fairly performed, that the enemy durst not follow us, as having now learned by experience that our giveing ground hath been much to their disadvantage.[58]

Waller was right in this judgment of the situation. The royalists had lost the heart to fight. Indeed, their commanders had given order to the men during the night that if the enemy fell upon them, every man was 'to shift for himself' - and had already moved their cannon off to clear the way for the rush.[59] Slingsby and his companions therefore breathed a heavy sigh of relief when their messenger reported Waller's withdrawal - 'wee were glad they were gone, for if they had not, I know who had within an hour'. His dry humour nevertheless underlines their exhaustion and loss of morale. The death of Grenvile and the cowardice of the cavalry played heavily on their minds - 'but indeed had our horse bin as good as the Enemys, the rebells have never gone of the field unruin'd'.[60] Henceforth the Cornish infantry, who had made such great personal sacrifices, showed their contempt by calling the cavalry the 'run-away horse'.[61]

Sir William Waller's standard

Early next morning, the royalists admitted their defeated condition by withdrawing to Marshfield. This finally underlined the extent of their folly in attacking the ridge on the previous day. Grenvile had gained a hero's reputation, but had lost his own life; the infantry had gained the ridge, but had lost their morale - and most of their cavalry, too; the royalists had gained ground, but in doing so had ensured that the battle itself could never be won. Already short of ammunition at the start of the fighting, they had wasted so much during the day that any thought of attacking Bath was futile.

Before leaving Lansdown in the early dawn, royalist soldiers were sent out to plunder the battlefield. To their joy they found '3 or 400 of the enimy's armes, and 9 or 10 barrells of theire power'[62] - a most welcome windfall. Their joy was shortlived. Fate intervened in a curious and ironical manner. About 8 o-clock in the morning, the horse and foot were ordered to withdraw down the steep sides of Lansdown and rendezvous on the gentle upper slopes of Tog Hill. Richard Atkyns, a cavalry captain, went with Major Sheldon to speak to Sir Ralph Hopton:...

> who was then viewing the prisoners taken, some of which were carried upon a cart wherein was our ammunition; and (as I heard) had match to light their tobacco;...I had no sooner turned my horse, and was gone 3 horses lengths from him, but the ammunition was blown up, and the prisoners in the cart with it; together with the Lord Hopton, Major Sheldon, and Cornet Washnage, who was near the cart on horseback, and several others: it made a very noise, and darkened the air for a time, and the hurt men made lamentable screeches. As soon as the air was clear, I went to see what the matter was; there I found his Lordship miserably burnt, his horse singed like parched leather, and Thomas Sheldon complaining that the fire was got within his breeches, which I tore off as soon as I could, and from as long a flaxen head of hair as ever I saw, in the twinkling of an eye, his head was like a blackamoor...[63]

This unfortunate incident further weakened the royalists' crumbling morale. The sight of Hopton's injuries was enought to turn over the stomachs of even the tough Cornish infantry - 'Sir Ralph Hopton made a miserable spectable, his head swolne as bigg as two heads and his eyes neare burnt out'.[64] Hopton was without doubt the commander they most admired, as Slingsby noted- '...this disaster encourg'ed the rebells and discourag'd us. Our horse were bad before but now worse, our ffoote drooped for theire Lord whom they lov'd, and that they had not powder left to defend him, for as I remember we had then but nine barrels left.'

The Old Rectory in Cold Ashton, where Sir Bevil Grenvile lodged the night before the battle of Lansdown and where he died after being carried off the battlefield mortally wounded.

The parliamentarians, meanwhile, according to their original plans, had prepared themselves for another early march to the top of Lansdown. Just as they were ready to leave, information was brought of the royalist retreat 'and so frustrated our expectation of fighting with them, as wee intended'.[65] Nevertheless, refreshed by their overnight stay, strengthened by recruits and encouraged by the news from the royalist camp, Waller's army had taken possession of Lansdown by late afternoon. From there they made harrying attacks on the enemy first at Marshfield and then, as it retreated, along the road to Devizes. Apparently, five hundred or so royalists deserted, 'many of them being taken by the country people and brought to Sir William'. Waller immediately adopted the normal practice of making them promise on oath not to take up arms against parliament again - and then let them 'return to their dwellings'.[66] It was much too costly and inconvenient to keep large numbers of prisoners.

A parliamentarian prisoner, similarly released by the royalists after four or five days' captivity, reported back to the Mayor of Bristol 'that he left them in a sad condition, confessing themselves to have the rout'. In all the royalists suffered the loss of three senior officers and ten captains, 'of ordinarie men, we know not the number; seven cart loads of dead men were carried from the place, divers wounded, twenty in a house and not one like to live, and more in other places; they wanted chirugeons much.'[67] Sir Bevil Grenvile had been carried off the battlefield badly wounded and taken to the Old Rectory in Cold Ashton, where he died in the place which had been his billet the night before the battle. Another report estimated royalist casualties at 200 dead and 300 wounded. The parliamentarians, on the other hand, claimed much lighter losses for themselves - a Major, a Lieutenant, 2 Cornets and 'for common souldiers we finde but 12 dead upon the place; the enemy having buried and carryed away their own, we may be confident would not be so kind to conceal any of ours. We have about 60 wounded; whereof 4 already are dead'.[68] Amid all this suffering, John Ashe, who had given so freely to the parliamentarian cause, received an unexpected bonus, having 'his ground well stocked with 60 cavalier horses, who fled from the Army the night after the Battell'.

Parliament had no hesitation in claiming a complete victory. The Commons, on hearing the news, voted £5,000 'to be sent down to Sir Wm. Waller to be given as a largisse to his souldiers for the good service they have done'.[69] The roundhead newsheet, *Speciall Passages,* boasted of 'the late successe of the truly valiant and magnanimous commander Sir William Waller in the western parts, and of the victory obtained by him against Marquesse Hartford, Prince Maurice, Sir Ralph Hopton and others, on Wednesday July 5 near Marshfield'.[70]

The royalist paper, *Mercurius Aulicus,* bitterly described how Waller succeeded in recruiting large numbers of local people after the battle by sending his officers round 'to the parts adjoining to informe the people that he had given a notable defeate to the Princes Army, and broken the whole body of his Force; and therefore if they would now cheerfully come in and show their zeal to Religion, Lawes, and Libertie by joining with him in pursuit of so great a victory, they might soon make an end of the cavaliers and conclude the warre'.[71] That the people accepted this summons is another clear indication that the area naturally felt included towards the parliamentarian cause.

Alexander Popham's Bath Regiment had fought alongside Sir William Waller at the Battle of Lansdown with the general populace lending active support. Wagons had again been filled with supplies (in a manner reminiscent of the Mendip rising a year earlier) and despatched to Lansdown by the country people living in such villages as Compton Dando, Whitchurch, Chelworth, Charleton ('3 hundred weight of cheese'), Farmborough and Thrubwell;[72] royalist soldiers fleeing during the night after the battle were, according to Waller, 'taken up by the Country people and brought in to us';[73] at the same time, according to Hopton, Waller ' recrewted himself from... the present generall inclinations of the Country, with fresh men and ammunition, and all other things necessary' to enable him to pursue his enemy with vigour to Devizes; and throughout the campaign,

Sir Bevil Grenvile (1596 - 1643), who commanded the Cornish infantry in the Marquis of Hertford's royalist army.

according to Clarendon, Waller was able to rely on support from 'the most absolute disaffected parts' in the region, namely the area around Bath.[74]

Royalist historians, in concentrating on the courageous exploits of the Cornish foot, have had their judgment blurred by the clouds of admiration so raised. A curious assumption has inevitably followed - that because Grenvile's men succeeded in storming the ridge, then the battle had been won. The reverse, indeed, was true. It was because the Cornish foot had insisted on reaching the ridge that the battle was lost - the cavalry had deserted, the infantry was mauled and exhausted, the ammunition was spent. Little account has previously been taken of the nervous condition of the royalist forces on the ridge as - by their own admission - they prepared to flee into the night; little stress has been placed on the speed with which they left Lansdown on the following morning.

The capture of the ridge was one of the most purposeless acts in the war. It raises a serious question mark against the competence of the royalist High Command (Hopton apart). Certainly they allowed Grevile's 'rush of blood' at the bottom of Tog Hill to dictate their tactics. Waller, on the other hand, was always in control both of his own army and of the general situation. Once he had seized Lansdown early on the Tuesday morning, he retained the initiative throughout. By choosing his fighting positions carefully, by rapid movements under the cover of darkness, by making the most of his resources in Bath, Waller outwitted the enemy. In the space of four days he had transformed the situation. His seemingly unbalanced and depressed forces, who had recently been sent scurrying across Mendip, had now themselves halted and turned the same royalist troops, who had confidently driven all before them through Devon and Somerset.

On Thursday morning, 6th July, the narrow streets of Bath were crowded with soldiers, many wounded, most showing the scars of battle. The smell of war hung heavy over the city. Inns were packed with roundhead officers. Excited local citizens crowded around clusters of troops to hear the gory details of the previous day's fighting. Generosity was doubtless given a new lease of life. Exhausted horses were watered and refreshed at the conduits around the city. Messengers clattered through the north gate bringing news of the latest movements of the royalist camp.

Sir William Waller worked his way amongst this bustling throng in search of royalist prisoners. He found a cavalry lieutenant, Thomas Sandys, who had been shot twice by a Scotsman after he had been taken prisoner. Waller 'seemed exceeding angry at the inhumane action that befel him and sent for his own chirugeon immediately and saw him dressed before he went away; he gave the innkeeper charge that he should have whatever he called for, and would see him paid; that whatsoever women he sent for to attend him, should be admitted, and lent him ten broad pieces for his own private expenses'.[75] Waller was so concerned for him that he visited him again on his way to Bristol, after the battle Roundaway Down. Such were the courtesies of war. Humanity and brutality were close bedfellows.

The parliamentarians did not tarry in Bath. Shortly after that incident, Waller led out the whole of his force - including Popham's Bath Regiment - in pursuit of the enemy. They had by this time received welcome reinforcements of men and equipment from Bristol. In particular, Nathaniel Fiennes had sent sixty barrels of gunpowder to replenish Waller's stocks, 'he having but six barrels of powder left him after the fight at Lansdowne'.[76] Eventually, after severely harassing the royalists' retreat from Marshfield, they finally caught up with them at Devizes. The town was confidently invested and it seemed only a matter of time before the roundheads completed the inevitable destruction of Hertford's weary army. But suddenly the initiative was lost. Within the space of three days the fortunes of war had been dramatically reversed.

During the night of 10th July, Prince Maurice broke out of Devizes with his cavalry and made for Oxford, leaving Hopton behind with the infantry. On Wednesday the 13th, he returned with nearly 2,000 fresh horse reinforcements. Waller, who through lack of infantry had failed to take Devizes by storm, now led his army out onto Roundaway Down to face this newly-arrived royalist cavalry. The battle was an utter disaster. First Haselrig's Lobsters, then Waller's own regiment of horse was routed and fled the battlefield in total disorder.

Waller and Popham tried desperately to rally the foot, who fought on bravely for a while. Then, seeing the approach of the royalist infantry from Devizes, the parliamentarians attempted a disciplined retreat, but were so harried by Byron's horse that panic quickly set in. Waller and Popham took to their mounts and raced back to Bath; their men threw down their arms and made for the cover of the woods. Many of them were killed or captured in the turmoil that followed. Those who escaped crept back to the security of their homes utterly sick of war. Popham's Bath Regiment had been destroyed at Roundaway Down. Many of its members, of course, would fight again for the cause, but the day of local volunteer regiments was over. Waller's experiences in the west had merely underlined the need for a more professional army - an idea which was to reach its fulfilment in the establishment of the New Model in 1645.

Waller and Popham had meanwhile arrived back in Bath, where they gathered together what survivors they could before marching on to Bristol. Bath was left unprotected. Their stay in Bristol, too, was short. After leaving a garrison force under Nathaniel Fiennes, the governor, the two dejected leaders took their sickly troops northwards to Gloucester and Warwick. From there Waller was summoned to London to recruit a new army in the area around London with Alexander Popham as colonel of one of his foot regiments. Later Waller's new army was amalgamated into the New Model, though Waller himself played little further part in it. Popham, however, continued to take a considerable interest in the fortunes of North-East Somerset and, although for the time being his regiment was no longer composed of local people, his military service on their behalf was just an energetic as ever.

5
The Community Under Royalist Control, 1643-45

(i) Sullen cooperation, 1643-45

Shortly after the battle of Roundaway Down, the royalist troops took possession of Bath where they welcomed the opportunity to refresh themselves. A few days later they were joined by Prince Rupert and a strong body of reinforcements from Oxford. By 22nd July, the combined army had laid siege to Bristol which fell after only four days' resistance. The capture of this wealthy port placed the west firmly in the King's hands and seemed to brighten the prospects of a general royalist victory.

In the north, too, the Earl of Newcastle had been making great progress in his march southwards with the capture of Gainsborough, Nottingham and Lincoln. The idea of a triple attack on London by the northern, western and Oxford armies became a distinct possibility. But Charles had reckoned without the strong parochialism of his locally-recruited forces. Just as Newcastle's men were reluctant to leave the north while Hull held out for parliament, so Hopton's Cornishman refused to march further eastwards until the garrisons of Plymouth, Lyme and Gloucester had been reduced. To make matters worse, the Earl of Essex successfully relieved Gloucester with a large army from London and then held the King's forces at Newbury as they made a dash for the capital

King Charles I with Sir Edward Walker, secretary of his council of war. Portrait by an unknown artist.

(20th September). By the end of 1643, the royalists had lost their best chance of success. Parliament had made an alliance with the Scots, which turned out to be a decisive factor in the defeat of Rupert a few months later at Marston Moor (July 1644). From that moment the final result of the war was never seriously in doubt.

Meanwhile, the capture of the area around Bath by royalist forces in July 1643, following Waller's decisive defeat at the Battle of Roundaway Down, had not only destroyed Popham's Bath Regiment as an effective fighting force, but had also presented the inhabitants of North-East Somerset with a severe new challenge - royalist occupation. For the next two years local people submitted to their new rulers with a sullen sense of inevitability. There was no underground resistance movement, no sabotage and no acts of heroic defiance. They concentrated instead on maintaining the flow of daily life, farming their fields, weaving their cloths and keeping open their markets. The Bath Corporation continued to meet, as it did throughout the war, royalist and parliamentarian sympathisers sitting together side by side to ensure that the local economy survived and that essential business was not neglected. Given this attitude, it is easy to accuse them of neutralism during this period. In one sense, of course, they were acting in a neutralist manner but, as Professor Underdown has pointed out, 'neutralism ... was not always absolute'.[1] The Civil War, it must be remembered, was not a total war. Local people had every right, therefore, to regard the preservation of life as their first priority. But this did not mean that they approved of their new masters. There were, after all, other ways of expressing their feelings and maintaining their loyalty.

Cooperation was kept at a minimum. This applied, in the first instance, to a system of taxation designed in November 1644 to support local royalist garrisons by raising £2000 per week from the whole region around Bristol, including £850 a week from the eastern division of Somerset. After the first six months of operation, in spite of the use of troops in 'levying and collecting' the contributions, Edmund Turner (Treasurer of the Garrison) was forced to admit that he was averaging only £90 per week in total - largely because 'the contributions coming from Somersetshire are so small'.[2] The residents of Bath had been dragging their heels on payments even before the new system had been invented, because in March 1644 the Council had been forced to appoint six officials 'to rate the inhabitants of the Cittie for raseing of £150 for arreres to the Kinge'.[3] It is true that the Mayor and Corporation felt obliged to obey instructions from the royalist governor of the city to provide a court of guard and to improve the fortifications at their own expense - a fact witnessed to by numerous items in the Bath Chamberlain's Accounts between 1643 and 1645 (see Chapter Six). They also agreed, under compulsion in February 1644, to provide 'tenn barrells of powder at their owne cost and chardges for His. Ma.ties service' (bought shortly afterwards for £50) and to provide storage for the powder required by neighbouring Hundreds. Their true feelings, however, were expressed at a later time, after the recapture of the city by the New Model Army, when someone vented the anger and shame of the Councillors by vigorously striking out the offending item from the Minute Book (see below).[4]

The citizens of Bath had further ways of making their unwelcome guests feel uncomfortable without ever stepping out of line. In 1643 and 1644, for instance, they suddenly began the tradition of celebrating Gunpowder Treason Day (5th November) and Crown Nation Day (the anniversary of Queen Elizabeth's accession) with bonfires and the ringing of church bells. These anti-Catholic occasions gave local puritans the opportunity to reaffirm their Protestant faith, linked with a desire to return to the Elizabethan system of government. They provided, within the context of the situation in North-East Somerset, a means of symbolising visually their hatred of Laudian doctrine and their commitment to the Mendip spirit. There had also been a longstanding custom to offer lavish gifts to eminent people who visited the city. In 1637, for instance, the Lord Bishop had been presented with 'one fatt sheepe', a salmon and some wine, while the Lord Chief Justice, the Deputy Lieutenants, Sir Francis Popham and the Recorder all qualified for rewards of different kinds. This pattern was repeated year after year - until

Extract from the Bath Council Minute Book, 18th March 1644. The entry was later crossed out. It reads:

It is agreed that the Chamber will provide
Tenn Barralls of Powder at their owne
costs and charges for his Maties Service.
And further that if the Severall hundres of
this Division doe desire to by in their
p[ro]portion of powder into a Magasein that this
Corporation will provide a place for it but
not to insure it if it should be taken from them
or come to any other mischance.

the time of royalist occupation when the practice almost completely died out. It is true that the King and Queen were both presented with silver plate on their visit in 1644, but there was not the slightest recognition for the Prince of Wales, Lord Goring, Prince Rupert, Sir Ralph Hopton or a host of other royalist dignitaries who passed through the city during this period. Indeed, there were no presentations at all in 1645 - until the arrival of the New Model Army when Sir Thomas Fairfax was presented with four separate gifts of 'wynn and sugar', Major Skipton received one and 'Mr Pryne' gained 'two quarts of sacke'.[5] Similar favours were later bestowed on Oliver Cromwell.

But it was not just visitors who were made to feel uncomfortable. Sir Thomas Bridges of Keynsham, who had been appointed Governor in 1644, became increasingly unpopular with local residents as demands for money and quarter increased. We shall consider in Chapter Six how the quality of life for local people suffered during this period, how fabric was neglected and streets were left uncleaned. The residents of Bath bitterly resented the highhanded methods of the new governor, the expense of maintaining his house, the cost of his linen allowance (£10 a year) and the 'one hundred pounds which Sir Thomas Bridges extorted from the Corporation during the tyme of his being Governor here'.[6] They not only sued him in 1646 for the recovery of that sum, but, according to parliamentarian accounts, did everything in their power to undermine the resistance of the garrison in July 1645 when a detachment of the New Model Army under Colonels Rich and Okey arrived at the gates (see below).

Throughout the years of occupation, the Mendip spirit was kept alive, awaiting its opportunity. Although several of the original local leaders were in temporary exile with the parliamentarian army elsewhere, by the summer of 1644 parliament had decided 'That Colonel Popham shall have leave to go into Somersetshire to raise forces there for the defence of that county.'[7]

In the meantime events had rather speeded up his departure for the west. Heartened no doubt by the news from the north, parliament had already established a new 'Committee in the West' on 2nd July to raise money in Wiltshire, Dorset, Somerset, Devon and Cornwall. This included many familiar faces from the Bath area - Alexander Popham, John Ashe, James Ashe, John Harington - and one new one, Matthew Clift, a member of the city council.[8] The task of this committee was clearly to lay the financial basis for the recruitment of a new local army. *Mercurius Civicus,* issued in mid-July, certainly gave the strong impression that the people around Bath anxiously awaited their opportunity to drive out the royalists - 'so that upon the comming downe of the westerne committees with horses and armes, the countrey will not be long under their tyranny, if they make use of the opportunitie of rising with them, which is apparent they are willing to doe'.[9]

This, however, was not entirely the view of the Earl of Essex when he passed through the area on his abortive campaign to the west. Writing to the Committee of Both Kingdoms on 10th July, he shrewdly summed up the local situation. Although Somerset and Devon showed great affection to the parliament and desired to be rid of the 'Egyptian slavery', there were two things which greatly hindered the aid he should have received from that area. The first, he said, was 'their desire to serve under their own countrymen and not be listed in my army'. Consequently, although many potential soldiers were available, these were useless until arms 'and the gentlemen who have the power over them be come down'. The second factor was the power exerted by royalist garrisons over the surrounding districts, making difficult the raising of money.[10]

This plea from Essex for men of local standing to be sent down to lead the rising in Somerset clearly hastened the return of Alexander Popham. It emphasised, too, that in spite of the continuing loyalty of the area to the roundhead cause, it clung hard to the tradition of local regiments, showing great suspicion of outside influences. How successful Popham was in his task is not evident, although a letter of 15th July suggested that the regiments of Popham and Weare numbered no more than 200 hundred in all.[11]

While Popham was busy attempting to stir up the inhabitants, attempts were being made by established forces to loosen the King's grip on Bath and Bristol. Colonel Edward Massey, Governor of Gloucester, marched his forces in an attempt to seize those cities while their garrisons were absent on operations in Wiltshire. The royalists returned in the nick of time. Nevertheless, on 4th September Massey 'drew out of our horse about 100 and myself marched with them to face Bath, where we gave an alarm'. He fully intended to return on the following day with the whole of his force, but was recalled to Gloucester.[12]

Waller, too, made several sallies into the west in order to redeem his previous loss of Bath and Bristol. From Newbury he wrote to the Committee of Both Kingdoms in London on 30th October, 1644 putting forward the case for an attack on Bath, which then housed both the King and Prince Rupert. 'If you command your forces to go up towards Bath, either the King will give us battle or retire to Bristol. If a battle, we have cause to desire it; if to Bristol we have as fruitful parts as are in England to quarter in, and then our victory will be prosecuted to the parliament's honour and profit.' The King he thought, was unlikely to move eastwards because 'it is not for men with horses here in winter to go far from their garrisons, for there are so many rivers in every county, and so much enclosure, and the lanes so deep (in mud), that cut up but one bridge and in places of advantage 500 foot might beat 5,000 horse'. In spite of the approaching winter, his awareness of 'the desolation and utter ruin which falls upon all sorts of people where armies come' urged him on to free the towns of north-east Somerset from the grip of the enemy. His request was nevertheless refused.[13]

He therefore had to wait until the Spring of 1645 before he was again allowed to enter the west country. By then, of course, the New Model Army was being recruited under Sir Thomas Fairfax. As a member of parliament, Waller had been excluded by the Self

Denying Ordinance from any active role in the new army. Nevertheless, on 15th January, 1645 he was asked, as a temporary measure, to lead a force of horse and dragoons into the west to hold the royalists in check until the New Model became ready for service in April.

By the beginning of March he had been joined by Oliver Cromwell and his Ironsides. After a resounding victory over royalist cavalry near Devizes, Waller sent Cromwell to relieve Taunton while he himself made a thrust at Bath and Bristol. According a *A Perfect Diurnall*, 'Sir William Waller went toward Bristoll with about 2,500 horse and dragoons; he faced Bristoll (tis said) with one part of them and Bath with another, but effected not his designe and returned backe without any losse, and was at Marlborough in Wiltshire on Munday night last'[14]. According to *Perfect Occurences,* Waller actually summoned the Bath garrison to surrender and, when the enemy refused, 'he strook petars into the gates to blow them open'.[15]

Later, in a letter to London, he again stressed the willingness of local people to rise in support of parliament, but blamed his failure on the lack of infantry at his disposal - 'yet I cannot but lament my want of Foote, and dare speake it with confidence, that if I had but those 3000 that were assigned unto mee, you might bee masters of the west, and of the places of the greatest importance in it, the people being universally disposed to receive us, but unwilling to engage till they see me with such a body as may give them assurance

I meane to stay with them, and not to bee gone tomorrow'.[16] The 'Mendip Men' were anxiously awaiting, therefore, for two things - the appearance of a strong army which they could support and the re-appearance of their own leaders whom they alone would follow. Their prayers were quickly answered.

(ii) The Recapture of Bath, 1645.

By the end of April 1645, Waller had surrendered his commission and witnessed the dispersal of his temporary army. But after its decisive victory at Naseby on 14th June, the powerful New Model Army was free to take over his work in the west. Moving with remarkable speed, it reached Somerset at the beginning of July. Its disciplined and well-

Sir Thomas Fairfax (1612 - 1671), commander of the New Model Army. An engraving by Engleheart after a drawing by Edward Bower.

equipped troops had already seized Langport and Bridgwater by the twenty-third of the month. From there they marched south to Martock with the original intention of pursuing Goring's defeated royalists and preventing them from rallying together.

Sir Thomas Fairfax, however, 'was at this time much troubled in his thoughts concerning his march further west, before Bath and Sherborn were absolutely reduced... Reckoning it also a service of importance to take in Bath, in order to the straitening of Bristoll and hindring P. Rupert for raising any considerable force in those parts.'[17] His Council of War shared his doubts about the wisdom of proceeding further into the south-west while large royalist garrisons at Sherborne, Bristol and Bath remained free to cause trouble in his rear. In particular, possession of Bath was regarded as 'very advantageous to the taking of Bristoll'. The plan was therefore changed. Whilst Colonel Pickering was sent with a brigade of horse to commence the siege of Sherborne, Fairfax took the rest of his army northwards to Wells, where he set up his own headquarters.

News reached him in Wells of terrible disorder within the city of Bath. The trouble had apparently started on Monday, 28th July when 'about 60 horse (most Welch) came from Prince Rupert to strengthen Bath; and other officers with them to governe the Towne, because that P. Rupert had found, when hee was there two dayes before, that Sr. Thomas Bridges was quite out of heart to keep it; for the very name of Sir Thomas Fairfax strikes a terrour to the enemy. But when they were come into Bath, the Towne cryed out as one man all against the Welch: No Welch, no Welch; Neither did Sir Thomas Bridges take it well, that he should bee displaced, and another put in; which caused a great division in the Towne, that the officers and horse would not stay to dispute it; nevertheless some Welch stayed in the Towne, which did much displeasure both the Governour, the officers, the Townsmen; yea and the Garrison souldiers also'.[18]

The citizens of Bath, of course, were prompted in their actions not merely by a dislike of Welshmen, but also by a determination to disrupt the defence of the city. They were also genuinely worried about admitting 'souldiers from infected Bristol', which was

A reconnaissance party from the New Model Army surveys the defences of the royalist garrison in Bath (29th July, 1645)

apparently 'so much infected that it is more like to take an army than be taken by it'. To make matters worse, Bridges (the Governor of Bath) had become so unpopular with the townsfolk that they were 'not willing to beare Armes'.[19]

News of all these squabbles greatly encouraged Fairfax and made him optimistic about taking the city with comparative ease. He therefore 'thought it fit to spare his Foot any unnecessary labour, and sent two Regiments of Horse under the command of Colonell Rich, and two Troops of Dragoons with Colonell Okey to give account of the condition of the towne, that orders might be given accordingly'. This force set out on the Tuesday on what was intended to be no more than a reconnaissance expedition. They arrived just before sunset on Holliwell, a hill to the south of the city, placing their dragoons 'within halfe pistoll shot of the gate on the Bridge of Bath'.[20]

As they came down the hill at the bridge end, 'the enemy in Bath took an alarm and discharged their ordnance, whereupon some of our dragoons let fly at them their musket shot'.[21] Colonel Rich immediately summoned the town, but the Governor refused to surrender. Just as the sun was setting, therefore, Colonel Okey took his dragoons forward on a most impudent plan. Creeping forward 'on their bellies' to the bridge gate unobserved, they suddenly 'seized on the small end of the enemies muskets, which they had put through the loop-holes of the gate, and cryed to the enemy to take quarter'. The royalist guards were so terrified by this unexpected attack that, leaving their muskets behind, they fled back across the bridge to the safety of the breastworks on the other side. Okey's men immediately set fire to the gate and 'became masters of the bridge'.[22]

During the night the garrison remained in a state of undisguised panic - 'In the night the enemie within took several alarmes and were in great fear of us, as I conceive they knew not our strength, onely before had some intelligence of the advance of our armie'. In point of fact, the parliamentarians had confined their troops to the south and west side of the city - 'But the north part of the towne lay open, for we came not to block them up, nor had we forces to do it then present there; The Enemie might have gone away on the north part of the towne, in despite of all that we could do to hinder them, but God did so infatuate them, that they had not power'.[23]

Sir Thomas Bridges certainly suspected that Fairfax had surrounded the city with his whole army and when, early on Wednesday morning, he heard rumours of troops approaching from the north, he felt utterly convinced of it. Lacking the will to fight, he immediately sent a messenger to Colonel Rich requesting a parley. By sunrise the town had surrendered under the following conditions:

1. All, both officers and souldiers to have quarter for their lives.
2. That Sir Thomas Bridges and all the officers be permitted to march away to Bristoll, without let or molestation.
3. That Sir Thomas Bridges, and all other Field Officers, and Captaines have liberty to march away with horse and armes.
4. That all officers under the degree of captains, march away without Arms (only staves in their hands) to Bristoll.
5. That Sir Thomas Bridges, with all the officers aforesaid doe immediately march out of the garrison and surrender it to Colonell Rich for the service of Parliament.
6. That all the Ordnance, Armes and Ammunition be surrendered also.
7. The common souldiers to be left all prisoners. [24]

The parliamentarians themselves were amazed at their own rapid success. Only the intervention of God could explain such things. 'And truly you may think it a strange thing for horse to take a town, and no foot within 15 miles of it; but you may see how God infatuates men and possesseth them with a feare, that deprives them of wisdome and courage.'[25]

Troops of the royalist garrison in Bath defend the bridge against an attack by cavalry and dragoons of the New Model Army (29th July, 1645)

Their spoil from the city was considerable - 200 muskets, 100 pikes, six pieces of ordnance, 10 barrels of gunpowder, 10 barrels of 'other ammunition', a great quantity of match and bullet, six colours (including the standard of Sir Thomas Bridges from the 'Royal Fort'), pistols, swords, all Sir Thomas Bridges' bag and baggage and 'a greate store of beefe, corne and other provisions'. One hundred garrison soldiers and one hundred Welshmen were also originally handed over as prisoners,[26] but many of these escaped over the walls while the treaty was being drawn up.[27] Rich's force, which found 'the works, besides the wall of the city, strong and tenable', had taken Bath just in time. Prince Rupert had apparently already set out from Bristol with a relief force of 1,500 horse and foot, but retreated when he heard the news of its capture.[28]

Fairfax had meanwhile drawn up the rest of his army on the Mendips in readiness to march in support of the reconnaissance force. He now decided to take with him only two foot regiments, which would be left to garrison the city. He quartered in Bath on the Wednesday night, 'staying there next morning, and settled things for the safety of that place'.[29] Then, leaving Colonel Birch as the new parliamentarian governor of the city, he returned to Wells. The garrison had been made 'so strong that it might bee a check to Bristoll; whereupon Colonell Birches and Colonell Waller's[30] Regiments of Foot were ordered to remain at Bath, and three Regiments of Horse, viz. Colonell Butlers, Colonell Cooks and Colonell Pophams[31] appointed to quarter thereabouts, that they might joyne together for the blocking up or straightning of Bristoll.'[31]

There is no doubt that parliament was overjoyed at the capture of Bath, regarding it as a base of prime importance for launching the drive against Bristol. Added to which, it was rated as a 'prestige' victory - 'Its a Bishop's See, or half a one, and a little of theirs is worth much of others'.[32] But perhaps even more important was the terrible psychological effect the fall of the city had had on the inhabitants of Bristol. 'The enemy are in much feare and distractions in that city for feare of Sir Thomas Fairfax his Army', wrote *The*

True Informer, adding sarcastically, 'They might do well to make Colonell Sir Thomas Bridges Governour of it!'[33] The consequences resulting from the lack of courage displayed by Bridges were also referred to in *Mercurius Britanicus:* '...which faire example of cowardice was given in an ill time... And more particularly in Bristol, for the redoubled fortifications without, will not keep the inhabitants from the palsie within; what will they do then when they are actually straitned and besieged?'[34] Certainly the reputation gained by Fairfax's army after the amazing capture of Bath caused widespread dismay amongst the royalists in the area - 'This makes their heads and their hearts to faint at Bristoll, And how can the lesse garrisons of Lacock, the Devizes and other places be able to withstand so puissant an army. I leave them to consider....'[35]

(iii) The Rise of the Clubmen, 1645

After the surrender of Bath by Sir Thomas Bridges, Fairfax wrote to his father stating his belief that four regiments would be enough to take Bristol 'with the assistance of the county with the well-affected thereabout.'[36] The country people now made their move - a possibility that had been firmly forecast by various observers since the summer of 1644.

Lord George Goring (1608 - 1657), who was appointed Lieutenant-General of Horse in the King's main army in August 1644, campaigned in the West Country in the spring and summer of 1645. Portrait from the studio of Sir Anthony van Dyck, c1638.

Country people had in fact been making their move for several months in many southern and western counties as a form of self-defence against the atrocities of war. Various 'Clubmen' or 'peace-keeping' associations had been formed out of sheer desperation to preserve themselves 'from plunder and all other unlawful violence'.[37] In all, clubmen associations were established in 1645 in Shropshire, Worcestershire and Herefordshire (January-March), Wiltshire, Dorset and Somerset (May-September), Berkshire, Sussex and Hampshire (September-October), and South Wales (August-November). Set partly against the background of the disappointing collapse of the Uxbridge peace negotiations between King and Parliament and partly against the abolition of the Prayer Book at the beginning of the year, the rise of the clubmen occurred chiefly in those areas which had experienced uncontrolled plunder from large numbers of semi-independent garrisons or from 'foreign' armies as they trampled their way in and out of the county. By the spring of 1645, for instance, Goring's army 'was running amok, unpaid and vindictive' in the south-west.

The clubmen associations shared a number of characteristics, quite apart from their bitter hostility to soldiers of any kind. John Morrill has emphasised their essential neutrality. Although this 'did not preclude Associations from assisting either King or Parliament in particular circumstances', it certainly 'need not imply a betrayal of their neutrality.' Tactical alliances, therefore, were possible with Fairfax in helping to get rid of Goring from Dorset. Secondly, the groups seem to have emerged spontaneously from below. 'In every case, the initiative seems to have come from within the peasant communities, particularly from amongst yeomen and other farmers.' Nevertheless, they united 'all segments of local society from minor gentry and clergy to poorer farmers. They show the same fierce localism, make the same appeal to community traditions, to ancient rights and customs against external, centralising innovations.' Thirdly, although the associations shared some common values and aspirations - including a determination 'to return to known ways' and to rid themselves of 'outside interference in local affairs' - each nevertheless 'retained its own personal characteristics and prejudices, reflecting local circumstances.'[38] Ronald Hutton, in studying the Marcher clubmen, also concluded that there was no unified movement, in spite of a 'general fever of anti-military feeling among the countrymen of the Marches.'[39]

Prince Rupert of the Rhine (1619 - 1682), commander of the Bristol garrison in 1645 at the time of its capture by parliament's New Model Army.

The first of the clubmen associations in the west, recruited from Dorset and Wiltshire, was established just outside Wimborne St Giles on 25th May 1645. By June and July the movement had spread into Somerset with similar associations formed in the south-east (near Castle Cary), the west (beyond the Quantocks) and the centre (near Bridgwater). Their objectives were much the same - to present peace petitions to both King and Parliament, to elect officers from each parish, to protect themselves from plundering soldiers, to enlist 'uncommitted' men and to raise cash through local rates. 'The whole programme', argues Professor Underdown, 'shows a degree of political sophistication that reminds us that however humble, these were men of independence, long familiar with processes of self-government.' The clubmen who took part in this 'organised neutralism' consisted of the humbler yeomen farmers - or 'the country, shorn of its upper echelon of politicised gentry.'[40] This popular movement remained largely neutral throughout, with slight leanings towards the royalists in both the west and the south-east and towards parliament in the centre.

The countrymen in the north-east of the county, however, showed no such inhibitions about declaring their allegiance. An association of clubmen was certainly in existence in this area by 15th July 1645 when Prince Rupert wrote to them from Bristol warning of intelligence reports he had received based on intercepted despatches between Parliament and the Army. Fairfax, he insisted, had been commanded to suppress the local clubmen 'by violence and force', 'to seize upon the ringleaders' and 'to destroy the seeds of sedition and rebellion'.[41] This propaganda campaign, designed to drive the clubmen into the royalist camp, was totally ineffective. But the Prince was clutching at straws. After Goring's defeat at Langport and the surrender of Bridgwater to the New Model Army, Rupert felt increasingly less secure with his garrison at Bristol. He therefore made several positive overtures to the local clubmen for their support. *The True Informer* reported on 2nd August: 'He hath had severall meetings with the Club-men .... about Lansdowne in Sommersetshire, but they refused to take up Armes or joyn with him, which is the thing he earnestly moved them to'.[42] An earlier meeting had taken place at Wraxall, near Bristol, when, according to this parliamentarian source, Prince Rupert with one thousand

Nunney Castle, which had formed part of the Bristol garrison under the royalist occupation of the area. It had belonged to Richard Prater. a papist, whose lands were subsequently sequestered. The castle was captured by a detachment of the New Model Army under Colonel Thomas Fainsborough on 20th August, 1645, after his cannon had breached the wall.

troops, two pieces of ordinance and 'a loade of match' had put on a show of force 'partly to flatter, and partly to affright' the local clubmen. They stubbornly refused to acquiesce, either by giving him a volley of shot 'in token of submission' or by allowing his force to pass through their ranks. Furthermore, when Sir Edward Gorges accused parliament's soldiers of tearing a book of Common Prayer to pieces in a local church, 'one clubman stepped forth and said that hee lyed like a knave'. With such defiant expressions ringing in the Prince's ears, the clubmen allegedly parted 'without expression either of love or feare to Rupert or his associates'.[43]

Two days after the meeting on Lansdown, on 30th July, Sir Thomas Bridges surrendered Bath in a most ignominious manner to a reconnaisance party of the New Model Army. By 23rd August, after Sherborne and Nunney Castle had also fallen, Bristol itself was in a state of siege. It was at this moment that John Ashe, who had 'attended upon Sr Thom. Fairfax and his army in all his marches and services downe in the westerne countys',[44] advised the General to issue warrants to the High Sheriff, Sir John Horner, to raise the northern part of the County. Ashe and Horner, who understood the local political situation to perfection, showed admirable timing in their move. If these parliamentarian pamphlets are to be believed (and there is some local evidence to support them - see below), the inhabitants of North-East Somerset responded to the call with great enthusiasm, enlisting into the ranks of the clubmen and assisting at the capture of Portishead fort on 28th August.[45] A few days later, a remarkable meeting took place on the hills overlooking Chewton Mendip, where great crowds of clubmen had been summoned by Sir John Horner for a meeting with representatives from Sir Thomas Fairfax. This, of course, was the scene - as *The True Informer* reminded its readers - of 'their old rendezvous' in August 1642, when multitudes of countrymen had assembled to resist the intrusions of the Marquis of Hertford. There can be little doubt that the convenors of this new meeting (Horner and Ashe), who had also been the inspiration behind the uprising three years earlier, had deliberately chosen this site to awaken memories, to forge unity and to symbolise the continuity of their resistance.

According to parliamentarian sources, about four or five thousand clubmen appeared on horse and foot to welcome a party sent by Sir Thomas Fairfax, including Oliver Cromwell, John Ashe and Hugh Peters, the army Chaplain. Cromwell thanked them for the 'willingnesse and good affection' already expressed and emphasised the vital importance of capturing Bristol - not least from their own point of view. Peters 'preached twice on horseback' to the assembled crowd, urging them 'to send in a final party to assist the designe in hand, 2000 would content'. He later claimed, in a report sent to London, that 'the issue was a generall resolution to come to us, which next day they did about 3000.' Other sources, however, reported that, although 'the people seemed willing to do what was desired', the consultations were abruptly interrupted by an urgent message warning of the King's advance to Cirencester. The meeting hurriedly broke up, but reconvened again a few days later at Dundry Hill, near Bristol, 'where the Clubmen agreed with great alacrity, and readinesse, to give assistance for the regaining of Bristoll'. The result, according to *Mercurius Civicus,* was that 'between 2000 and 3000 of the Somersetshire Clubmen with 25 colours' joined Fairfax at the siege of Bristol, with others 'that still come in to us every day, and will adventure their lives with us'.[46]

The descriptions given by these parliamentarian newsheets are to a large extent substantiated by the narrative of Joshua Sprigg, Fairfax's chaplain. He records that the decision by the New Model Army to delay their original plan of proceeding further west and to capture Bath instead was partly taken because they considered it 'a service of importance for .... the countenancing the well-affected countrymen thereabouts.' Their eventual success in raising the power of the county, after Fairfax had issued warrants to Horner, 'was much promoted by the interest and endeavours of Mr Ash.' Sprigg's most significant evidence regarding the eagerness of the local people to assist Fairfax comes in his entry for 10th September 1645:

The Gateway of Farleigh Castle in 1789. A drawing by S.H. Grimm. The castle, which formed part of the Bristol garrison during the royalist occupation of the area, was captured by the New Model Army on 15th September, 1645. It was surrendered to Sir Edward Hungerford (its owner) by his own half-brother, John Hungerford, who had held it for the King.

> This day, about two thousand well-affected countrymen, who with many more, upon treaty with the lieutenant-general at the beginning of the siege, had engaged their assistance to make good the same, marched with some thirty-six colours in the face of Bristol, had quarters assigned them, and kept guards. Two pieces of ordnance also were sent unto them for their encouragement; it not a little grieving the enemy within to see the forwardness of the country to come to our assistance; for which reason (and to lay an effectual caution against their revolt) it was held fit to make use of those forces from the country, rather than for any considerable service that could be expected from them.

Fairfax, therefore, readily acknowledged the political importance of local loyalty to the parliamentarian cause, even if their military efficiency was somewhat in question.[47]

Local clubmen not only contributed to the capture of Bristol on 11th September, 'but also assisted during the next two months by protecting the north-western edge against plundering raids by Goring's cavalry and by involving themselves in the mopping-up operation, which included the seizure of Farleigh Castle on 15th September. By this time, the clubmen had been given their own commander - Colonel Alexander Popham. In doing this, Fairfax had not only set the seal on the clubmen's loyalty, but had also granted official recognition to this local army. Popham was, after all, one of his own serving officers. After the surrender of Bath by Bridges on 30th July, Fairfax had left a garrison based on the city, consisting of two regiments of foot (commanded by Colonels Birch and Waller) and three regiments of horse (commanded by Colonels Butler, Cooks and Popham).[48] These duties had prevented Popham from involving himself too closely in the clubmen's earlier activities. He was not in evidence at Chewton or at Dundry. But now the situation had turned full circle with Popham again in charge of the 'trained bands' (or their 1645 equivalent) and his troops again pledged to fight for parliament. Local parishes supported the enterprise, as they had done in 1642. Sub-committee accounts give clear evidence that a local rate was charged 'for clubmen's pay'. The villages of Camerton, Dunkerton, Claverton, Publoe and Thubwell, for instance, all sent contributions to the clubmen 'then assisting Sr Thomas ffairefaxe, by vertue of Sr John Horners Warrant'. Publoe collected four pounds for 'the clubmen under the comand of Coll. Alexander Popham in the west of the county of Somerset', though many others from the tithing had joined the service 'at their owne chardge' - a further indication of the willingness of local people to become involved, and a further proof that the accounts given by parliamentarian newsheets of clubmen activity in the area are not totally without foundation.[49]

The clubmen of North-East Somerset were unique. Unlike their counterparts elsewhere, they did not consider their immediate aim to be that of neutrality or their ultimate mission to engage in a peace keeping role. From the outset they roughly rejected the advances of Rupert and awaited a call from Fairfax. It is certainly true that a population intent on protecting itself from plunder would tend to turn instinctively away from Goring's ruthless crew towards the disciplined troops of the New Model Army. Local people had clearly been impressed by the exemplary behaviour of Fairfax's men who had been quartered in the villages of North Somerset and South Gloucestershire. Special markets had been opened for the Army's use but, according to one eye-witness, 'the souldiers pay for what they have, and behave themselves so civilly and courteously that they have gained the affection of the countrey: and on the contrary, they are as much alienated from Prince Rupert and his souldiers'.[50]

Nevertheless, the immediate inclination of the local clubmen towards the newly-arrived forces of parliament was no sudden response brought about by the heat of war. Rather it demonstrated a remarkable consistency in their approach which had characterised their attitude throughout the conflict. As *The Kingdom's Weekly Intelligencer* pointed out, these people had been 'active clubbers against Hopton, Stawell, and the rest of the incendiaries of the western parts' in 1642.[51] 'Active clubbers' they had remained at heart, even though they had wisely decided against foolish risks during royalist occupation. But the men who had slept rough on the Mendips in 1642 were the very same men who had provided active assistance to Waller at Lansdown in 1643, the men who had lit bonfires under the nose of Sir Thomas Bridges to celebrate Gunpowder Treason Day, the men who had staged a street demonstration against Prince Rupert's Welsh reinforcements for the Bath garrison and the men who had outlined their willingness to rise again when visited by Essex in 1644 and Waller in 1645. Their only conditions had been first, 'their desire to serve under their own countrymen' and second, the reappearance of a strong army which would stay with them 'and not bee gone tomorrow' (see above). These conditions had now been fulfilled. The emergence of the clubmen of North-East Somerset witnessed not so much the steady growth of a peace-keeping association as the spontaneous, but long-awaited revival of the old trained bands under their former leaders and pledged to their former cause. The term 'clubmen' is therefore something of a misnomer. There was, however, one significant difference between the situation in 1642 and that of 1645. Whereas, at the start of the war, the trained bands of part-time volunteers had actually *formed* the army of Parliament in its resistance to Hertford, by 1645 they had been superceded by the fulltime professionals of the New Model Army. Therefore, although their role could no longer be such a dominant one as it had been in 1642, they keenly awaited their invitation from Fairfax to play a supplementary, but nevertheless vital, part in ending the war.

For a second time within the space of three years, therefore, a popular rising had succeeded in driving royalist forces out of the area and establishing control in the hands of parliament. The reasons for their action in 1645 were perfectly consistent with their reasons in 1642. As Professor Underdown has pointed out: 'The yeomen and clothworkers had more to gain from a parliamentarian than a royalist victory, and if left to themselves without interference from cavalier gentry and clergy, they knew it'.[52] Cromwell had made a similar point to them in his speech on the Mendips, commenting on the siege of Bristol 'that as England would be happy in it, so they chiefly in their particular if the City was taken; and on the other side, the great danger they were in if Sir Thomas should now rise from it'.[53] For them, the danger lay in a return to the corruption and tyranny of the 1630's. Whereas 'country people' in general stood rather vaguely for 'liberty and property,' the protection of 'the ancient and fundemental laws of the Kingdom', the defence of religion against popery and a return to the harmony experienced in the 'good old days' of Queen Elizabeth, the country people in North-East Somerset stood for something much more specific. They stood for a personal brand of puritan religion, which encouraged thrift, morality, family discipline and sober pastimes. The memory of their experience in the 1630's, when both their religion and their livelihood had been seriously threatened, still loomed vividly before their eyes. In 1645, as in 1642, local people again turned to Horner, Ashe and Popham, not so much out of deference to their natural leaders, but because those leaders were again 'in step with the general opinion in the neighbourhood'. And the general opinion in the neighbourhood was again intent on defending its own distinctive culture. There was, however, one important difference between the two risings. In 1642, the willing multitude on Mendip had, from the outset, been created, inspired and led by the local gentry. In 1645, a grass-roots movement in the villages had first created the clubmen's association and only later turned to the gentry for leadership. This, together with the consistent attitudes which had been maintained during the intervening years, goes a long way to disproving Underdown's theory that active commitment in the area 'was confined to a politicised minority' which had struggled in 'a sea of neutralism and apathy.[54] Even if their parliamentarianism had been partly submerged during the years of occupation, it existed nevertheless - and it existed at levels far lower than the gentry and the wealthy clothiers.

6.
The Impact of War on the Local Community, 1642-46

(i) Impact on the Farming Community

(a) Taxation

'God preserve our Kingdom from these sad troubles much longer', wrote the Mayor of Bath to John Harington in 1646.[1] This heartfelt cry expressed the pent-up feelings of thousands of ordinary people who had endured the ravages of war in the parishes of North-East Somerset over the past few years. It was an area which had apparently suffered greatly from the cross traffic of competing field armies, from the incessant demands of the Bristol garrison and its satellites at Bath, Nunney, Berkley, and Monkton Farleigh, from the build-up to both the Battle of Lansdown in 1643 and the siege of Bristol in 1645, and from the mounting demands of the official tax collector.

'There is no counting the cost of the civil war', wrote Dr Morrill.[2] It is nevertheless possible to estimate something of the financial burden of the war imposed by Parliament and experienced by particular villages with all its attendant human suffering. Part of the task of the subcommittee of accounts, established by parliament in 1646 as a branch in each county of the Committee of Accounts in London, was to ascertain the wartime losses of each local community. The Somerset subcommittee, largely nominated by William Prynne and composed of local worthies from the area around Bath,[3] included John Gay, Thomas Cox, Giles Broade, John Rosewell and Peter Rosewell.[4] They met regularly in the Guildhall at Bath during June and July of that year to receive accounts from the constables and churchwardens of each parish within the Hundreds of Bathforum, Wellow, Kilmersdon, Frome and Keynsham, giving details of 'all the armes, horses, plate and moneyes paid, lent, delivered, taken and received .... as allso quartering of soldiers to and for the use of the Parliament since the beginning of this unhappie warr'.[5] The claims for losses sustained by individuals, compiled 'by the Churchwardens and two or three of the discreete and honest men of the inhabitants', give a graphic picture of the daily misery endured by many, at least during certain phases of the war in North-East Somerset. The returns for the Hundreds of Wellow and Keynsham, have survived intact; those for Bathforum and Frome appear in a somewhat fragmented form - whereas those for the city of Bath have disappeared altogether.

Taxation in all its forms put mounting financial pressure on local inhabitants as the war progressed, totally overshadowing the spectre of Ship Money and other 'illegal' charges made by Charles I during the 1630's. The Subsidy of £400,000, voted as early as 11th March, 1642 in the form of a land tax for the payment of debt in Scotland and war in Ireland, was collected in earnest from May and applied generally to the needs of parliament.[6] In Bath itself 105 people were wealthy enough to be assessed for this tax and paid between them £66 8s 4d for the half year. The parishes of Claverton and Bathampton together contributed a total of £21 10s from July in that year 'for the defence of England and Ireland in payment of the subsidie of £400,000'.[7] Between them they had a total of sixteen houses in the Hearth Tax returns of 1664-65, which would put the population at no more than about 92.[8] Similarly, Stanton Prior paid two instalments of £9 11s each in November 1642 and February 1643, while Whitchurch contributed a total of £24 19s 2d. Most of the villages within the Hundred of Wellow refer to the payment of

An army in camp - ominous news for local people.

'The Great Subsidie or Landscott' in two 'moieties', although the inhabitants of Camerton confessed that 'part paid to several constables and the rest not paid'.[9] These were in themselves heavy burdens for small villages to bear. But this was only the beginning.

On 10th June 1642, parliament issued orders for 'the bringing in of money or plate to maintain horsemen, and arms, for the preservation of the public peace, and for the defence of the King and both Houses of Parliament'.[10] These Propositions encouraged voluntary contributions of money and individual provision of horses and arms by the promise of an eight per cent interest rate (which was never repaid). The Somerset County Committee, which had been established on 20th July partly to implement these orders, quickly got to work under the influential leadership of John Ashe, Alexander Popham, and John Horner. It wasted no time in raising money to support and enlarge the forces under its command. Assistant collectors were appointed to visit 'people of ability' and receive their subscription. The parishes of North-East Somerset on the whole responded most generously to these initial demands, for reasons which have been explained (see Chapter Three).

In Keynsham, for instance, forty people lent between them a total of £82 15s 'towards the setting forth of dragoones'. Individual donations varied between five shillings and ten pounds, some of them in the form of plate. A further twenty-eight people together provided eighteen horses (most of them fully equipped), twenty-two muskets, eighteen swords, eleven bandoliers, four pistols, five pikes, one halberd, one 'birding peece' and one 'new corstlett and headpiece' at a total cost of £133 2s 8d. The same pattern was repeated to a greater or lesser extent in all the parishes of North-East Somerset. Widdow Elizabeth Jennings of Publow even donated to Nathaniel Fiennes, Governor of Bristol, 'one peece of ordinance' valued at £20 and belonging to her late husband. In 1642,

Whitchurch provided four horses, seven muskets, two swords and a carbine, as well as sums totalling £23 8s - all 'sett out under the command of Parliament for Colonel Alexander Popham'. Gifts and donations were received at the Guildhall in Bath by John Lock of Pensford (a client of Alexander Popham) on behalf of the Committee and made available to local military commanders. In this way Popham was quickly able to raise the arms and horses which had been so sorely lacking in the first local skirmish of the war at Chewton.[11]

At the same time, his officers were also endeavouring to recruit local men to fight in the war, part volunteers and part conscripts. Pressure was firmly applied as villagers in the northern hundreds were visited with systematic efficiency. It was, however, possible to buy exemption, as the men of Publow found to their relief. In 1643, it cost William Gage and Nathaniel Lott twenty-eight shillings each to be 'freed from the service' plus the donation of either a musket or a pike. Such payments were also received by John Lock in the Guildhall at Bath. The anguish suffered by relatives in war is illustrated by the action of Thomas Elme, who put up the necessary money together with a musket 'to free his kinsman Wm Elme from bearing his armes under Coll. Popham'. Early recruitment anxiety was, however, nothing compared with the experience of Bristol citizens in November 1644, when the royalist garrison suddenly issued an order to impress 1,000 men from the vicinity.[12]

Voluntary contributions alone were unlikely to win the war. People's generosity and enthusiasm, inspired perhaps by a sense of idealism at the start of hostilities, were quickly choked by the incessant demands of busy commissioners and hungry soldiers. The element of compulsion was now added in two ways. First, the collection of the fifth and twentieth part (or forced loan) from those 'malignants' who had not given freeiy in response to the Propositions. The Somerset Committee, empowered by parliament on 27th January 1643, set to work on the task. Although it is not easy to discover the extent of its success, largely through the destruction of its records, some local royalists suffered from the imposition of this tax, including Sir Thomas Bridges of Keynsham who paid £161. There is far more evidence, however, on the impact of the second compulsory aspect introduced by parliament to raise and equip urgently-needed forces, namely the Weekly Assessment. This new tax on each individual according to the value of his property was imposed by ordinance on 24th February, aiming to produce a weekly figure of £33,518 in the country as a whole.[13] By August 1643 the County of Somerset had been assessed at a total of £1050 per week, while the City of Bristol was expected to raise the weekly sum of £55 15s. The task of gathering in this money throughout the county was again entrusted to the Somerset Committee, with John Ashe as its newly-appointed Treasurer for the Eastern Division.[14]

There is no doubt that Ashe applied himself to the task with characteristic energy and concern. There is certainly some evidence that this more centralised scheme worked successfully and efficiently until the royalists gained control of the area in the summer of 1643. The parish of Whitchurch, for instance, paid nineteen weeks contributions in 1643 'for the use of the garrisons of Bristol and Bath' - a total of £32 16s 7d.[15] Most of the villages in the Wellow Hundred also claimed substantial 'contribution' payments for this period - Dunkerton £46 0s 0d, Englishcombe £48 18s 12d, Hinton Charterhouse £35 9s 2d, Foxcote £26 8s 0d ('four months contribution att Sir Wm Wallers being in this Countie'), although Wellow, Combe Hay and Corston make no mention of it at all. The Constables of Twerton and Newton St Loe, on the other hand, could both recall that 'much more hath bin paid before the King's forces tooke Bristoll', while at the same time confessing that they 'cannot for the present finde out our accompts'.[16]

In spite of this initial success which varied from place to place, the collectors gradually found it more and more difficult to gain the co-operation of local inhabitants who had already been squeezed dry in other ways. A despondent letter written from Bath by John Ashe to Nathaniel Fiennes, Governor of Bristol, on 1st June 1643 illustrates the extent of his problem. The continuing practice of free quarter clearly made most people reluctant to contribute to the Weekly Assessment in addition. 'The inhabitants and constables of the hundred of Keynsham', he wrote, 'bring in very little money, alleageing that they are eaten up and charged more then comes to thire share by the Bristoll Troopers and dragoones'. Furthermore, Colonel Popham, had apparently 'ordered them to pay no more upon the weekly assessment' until their expense claims against these soldiers had been met. Such were the complaints of constables from the whole area that Ashe was 'extreamely perplexed with them', receiving only 'very small summes'. He urged Fiennes to ensure not only that the local people received satisfaction for their complaints, but also that 'the refusers be compelled to bring in thire money' - an early hint that military force was to be used where necessary in tax collection. Ashe was clearly in a distraught state, because he begged Fiennes to 'excuse this scribbling, for its in the midst of a passionate debate amongst the negligent constables'. Nor was his problem simply confined to that of collection. He was also responsible, as Treasurer, for making payments to local commanders for the troops under their care. As far as possible he tried to earmark the revenue from certain parishes to support particular companies. For example, on 5th June he again wrote to Fiennes explaining that he had set aside for Captain Richard Hippesley 'the receipts of £105 weekly out of 4 hundreds next adjoyning the City of Bristol.'[17]

It was often necessary to double-check claims and insist on properly signed warrants. These points are again illustrated by Ashe's letter to Fiennes, in which he explained why payment had not yet been made for those soldiers from Popham's Bath Regiment who were then quartered in Bristol: '.... he tolde of 2 companys and you spoke of 3 companys. I pray you lett it be ordered, and send me your warrant signed by Collonell Popham, and I shall, upon sight thereof, appoint soe many hundreds adjoyneing as shall make good that weekly charge out of the weekly payment ....'. There is no doubt that income from this source was never sufficient to maintain local troops in the way that Ashe had envisaged. Accounts of Colonel William Strode, submitted on 3rd August 1643, for 'arms, horses, payments to maintain various companies payments to Waller, plate sold' etc., told their own story of inadequate supply coming in from his supporting parishes.

Paid out:	3402 07 04
Received from parishes:	1922 15 03
Owing	1779 12 01

It was small wonder that the troops had no money to pay villagers for their food or lodging - and, as the vicious circle rotated, small wonder that the villagers resented deeply the payment of this persistent tax. Similarly, commanders sometimes had great difficulty in moving their troops, because of lack of pay. In May 1643, for example, in spite of the threat of the advancing royalist army, Alexander Popham 'could not get the troops that lay in towne to march with him, although he promised them very largely, viz. to give 20s a man to them before they stirred.'[18]

After the recapture of the area for parliament by the New Model Army in the summer of 1645, the Weekly Assessment was again revived in Somerset and increased to £1250 a week. The parish accounts indicate that this time the local officials were much more successful in gathering in payments on a regular basis. The village constables of the Wellow Hundred, with detailed exactions fresh in their memory, are quite specific in their returns for the period August 1645 to September 1646 - Twerton £42 18s 11d (5 months contribution), Camerton £52 2s 5d (11 months), Newton St Loe (10 months), Dunkerton £45 14s 0d (11 months), Englishcombe £63 8s 0d (9 months), Hinton Charterhouse £52 7s 3d (10 months), Norton St Phillip £43 7s 3d (11 months). Most of these payments went to support 'the Garrison of Bristol' or 'the Governor of Bath', although additional contributions were also taken in several cases for 'the Brittish Armie in Ireland'.[19]

In matters of taxation, the royalists made even greater demands on the local community but enjoyed even less success when they occupied the area of North-East Somerset between July 1643 and September 1645. The Bath garrison, together with those of Berkeley Castle, Nunney Castle and Farleigh Castle, came under the direct control of Bristol. By 1st November 1644 a total establishment of three regiments of foot (with 1,200 in each regiment) and seven troops of horse (with 60 in each troop) had been assigned to cater for the needs of these garrisons. It was an expensive arrangement. The total *weekly* pay of these forces was estimated at a cost of £1,185 19s with Colonels of Foot receiving £5, Captains £2 10s, Corporals 5s, and common soldiers 3s 6d. Nor did that figure include either the salaries of the garrison officials (the Treasurer, the Quartermaster General, the Keeper of the Stores, etc.) or the cost of arms and ammunition. It was essential, therefore, that money should be raised locally, in the manner of parliament's weekly assessment, to support these needs of war.

Letters patent issued by Charles consequently granted full powers to Edmund Turner, Treasurer of the garrisons previously named. All sheriffs, justices, mayors and constables were commanded to assist him and his collectors in levying contributions on the neighbouring districts. Local army officers were also to help by 'sending forth such parties of horse or foote as you shall think fitt and necessary for the due leavying and collecting of the contributions aforesaid'. Two months later, Turner was appointed Captain of his own troop of cuirassiers to aid him in this work of tax collection. Their task of raising £2,000 per week was enormous. Of this £150 would be contributed by Bristol, £500 by Wiltshire, £300 by Gloucestershire, £200 by customs duties from the port and £850 by the eastern division of Somerset. A heavy burden, therefore, fell on Bath and the neighbouring hundreds of Keynsham, Bathforum, Kilmersdon, Wellow and Frome.[20]

By May 1645, it was fast becoming clear that the royalists were no more successful in money-raising than their parliamentarian predecessors. Richard March, Keeper of the King's Stores of Ordnance in Bristol, wrote a pitiful letter to Sir Edward Nicholas, the King's Secretary of State, complaining of the lack of cash. Under the terms of the original establishment, he should have received £350 per week to be spent specifically on ammunition and the making of new weapons for Bristol and its outlying garrisons. But in the first twenty-nine weeks of the scheme, Turner (the Treasurer) had only paid him a total of £2,490 instead of the expected sum of £10,150 - i.e. under £90 per week. Apparently the main reason for this was that 'the amounts expected from the customs here and the contribution coming from Somersetshire are so small'.[21] The reluctance of local people to support the royalist cause has already been explained (see Chapter Three), but even before this new system had been devised, Bath itself had fallen seriously behind in its payments. Indeed, on 18th March 1644 the Council had been obliged to appoint six officials 'to rate the inhabitants of the Cittie for the raseing of 150 *li* for arreres to the Kinge'.[22]

Richard March was clearly not lacking in either material or skilled workmen to produce a vast store of weapons - 'If constant payment were settled I would undertake to arm for his Majesty 20,000 men a year, viz. 15,000 muskets and bandoliers, and 5,000 pikes'. Without a regular supply of money, however, this vital work of arms manufacture would collapse - 'the artificers cannot continue at the work, their arrears now owing being above £1,200'.[23] Because of the urgency of the situation, therefore, renewed pressure was applied on the reticent tax payers of North-East Somerset.

According to the newsheet, *Mercurius Civicus,* the royalist governor of Bath in July 1644 was 'one Ridgley, that long since escaped out of Newgate'. If their rather colourful report is to be believed, he was prepared to use a good deal of violence in collecting the local contributions:

'He hath about 300 Irish under his command there; whom he sends into the country to fetch in contributions at his pleasure; He daily offers many affronts and commits many insolences against the inhabitants, forcibly taking away their goods and lately offered to pistoll the Mayor of the Towne, had not the women there in the absence of most of his souldiers threatened to pull him in peeces. On Saturday night last he sent out a party, who fetcht in about 30 of the countreymen thereabouts, and brought them in two by two for not paying the unreasonable taxes assessed upon them, most of them they imprisoned, drowned two and murdered two others that seemed to adhere to the Parliament. These Irish souldiers have not (as was observed by one that saw them march) above six swords in 7 or 8 files, and sometimes scarce one in ten of them have a sword.'[24]

As the need for money became desperate, a certain amount of force was unquestionably used. It should be remembered, however, that both the royalists and the parliamentarians made provision in their ordinances for the use of troops and the confiscation of property in cases where weekly payments were refused. But although this report possibly contained some grain of truth, it should certainly not be taken as proof of a general reign of terror - quite apart from any exaggerations in detail which were added for propaganda purposes. The Irishmen concerned in this episode were probably some of the troops brought back from fighting in Ireland after the King's truce with the Catholic rebels at the end of 1643.

In order to set all these taxation figures properly into context, two general points must be made. First, the people of North-East Somerset were certainly no worse off in matters of taxation than those living elsewhere in the country and, in some ways indeed, were very much better off. They were not, for instance, subject to those sudden demands for additional payments which affected the population of key garrison towns vulnerable to siege. The citizens of Worcester, when faced with a demand for a £4,000 loan in September 1643, protested that they could not raise so large a sum 'in respect of the decay of trade in clothing, the weekly burdens and taxes laid on the inhabitants for making fortifications and scouring the ditches'. They were even more horrified in June of the following year when the Council received a further demand for a grant of £1,000 'to be suddenly raised in money by tomorrowe night'.[25] In Nottingham, quite apart from their regular contributions, the inhabitants were confronted by a series of four extra payments in July and August, 1643 - £115 10s. collected to pay Cromwell's soldiers, £104 11s 'lent' to Sir John Meldrum, £540 8s 4d raised on the Committee's warrant and a further sum assessed by the Corporation itself for the urgent repair of the bulwarks and the supply of light and coal for the night guard.[26] In Leicester, Prince Rupert's initial demand in 1642 for £50 was quickly followed by another for £2,000. Such were the financial pressures in that city that, even as early as May 1643, the Corporation agreed 'that ye Towne plate, or soe much thereof as Mr Major and the Chamberlain shall think fitt, shal be sould forthwith at the best rate and the money thereof raised to be imployed towards the payment of the Townes debts'.[27] Indeed, so complex had become the tax system in certain areas that in the Eastern Counties, for example, the account books at the end of the war listed all the levies and loans taken since 1641 under no fewer than forty-seven headings![28] At least in North-Somerset, life was a little more straightforward than that.

Secondly, it should be remembered that local people were perfectly accustomed to the notion of paying taxes both on a regular basis and on extra occasions to cover emergency needs. The war merely added to the frequency of payments, depending to a large extent on where you lived. The parishes of Claverton and Bathampton, for instance, which together had paid £21 10s in 1642 towards the Subsidy of £400,000 (see above) had paid substantially more on a poll tax (August 1641) long before the civil war had started. Their combined charge of £266 1s 6d even excluded the assessment for William Bassett, who had paid in London.[29] On the other hand, the response of the people of Keynsham to the Propositions of June 1642, which voluntarily raised £215 17s 8d (see above) far exceeded the amount demanded from them by the Ship Money assessment of 1628 (£20 15s) or the Subsidy of December 1641 for the relief of the army in the North (£19 4s). [30] On an individual level, James Smith and John Weeks of Farmborough, who had been assessed for 10s 3d and 7s 11d respectively towards Ship Money in 1628, gave in response to The Propositions of 1642 £1 5s and £1 14s 6d. [31]

Nevertheless, certain war taxes were much more oppressive and persistent than their peace-time equivalents. For instance, a subsidy in 1641 had cost the village of Englishcombe a total of £6 2s 8d, whereas they had allegedly paid £48 18s 12d in 1643 and £66 8s 0d in 1645-6 towards the Weekly Assessment. Furthermore, the Hundred of Wellow had paid a combined sum of £83 1s 4d for the 1641 subsidy, but their estimate of expenditure on taxation for the two years of parliamentarian control during the war totalled £867 2s 9d. [32] This ties in with a similar experience by the inhabitants of Stratford-on-Avon in Warwickshire who had paid £150 to all the levies of 1640-2, compared with the £1,528 paid in Weekly Assessment in two-and-a-half years between 1643 and 1646. [33]

Although, as Dr Morrill has stated, 'taxation became an institutionalised version of the seizing of supplies by armies and garrisons from the countryside', [34] it was in fact far less productive during the war in North-East Somerset than either free quarter or direct methods of requisitioning. This is illustrated by a close examination of the returns submitted by the Wellow Hundred in 1646. Contributions made by each tithing in various ways towards parliament's war effort were detailed as follows: [35]

Twerton	219 11 11
Tellisford	36 15 00
Camerton	192 18 01
Newton St Loe	375 10 11
Corston	150 15 00
Dunkerton	141 11 04
Inglishcombe	289 05 05
Combehay	470 07 09
Hinton Charterhouse	864 12 10
Norton St Philip	390 15 06
Wellow	513 12 09
Total	3578 08 06

A breakdown of these figures reveals that taxation (including money raised from the Subsidy of £400,000, the Propositions, the Weekly Assessment and the contributions to Ireland) raised only £867 2s 9d of this amount. Free quarter, on the other hand, accounted for £1201 10s 0d of the total, leaving no less than £1508 15s 9d to cover requisitions, losses, sequestrations and forced labour.

This situation was repeated in other parts of the country. Dr Morrill has shown that in Buckinghamshire the total war taxation to the end of 1646 amounted approximately to £65-70,000, whereas 38 out of the 210 townships in the county alone provided £17,636 in free quarter. A similar story was true in Cheshire. As in the Thirty Years' War, the major economic cost to local communities stemmed from free quarter and billeting. In consequence, no fewer than twenty-five counties petitioned parliament between 1645 and 1647 that they would be unable to bear the burden of maintaining forces at their current strength. [36] Dr Hutton has shown that the suffering of ordinary people was just as severe in areas under royalist control as those under parliamentarian. In spite of early attempts to avoid using the system of free quarter at the start of the war, by August 1643 it had become the practice of the royalist field army on campaign. It later developed into the general rule for all counties where large congregations of troops were garrisoned.[37] In some cities, the Corporation itself undertook the task of organising the allocation of billets. In Gloucester, for instance, faced with the arrival of Massey's regiment, councillors agreed in February 1643 to accommodate these 1500 temporary residents by imposing a system which gave six soldiers to each alderman, five to each sheriff, four to each councillor and the remainder to other citizens in proportion.[38] In the countryside, things were arranged on a more ad hoc basis.

(b) Free Quarter

However much ordinary people disliked the regular demands of the tax collector, this was nothing compared with the horror, fear and disgust with which they greeted the arrival of troops in search of free quarter. The unlucky householder could only submit to the demands of armed men for board and lodging, hoping that the 'ticket' given in return would one day be exchanged for cash or taken in part payment of the next assessment. Although this much-detested practice of quartering the armies, both royalist and parliamentarian, upon private citizens did not reach its climax in North-East Somerset until later, there is strong evidence that it was already widespread by 1643. As Waller awaited the arrival of Hopton's royalist army from Cornwall in the summer of that year, he gradually staged a rendezvous of all parliament's western forces on the downs around Bath. This build-up of military strength and activity was to cause severe discomfort to the local community as billeting officers and quartermasters went out in search of both accommodation and supplies. Keynsham, for instance, was ordered to support 'Captain Rawlins and his Troope being about the number of 50 men and horse for 4 weeks' at an estimated expense of £70. Similarly, the inhabitants of Norton St Philip were faced with the prospect of quartering the whole of Popham's Bath Regiment, 'being 700 of them'. Although they stayed for only two nights, it cost the village something like £53 in provisions.[39]

A billeting officer arrives at a house to check in soldiers on free quarter.

One of the worst horror stories from the period of the war was undoubtedly the experience of the inhabitants of Combe Hay, who discovered that their village had become the main daily meeting point for the whole parliamentarian army. Waller had based himself on Bathampton and Claverton Down, thus gaining a strong vantage point from which to protect the city against any sudden royalist thrust along the Avon valley. The unfortunate villagers were consequently forced to endure not only Captain Sanderson's troop of sixty horse on free quarter for two weeks 'and odde dayes', but also 'ye dayly concourse of ye whole armie to our village, during Sr Willm Wallers beinge about Bath downes and Odde downe'. This caused considerable damage to the crops, 'spoylinge our grounds ready for mowinge' and a constant demand for hay and other commodities to be 'caryed to ye countrie to them'. Worst of all, the troops showed their ingratitude for the hospitality offered by the village by stealing eighty of their sheep and pressing Elizabeth Bailey's grey mare into service 'to carry amunition after ye armie of Sr William Waller'. The estimated cost of this short episode in the history of Combe Hay was £114 0s 0d - an enormous burden for one small community to shoulder.[40]

Some villages suffered much more heavily than others from the threat of free quarter. Their vulnerability depended partly on luck, but more particularly on their geographical location - their proximity to the site of a battle, a city under siege, the garrison of the town or the route taken by armies as they marched on campaign. Twerton, for instance, which lay just outside Bath on the road to Bristol was easy prey throughout the entire war - to a company of Waller's own regiment, to two hundred of Captain Abbot's cavalry 'when they marched against Bristoll', to forty-seven men from Sir Thomas Fairfax's own Lifeguards, to thirty-one soldiers from the Bath garrison (who stayed for over six weeks), to ten New Model Army troopers from Cromwell's regiment and finally to '800 soldiers of Collonell Montagues Regiment when they marched from Bristoll to the Devizes for 1 night with 30 horse and 18 oxen'. In between times they had also accommodated thirty-one of 'Sr Thomas Ffairfax's souldiers beinge sicke men, some a week, some a fortnight and some a month'.[41]

There is little doubt either that some villages acquired a reputation which, passed on by word of mouth, succeeded in attracting in troops who might otherwise have passed it by in peace. Such, alas, was the fate of Combe Hay which had no fewer than eight visitations between July 1645 and January 1646, experiencing in the process the almost identical misery previously inflicted in 1643. Their first intruders seemed innocent enough (twenty-five officers and men from the New Model Army who were part of the reconnaissance party which surprisingly frightened the Bath garrison to surrender in July 1645), until they demanded on departure 'beere, flesh, cheese, bread' for four hundred men at the rendezvous on Bathampton Down. But worse was to follow. After a whole regiment of eight hundred infantry had descended on the village 'movinge from Bristol to Devizes' for one night on 17th September, they were followed hard of heel on the next day by 'one foot company more of thirteen hundred, as they themselves reputed .... which companyes spoyled and killed 80 sheepe'. History had a nasty habit of repeating itself when the horrors of free quarter had once been experienced.[42]

Nevertheless, some villages, such as Thrubwell and Charleton, escaped entirely from this sickening trauma. The table below analyses the total expended in the war effort on behalf of parliament by the Hundred of Keynsham, with the proportion taken by the cost of providing free quarter.[43]

KEYNSHAM HUNDRED

	Total spent in war	Cost of free quarter	percentage of whole
Keynsham	394 06 02	114 11 02	31.1
Farmborough	71 12 01	45 13 02	56.5
Marksbury	79 18 00	122 10 00	63.7
Thrubwell			
Saltford	173 08 00	74 05 06	42.8
Stanton Drew	178 12 08	26 01 08	14.6
Stanton Prior	193 08 06	89 08 00	46.2
Priston	375 18 04	112 00 00	29.8
Burnett	48 19 09	7 00 00	14.3
Brislington	147 00 08	35 00 00	23.8
Charleton	51 12 03	-	-
Chelworth	118 04 03	13 12 00	11.5
Whitchurch	302 18 01	104 04 00	34.4
Compton Dando	155 02 06	30 15 00	19.8
Publow	321 07 06	166 10 00	51.8
Belluton	85 02 08	63 05 04	74.3
	2812 02 07	956 14 08	34.0

Even as late as October 1644, Waller and Haselrig still considered that northern Somerset provided 'as fruitful parts as are in England to quarter in', eyeing with envy the royalist-held area around Bath.[44] But if the Hundreds of Bathforum, Wellow, Keynsham, Frome and Kilmersdon had escaped rather lightly during the early years of the war, the situation was speedily corrected with the arrival of the New Model Army in the summer of 1645. Although the campaign was comparatively short, including the siege of Bristol, the suffering and inconvenience here was great for the local inhabitants. The village of Wellow, for instance, had fourteen visitations from Fairfax's army in quick succession between July and September, including Colonel Waldren's foot regiment of two thousand men for one night - a total of over three thousand troops at a cost of £282 0s 0d to the small farming community. In the Hundred of Keynsham, forty-two of the sixty-two households in Publow, during the same period, quartered 1381 men (averaging 32.8 per household), 511 horses (averaging 12.1) and the artillery train of 140 oxen. Although a few individuals were inflicted with impossible numbers for one night's stay - Lyson Hopkins had a hundred to contend with on one occasion and Widdow Jennings fifty - for most the effect was cumulative as fresh soldiers arrived almost daily in a village which became increasingly devastated.[45]

Alexander Gage, Churchwarden, was visited on ten occasions, while the Gage family's five dwellings in Publow (belonging to William, a yeoman farmer, Alexander, Richard, Samuel and Widdow Priscilla) together suffered a total of thirty-six visits, accommodating 201 men and 120 horses at a cost of £25 7s 8d. John Hedges, however, had the most varied experience. His seven requests for quarter included one from the General's gunsmith, who brought along his wife and boy, and one from a sick soldier who stayed for thirty-five nights. Hedges, like others in the village, found himself forced not only to stock up his visitors on departure with provisions 'for ye leaguer' at Bristol, but also to witness the galling sight of Colonel Fleetwood's men carrying away '3 wayne loads' of his oats at the end of their stay. James Palmer, the Tythingman, was obliged to supply 'hard wood, faggots and helme wch was carried to the League att Bristoll', while Nicholas Martin (who was licensed to buy barley and make malt[46]) had the unenviable task of looking after the Train of 140 oxen for three nights.[47]

The recapture of North-East Somerset by Sir Thomas Fairfax in the summer of 1645 and the subsequent departure of the New Model Army, did not bring an end to the suffering of ordinary people at the hands of the military. The problem of local garrisons remained. After the fall of Bristol, Bath had been left with a garrison force of one infantry regiment, numbering just over a thousand men, under Colonel Birch as Governor. During the autumn of 1645 conditions in the west remained uncertain, even though the New Model Army successfully continued its mopping-up campaign of royalist strongholds. It was therefore important, at least until tension eased, to maintain the outer defences of the city. The Corporation itself spent money on repairing damage to Gascoyn's Tower and the main borough walls.[48] Neighbouring parishes, too, were called upon to help both with the expense and with the labour. In October, for instance, the inhabitants of Bathampton and Claverton paid 17s 2d 'for two mens worke thirty dayes at the Bullworke at Bath' and later paid further sums totalling £3 5s 'towards the making up of the breaches in the works at Bath', having received 'a warrant from Captain John Burges (Bridges) Governour there'. In the same way, the village of Dunkerton paid money to 'Coll. Birch for Pioneers to worke at ye bullworkes of Bath'.[49]

As we have seen, Bath and its surrounding area had already suffered greatly, at the hands of royalist and roundhead alike, from the hated practice of free quarter. This suffering had, if anything, been intensified by the re-capture of Bath and the arrival of Colonel Birch's regiment of garrison troops. Bath and its neighbouring villages became the temporary home for over a thousand soldiers 'under the command of Colonel Burch'. The periods varied from four days to over a month. The same story was re-told at Twerton; at Dunkerton; at Combe Hay; at Hinton Charterhouse and at Stanton Prior (where the parish eventually claimed costs of 4d a day for each soldier billeted and 10d a day for a trooper and his horse). In addition to these burdens of free quarter, the same villages were also expected to provide regular financial contributions to the costs of the war and to suffer the requisitioning of supplies when demanded by Colonel Birch. Charlecombe, for instance, had twenty loads of hay taken in this way, while the people of Dunkerton were obliged to send provisions to Farleigh Castle.[50]

These tribulations were by no means ended with the departure of the main garrison under Colonel Birch in January 1646 or by the final removal in the following month of the skeleton force of two companies which had been left behind under Captain John Bridges.[51] In the early months of 1646, the western counties were alive with the constant movement of troops as the last groups of armed royalists were sought out and destroyed. These soldiers, with no local loyalty and little human sympathy, descended on Bath with monotonous regularity for temporary shelter and sustenance. By February, the citizens had had enough. The Corporation, meeting to discuss the grave situation, decided as a first step 'that a petition shall be preferred to the houses of Parliament for release of ffree quarter'. Two of their own councillors made the journey to London to deliver the petition by hand.[52]

At the same time more subtle methods were used to relieve the problem. The Mayor, John Biggs, wrote a personal letter to John Harington of Kelston, a good friend to the locality, imploring him to persuade his son, Captain Harington, to use his influence in the army on behalf of the city. In particular, he was asked 'to get favour from the Commander to spare further levies' in view of the city's terrible distress. Visits by previous troops had caused devastation in private homes as soldiers on the rampage had indulged in looting and wanton distruction. 'Our houses are emptied of all useful furniture, and much broken

The quartering of soldiers in Bath Abbey

and disfigured; our poore suffer for want of victuals', complained Biggs. 'We have now 400 in the town and many more coming; God protect us from pillage'. This personal approach clearly did more immediate good than the petition. Captain Harington eased the situation by bringing his own company to quarter in Bath so that he could take good care that local people were treated fairly.

A letter written subsequently by the Mayor to Captain Harington, expressing their gratitude for his efforts, gives a graphic picture of free quarter and its dramatic impact on the lives of ordinary people - even though Harington's presence had prevented 'such disorder as doth often happen, too oft, under soldier-like quarterings'. On the arrival of the troops, a levy was immediately demanded of the inhabitants based on 'the rate observed all over the west'. The demand was backed by the threat of pillage to those many citizens who 'had not monies ready'. Although Bath was spared the usual demand for conscripts on this occasion, it was nevertheless required to produce eighteen valuable horses for Harington's use. There was little plunder, 'excepting in liquors and bedding', but food set aside by families for the day's meal was taken at will by a troop from Marlborough (though 'they restored it again to many of the poorer sort'). The discomfort endured by local people in a tightly confined city seething with disreputable humanity cannot be overstated. Family life was disrupted ('our beds they occupied entirely'); city administration.was disrupted ('the Town-house was filled with troops'); and religious worship was disrupted ('the Churches are full of troops, furniture and bedding'). People lived in a state of fear, terror and suspicion. Even the Mayor was obliged to find a poor man to smuggle his letter to Harington: 'I dare not send a man on purpose on horseback, as the horse would be taken'.[53] Although the system of free quarter was to continue for several more years, Bath was shortly to be relieved at least of the need to maintain its fortifications. The Mayor and Aldermen received authority from the Committee of Both Kingdoms on 29th May 1646 to 'slight the works'.[54]

(c) Requisitioning

Although free quarter did much to damage the livelihood and morale of the rural community, the agricultural economy was much more seriously undermined by the common practice of requisitioning food, animals, equipment and farm labour. The greatest setback of all was for a farmer to lose his horse, which was vital not only for personal transport, but more particularly for work on the fields and carriage of goods to market. Claims abound in the parish accounts submitted at the end of the war for horses seized during the conflict and normally valued at about £6 0s 0d each. The Hundred of Wellow, for instance, lost a total of twenty-nine horses, including seven from Camerton and ten from the village of Wellow itself. Sometimes such property was temporarily 'borrowed' rather than permanently requisitioned such as the two horses from Corston 'prest by Sir William Waller's warrent and left att ye Devises' or the two horses from Norton St Philip which were loaned to Waller 'to carry ammunition from Bath and never returned'. Mention has already been made of the one hundred-and-sixty sheep stolen from Combe Hay. This practice was not uncommon in North-East Somerset, as the inhabitants of Whyttoymead found to their cost when a marauding company of soldiers 'kilde and carryed away 7 sheepe'. Animals, unlike furniture and equipment, could not quickly be repaired or replaced, and could scarcely be hidden. Farmers who suffered in this way, suffered more deeply than most.[55] In an attempt to silence the growing volume of complaints, parliament stipulated in May 1643 that in future officers needed to obtain the written authority of two Deputy Lieutenants or Commissioners before a horse could be taken. It had little lasting effect.[56]

The immediate harvest could also be ruined - and with it a substantial part of the farmer's income - by the thoughtless or deliberate actions of a visiting regiment. We have already seen how crops were recklessly trampled down by the gathering of Waller's army in Combe Hay. But soldiers could also requisition a meadow, thus depriving the farmer of valuable fodder for his own animals. Just before the Battle of Lansdown, for instance, Captain Butler's troop of horse, which formed part of Haselrig's Regiment, visited Hinton Charterhouse and did 'eat upp a meade of grasse belonging to Gyles Parsons', before moving on to Inglishcombe where they 'had freequarter in one meadow of John Clement for one whole day about mowing time'. Seed-time and harvest alike could equally be wrecked by a sudden demand from a local garrison for labourers and ploughs to work on the fortifications. Norton St Philip was called upon three times to provide a plough for three or four days to labour on the earthworks at Bristol, whereas Whitchurch was expected to maintain two men over a period of eight weeks 'for raising of the Bulwarks of Bristol'. Both Dunkerton and Inglishcombe, however, opted to pay money instead of releasing further workers in this manner from their already depleted landforce. [57]

Nor was the farming community any safer when crops had been finally harvested. A hungry troop could quickly sniff out their much-needed supplies. Newton St Loe suffered in this way when five loads of hay were taken for Sir William Waller's troops, two for Sir Arthur Haselrigg's cavalry and 'one load for Mr Ashe's own horse'. Widdow Hales of Littleton lost corn valued at £1 16s 0d to Waller's men just prior to the Battle of Lansdown, while on the same occasion the village of Whyttomead forcibly supplied 'two horse loade' of provisions for the army rendezvous on Bathampton Down. When, two years later, dragoons from the New Model Army came to reconnoitre Bath, Hinton Charterhouse was compelled to provide beer and provisions for their camp on Odd Down. In addition to these occasional demands from soldiers passing through the area, local communities were also obliged to send regular provisions to the garrisons of Bristol, Bath and Farleigh Hungerford. But even transporting supplies was a thankless task. When the parish officers from Combe Hay arrived at Farleigh Castle with provisions and money intact, having safely guarded their cargo with personal muskets, they suffered the indignity of having their muskets requisitioned at the same time. [58]

The requisitioning of a horse and supplies

These experiences were not unique. Donald Pennington and Ronald Hutton have both drawn attention to the plight suffered by communities throughout the country from plundering parliamentarian and royalist troops alike in the form of visiting field armies and local garrisons. Quite apart from the special levies demanded on arrival, the field army would also seize what it needed by way of equipment and supplies. Royalist officers were granted compulsory purchase rights on horses (although the 'purchase' part of the agreement was not always honoured), such as the 100 draft horses taken from Worcestershire in March 1643. Despite parliament's efforts to regulate the levying of horses for military use - the allocation for Manchester's army, for instance, was fixed at 6,500 from London and the South-Eastern Counties in 1643 - their instructions largely went unheeded by front-line commanders. In 1644, Tavistock was said to have been 'clean stripped of horses', while few at all could be found in Staffordshire. Such had been the loss of cattle in Buckinghamshire that, by the same year, farmers were showing a great reluctance to re-stock their lands. Little mercy or moderation was shown. The foraging party sent out by Lt. Col. Michael Jones in 1645 returned with 6000 sheep! Problems were particularly severe in 'corridor counties' like Worcestershire, which witnessed the frequent traffic of armies. The Governor of Worcester calculated that he had spent £1,813 in 1643 in assisting the passage of 'foreign' troops. Further trouble could be expected from armies retreating after a campaign, when discipline became ragged. Aston's horse, returning from Cheshire, plundered the district around Droitwich and Bromsgrove so severely that the inhabitants were unable to pay their monthly assessment. Some areas escaped lightly, like Kent, South Wales and East Anglia, but others were totally devastated by successive waves of plundering troops - especially north Nottinghamshire and Lancashire. John Morrill found evidence of 'systematic plundering' from thirty counties and petitions against the behaviour of the soldiers in twenty-two.

The people who suffered the most, however, were undoubtedly those who lived inside a garrison or in the area controlled by it. The tribulations suffered by the citizens of Bath in quartering a succession of garrison troops have already been described. Both sides used a system of main garrison towns, each supported by a network of satellites. This enabled them to control large areas of territory and to gather in supplies more easily from a hostile countryside. The aim was partly to ensure adequate sustenance for the garrison forces themselves and partly to stock-pile for the use of visiting field armies. Winton Castle in Hampshire, for instance, became a depot in 1645 for '15,000-weight' of cheese, '7000-weight' of biscuit plus large quantities of beef, pork, salt and beer. Even as early as 1643, an inter-locking network of thirty-four garrisons had been established in Shropshire, while the parliamentarian garrison at Newport Pagnell had received authority to set up a complicated system stretching over eight counties to support its 1500 men. The royalist garrison at Newark sent out foraging parties as far as Lincoln and Grantham in order to maintain its stocks, whereas Massey at Gloucester controlled an enormous area around the city through his subsidiary garrisons at such places as Stroud, Dymock, Strensham, Sudely, Beverstone and Slimbridge. An idea of the impact of this system on ordinary individuals is illustrated by the experience of one farmer living at Standish who was visited by soldiers from the Bolton garrison. He lost 24 steers, 9 oxen, 2 bulls, 10 calves, 15 pigs and 26 sheep at a personal cost of £81 2s 0d. The men who controlled these operations were career soldiers, not local gentry. By the end of 1643, the King had abandoned the idea of maintaining the war effort by using local leaders to encourage local populations. As Ronald Hutton remarks: 'Local gentry would hesitate to ruin their neighbours; geographical and social outsiders would not suffer this handicap. They served the war itself, and their only loyalty was to their commanders.' The experience of North-East Somerset in terms of plunder by visiting armies and requisitions by the Bristol network of garrisons was not untypical, therefore, of the country at large, although it probably avoided the worst extremes.[59]

(ii) Impact on the Citizens of Bath

Although the City Council continued to meet regularly throughout the whole course of the war, there is no doubt that the normal flow of life was badly disrupted during the years of royalist occupation (July 1643 to August 1645). An examination of the Bath Council Minute Books and Chamberlain's Accounts reveals that, in many ways, city life continued as normal when the parliamentarians were in control of the area. The majority of members of the Corporation were happy to work in close harmony with the garrison in maintaining all essential services and administration for the welfare of the community. The situation changed dramatically once the city had been taken by the King's forces after the Battle of Roundaway Down. Although outwardly co-operative, local people found themselves increasingly incensed by the demands of their new occupiers, particularly under the governorship of Sir Thomas Bridges.

A close analysis of the Chamberlain's Accounts over the ten-year period, 1637-1646, gives a clear indication of both the extent of the dislocation and the cost of the war in terms of the quality of life (see Table). Although the theoretical income of the Council remained fairly constant throughout the period, there is no doubt that it proved increasingly difficult for the Chamberlains either to collect all the rents due, or to finalise their accounts at the end of their term of office. John Parker, for instance, submitted even as late as 1649 'a note of rents yett behind and due to Chamber' from the year when he was Chamberlain in 1642. Similarly, John Atwood, who was Chamberlain between 1644 and 1646, did not finally settle his accounts until January 1649, again writing off a 'rent roll of several rents uncollected'.[60] This breakdown of basic administration, particularly during royalist occupation, is again illustrated by the fact that, whereas the Council granted an average of eleven freedoms a year between 1637 and 1643, there were only two recorded for 1644 and four for 1645. Property transfer also suffered in the same way. Although the accounts show a yearly average of 10.5 entries relating to fines and seals, this figure slumped to six for 1645 before rising dramatically to seventeen for 1646, when the city was again under parliamentarian control.

Bath's experience over this temporary breakdown of general administration and rent collection was not untypical of the situation elsewhere. In Bristol, for instance, it was estimated that about £200 in rent was 'utterly lost', because many had fled the city, leaving their homes unoccupied.[61] The Council in Gloucester also suffered a severe decrease in the amount of money raised in rent collection. Whereas there had only been a 5% deficit on the rent roll in 1641-2, this figure rose to 42.8% in 1643-4. Furthermore, in 1644-5, there was not only a deficit of £149 12s 11d for the year, but also a backlog of £242 6s 2d from previous years due in part to damage sustained by local property. As in Bath, the Council tried hard to keep the machinery of government intact and to concentrate on maintaining the flow of everyday life.[62] Great disruption, however, was encountered in Barnstaple, where the session court records ended abruptly in 1642, implying a takeover by military government; in Newcastle, where not only did numbers decline in apprentice enrollments and freemen admissions, but the Council itself fell into abeyance between 20th October 1642 and 28th March 1645;[63] and in Worcester, where no meetings of the Corporation took place between 29th August and 7th October 1642, but where meetings more than doubled in number thereafter as the war progressed.[64]

Council meetings in Bath were not in themselves halted. Indeed, during the first year of the royalist garrison, the Corporation met almost in a frenzy, calling an unusually high total of sixteen meetings. This compares with a mere six for the following year (1644-45) and eleven for the year following the recapture of the city by the New Model Army. Attendance by Aldermen and Councillors remained consistently good with an average of 17.5 for 1643-44 and 19.5 for each of the following two years, although one meeting on 30th June 1645 was cancelled - 'Nothing done because a full hall came not'. Individuals attended meetings with a fair degree of consistency throughout these three years with the exception of Henry Chapman, Philip Sherwood, Thomas Gibbs, George Chapman

BATH CHAMBERLAIN'S ACCOUNTS, 1637 - 46

Year Ending October	INCOME			EXPENDITURE				ANALYSIS OF EXPENDITURE UNDER GENERAL PAYMENTS (percentage of whole shown in brackets)					Balance in hand	No. of	
	Rents of Assize	Increased Rents	Casual Receipts	Stipend and Outrents	Gifts and Rewards	St. John's	General Payments	The Poor	Defence	Fabric	Water	No of Entries		Freedoms	Fines & Seals
1637	117.9.6	5.2.4	167.19.8	134.18.2	58. 5.11	39. 0. 0	68.17. 4	23.15. 5(34.5)	1.14. 0(2.4)	36.19.10(53.7)	8. 2.8	136	33. 8. 9	9	9
1638	117.4.0	5.2.4	231.17.3	134.18. 6	2.12. 6	52. 9. 2	212.17.11	34. 3.10(16.0)	6. 7.10(3.0)	81. 3.10(38.1)	18. 1.1	181	20.12. 5	11	12
1639	117.4.0	5.7.5	207. 8.6	134.18. 6	45.12. 8	37.18.11	148. 4. 9	22.10. 1(15.1)	24.16. 6(16.7)	6.19. 7(4.7)	11. 7.7	106	20.10. 6	9	10
1640	117.4.0	6.0.4	300. 7.8	142.14. 6	10. 4. 5	56.11. 2	178.18. 4	33.12. 8(19.2)	12. 5. 7(7.0)	13.12. 9(7.8)	5.18.1	160	56. 5. 0	13	17
1641	117.4.0	6.4.4	148.19.2	148.18.10	5. 2. 7	43. 1. 1	180.10. 1	50. 4. 8(27.8)	46. 7. 2(25.6)	27.12. 8(15.3)	17. 1.3	118	-	17	10
1642	117.4.0	6.9.4	219. 8.8	142. 9. 4	5. 3. 8	57. 4. 3	83.11. 6	34. 8. 0(41.1)	22. 1. 3(26.4)	8. 1. 2(9.6)	3. 4.2	118	89.11. 5	12	8
1643	117.4.0	6.9.4	119.17.6	144. 8. 0	5.12. 4	42. 8. 8	127.14. 2	53.19. 6(42.2)	50. 9. 7(39.5)	13.10. 1(10.5)	4. 5.1	148	52. 6. 6	7	8
1644	117.4.0	11.4.6	223. 0.0	142.13. 0	1.10. 4	50. 1. 5	116.12. 8	27.13. 0(23.7)	36.18. 6(31.6)	0.13.10(0.6)	8. 5.2	79	75.19. 3	2	9
1645	117.4.0	24.7.8	203. 1.8	140. 8. 4	-	37.14. 4	97.13. 3	28.15. 8(29.5)	54.11.11(55.9)	3.11. 2(3.6)	7.15.8	108	180. 2. 0	4	6
1646	117.4.0	24.5.2	302. 5.4	142. 0. 6	3. 7. 0	41. 9. 2	239. 2.10	41. 3. 6(17.2)	95. 4. 0(39.8)	27. 8. 3(11.4)	8.16.1	115	229.15.10	5	17

and Matthew Clift, all of whom were actively involved in the war effort for one side or the other. Two new councillors, Giles Long and Anthony Tanton, were elected in 1644.[65] There was therefore a clear desire by all members of the Council, whatever their own political inclination, to work together in maintaining the economy of the city and the necessities of everyday life.

They did not always succeed. Throughout the entire war, priority was given to public health, the markets, the common and, in basic essentials, the poor. Bath's reputation as a health resort had made local people noticeably conscious of the need to preserve their considerable advantages over such plague ridden cities as Bristol. Even at a time, therefore, when considerable neglect was affecting the rest of its fabric (see below), the Council took good steps to ensure that its pure water supply was kept intact. Although major improvements to the system were now out of the question, plumbers were regularly called in to mend the pipes as leaks appeared (even during the worst moments of royalist occupation) and Thomas Comming was paid an annual stipend of £1 6s 8d 'for lookeinge to the water on Walcotside. The proper disposal of sewage was of equal importance, particularly in a city crowded with soldiers, visitors and the poor. Although the Council Minutes have been destroyed for the years 1639 - 1643, it is significant that one of the earliest appointments recorded in the Spring of 1644 was that of Richard Riall as Scavenger. It was later agreed that he should be authorised 'to carry and spread the soile' on the Common, receiving 1d per load for doing so.[66]

After health, the opportunity to buy and sell in local markets was of prime importance to the producers and consumers which made up the community. Farmers, craftsmen, clothiers and innkeepers alike, who depended on the market for their livelihood, were not affected in the way so vividly portrayed in the propaganda report of *Perfect Occurrences:*

> 'What misery do the country people lye and groan under about the Bath and the Vizes in Somersetshire, and indeed in all places where the enemy hath power; No Faires, no wakes, no trading to any purpose, but the people driven from house and home and many villages looking like the ruines of Germany'.[67]

All the evidence points to the fact that trading continued uninterrupted in Bath, even if some aspects were curtailed by the war. Supervisors of Leather, for instance, were not appointed during the hostilities, whereas Aletasters and Supervisors of Fish and Meat were regularly nominated. The Council also maintained the fabric within the Market House itself, indicating at least some level of activity. A stook was bought for the 'Butchers' Shambells' and John Beacon was paid £1 15s 0d 'for worke done at the Markett house'. Nor was the control and organisation of the common, an important source of profit to the freeman, neglected at any time. The Council not only continued to appoint Overseers, Haywards and Supervisors of the Bounds, but also introduced new regulations in April 1645 which limited the use of the common for cattle until after the hay crop had been taken.[68] All-in-all, the leading citizens of Bath would certainly have concurred with the advice given to the Mayor of Chester in 1644 urging him 'to have a special eye to the preservation of the Markett.'[69] They were only too well aware of the fact that their existence depended upon it.

Those members of the community who were dependent on charity for their livelihood were also given a measure of priority by the local Corporation. Throughout the war, it fulfilled its obligation to maintain the staff and inmates at St John's Hospital, spending on average over £45 per year, a very similar figure to the pre-1642 total. In addition, it continued to make its regular annual payments to the poor of the city 'in bread at Lent', 'in coals at Michaelmas', 'in wood at Christmas' - together with further payments to inhabitants of two hospitals (St John's and St Catherine's) and the Alms House of St Mary Magdalene. Indeed, total spending on the poor (i.e. in addition to the financial support given to St John's Hospital) reached an all-time record of £53 19s 6d (or 42.2 per cent of the general payments made by the Chamberlain) between October 1642 and October 1643, the first year of the war (see Table). Quite apart from their regular donation of seasonal gifts, the Corporation in that year paid for new gowns to be made for the inmates of St Catherine's Hospital, for 'bread at lent above the ordinarie allowance' and for many casual acts of kindness. Twenty separate items were listed which helped to relieve individuals in distress, including soldiers injured, imprisoned or unwell: 'a shroud for James Bradly and makeinge the grave', 'cheese for the prisoners that were in St James Church', 'a shroud for a poor soldier', 'strawe for sicke and maymed souldiers', '10 dozen of bread to the prisoners' etc. [70]

The positive action undertaken by the Bath Corporation towards its poor throughout the war was echoed by the Council in Gloucester. Although hostilities there caused a fall in revenues for the local hospitals, every attempt was made to keep them going. Similarly, apart from a lapse in 1645, funds were also maintained for the supply of doles in wood and coal. The victims of war during the siege together with those who were drafted to work on the fortifications (and thus unable to provide for themselves) were relieved by a double poor rate. [71] At least resources were found in both cities to finance this vital task and the Councils there never resorted to extensive borrowing from charity endowment funds in order to subsidise the cost of war - as was the case in Worcester when, 'according to the Order Book, 'the revenue of this cittie is very small and the debtes of this cittie are very greate.' [72]

However, the two years of royalist occupation in Bath saw a dramatic fall in the total spent on relieving the poor - £27 13s 0d (or 23.7 per cent of general payments) in 1643-44, and £28 16s 0d (or 19.5 per cent) in 1644-45. Although regular payments were maintained, as already stated, the people who suffered most from the neglect of policy were impoverished individuals living outside the hospitals or almhouses. These people could previously have counted on the charity of the Council for immediate relief from a particular crisis, as in 1640 when Sly's daughter was clothed with a peticoat, waistcoat, shoes and stockings, or thirty-two poor widdows were give a shilling each, or Joan Edmonds had her chimney mended, or Goody Tysoe her windows glazed. There was little generosity of this nature between 1643 and 1645. Over the course of two years, only eight casual payments were made to individuals in distress, chiefly for shrouds or burials, including one for 'a stranger wch drowned in the kings Bathe'. Nor can it be argued that the Corporation was lacking in financial resources as a result of the war effort. The accounts show clearly that there was a large unspent balance which increased yearly between 1643 and 1646, reaching a peak of £229 15s 0d by the end of the war (see Table). It rather seems to suggest that administration became much more unreliable and irregular during the confusion caused by the royalist occupation; that the Council, though largely identical in composition and outlook, became either dispirited, disorganised or frustrated in its efforts to maintain its previous policies. [73]

This theory is further supported by the alarming neglect of the city fabric, which took place between 1643 and 1645. Bath had always prided itself on the splendour of its buildings as it welcomed its annual crop of visitors. Indeed, as a developing 'Spa Town', the city had probably done far more than most. Elsewhere, in the sixteenth and seventeenth centuries, the only major new buildings evident in towns were town halls - for instance, in Abingdon, Aylesbury, Exeter, Gravesend, Guildford, Leicester and Newcastle. Bath had gone somewhat further. [74] During the first part of Charles I's reign, the Council had invested in a major programme of development which had included a House of Correction (1623) and a new Guildhall and Market House (1626), a new 'Conduit House' (1636), replenishment of the Guildhall interior (1637), a major restoration of the city's water pipes (1638) and a costly tree-pruning operation (1638). Each year, in addition, the Chamberlain had regularly made generous payments to ensure that Corporation property did not deteriorate.

The tomb of Lady Jane Waller, Sir William's first wife, in the north transept of Bath Abbey. Built by the sculptor Epiphanius Evesham in 1633, it displays alabaster effigies of the couple and their two children. Their features were damaged by cavalier soldiers during the royalist occupation of Bath, 1643 - 1645.

Their interest centred particularly on the condition of the Guildhall, the Market House, the Baths, the Prison, the School, the House of Correction, the bridge, the walls, the roads and the gates. From an average annual expenditure on fabric of £26 17s 0d between 1637 and 1643, the total slumped to a mere 13s 10d in 1644 and £3.11s.2d in 1645, before rising again to £27 8s 3d in 1646. Just fourteen items were recorded during those two years as needing repair, including the Guildhall windows, the pound door, two locks and the School windows (the most regular item of all!).[75] It is possible, of course, that some buildings had fallen into disuse because of the war and did not therefore require such lavish attention. This was probably true of the School itself. According to his son, Thomas Rosewell had attended the School 'till the Civil Wars began to rage; And the King's Army taking that garrison, their school was broke up, and the youth were scattered'.[76] Many cities, of course, suffered a similar neglect of fabric during the war, particularly those that were frequently under siege. In Worcester, for instance, which had experienced considerable damage and destruction during the hostilities, the Corporation only spent on average £4 to £5 a year on repairs in the years 1642-1646. This figure rose dramatically to £101 9s 8d for the financial year 1646-47, when an energetic policy of reconstruction was pursued.[77]

There is another pointer to the reasons for disruption which clearly took place with the departure of the parliamentarian garrison - disruption which had affected the granting of freedoms, the transfer of property, the collection of rents, the care of the poor, the maintenance of council fabric and the continuity of education. The truth of the matter is that although ordinary people remained totally preoccupied with their own existence, the city council became - whether they liked it or not - totally obsessed with the defence of the city. Spending on the armoury, gates, walls, barricades and special guards rose from £1 14s 0d in 1637 (a mere 2.4 per cent of the council's general expenditure) to £54 11s 11d (or 55.9 per cent) in 1644-45, and £95 4s 0d (or 39.8 per cent) in 1645-46. The extent to which the war dominated the annual budget during the royalist occupation and discouraged other spending is emphasised by a close examination of the Chamberlain's Accounts. Whereas between 1637 and 1643 there were on average 138 general payment entries per year, in 1643-44 there were only 79 (including 30 on defence) and in 1644-45 just 108 (with as many as 71 on defence). These were the years when quality of life within the city suffered its greatest setback; when the Corporation lacked either the time or the inclination to deal with routine matters which normally were close to their hearts. They were certainly not lacking in money. The city could well afford the total of £350 16s 4d spent on defence during the ten-year period, 1637-46 (see the annual balance-in-hand shown in Table). Its spending on the poor during the same period (in addition to the support of St John's Hospital) was almost exactly the same (£350 6s 2d), whereas that on the repair of property, roads and water system slightly less (£312 12s 0d).[78]

Bath's comparative affluence throughout the war contrasts noticeably with that of both Gloucester and Worcester, though it must be remembered that both these cities suffered far more severely from prolonged siege. In Gloucester, the Council plunged from a credit balance of £213 19s 8d in 1639-40 to a deficit of £161 19s 7d in 1642-3. Thereafter, they remained seriously in the red until 1645-6, when something of a miraculous financial recovery was staged.[79] In Worcester, where 'civic insolvency was common enough even in time of peace', the Corporation's annual deficit rose from £249 10s 11d in 1642 to £606 14s 6d in 1645. It was forced not only to take up loans at 8% interest, but also to borrow heavily from charitable funds in their custody. Furthermore, part of the Corporation estate was placed in trust so that the debt of about £800 could eventually be paid off. One of the basic problems at Worcester was its low level of annual rents which, even before the disruption of war, only amounted to £104 14s 8d in 1641, in spite of a population of 7000. Bath, on the other hand, with just 2000 inhabitants enjoyed a rental of £123 4s 4d in the same year (see Table). During the five war years, whereas Worcester's *total* income averaged c£270 per annum, that in Bath amounted to c £363; and whereas the total expenditure incurred by the Worcester Corporation substantially increased during the years 1643-5 from its pre-war average (reaching a peak of £961.0s.4d in 1645), the expenditure in Bath over a similar period noticeably declined, in spite of increased spending on defence (see above).[80]

Anxiety over attack from without seemed to be prevalent in Bath even as early as 1639 with somewhat feverish activity to replenish the armoury within the Guildhall. The Chamberlain issued payments for new muskets, bandoliers, pouches, 'a spanish picke', barrells of powder, and 'reade cloth for the pickes'. John Gray, the corporation's armourer, busied himself with scouring the armour and repairing two muskets belonging to individual councillors. Expenditure that year leaped to £24 16s 6d. The following year (1640) saw the despatch of twelve local men on the 'Northern expedition', each equipped with swords and ten shillings in cash provided by the city council. It also heralded an era of anxiety and fear of attack as the Chamberlain made the first of many future payments 'for beare and for bread when the souldiers did watche the cittie'. By 1641, with anxiety fed by rumour, the corporation had realised the vital importance of ensuring that the fortifications were adequate to withstand a siege. In addition to the minor repairs which were undertaken at the North, South and East Gates, they ordered a major rebuilding of the wall in the north-eastern corner of the city, near the prison. This alone cost £36 0s 0d.[81]

Once the war had started, regular attention was paid to outer defences, internal security and weapon supply. During 1642 and 1643, all fortifications were further strengthened, especially at their weakest points. Barricades were erected outside the East and West Gates; breast works were dug outside the North and South Gates; the height of the city wall was raised at St James's Churchyard and considerable work was done on the platform at Gascoyne's Tower. All the gates were repaired - Matthew Clift was paid 'for keyes and mendinge the lockes of the Cittie gates', new bars were made for the North and East Gates, whilst a small door was walled up at Westgate House. One of the

Payments Imprimis payd for placing the Barrells of Match in the hall — 00-01-00

Item paid for mendinge a Locke — 00-00-04

Item paid for paper to make upp powder in — 00-00-04

Item paid for hoopinge the Markett pecke and two old Barrells to hold the Bulletts in — 00-01-00

Item paid to sev(er)all men for Timber for posts at the Chaines — 03-00-09

Item paid for Carriinge a Letter to Honad Streete — 00-01-00

Item paid Joseph Holder for cleansinge the way by the Burrowalls — 00-01-00

Item paid to Laborers for settinge upp and takeinge downe the Barricadoes at East and West gate — 00-08-06

Item paid for mendinge the Lanthorne — 00-01-00

Item paid for the Criers Coate and makeinge — 01-01-01

Item paid for bread and Beare for them that brought the great guns — 00-02-06

Extract from the Bath Chamberlain's Accounts, 1643

major difficulties, of course, was to offer some protection to the houses outside the North Gate in Walcot Street and Broad Street. Those in Southgate Street were already guarded by the gate on the end of the bridge. To solve this problem, the Council ordered metal chains to be made and erected across of the top of those streets. Christopher Brewer in Broad Street and Thomas Deane in Walcot Street were paid to look after the chains, which could be locked securely in position between wooden posts.[82]

The Council also sought to improve its armoury. Old muskets were repaired by Gray, who was paid for 'two new locks and six new cockes and other worke to the musketts'. Richard Bleckley was employed 'makeing staves for muskett rests', which Gray again completed with 'iron worke done to 12 rests'. 'Three paire of Bandaleers' were purchased to carry the charges of gunpowder needed by musketeers. Barrels of match, barrels of bullets and stocks of paper 'to make up powder in' were placed inside the Guildhall store. Then, in 1643, the city received some 'great guns' and a large magazine from Sir William Waller's army. Men were employed in 'drawinge up the greate guns from the bridge end' to the platform on Gascoynes Tower, where 'worke and iron about the carriages of the great guns' was completed. The powder and shot were carried up into the Guildhall, which now contained a sizeable stock. From this it was possible to send out supplies of powder, match and bullets to assist other garrisons like Malmesbury.

Apart from these practical improvements, the city authorities also endeavoured to increase the general state of alertness to the danger of attack. An 'extraordinary watch' was started as early as 1642 to supplement the work already being done by the regular nightly patrol. By 1643 three 'courts of guard' were in operation each night, one of them certainly based at the South Gate. Once the system had been organised, it cost the city an average of £3 10s 8d per month for 'wood, coale and candells'. But at least this eliminated some of the rather irregular payments made in the early days for such items as 'beare and fier at the Nagg Heade, there being a Court of Guard - 4s 6d'. Security was perhaps further strengthened by the purchase of 'a drume for the Cittie use' and the removal of the firebuckets from the Guildhall to a more central position in Stall Street.[83]

Bath was certainly not alone in making its anxious preparations against unknown threats from outside. Many cities had also been repairing defences and stockpiling arms over several months prior to the outbreak of civil war. As early as November 1641, for instance, the Corporation of Gloucester had ordered that, 'by reason the tymes are dangerous', twelve men were to keep watch and ward. Nor did their nervousness decrease. By February 1642, they had ordered sixty new muskets and other weapons; and, by August, they had not only spent £198 2s 5d on emergency work on the fortifications, including the purchase of new ordnance, they had also appointed a Committee of Defence 'to doo anythinge ... that they, in their discretion, shall conceive may concerne the defence of this City.[84]

The royalist occupation of Bath saw a dramatic increase in the number of special guards on duty in the city throughout the night, an indication of a growing sense of insecurity. Three regular courts of guards, comprised of local trained bands, were established at the North, West and South Gates under the command of Captain Henry Chapman and Captain Philip Sherwood, both members of the royalist faction on the city council. The corporation again provided the ordinary soldiers with 'wood, cole and candells' and their officers with 'wynn at the New Taverne' (owned, of course, by Henry Chapman).

Of greater significance, however, is the fact that council spending on these special guards escalated from £23 15s 1d in 1642-43, when the parliamentarians held the city, to £36 18s 4d in 1643-44 and £58 2s 5d in 1644-45 when the royalists were in control. Local people were therefore much more conscious of the intrusion of soldiers into their *daily* lives during the two years of royalist occupation. The garrison itself was distinctly edgy. One of its first tasks was to change the locks on the city gates![85]

Shortly afterwards, the Council agreed to a request that all the doors which had been made in the city wall by individuals from their private property should 'be damed up and taken away and the Hame gate to be alsoe damed up'. The Chamberlain then made payments for 'walling up gates and doors about the cittie wall', thus tightening further their security against attack. At the same meeting they decided that 'a Turnepicke be sett up at the Westgate or els the said gate to be walled up'. Eventually, they settled on a turnpike which cost them £3 1s 8d to manufacture. Concern over the growing restrictions to the free movement of local people was voiced at the Council meeting on 18th April 1645. It was therefore decided to erect a drawbridge at the West Gate 'to the end the same gate may be opened and left open for the general ease and use of the said cittie'. Although the Governor agreed to find the timber, the council levied a rate to pay for the cost of building.[86]

What is difficult to uncover in Bath however is the amount of daily discomfort endured by ordinary people as a result of the war and the intrusions of the garrison. Just occasional glimpses are revealed of the damage and debris that became part and parcel of everyday life. In 1652, for instance, Mr Ernley of Westgate House gained a rent rebate from the Council as recompense for the 'losse and damage suffered by reason of the Court of Guards kept there in the tyme of this City being a garrison'.[87] The inhabitants of Widcombe also had war damage on their minds when they petitioned the County Assizes in March 1647 - but damage to the 'three great travaylinge rode wayes' that ran through their parish. 'Since these unhappy warres', they stated, 'by reason of the often passage of armies and carriages through those wayes and want of tymely repaire, the wayes are growen soe ruinous that the inhabitants, being for the most parte very poore and eaten oute with free quarter, taxes, contributions, and billitinge of souldiers goinge to Ireland .... are not able sufficiently to repair them without some competent contribution from the said citty of Bath'.[88] The citizens of Bath had also suffered from the mess which armies had left on the narrow streets and pavements of the city. After the Battle of Lansdown, for instance, the Chamberlain paid men to remove what filth they could. A dead horse had to be dragged out of the water course, another out of a street corner. Richard Barnett and Barnaby Singer were rewarded for 'cleansinge the streets'.[89]

The discomforts experienced in Bath, however, were nothing compared with those in other cities, where the damage inflicted was often considerable. Particularly vulnerable at the time of an enemy advance were the houses of those people living outside the city walls. The Corporation of Leicester, for instance, issued an order on 19th April 1645 'for the necessary defence and safety of the towne and to prevent the enemys approache to the fortifications thereof.' Two hundred houses on the south side of the city were to be taken down and the ground levelled 'before Wednesday next'. Sudden homelessness continued to be a problem even after the war. In 1647, Sir Thomas Fairfax pulled down a further 120 houses in a move to strengthen the defences. The Mayor petitioned parliament on behalf of the poor men thus affected who were 'now destitute and exposed to much hardshipp and miserie'.[90]

A similar story applied in Gloucester, where a 1646 valuation of 241 houses destroyed during the siege was put at £28,720,[91] and in Worcester, where houses were 'pulled downe for fortifications'[92] by Waller in 1643 - a task undertaken by 400 of 'the ordinary sort of women out of every ward ... striking up with spades, shovels and mattocks ... in a warlike manner'. Nor was this the only damage inflicted. During the occupation of the city by a parliamentarian army of 15,000 under the Earl of Essex, the cathedral was sacked, the organ destroyed, the stained glass smashed and the library rifled. Furthermore, a later estimate of the cost sustained when the suburbs and hospitals were deliberately burned put the damage at £100,000.[93] Many towns had equally gruesome tales to tell. Churches were destroyed in Scarborough and also in Torrington, where a powder magazine stored in the church exploded.[94] In view of this evidence from elsewhere, it is fair to conclude that Bath escaped somewhat lightly. This was also the feeling of a visitor to Bath in 1646, who noticed the absence of serious damage and attributed it to the fact that 'Mars made it not his house but his thoroughfare, and rather baited than dwelt therein'.[95] The citizens of Leicester, Gloucester and Worcester had not been so lucky.

(iii) Impact on Traders.

According to one report, Bath's trade as a health resort was badly hit in the summer of 1642. Many of its regular clients apparently had already joined the King in York:

> "The inhabitants of Bath express great griefs that they have had little company this summer; they fear that their chief benefactors bend towards the north, and that cold climate makes them think the less of bathing, for having had recourse to the waters of Knaresborough, their heat is allayed. The poor guides are now necessitate to guide one another from the alehouse lest they should lose their practice. The ladies that are there are fallen into a lethargy for want of stirring cavaliers to keep them awake .... The poor fiddlers are ready to hang themselves in their strings for a pastime for want of other employments."[96]

Nevertheless, the indications are that, as a health resort, Bath was not thrown out of business once the civil war had started. Hot water baths and inns were very much in demand, even though the clientele was somewhat different. Visitors still came - but to cure mutilated limbs instead of aching joints. For their part, the Corporation ensured that the baths were maintained in good condition for their reception. Others arrived for political or military reasons, but they too helped to maintain the flow of life which ensured a steady livelihood for the traders, innkeepers, craftsmen, clothiers, and food producers of the locality.

Bath therefore remained a bustling and vigorous centre, attracting a large number of distinguished guests. Charles I, with 7,000 troops, stayed for a while in July 1644, when in pursuit of the Earl of Essex, who was campaigning in Cornwall. Earlier, in May, the City Council had bought special 'candells for the Queenes comminge to Towne'. Henrietta Maria was in fact on her way to Exeter, before leaving for France with her newly-born child. The King and Queen were both presented with plate by the Mayor and Corporation.[97] Their son, the Prince of Wales, stayed on a number of occasions in 1644, while Lord Goring arrived for a few days in April 1645 with the hope of curing 'his lameness'.[98] Perhaps the best example, however, of Bath's continuing fame as a health resort in time of war is the case of Sir Gervase Scroope in April 1644. The King felt so strongly that only the waters of Bath could revive his valiant servant, who was then in enemy hands, that he was even prepared to send a hostage to gain his temporary release:

> "His Majesty is informed from London that Sir Gervase Scroope's extreme indisposition of body, occasioned by his wounds is such, as according to his physicians, in probability nothing but the present use of the Bath can relieve him. His Majesty's pleasure is that you forthwith despatch a trumpet to the Earl of Essex to desire that Sir Gervase Scroope may have liberty to repair upon parole to take the benefit of the Bath. If that assurance will not satisfy, offer his son Mr Scroope to be sent to London as hostage for him till his return."[99]

Bath also gained heavily from the fact that political leaders of both sides found the city much more healthy to live in than Bristol. During the time of royalist occupation, refuse there was left to accumulate in the streets with an every-increasing stench. An observer wrote: 'the city itselfe is now so nasty and filthy that a traveller that comes out of the fresh aire can scarce endure it'.[100] Epidemics thrived in these conditions. 'The new disease is very hot in that city', commented one visitor, 'and neere 200 die weekly thereof, for which cause it is thought the King hath diverted his intention of going thither.[101] Both Charles and his son preferred the purer air of Bath where at least the water was uncontaminated and fresh from the springs. In 1645, for instance, a report reached London that 'the sickness increases fearfully in this city .... (so that) the Prince is resolved to remove upon Monday to Bath'.[102] Sir Thomas Fairfax, Major-General Skippon and General Cromwell were all to follow in his footsteps later in the year and were duly honoured by the Council on arrival with gifts of wine and sugar.[103] Bath's exceptional fortune in remaining an essentially healthy city throughout the seventeenth century was beneficial not only to the prosperity of the spa, but also to the welfare of its own citizens. Like Bristol, many towns frequently suffered from the scourge of the bubonic plague which devastated the population and ruined trade. Norwich had six major epidemics between 1579 and 1665; Bristol lost a sixth of its population on three occasions between 1565 and 1603; the epidemic in Newcastle of 1636-37 carried away over thirty per cent of the population, while that in Colchester took a toll of almost half the population in 1665-6.[104]

Business life in Bristol was also seriously disrupted by the garrison's need of new fortifications - 'and the tradesmen and other inhabitants are summoned in by tickets set up in severall places to shut up their shops and goe forth every Monday, Tuesday and Thursday for the raising of new fortifications .... There are at no time but few shops open in the City, for the most part scarce one in ten, the rest are gone away'.[105] At least the innkeepers, bath attendants, clothiers and shopkeepers of Bath did not have their business interrupted by the need to labour on the town walls.

Trade in North-East Somerset was, however, dislocated in one particular and vital way. The goods of west country clothiers were always liable to be intercepted as they made their way in convoy through hotly disputed areas like Wiltshire to the main markets in London. Trade certainly continued throughout the war years with routes becoming increasingly secure after 1644. Just how far production suffered is not clear, but the following report from the royalist newsheet, *Mercurius Aulicus*, of 16th March 1643 gives a glimpse of the difficulties. It also illustrates vividly the sort of cloak and dagger work that John Ashe was undertaking on behalf of parliament. His energy, spirit and organising ability impressed even the royalists who recognised him as one of the mainstays of the rebellion in Somerset:

> "Certain newes also came this day that Sir Arthur Aston [the royalist Governor of Reading] had seized on seven cart-loades, one waine-loade, and 24 horse loades of broad fine cloth, amounting in the whole unto 380 clothes, and that in many of the packs were found some *Belts and Bandoleers,* and great store of *Match,* and a considerable summe of *Money*. All which were sent towards London from one Mr Ashe, the greatest clothier in the Kingdome, as it is conceived, but of so turbulent a spirit and so pernicious a practicer in the maintaining and fomenting of this Rebellion, that he stands expected by His Majesty amongst some others, out of His Majesties genrall pardon for the County of Sommerset".[106]

A few days later, on 24th March, parliament sent a letter to the King's Committee at Oxford demanding the return of Ashe's cloth. Charles had, in fact, recently issued a proclamation granting free passage to merchants' goods in an attempt to prevent a complete breakdown of the economy. He now ordered the release of all goods seized by the Reading garrison to the various owners - except those belonging to Ashe. Parliament rather naively protested that they really could not understand why 'those cloaths belonging to Mr John Ashe, by what occasion they know not, are refused to be delivered'.[107]

From 'The Groot Boeck' of accounts kept by the Ashe firm in London between April 1640 and February 1643, we know that trade from North-East Somerset was certainly disrupted during the early months of the war. Whereas John Ashe had regularly sent a

The interception by royalist soldiers of a cloth convoy bound for London.

convoy up to London once a week until the end of October 1642, there were no deliveries at all from Freshford in November, only one in December, one in January and two in February. There is also a clear indication that the problem he faced was with delivery rather than production because, whereas he had been despatching an average of fourteen cloths a week from his own workshops, he suddenly sent fifty in one batch in December followed by a further forty-eight in the January consignment. The 80 cloths which were intercepted by the Reading garrison in March were clearly not all owned by John Ashe, although it is highly probable that he personally organised these convoys of goods destined for his brother's shop in London. The other local suppliers, who all feature in 'The Groot Boeck', were John Curle, Anne Davison and Jonathan Ashe of Freshford, together with James Ashe and Samuel Ashe of Westcombe. Whereas none of these clothiers managed to send any cloths through in November, John Curle, Anne Davison and Jonathan Ashe also failed to deliver their regular supplies in September and October.[(108)] There is little doubt that the disruption experienced in November 1642 was the result of the King's abortive attempt to regain London. Advancing with his army from Oxford, Charles reached Reading on 4th November before sending Prince Rupert out to take Brentford by storm eight days later. After the Earl of Essex had blocked his advance at Turnham Green, the King withdrew to Reading on 19th November before establishing winter quarters at Oxford. The route to London from Somerset, which was far too perilous for traders to use during those four frantic weeks, continued to be fraught with difficulty until the royalist garrison finally abandoned Reading on 18th May 1644.

In the meantime, North-East Somerset had fallen into royalist hands after their decisive victory at Roundaway Down on 13th July 1643. Both Bath and Bristol therefore housed garrisons loyal to the King until the arrival of the New Model Army almost exactly two years later. In view of the fact that markets continued to be held (see above), it is more than likely that the small independent clothiers of Bath and its surrounding area continued to make a living themselves - supplemented no doubt by their agricultural interests - and to provide some sort of livelihood for their dependent workforce of spinners and weavers. There is little doubt however that John Ashe, on an individual basis, suffered considerable loss as a result of the war. This was not entirely due to the interception of his cloth convoys by marauding soldiers. As one of the prime leaders of parliament's war effort in Somerset, he was a marked man. Wisely, therefore, he withdrew from Freshford and based himself in London until the local hostilities were brought to an end, occupying his time from September 1643 as a member of the Goldsmith's Hall Committee responsible for the sequestration of royalist estates. It is hardly surprising, therefore, his enemies took advantage of his absence to vent their spite on his property in Somerset and Wiltshire.

Ashe himself later claimed that he had 'lost ye greater part of his personal estate and 3 whole years revenue of his lands by ye plunder and cruelty of ye said enemy'.[109] In the light of Ashe's own claim in 1637 that his absence in London attending a summons of the Privy Council had seriously imperilled 'the livelyhoods and welfare of thousands of his poore people, his workfolks'[110] who totally/depended on his personal direction, it seems likely that his cloth business in the Freshford area suffered serious damage from his enforced exile. There is, however, no hint in his petition to parliament for compensation in July 1646 that his business was totally destroyed or that his machinery was vandalised.[111] In view of the fact that he itemised claims for every other type of loss, it seems unlikely that he would have spared himself from including an area so dear to his heart. It is more probable that the business itself continued to run throughout the war under the direction of his wife, Elizabeth, as it did after his death in 1659 - for he bequeathed to her, rather than to his sons, his 'utensells for trade'.[112] Even after the recapture of the area by the New Model Army in 1645, Ashe continued to spend much of his time in London as a Member of Parliament and a leading member of various committees - and yet, as already described, his business went from strength to strength. It had clearly become far less dependent on his own personal supervision.

The cloth trade of North-East Somerset was by no means unique in the dislocation it suffered throughout the war. Traders in most areas faced a similar problem, especially after the King's prohibition of trade with London from the summer of 1643. In the face of this severe threat to their livelihood, clothiers from Wales, Worcestershire and Gloucestershire petitioned the King. Although he eventually compromised by issuing special licences to trade across areas held by his troops, local garrison commanders continued to intercept convoys bound for London. Worcestershire clothiers had their horses and cloths seized en route for the capital in 1644; west country clothiers, escorted along country lanes by parliamentarian guards, were nevertheless intercepted by the Banbury garrison in 1645, losing 72 woolpacks in the process; Wiltshire clothiers, even after paying the toll money demanded, still lost the whole of their consignment to the Wallingford commander in 1645.[113] The citizens of Worcester, who had petitioned the King 'for freedom of trade for the cytie to London' in 1643, were so frustrated by the end of the siege that they threatened to throw the soldiers over the walls or to club them to death if they rejected the surrender terms, 'being now, as all quiet people are, weary of war, desiring their trading may go on'.[114] Even local trade had been badly affected with the closure of markets, like Shrewsbury, and the suspension of fairs in such places as Bristol and Evesham, 'where the fair should have been kept, but the King, Prince Rupert and their force, coming in about 12 o'clock, spoild the Faire'.[115] However, perhaps the most humiliating loss suffered by clothiers and traders occurred in Chester in October 1645, when Lord Byron took emergency measures to strengthen the defences of the city. He ordered his men to take 'what quantities of coarse woole he pleased to be made into packs, and imployed in filling up the breaches'.[116] At least the clothiers in Bath were spared that particular anxiety.

The account books of the Ashe firm of clothiers in London not only cease, but are quite deliberately rounded off at the end of February 1643 - a sign perhaps of a feeling that the dislocation of supplies from Somerset had become too serious a matter. Nevertheless, a 'Notebook of Debts owing to Grace Ashe' dated 1646, indicates that the firm itself continued throughout the war. Indeed, at the very time when the North-East Somerset clothiers were experiencing difficulty in managing delivery, business was booming for the Ashe firm in London. Whereas they had sold on average 90.3 cloths a month at a total cost of £1925 between January 1641 and October 1642, their sales figures jumped dramatically to an average of 102.6 cloths a month valued at £2240 between October 1642 and February 1643 - perhaps an indication that armies were beginning to clothe their troops in a systematic manner.[117]

Local clothiers and other traders clearly benefited from orders placed by army officers and garrison commanders as they set about the task of equipping their forces. Although recorded evidence is thin, at least two Bristol-based customers of the Ashe firm in London picked up welcome orders from troops under the command of John Fiennes, Colonel of a Regiment of Foot and Captain of a Troop of Harquebusers. Michael Pope and Richard Horton had each purchased cloth from James Ashe before the outbreak of war for re-sale in their drapery businesses. Spurred on by the advance of the royalist army under the Marquis of Hertford and Sir Ralph Hopton in the summer of 1643, Colonel Fiennes was clearly anxious to ensure that his men were adequately clothed for their operations in North Somerset. Various drapers, including Pope and Horton, were therefore called upon to provide cloth worth £106 16s 8d in all, while mercers, Robert Flower and James Powell, supplied other goods valued at £74 2s 11d. Unfortunately, a few days after these items were delivered, Prince Rupert took Bristol by storm. In the resulting confusion, the debts remained unpaid and these transactions with Bristol traders merely listed in the accounts of Colonel Fiennes as 'money owed'.[118] Such were the opportunities and frustrations provided to local businessmen by the war - frustrations echoed even as late as 1662 by Bath butcher, John Russell, who, in a petition to the Bath Corporation requesting reimbursement, complained that 'in the last late warres upon the comeing of the King's Army into this cittie, he delivered by order of the then Mayor and Justices so much beef unto the Constables of this Cittie for provision of the said Army as came to the value of three pounds and 15 shillings'.[119]

There is clear evidence from other parts of the country that some manufacturers and tradesmen reaped substantial benefits from the war as armies moved around in search of uniforms and equipment. The ironworks of Dudley and Stourbridge were commissioned to cast bullets and cannon balls for the royalist commanders, while the forges of Worcestershire and Shropshire manufactured tons of cannon, grenades and pikeheads for the King's field army at a cost of £1074.[120] In Bristol, the Council submitted to the King's demand by providing 1500 pairs of shoes and stockings from local craftsmen - even though they were paid for by means of a weekly levy on the populace.[121] A major garrison could provide considerable employment for local workers. The Reading garrison, for instance, called on resident traders to supply over 3000 coats, shirts and shoes, while, in Warwick, one cattle dealer charged the garrison £335 for beasts, hides and tallow within the space of six months. In Bewdley, the local haberdasher won a contract to supply parliamentarian forces with Monmouth caps for twenty-three shillings a dozen. Oxford became the centre of a supply system for the royalist cause. Contractors organised metal-smiths, gunsmiths and swordmakers who bought up raw materials over a wide area in order to satisfy the demand. The construction and strengthening of fortifications in many cities created an urgent need for tools and raw materials, including lime, coal, lead and timber, not to mention the local expertise of masons, carpenters and blacksmiths.[122] Perhaps the best illustration, however, of the benefit gained by local tradesmen comes from London where, between August and October 1642, the sum of £6502 3s 4d was spent on equipping the train of artillery in Essex's army with tools and equipment. John Pace, one of many shopkeepers listed, provided 200 shovels, 24 scoops,

100 baskets, 50 lanterns, 12 pails and 12 pickaxes for £24 14s 4d; Richard Yates sold 200 hedging bills for £21.13s.4d; and Thomas Fossam supplied shot, nails, paper, sheepskins and lintocks for £21.[123] In view of what visibly happened elsewhere, it is perfectly reasonable to assume that manufacturers, craftsmen and traders in North-East Somerset greatly benefited from resourcing the war effort, even if the demand from the Bath garrison was on a slightly smaller scale.

❖ ❖ ❖ ❖ ❖ ❖

How badly, then, was the community of North-East Somerset affected by the war? There is no doubt that the war caused temporary disruption to daily routine and economic activity. There is also no doubt that the war seriously reduced the quality of life for both countrymen and townsfolk, all of whom were forced to endure discomfort, humiliation, anxiety and deprivation at the hands of soldiers. Villagers looked on with disgust as their homes were turned into barracks; citizens watched with horror as their health resort was transformed into a garrison. Fabric was neglected, privacy lost and morale lowered. But more than anything, the hostilities induced a state of war weariness and a deep loathing of military intrusion.

Nevertheless, in spite of it all, the markets continued to function, the health trade was revived, the cloth industry survived and the people were fed. There was disruption, discomfort and disgust, but no permanent damage. Even Bath's fortifications escaped largely unscathed. The records which exist give no hint of large-scale unemployment or food shortage within the war period. In some ways, of course, army recruiting-officers helped to solve the problem of unemployment and poverty by mopping up surplus labour from the countryside. But the people themselves were resilient. After all, to a community accustomed to natural disasters, harvest failure and unemployment in the 1620s and 1630s, the Civil War was just one further set-back to normal life. The area's inbuilt affluence, epitomized by the City of Bath's constant balance-in-hand, enabled it to survive this latest crisis in the series.

Even the agricultural community enjoyed a hidden benefit which made belt-tightening over a limited period not too uncomfortable an experience to bear. The system of land tenure, which operated in North-East Somerset, was based on the granting of land on long leases, normally for three lives. These lifehold tenancies provided the landlord with income not so much from annual rents, which tended to be minimal, but from sizeable fines which were paid when a new life was added to the lease. These arrangements, which were protected by manor cutom, were very beneficial to the tenant during a period of inflation or economic crisis, because the landlord was unable to raise the rent to its true market value. For instance according to surveys taken at the time, the real value of 329 acres in Walcot was £343 per annum in1638, whereas the actual rent produced was just £10 3s 10d; similarly, the Lord of the Manor of Farmborough drew only £33 14s 9d in income from 1188 acres in 1630, in spite of the fact that the open market value was £387 5s. It is perhaps significant that Farmborough, which suffered all the usual hardships during local hostilities, put in a claim later for war compensation which amounted on average to a mere £57 5s 6d per annum. [124] Local people in general therefore were able to absorb the costs of the war comfortably without permanent hardship or distress.[125]

7
The Community in the Aftermath of War, 1645-50

(i) Clearing up after the war

The recapture of Bath and the ending of the war gave the Corporation a long-awaited opportunity to undertake a series of much-needed repairs. Although Bath itself had never been the centre of bitter fighting or the target for destructive siege guns, damage had been caused by the movement of armies and the sheer neglect of the fabric. What money the city had had at its disposal throughout these four years of turmoil had been largely devoted to essential military and human needs. Now at last, the councillors could afford to work more generously at the broader requirements of a war-weary city.

Between 1645 and 1647, therefore, priority was given to the task of restoration. Work was done at the Bridewell and windows were mended at the Black Alms House (where the paupers also received ten new gowns); the School House door was repaired; the cobble-stone surround at the Hot Bath was re-pitched, and new padlocks bought for the King's Bath. The Market House and Guildhall were given a similar face-lift. New tiles and two lead gutters were placed on the roof; a new rope was purchased for the market bell, while three new mats, two pewter chamber pots, an inkstand and two iron dripping pans were added to the internal furnishings.

A great effort was also made to improve the appearance of the streets. Highway repairs were carried out in Southgate Street, Binbury Lane, Westgate Street and the Market Place, while Thomas Bullman was paid 'for makeinge a hedge under the Burrowalls'. Considerable work was also undertaken on the bridge - the scene, of course, of hand-to-hand fighting when the city was re-captured in July 1645. Thirty-four loads of stone and gravel were used and two hundred and eight yards of pitching was done on the surface of the road. At the same time a man was paid 'for takeing up of the stones out of ye water that fell from ye bridge'.[1]

The city's piped water supply had also clearly suffered from neglect during the war. Much effort now went into making it fully serviceable again so that privileged individuals could recover their benefits. Thus pipes were mended, in 'Saunders ground, at Thos. Phelpes doore .... at Mr. Clifts doore'. The general public benefited, too. Rails were erected at the conduit in Stall Street, stones were laid at the Upper Swan conduit, improvements were made at 'the water works', while many pipes were dug up, 'soldered' and re-buried. The impression generally was one of feverish activity aimed at restoring the peaceful life of the city.[2]

There is, in addition, a clear indication that the suffering and turmoil of the last four years had served to jog the community as a whole out of a complacency brought about by years of prosperity. When the war ended, therefore, there was a general determination not only to restore that quality of life which had temporarily been lost, but to improve it. Under such stimulus, the Corporation at long last- took advantage of the powers conferred on them by Elizabeth's revised charter. Thus after a lapse of over half a century, they acted on their right to 'frame and execute local laws for the good-ordering of the city'. These bye-laws were first drawn up on 2nd September 1646[3] before being finally ratified on 28th October 1650.[4] They dealt with such matters as controlling the ordinary citizens,

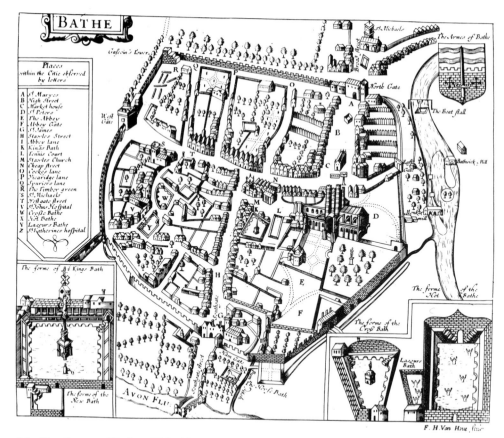

John Speed's map of Bath, published in 1610, shows a small compact medieval city with houses largely situated within the walled area.

restricting the trading activities of the town, regulating the members of the Corporation, administering the property under their jurisdiction, improving the management of the baths, cleaning the streets, removing nuisances, controlling the market, expelling certain kinds of undesirable inhabitants, rewarding the officers of the city and appropriating the goods of felons.[5]

A particular attempt was made to control the activities of traders. Indeed, because the charter decreed that 'no foreigner should sell or put to sale within the city .... any merchandize (except in the market or fair) without license of the mayor', it was first of all stipulated that only freemen would be permitted to keep a shop. A person who was privileged to be in this category would in future not be allowed to 'open his shop or shop-window or sell any wares or commodities upon a Sunday, upon pain to forfeit for every such offence three shillings and four pence to the use of the poor of the parish where the offence should be committed'. Butchers came in for special consideration. They were not to bring any live beasts into the city for slaughter on a Sunday. Furthermore, in order 'to prevent improper meat from being sold in the city', they were also banned from bringing pork into the market 'till St Michael's day' and ram mutton 'from St Lawrence's day to All-Saints day' - under penalty of six shillings and eight pence for every pork or ram so brought for sale.[6] A careful check was also maintained on other traders in the market - the butter scales were repaired, a new corn-measure purchased and an inspector employed 'to vew the Cornebuyers'.[7] The Supervisors of Fish and Meat, the Aletasters and the Supervisors of Leather continued to do their work, but with a more watchful eye.

The Corporation showed similar concern for the condition of the streets and the purity of its water supply. In future no person would be allowed to water horses or other animals at the city conduits or within twenty feet of them; nor could they wash their clothes there or even in the open streets of the city. Both contamination and stench were to be avoided at all costs if Bath was to enhance its growing reputation as a health resort. Consequently, in what is possibly the first recorded parking restriction, no-one was permitted to 'tie or feed, or suffer any kind of beast to stand in any of the said streets (except at farriers doors) above the space of one quarter of an hour'. Animal dung could quickly sicken the atmosphere in the confined area of the city. The householder, too, faced much stricter regulations over his own refuse. He was prohibited from throwing 'any soil, dung, filth or carrion, in or near any open street .... which shall be offensive to such street'. He was also required to 'sweep and make clean the street before his house every Saturday, on pain of forfeiting one shilling for every offence, to be applied towards repairing and cleansing the said streets.[8] There is real evidence, too, that these fines were put to good use; Barnaby Singer was henceforth regularly employed by the Council in 'makinge cleane the streets'.[9] Similarly, butchers were not permitted to kill their animals in the streets or 'hang out any flesh, newly killed, so as to soil and annoy the said streets' nor could they allow their pigs to wander about freely.

At the same time the Corporation made a determined effort to exercise a tighter control over the very considerable amount of property it owned within the precincts and environs of the city. Many abuses had clearly crept in during the wars concerning both the terms of leases and the collection of rent. It was vitally important that these should now be rectified. In the first place, ownership of virtually all the buildings gave it considerable power over the type of people who were permitted to live in Bath. Recent experiences confirmed the desirability of this selective process. It was therefore decreed in the bye-laws that leases would only be granted by the Corporation at quarterly meetings; that they would only be issued either for a total of twenty-one years or for a period of ninety-nine years spread over three lives; that such leases should not be transferred to another person 'without a license in writing first obtained from the Corporation'. Thus in October 1647 William Chapman was granted the lease of a tenement and garden for the lives of his children Robert, John and Katherine.[10] In this way the Council was able to keep the city very much 'within the family' of people known or recommended to them personally. Furthermore, no inhabitant was to be allowed to take in lodgers or under-tenants without the Council's permission.[11]

But the Corporation and townspeople were not allowed to forget too quickly the requirements of war. After the fall of Bristol, Bath had been left with a garrison force of one infantry regiment, numbering just over a thousand men, under Colonel Birch as Governor. During the autumn of 1645 conditions in the west remained uncertain, even though the New Model Army successfully continued its mopping-up campaign of royalist strongholds. It was therefore important, at least until tension eased, to maintain the outer defences of the city. The Corporation itself spent money on repairing damage to Gascoyn's Tower and the main borough walls[12] Neighbouring parishes, too, were called upon to help both with the expense and with the labour. In October, for instance, the inhabitants of Bathampton and Claverton paid 17s 2d. 'for two mens worrke thirty dayes at the Bullworke at Bath' and later paid further sums totalling £3 5s. 'towards the making up of the breaches in the works at Bath', having received 'a warrant from Captain John Burges [Bridges] Govenour there'. In the same way, the village of Dunkerton paid money to "Coll. Birch for Pioneers to worke at ye bullworkes of Bath'. [13]

However, in January 1646, the Committee of Both Kingdomes in London (which was responsible for the running of the war) decided that the Bath garrison would be better employed in assisting in the attack on Hereford. Colonel Birch was therefore ordered to march out with this regiment, leaving behind the big guns of Gascoyn's Tower and two companies of foot - about two hundred troops in all with Captain John Bridges as the new

The army continued to intrude into daily life after the hostilities ceased.

Governor. Major-General Skippon, the Commander of the Infantry in the New Model, was at the same time warned to keep a watchful eye on Bath now that it was virtually unmanned - 'Therefore take care that Bath be not possessed by the enemy till the works there can be slighted, which we have determined shall be done so soon as the season of the year will permit'[14] By 2nd February, it has been decided to withdraw both the guns and the two remaining companies of soldiers for service at Hereford.[15] Bath was therefore left without an official garrison force.

It was not however until later in the year that the city was at last relieved of the need to maintain its fortifications. Action to 'slight the works' which had been promised as early as January, had still not been taken by 11th May when the Corporation met to discuss the matter. It was decided that 'a letter be sent to Mr Ashe to procure an order from Parliament for slighting the garrison within this Cittie with all speed'.[16] James Ashe acted without delay and clearly used all his father's enormous influence in the House to secure the wishes of his constituency.

Shortly afterwards, on 29th May, the Committee of Both Kingdoms wrote to the Mayor and Aldermen of Bath stating that, as the need for a garrison had ended, they should start work immediately on dismantling 'works and fortifications'. While these remained intact, there was always the danger that they would suddenly be seized by a group of royalists.[17] The Bath Chamberlain's Accounts bear some evidence that this task of demolishing the earthworks outside the main gates and removing other specially erected barricades was completed without delay. Payments were certainly made 'for pooleing upp the rayles at the Towne Walls' and 'to the workmen for bringinge the bords from the Mounts'. The drawbridge over the earthworks at the South Gate was also removed and the normal road re-made. In spite of these changes, however, the Council continued to keep the city walls and main gates fully maintained during the coming years. The armoury, too, was re-stocked for future emergency. Seventeen muskets and a broken sword were repaired; over twelve pounds of gunpowder, one pound of match and twenty-eight pounds of bullets (at 3d per pound) were bought to replenish the stores.[18]

Nevertheless, Bath had at least freed itself from the outward symbols of war. The garrison had gone and the earthworks had been dismantled. The citizens now longed for peace and a return to normal life. Although they had come to hate the sight of soldiers, they still continued to show gratitude to the leaders of the parliamentarian army. Sir Thomas Fairfax, Major-General Skippon and General Cromwell were all honoured on their arrival with gifts of wine and sugar, while the local heroes were not forgotten. William Prynne received 'two quarts of sacke' and Alexander Popham, perhaps doing best of all, accepted 'one gallon of claret, one loafe of sugar and 1 ounze of Spanish tobacco'.[19] Even though local people wished to forget the war, they did not forget the cause for which it had been fought.

Oliver Cromwell (1599 - 1658), cavalry commander in parliament's New Model Army in 1645 and a visitor to Bath at the end of the war. Portrait after Samuel Cooper.

This feeling, coupled with a genuine desire for the settlement of the Kingdom, probably accounts for the large-scale celebrations which took place in the city during the spring of 1647. It coincided with the news that the King (who had surrendered himself to the Scots) had now been handed over to parliament. At that moment he was being held in honourable confinement at Holmby House in Northamptonshire, where negotiations for a return to normal government were then taking place. The Bath Chamberlain's Accounts give clear hints of a general rejoicing at the thought of the coming peace. Stirridge was paid 'for beating the Drume, the 23rd of March' - presumably to launch the celebrations to which, not only the local people,but also men from Keynsham, Newton St. Loe, Batheaston, Swainswick and Saltford had been invited. Certainly '2 barrells of beare of 18 gallons' were placed in the streets, while one pound of tobacco and three dozen pipes were 'given then to Keinsham men'. Meanwhile, the local dignitaries - the Mayor, the Justices of the Peace and high-ranking army officers - were having their own celebrations (at the Corporation's expense) in The Hart. [20]

(ii) The Struggle between Local Radicals and Moderates.

The part played by members of both the local gentry and Bath Corporation during the civil war has already been described in Chapters Two and Three It has been suggested that the community of North-East Somerset, though divided in its loyalty, remained consistent in its attitude throughout the hostilities. With the exception of Sir William Bassett, none of the local leaders previously mentioned could stand accused of being either a turncoat or a neutral. On the royalist side, Henry Chapman's faction continued their struggle against the puritan elite long after the war had ended (see below), while Sir Ralph Hopton served his master to the bitter end, eventually dying as an exile in Bruges in 1652. The reappearance of Horner, Ashe and Popham as leaders of a second popular rising in 1645 in favour of parliament was a clear indication that the 'Mendip Spirit', which had been kindled in 1642, had been kept alive during the years of royalist occupation. Leading members of the local puritan elite, including both the gentry themselves and Matthew Clift's faction on the City Council, possessed the same militancy that characterised the 'war' party in parliament. Although they remained, throughout the conflict, largely 'Presbyterian' in religion, they emerged increasingly as being 'Independent' in politics. For them, a victory in the war was vital to safeguard their religion, their values and their culture. It is not without significance that the only local people indicted for treason by the King between 1644 and 1646 were Alexander Popham, Edward Popham, John Ashe, Samuel Ashe and John Horner from the gentry and Matthew Clift and Edward Parker from Bath Corporation. These, more than any, were the men who had spearheaded the rebellion in North-East Somerset. [21]

Once the war was over, however, their political attitudes gradually changed. Moderation, rather than militancy, became the dominant feature in their outlook, although individuals within that wartime alliance shifted their stance at varying rates. North-East Somerset, during the period 1645-1649, echoed the revulsion felt throughout the whole county to the oppression of military rule linked with a general yearning to return to the stability of traditional forms of county government. Discussions in July 1646, for instance, at the Council of War for the army operating locally, portray a county increasingly hostile towards the County Committee over troop outrages. 'If they lie above a night in a place, the country rise' they observed. It was little comfort that soldiers found guilty were harshly punished - Captain Edward Starkey and six others imprisoned 'for several robberies upon the high waie' in North Somerset; trooper Robert Bird, hanged for murdering 'a countryman' at Hinton St George; trooper Tobias Grey, 'burnt through the tongue with a hot iron' for cursing, swearing and profaning. [22] Local people were totally weary of these intrusions. Leadership within the area, therefore, gradually took on a new role, namely that of challenging and controlling a dominant radical minority which had ruthlessly seized power within the county towards the end of the war.

Amid the confusion that reigned in Somerset from 1645 and in the absence of any legally-appointed justices, there was only one body capable of maintaining any semblance of local government - the County Committee. Its business included the sequestration of royalist estates, the payment of hardship allowances to those who had suffered in the war, the collection of taxes (until 1647), the control of the militia, the maintenance of law and order (until new justices were appointed in (1646) and the removal of unsuitable clergy.[23] Membership of this new omnipotent body had been transformed in character since its inception in 1642. Whereas previously it had been dominated by the families of well-established gentry, under changes made necessary through natural wastage new members had been recruited from widely differing backgrounds. These consisted of not only men of local stature (including Alexander Popham, Edward Popham, Sir Edward Hungerford and Samuel Horner) and eminent lawyers (including William Prynne), but also men of much humbler birth - minor gentry, yeomen, maltsters, merchants and drapers (including Matthew Clift).[24] From 1645, this newly constituted Committee came increasingly under the control of Colonel John Pyne of Curry Mallet - the very same man who had been defeated at Marshall's Elm, while trying to bring reinforcements to assist Sir John Horner outside Wells in 1642. Pyne and Horner now found themselves in political opposition as the Committee became deeply split over the burning issues of the day. On the one hand, Pyne's radical faction (which included the Pophams, Matthew Clift and many of the more obscure members) advocated vigorous action against both royalists and episcopal clergy and the speedy enactment of a 'godly reformation'. On the other hand, the moderate faction (which included Sir John Horner, William Strode, John Ashe and William Prynne) campaigned for a compromise settlement with the King and the gradual healing of old wounds within the framework of county society.[25]

In spite of repeatedly determined efforts by Horner, Prynne and Ashe to baulk the designs of the radical minority, Pyne skilfully outmanoevred them at every turn. The moderates had already lost one of their most respected members from the north-east of the county, John Harington, who withdrew from the Committee in 1645 because he wished to avoid entanglement with factions. Although his diary shows that he was particularly friendly with John Horner, John Ashe and William Prynne, his political views - according to Margaret Stieg - were 'more consistent with the Middle Group' in parliament than with those of either the Presbyterians or the Independents. Anxious above all to keep his integrity and his freedom of action, he steered clear of political groupings and became instead 'a true independent'.[26] The loss of Harington was further compounded by the frequent absence in London of Ashe, who was Chairman of the Committee for Compounding, and Prynne.

This left Sir John Horner to bear the brunt of the resistance to Pyne's policies. Horner, a man of immense prestige within the local community, in many ways epitomised the old 'country' attitudes. Although he advocated moderate reform in state and church (including the replacement of episcopacy by the presbyterian form of religion), he also believed in 'the ancient and fundamental laws of the Kingdom' which would ensure that reform was brought about through constitutional means. He, like the majority of people in Somerset, looked for the restoration of the old framework of society and, with it, the return of stability and order. He was therefore deeply distrustful of Pyne who was far less compromising in his attitude and far more committed to the doctrine of change, even if that implied the use of non-constitutional methods.[27] Furthermore, although Pyne was himself a Presbyterian in religion, he associated closely with Quakers, Independents and Baptists, showing a willingness to tolerate and encourage those of a more extreme persuasion.[28]

The first round in the struggle for power undoubtedly went to Horner. The 'recruiter' elections of 1645, designed to fill fourteen vacancies caused by death or expulsion from the Long Parliament, provided an opportunity for Pyne's faction to strengthen their influence and for Horner's group to challenge it. The prestigious county election on 1st

December produced four candidates - George Horner (Sir John's son) John Harington, William Strode and Henry Henley (Pyne's candidate). As High Sheriff, Sir John Horner was responsible for the organisation and control of the election - and he had no intention of allowing his son to suffer defeat! As soon as the freeholders had convened at Ilchester, Horner adjourned the election to Queen Carmel, some four miles away, on the pretext of plague. Strode and Henley, believing that Horner would repeat the ploy until the freeholders had been exhausted, decided to boycott the election. George Horner and John Harington were subsequently elected unopposed.

A written objection to the Commons concerning the conduct of the election was signed by John Pyne, Edward Popham and twenty-two other members of their radical faction (but none from North-East Somerset). In it they described the High Sheriff's action as 'one of the saddist and most unpardonable breaches made upon this county' and condemned 'the greate scandall and discoragement given to the well affected party .... many having travelled on foote above thirty miles, notwithstanding the extremity of the weather'. They resented the undermining of the freedom of the election, which had prevented their 'free choyce' of Henley and Harington, 'for whom the greater number by far did publiquely professe themselves'.[29] The protest resulted in the election being declared invalid (5th June 1656). When a new election was called for 13th July at Castle Cary, the Commons ordered all its MPs from Somerset to return to London in an attempt to reduce the tension. Pyne's allies on the County Committee, led by Matthew Clift, wrote to the Speaker urgently requesting that he should be allowed to remain with them. 'Your best affected people', they pleaded, 'have been much amazed to heare such reports that he should be sent for by a Troope of Horse'.[30] The original four candidates campaigned vigorously, although Harington characteristically declined Horner's suggestion that they should run in harness. 'I refuse', he wrote in his diary, 'saying I would join with no man.'[31] Nevertheless, Horner and Harington again emerged triumphant, in spite of mild protests that Sir John had improperly conducted part of the election in private while he was eating dinner![32]

Although Pyne's candidates met with more success in the borough elections at Bridgwater, Minehead and Taunton, he encountered yet another rebuff at Bath. The Mayor and Corporation, who were beginning to reflect the spirit of moderation which was now afoot in North-East Somerset, had originally sent a letter inviting John Harington to represent them alongside Alexander Popham, as a replacement for the disabled William Bassett . [33] However, in view of Harington's election for the county a few days earlier, they now settled for John Ashe's son, James, who defeated by 16 votes to 3 the only only other candidate in the election, Pyne's accomplice, Edward Popham - another clear indication that the citizens of Bath were no longer inclined to follow a more radical line in politics.[34] It is also worth noting that Alderman Matthew Clift, who had previously led the war effort in Bath on behalf of parliament and was now one of Pyne's most loyal supporters, no longer commanded quite the same authority within the city council as he had previously enjoyed. Whereas he had already been elected Mayor on two earlier occasions in 1629 and 1640, he was defeated in three successive contests for that office - by John Atwood in 1646 (when he received only one vote and was also bottom of the poll in the election for Justices), by moderate Walter Chapman in 1647 (when he totalled six votes) and by moderate Richard Druce in 1648 (when his tally was eight votes). Indeed, it was not until the following year that he scraped home by just three votes in a contest with John Pearce (i.e. after the trial and execution of the King).[35]

Matthew Clift, however, was aspiring to even greater power as a key member of the County Committee's 'standing committee'. In the cause of efficiency, the ordinance of 1644, which authorised the new arrangements, had instructed the large committee to meet only as a standing committee of seven on a rota system for periods of a fortnight. Taking advantage of the apathy of others, Pyne quickly ensured that his close associates attended the committee with increasing regularity, whether or not it was their turn on the rota, thereby controlling the vast amount of business to be conducted. Documents relating to the Committee of Accounts and the Committee for Compounding confirm that the most frequent attenders of this standing committee were not the gentry, but the humbler members of the radical faction - Matthew Clift (whose signature invariably appears first), Edward Ceely, Henry Minterne, Henry Bonner, Thomas English, Richard Trevillian, Jonathan Pitt and Christopher Pittard.[36] These men, therefore, became Pyne's effective working group - a fact which helps to explain Matthew Clift's repeated absences from meetings of the Bath Council between 1645 and 1649.[37] In this way, Pyne was able to dominate policy and to outwit most of the moderate gentry, including Sir John Horner, although he was soon to discover a much more resolute adversary in the form of William Prynne.

According to the *Perfect Weekly Account,* Pyne had attempted to outflank Prynne's expected opposition to his policies by adjourning the committee whenever the latter came down from London 'to examine and reform the abuses and grievances which the county generally complain of.'[38] Prynne was furious and later complained in a letter to the Committee about their 'carriage' towards him in this manner at Bridgwater. In reply, Matthew Clift and four others admitted the irritation they had caused and that his annoyance stemmed from 'the Committee adjourning before you came thither' and that 'you were displeased because the gentlemen then present served not your humour'.[39] Similarly, Prynne's attempt to ensure that only moderates were appointed to the new subcommittee of accounts in 1646 (responsible for auditing the accounts of the County Committee's officials) was frustrated when Pyne successfully infiltrated its membership.

His grip on local government in Somerset was further strengthened through the powerful control he quickly established over the first post-war Commission of the Peace, which had been issued in 1646. Although ten inhabitants of North-East Somerset, including moderates Prynne, Harington, Ashe and Horner, served as Justices of the Peace in the years before 1649 (out of a total membership of 68), very few of these were active outside their own locality. The work of county administration, therefore, was surrendered to Pyne's faction which packed the Quarter Sessions and dominated follow-up assignments at the Assizes. The appointment by parliament in June 1647 of a separate Assessment Commission for Somerset (to replace the tax collection role of the County Committee) seemingly gave an opportunity to the moderates to re-gain authority over that vital area. But although the Commission at first contained a majority of that persuasion, including all the leading gentry from North-East Somerset, Pyne, through active persistence, eventually gained places for his own list of radicals, including Matthew Clift. Pyne's clever strategy, which he pursued with ruthless determination, ensured that the gentry and leading citizens of North-East Somerset were temporarily outwitted and reduced to an insignificant role in the affairs of the county.[40]

(iii) The Punishment of Royalists

Throughout this early post-war period, Pyne's tactics in outmanoeuvering his political opponents were designed with one objective in mind, namely to mount a speedy offensive against their real enemies - the royalists, the episcopal clergy and the ungodly. The success of this campaign would clearly be dependent on the availability of an army, because the 'saints' would need to use force if they were to impose their godly reformation on an ungodly majority. The Committee's main task of sequestering or confiscating royalist estates therefore served two vital purposes - it meted out fit punishment to all delinquents and, at the same time, it generated financial resources with which to maintain the local militia. Although the composition fine itself, which enabled the royalist to recover his estates, was payable only to the Committee for Compounding in London, the revenue of these estates, during the period of sequestration while the fine was being calculated, was enjoyed by the County Committee itself. It is not surprising, therefore, that the Committee employed up to three hundred sequestration officials to bring to heel as many delinquents as possible and that sequestration proceedings were often long drawn out! Even the moderate gentry who actually belonged to the Committee felt unable to use their influence to stem the rushing tide of Pyne's investigators. Sir Edward Hungerford, for instance, was reluctant to promise any help to the wife of one royalist acquaintance threatened with sequestration. He said he would do all he could in the business, 'but that if he had been in any other place, he should sooner have prevailed with the Committee than with this Committee of Somersetsheere, who are very hard to the gentry.'[41]

The oppressive tactics of Pyne's sequestration officials are best illustrated by the case of William Prynne's chaplain, Lawrence Walroad, in 1647. In a letter to the standing committee, Prynne complained that they had 'caused the sheepe and cattle of Mr Walroad, without any notice or demand, to be driven away by the sequestrators troopers' and that he had been banned from further preaching. This high-handed action was, in Prynne's opinion, 'not out of zeale to justice, or the public good but particular spleen and malice against me' as a result of his previous quarrel with the Committee at Bridgwater. The point at issue was that, although Walroad had admitted serving under Hopton during the period of royalist occupation, he had been tried by the Committee (which had then included Sir John Horner), imprisoned for six months and later restored to his ministry after a further hearing by the Committee; he had since taken the League and Covenant and had preached faithfully, conforming to the Directory and the ordinances of parliament - and yet he had just been sequestered on the old charge exactly two years after his release.

Prynne concluded that, as this was clearly a personal vendetta against him, he would raise the county against them and 'pursue right and reparations' from them for all their past and present injuries, 'in the highest Judicatory in the Kingdom'. Furthermore, he would publish their 'malitious actions and proceedings to the world, that others may blush at them.' The standing committee, led by Matthew Clift, was totally unmoved by these extravagant threats and wrote a somewhat mocking letter in reply.[42] However, the irony behind this episode is that, by the time Prynne wrote his letter (15th January 1648), he had already been elected Recorder of Bath (13th December 1647) - a position that would entitle him to sit alongside Clift in the council chamber.[43] This was, of course, another indication that local opinion increasingly favoured a more moderate approach. Before the year was out, Prynne, who had thus suffered abuse at the hands of Clift's radical faction on the County Committee in the winter, would suffer further insults from Henry Chapman's royalist faction within the city during the bull-baiting riots in the summer (see above). He was not the man to be deterred.

Meanwhile, the work of sequestration continued apace. Nevertheless, it is interesting to note that of 303 delinquents referred to the Committee of Compounding from the county of Somerset, only twenty-one lived in the five hundreds of North-East Somerset. Most of the leading royalists in the area had applied for composition by February 1648, although Sir Ralph Hopton had been denied permission to compound. Among the first to do so was Sir Thomas Bridges of Keynsham, former royalist governor of Bath. While he admitted his delinquency, he claimed that the whole of his personal estate, amounting to £4,000, had been confiscated by the County Committee at the start of the war. He was originally faced with a fine of £1,380 which, by December 1646, had been reduced to £868 - on condition that he handed over the rectory (i.e. his income from tithes, etc.) of Keynsham church to the minister.[44] Many local people were doubtless pleased at the firm treatment meted out to Bridges. He was particularly disliked in Bath for his heavy demands during his period of residence during the war. The Corporation were already sueing him for the recovery of a 'forced loan' of £100. On 26th August 1646, they had agreed that 'Mr John Atwood, Chamberlain, Mr Walter Chapman and John Pearce shall go unto Mr Valentine Tenne, to demand a bond which the Towne Seale is fixed unto for one hundred poundes, which Sr. Thomas Bridges extorted from the Corporation during the tyme of his being Governor heer.' The claim was pursued with vigour by incensed not councillors. Later in the same year, a payment was made 'for serveinge Sr. Thomas Bridges with a subpena and for makeing his affidavit in London.' But although a further sum was paid to a lawyer in May 1647 'for following the suit against Sr. Tho. Bridges,' it is not clear whether the city ever recovered its money.[45]

Nevertheless, although local people had no great affection for Bridges in view of their experiences during the occupation, they were much more anxious to ameliorate, where possible, the sufferings imposed by the County Committee on other royalists, who were often their friends, neighbours, or close relatives. Henry Chapman had been lieutenant to Bridges during the royalist occupation and by 1664 was certainly one of the city's largest property owners.[46] When charged, however, he admitted that he had served as a captain of a foot company for six months, but pleaded that his estate was not worth £200. This plea was rejected, and he was fined £62 13s 4d., one-sixth of his estimated wealth.[47] George Chapman, for his part, confessed that he had been 'in arms against Parliament, but was convinced of his error and laid them down three years ago'. The Committee accepted both his story and his statement that his estates were worth less than the stipulated £200. He therefore escaped without a fine.[48] There is little doubt that some delinquents clearly concealed the true extent of their wealth and that local commissioners were sometimes willing to turn a blind eye to royalists who were acceptable as neighbours in all but politics.

John Ashe, as Chairman of the Goldsmiths' Hall Committee responsible for hearing the cases against royalists, certainly came to the assistance of the family of Richard Gay from Widcombe, near Bath. Originally fined £180 for his delinquency, Gay by 1650 was languishing in prison for debt. Ashe made a personal intervention when Gay's five children petitioned the Committee for the release of one-fifth of their former estate. 'The petitioners', he wrote, 'are my near neighbours, and are in very great want; and their father to my knowledge in very great misery, by reason of his debts and imprisonment.' Their request was granted and Lyncombe Farm was later released from sequestration.[49] Ashe took similar personal interest in the case of Philip Sherwood, a well-known member of Bath Council, who had been a close associate of Henry Chapman during the royalist occupation and had been 'in armes against the Parliament forces'. Sherwood begged to have his property released from confiscation because it was not worth £200. Ashe immediately wrote a letter to the County Committee supporting Sherwood's request. 'It is my opinion that if the petitioners estate be not worth two hundred pounds, he ought to be acquitted and discharged from sequestration.'[50]

William Prynne showed equal kindness and consideration to William Bassett - even though they had been on opposite sides in the war. Previously M.P for Bath, Bassett had finally decided, after much wavering, to join the King. In his petition to the Committee for Compounding, he claimed that he had originally left parliament and returned to his own home at Claverton 'by reason of an extreme sickness then on his wife'; that, following the capture of the district by the royalists in 1643, he was unable to leave his property 'without the apparent ruin of himself and family'; that 'he never bore arms against the Parliament and was imprisoned many days in Bath by the King's party for not complying with them, but opposing taxes dishonourable to his Majesty and grievous to his people'. He had finally surrendered to parliamentary forces on 25th October 1645 but had not been allowed to go up to London to plead his case before the House of Commons.

It was at this point in the story that Prynne had obliged him by securing a special pass from the Speaker. Even so he had been waylaid by royalists on the road to London and had been imprisoned by them for five months in Wallingford.[51] He pleaded with the Committee for leniency, bearing in mind that personal belongings worth £3,000 had already been sold by the local commissioners. The initial verdict was in favour of a fine of one-third, amounting to £2,512 17s. Bassett sold off some of his lands in Somerset, Gloucestershire and Cornwall to assist him in paying the fine, which was eventually reduced (in 1651) to £1,937 7s.[52]

A further act of kindness and sympathy was shown by Walter Chapman (Mayor), Matthew Clift, Thomas Atwood, Thomas Burford, John Parker and John Pearce (Aldermen) in signing a certificate in 1649 which stated that one of their colleagues on the council, Robert Fisher, 'aged threescore and fowerteene yeares and upwards, by reason of his said age, impotence and weakness of body is not any waies able to travell without danger of his life' - thus averting his need to appear before the Goldsmiths' Hall Committee in person. Fisher, who had admitted supplying royalist forces with food during the war, was eventually fined £57 2s., or a tenth of his estate. [53] A similar certificate excusing travel was also sent by councillors on behalf of their colleague, Thomas Gibbs in 1647, whose case provides a good example of the suffering experienced by many following the confiscation of their lands and the harassment inflicted on them by local commissioners.

Thomas Gibbs was a councillor and Justice of the Peace on the Bath Corporation. In February 1648 he compounded for his delinquency 'in adhering to the forces raised against Parliament' and for taking away arms from the well affected in and about Bathe, which accordingly he disarmed.' His initial fine of £68 was later reduced to £48, not in itself an insufferable burden. However, although he had paid his fine, he found it very difficult to regain possession of his property which the County Committee had leased to a tenant. The tenant requested Gibbs to allow him to continue in possession for a further year on payment of a reasonable rent. Gibbs anxious to regain his own property, refused and forceably took possession. Whereupon the tenant, urged on by his friends, prosecuted Gibbs for riot at Taunton Assizes and at the same time reported him to the County Committee for undervaluing his own property. Certain of the more militant members of the Committee then took it upon themselves (apparently without the Chairman's knowledge) to re-confiscate the property - 'upon which a party of horse forced him out of his possession, and carried him to Taunton Bridewell, where he still remains, to the great hazard of his life, being an aged and infirm man'. [54]

Perhaps the most extraordinary illustration of this healing process, however, relates to Henry Chapman himself - the man who had been such a constant thorn in the side of the puritan elite. Despite Chapman's flight into Wales after the capture of Bath by the New Model Army in 1645, he was welcomed back onto the council after the war and elected as bailiff in September, 1647. [55] Although he was shortly afterwards to lose his seat by order of parliament (see below), he apparently remained on cordial terms with the council, which never hesitated to involve him in business operations. Not only did he rent from them the House of Correction in 1648 (the year of his bullbaiting escapade) and maintain on their behalf the water course 'from ye upper conduit to south gate' for an annual fee of £2, he was also granted the use of the Bath Common in 1652 for a rent of £110. They raised no objection in March 1653 when he requested permission to make a new door from his tavern, The Sun, into the Shambles (or meat market) next door - and they were perfectly happy to purchase two 'pottles of canarie' from him for eight shillings in 1655, the year of his protest over tithes (see below). It was clearly not their policy to ostracise even the most vehement of opponents, especially when men like Chapman still had a useful part to play in the successful operation of everyday life in the city. [56]

Meanwhile, there had been another example of the solidarity of the Bath Corporation in the face of pressure being applied by militant radicals both locally in the county and nationally in parliament. The council, as we have seen, was composed not merely of friends and neighbours, who did business with one another in the local market, but of close relatives whose bond in blood worked in favour of sympathy and leniency during times of stress. Membership of the council remained virtually unaltered throughout the whole period of the war, in spite of sharp differences of political opinion, with royalist and roundhead continuing to sit side by side no matter which army was actually in control of the city. Their joint concern, which far outweighed the importance of any national issue, was to secure the livelihood of local people.

When the war ended, there seemed to be even more reason for continuing this close relationship. Certainly the debates recorded in the Council Minute Books give no indication of any intention to remove the royalists from their midst - not at least until 27th September 1647. On that day the Corporation decided quite suddenly by a majority of 18 votes to 10 'that Sergent Hyde shall be removed from his place and a new Recorder chosen'. The important office of Recorder had been held for several years by Robert Hyde, a member of the well-known royalist family, who had served in person with Prince Rupert during the war. Even so, the Corporation's action had only been prompted by the passing of an ordinance by parliament on 9th September requesting the removal of royalists from local government. Most of the local councillors were more than happy to forgive and forget - a fact vividly illustrated when, three weeks later, they agreed to quash their original decision and agreed 'that there shall be no election for a new Recorder, but the Sergt. Hyde shall stand'.[57]

The Commons, however, thought otherwise. On 4th October they therefore passed a more precise and forceful ordinance, which put irresistible pressure on local authorities:

'Be it declared, ordered and ordained by the Lords and Commons in Parliament assembled, That no person whatsoever that hath been in arms against the Parliament, or hath been aiding or assisting the forces of the enemy, or hath been or is sequestered, shall be elected, constituted Mayor, Alderman, Bailiff, Sheriff, Justice of the Peace, Steward of any Court, Constable, or any other officer .... And in case any such persons as aforesaid be elected into any of the Offices aforesaid .... the Lords and Commons do declare all such elections to be void and null'.[58]

Faced with this ultimatum, Bath Corporation had little choice. On 13th December 1647, they reluctantly agreed to expel the royalist group en bloc. Samuel Wintle, Philip Sherwood, Henry Chapman, Robert Sheppard, Robert Fisher, Robert Hyde and Thomas Gibbs all relinquished their places with the first four of these actually present when the decision was taken.[59] It has to be said, however, that they had lasted longer in office than their counterparts in Exeter, where the Chamber had been remodelled by a specific ordinance of parliament and twelve out of the twenty-four had been purged from their places as early as April 1646. In Bath, as in Newcastle, Bristol, Chester, Wells and Weymouth, the social background and general outlook of the post-war replacements showed little change from that of the members who had been ousted. They were still essentially ordinary local businessmen, typified by baker Richard Druce who, in 1649 when mayor, gave lodgings to the water poet, John Taylor. 'I went to his stall or shop window', wrote Taylor later, 'Mr Mayor was pleased to entertain me most kindly (with his hands in his pockets) and like a man of few words, forebode to say welcome to town; so we parting I duly left him in his shop, Lord Baron of the Brown Loaves and Master of the Rolls'.[60]

Bath Corporation was not alone in its desire to maintain continuity and to resist interference from outside. In Chester, for instance, the aim of the Assembly throughout was to adhere to the city's constitution and ensure that civil government was properly carried out. In spite of a purge in 1646, there was little local recrimination, but considerable continuity of membership in the Assembly.[61] The strong sense of public service, which most councillors felt, was illustrated at Gloucester, where the Corporation attempted to keep itself aloof from the detail of war so that the machinery of government could be freed to maintain the flow of daily life. 'For your aims ought to be as public as your places', said Mayor Dorney in his address to the new officers in 1646, 'and you are to consider that you enter upon an office, not a benefice'.[62] Many civil authorities showed a reluctance to cooperate with outside instructions to purge their membership. The Corporation of Shrewsbury, for example, agreed to only three ejections from a list of ten submitted by the King in October 1642. Other governing bodies procrastinated for even longer than

Bath. Although the ordinance banning royalists was issued in October 1647, Worcester delayed until January 1649 before expelling two of its royalist members - as did Weymouth and Melcombe Regis when, with considerable reluctance, it removed fifteen councillors.[63] In Worcester, as in Bath, royalists and parliamentarians sat alongside each other for long periods during the war, illustrating again a desire 'to maintain the Chartered rights of self-government against external pressure'.[64]

(iv) Disturbances in Bath, 1648

Parliament doubtless felt justified in removing known delinquents from positions of authority. They considered it wise, during the period of reconstruction and settlement which followed the war, to render all potential trouble-makers politically impotent. Their action had disastrous consequences in Bath. There, at least, the royalist group—under the inevitable leadership of Henry Chapman— was transformed into an embittered and rebellious action. Forcibly isolated from the sobering influence of their parliamentarian friends on the Corporation, they sought an opportunity for revenge. They did not have long to wait.

Charles 1, now in the custody of the Army at Carisbroke Castle on the Isle of Wight, had rejected all offers of a settlement and had secretly made an Engagement with the Scots (26th December, 1647). This provided for a rising of royalists in England to coincide with an invasion by a Scottish Army aimed at restoring Charles to his throne. In return he agreed to establish a Presbyterian system of religion for a trial period of three years. The Second Civil War, which emerged from these plans in 1648, ended in dismal failure. The sporadic risings of royalist groups, which occurred in England between February and May, were quickly dealt with by a watchful government. Furthermore, when the Scots finally invaded, their inexperienced army was ruthlessly crushed by Cromwell at the Battle of Preston (17th August). By September, the war was over.

Meanwhile on 3rd May, *The Moderate Intelligencer* gave news of a rising at Bath.[65] This, in fact, turned out to be a slight exaggeration, but *The Perfect Weekly Account* of the following week carried a full account of the ugly and provocative scenes which had been duly reported to parliament at the end of April: '...One Henry Chapman of the city of Bathe, a Captain of the Kings in the late wars, a desperate Malignant, had not only openly affronted Mr Long, the Minister there lately settled by the Parliament, but likewise caused on Doctour Jones, a great plunderer and late Chaplain of the King's Army, to read the Booke of Common-Prayer and Preach publickley against the Parliaments proceedings in St James Church'. This clearly offended both the puritan consciences and the parliamentary convictions of the Recorder (William Prynne), the Mayor and the Justices of the Peace 'who sent their officers twice to the church to inhibit him to reade the Booke of Common-Prayer or Preach'. It was all to no avail. Urged on by Henry Chapman to defy the threat of arrest, Dr Jones preached yet again in the church which was 'as full of malignants as it could hold'. After the service he 'was guarded from the Church by about one hundred Malignants to Chapman's house, some of them armed with swords, and after dinner he was in like manner guarded by them to the same Church where he read Common Prayer againe.'

This open defiance and the inability of the authorities to take action caused considerable anxiety amongst the 'well affected people .... who are now in great fear of having their throats cut and of a party there sodainly to be raised for the King against the Parliament'. The Corporation paid ten men to keep special watch at night.[66] Their suspicions of an imminent rising had been increased by the recent steady influx of royalist supporters from neighbouring districts under the pretence of visiting the hot water baths. To enable these visitors to confer freely with local royalists, Chapman and his friends had 'for some weeks before set up a Bulbaiting every Monday neere the city wals, but without the precincts, to which disaffected people flocked from the Adjoyning Counties'. Vigorous complaints against this were made at the city Quarter Sessions, but their authority did stretch outside the city boundary. To emphasise his contempt for the local authorities, Chapman arranged a special bull-baiting assembly on the very day of the Quarter Sessions. He and his followers, showing utter disregard, 'marched to it with a drum before their dogs in affront of authority'. When they heard of the outrages, the House of Commons ordered on 1st May that Henry Chapman and Dr Jones should be sent for as delinquents to appear before them.[67]

This episode reveals in a most vivid manner the sense of frustration felt by the traditionalist faction at the overthrow of their ancient culture by the puritan elite - a frustration which suddenly burst forth during the fleeting opportunity created by the Second Civil War. It is highly significant that Chapman and his supporters chose three symbols to express their attitudes - namely, the Book of Common Prayer, the public demonstration against Prynne and the bull-baiting ceremonies - symbols which epitomised the pre-war struggle that had taken place over the form of religion and the survival of popular recreations. It is also interesting to note first, that the frustration of the local minority was evidently shared by others from within the area, judging by the numbers who gathered both inside the church and outside the walls; and secondly, that the indignation at these outrages shown by William Prynne and the Bath Corporation merely emphasised the extent of the rift that now existed between local citizens - a rift which had been sufficient to divide the community in war.

(v) The Godly Reformation

Meanwhile, although Pyne and his henchmen were making considerable headway in their implaccable pursuit of delinquent royalists in Somerset, progress was much less satisfactory over the matter of the 'godly reformation'. By June 1643 an Assembly of Divines had been established at Westminster to work out a scheme for the reorganisation of the church on a presbyterian basis, with Humphrey Chambers, the Rector of Claverton, as a member of that Assembly. They eventually decided that in future the government of the church would be in the hands of local congregations, area 'classes' and a national Synod. By 1646 bishops had been abolished; a new Directory of Worship had been issued to replace the Anglican Prayer Book and Parliament had formally ordered the establishment of the Presbyterian system. The Speaker wrote to County Committees requesting them, with the help of reliable local gentry and clergy, to divide the county into 'classes' and nominate ministers and elders to be responsible for each. The County Committees were at the same time expected to continue their work of reporting disaffected or unsuitable clergy to the Committee for Plundered Ministers in London so that they could promptly be replaced.[68]

The response of North-East Somerset to these particular requests and to religious changes in the country at large during the period 1640-1662 illustrates, on the one hand, the strength and distribution of puritanism and, on the other, the survival of dormant anglicanism within the area. There is no doubt that puritanism was already strongly established in many parishes within this part of the county by 1640 and that a moral reformation had already taken place in consequence (see Chapter Two). Furthermore, Margaret Stieg has identified nine known puritan clergy who were instituted during the 1620's and 1630's - Jacob Aston of Kilmersdon (1624), Humphrey Chambers of Claverton (1623), Thomas Codrington of Keynsham (1639), John Cornish of Dunkerton (1634), Vincent Cupper of Wolverton (1638), William Long of Priston (1638), Thomas Spratt of Stratton (1620), Samuel Tilley of Keynsham, (1625) and John Warner of Bathford (1636).[69] It should be noted, however, that this only represents just over 10 per cent of the eighty-seven parishes within the five Hundreds making up our community of North-East Somerset. This is immediately indicative of the fact, confirmed by other evidence below, that puritanism was extremely vigorous in certain parts but that it had by no means taken root completely in the whole area.

A careful analysis of the 'scandalous' and 'malignant' clergy ejected from their livings, during the period 1640-1660, tells a similar story. A G Matthews in *Walker Revised* lists fourteen ministers who suffered in this way: Henry Ancktetyell [308], rector of Mells; John Bayley [309], rector of Berkley; Andrew Bowerman [309], vicar of Frome Selwood; George Collier [311], vicar of Nunney; William Crofts [311]; rector of Langridge; Richard Earle [312], rector of Hemington; Polydor Evans [312], rector of Marksbury; John Farwell [312], rector of Laverton; Robert Gayler [313], rector of Kelston; Richard Goodridge [313], rector of Combe Hay; William Hanson [314], vicar of Twerton; Alexander Huish [315], rector of Beckington; James Masters [316], vicar of St Peter and St Paul, Bath; and Henry Storke [319], rector of Saltford. [70] To these, Margaret Stieg adds four more 'suffering royalists' - Thomas Hull of South Stoke; Francis Standysh of Compton Dando; Benjamin Tanner of Charlcombe and Thomas Willis of Norton St Philip. [71] These eighteen clergy, ejected almost certainly following the evidence of ardent puritans who objected to their Laudian or royalist associations, together form just over 20 per cent of the clergy within the area of North-East Somerset - a surprisingly low total, bearing in mind that the national average for sequestration from livings was 28 per cent, with a peak of 86 per cent in London, and that the highest totals of ejections came in areas where puritan influence was most strong. [72] In Dorset, for instance, there were 85 extrusions from 239 incumbencies during the 1640's - or 35 per cent. [73]

Similarly, a study of the ejection of *puritan* ministers during the years 1660-1662 confirms the developing pattern. A G Matthews, in *Calamy Revised,* lists those local clergy who lost their livings as a result of the Act for Confirming and Restoring of Ministers (29th December 1660) and the Act for the Uniformity of Public Prayers (29th July 1662) - William Baker [24], assistant at Bath; William Green [233], vicar of Bath; George Long [327], vicar of Bath; John After [3], vicar of Beckington to 1658; Robert Pinney [391], rector of Charlcombe; Thomas Creese [142], rector of Combe Hay; John Humfrey [284], vicar of Frome; Thomas Grove [237], vicar of Kilmersdon; Richard Fairclough [187], rector of Mells; and Humphrey Chambers [107], rector of Claverton to 1645. [74] According to this evidence, therefore, just over 11 per cent of the eighty-seven parishes in North-East Somerset experienced the ejection of their puritan clergy at the Restoration - again a surprisingly low figure for what is generally considered to be a 'puritan' area. This is in marked contrast to the figure of just over 17% expelled in the county as a whole (i.e. 62 out of the 359 parishes listed by Stieg), [75] and to the 44 per cent expelled in Dorset. [76]

Furthermore, the 'Attestation', signed by a group of keen presbyterian ministers from Somerset on 9th August 1648 and one of a number of similar petitions to sweep the country in that year, was poorly supported. Demanding the speeding up of the 'much longed for settlement of church government' and 'the errors, heresies and blasphemies of the present time', the group included the ministers of Keynsham, (Thomas Codrington), Langridge (Richard Popjoy), Priston (William Long), Mells (Richard Fairclough), Combe Hay (Thomas Creese), Saltford (Thomas Ladde), Frome Selwood (William Wright), Norton-St-Philip (John Pinny), Chelwood (Richard Cheswood), Wanstrow (Christopher Reade) and Bath Abbey (Matthew Randall). These people wanted not only the establishment of a nationally-organised presbyterian church with rigid discipline and a set form of worship, but also the elimination of 'unwarrantable toleration' which permitted various sects to do as they pleased. [77] Nevertheless, in spite of their crusading zeal, they only represented some 12.6 per cent of the possible voting strength of the clergy in North-East Somerset compared, for instance, with the 20 per cent of Warwickshire ministers who signed a similar petition in March 1648. [78]

Out of all this evidence, a number of significant points emerge. First, only thirty-five out of the eighty-seven parishes in the area (i.e. about 40 per cent) demonstrated their clear commitment to the puritan cause - i.e. through their involvement either in the institution of known puritan clergy in the 1620's and 1630's, or in the ejection of scandalous and malignant clergy before 1660, or in the ejection of puritan clergy between

1660 and 1662, or in the signing of the Attestation in 1648, or in isolated references which indicate the presence of a puritan minister (such as the taking down of the maypole at Dundry or the lectures attended in Bath by John Harington and given by Robert Latimer from North Stoke and Samuel Gevinn from Bathwick).[79] Secondly, the distribution of these parishes on a map indicates that the main concentration occurred in the north of the area, especially along the Avon valley, and that there was comparatively little puritan activity south of Frome or in the Kilmersdon Hundred. Thirdly, the most active puritan centres, which featured in all four areas of the evidence presented above, were Bath, Combehay, Mells and Frome.

All this would seem to indicate that puritanism was particularly strong in those parishes closely associated with the clothing industry along the river valley; and in those districts personally dominated by the puritan gentry. It is not without significance that, of the eleven Elders from North-East Somerset listed in the draft scheme for a Presbyterian classis in the Bath and Wrington district (see below), no fewer than six were drawn from the Hundred of Bathforum - clothiers John Ashe and John Curle of Freshford, John Harington of Kelston, William Prynne of Swainswick, John Wood and Dr Tobias Venner of Bath. Two more, Alexander Popham of Hunstrete and John Collins of Priston were on hand to influence Keynsham, the other Hundred in the north of the area, while James Rowsell of Combe Hay (also nominated Elder for the Bath and Wrington Classis) and the Horners of Mells (nominated Elders for the Wells and Bruton Classis) clearly gave a decisive lead in those two puritan strongholds.[80] Dr Green, in commenting on the ejection of malignant and scandalous clergy, observed: 'There are strong grounds for thinking that it was pressure from above rather than from below that triggered off most of the attacks'.[81] In North-East Somerset, there are strong grounds too for thinking that it was 'pressure from above' which triggered off an ardent type of puritanism that expressed itself in about 40 per cent of the parishes *at some time* during the period 1620-1660.

These statistics also reveal the other side of the coin - namely that, in the remaining 60 per cent of the parishes, the clergy and congregations were apparently content to let the revolution slip quietly by. John Morrill, in his essay on 'The Church in England, 1642-9', observed that 'the greatest challenge to the respectable Puritanism of the Parliamentarian majority came from the passive strength of Anglican survivalism'. His study, based on a hundred and fifty churchwardens' accounts over ten counties, revealed that less than 25 per cent of the parishes acquired copies of the new Directory of Worship, that the prohibited Book of Common Prayer continued to be used in many places with comparatively little risk of retribution, that even in 1650 almost half of the churches held Easter communion and that between three-fifths and two-thirds of all parishes had the same ministers in 1649 as they had had in 1642. He concluded that 'there is a great deal of evidence of positive commitment to old values and practices'[82] - or, for what David Underdown has described as 'the comfortable certainties of the old religion'.[83]

There is more than a little evidence to suggest that Anglicanism survived during this period in many of those parishes in North-East Somerset that were not noticeably committed to puritan beliefs. This was due in part to choice, in part to neglect. There was quite clearly an attachment to the Book of Common Prayer, which proved difficult to dislodge, especially in view of the fact that copies of the Directory were in short supply. Eight months after the ban on the use of the Prayer Book in 1645, Colonel Martin Pynder, serving with the New Model Army in Bristol, wrote to the Speaker complaining 'that for want of able ministers, Directories and orders for the use of the same, the people here sitt in darkness and the collegiate men still chante out the Common-Prayer booke to the wonted height and *in private parishes they think of noe other discipline*'. Furthermore, he had noticed a certain degree of resentment among the local people concerning the replacement of the Prayer Book: 'in all places where we march, the country hardly beleeves you intend them either Liberty, Property or Religion, especially since you take away the Common-prayer booke'.[84]

Swainswick Church in 1790. A drawing by S.H. Grimm.

The Directory did in fact find its way into some of the parishes within the area. William Prynne, in springing to the defence of his chaplain at Swainswick, stated that the man had preached faithfully, conforming to the Directory and the ordinances of parliament.[85] Judging by the disturbances in Bath during the Second Civil War in 1648, the Book of Common Prayer had clearly been replaced by the Directory, probably after the institution of George Long at the Abbey in the same year.[86] The act of defiance by Henry Chapman and his royalist supporters consisted, at least in part, of encouraging Dr Jones 'to read the Booke of Common-Prayer' in St James's church. Ignoring the orders of the civic authorities, he twice more read Common Prayer to a packed church and 'was guarded from the Church by about one hundred malignants .... some of them armed with swords'.[87] This experience in Bath was very similar to that in other parts of the country. John Morrill has shown that 'the Prayer-Book rebellion of 1647', which had seen the reintrusion of ejected ministers brandishing prayer books in parishes nationwide, was the prelude to the second Civil War. 'Several of the incidents which sparked off the provincial risings of 1648', he concluded, 'were concerned with the suppression of Christmas or of the Prayer Book.[88]

In the main, however, puritanism failed to oust traditional anglicanism in many parishes within the area not because of the active opposition of inhabitants or clergy, but because of the difficulty in finding a sufficient number of ardent ministers to fill the vacancies. A letter from Somerset, written in the summer of 1646, emphasised just how desperate the situation had become. 'Ministers we have very few, our churches are interrupted. You talke at London of getting maintenance for them, but where are the men that must do the works?'[89] Even as late as January 1648, William Prynne complained in a letter to the Committee that they had removed his own chaplain from Swainswick, thus leaving 'three parishes together like sheepe without a sheppard, quite destitute of all spiritual food for their soules, in such a barren place, where there are 10 parishes more adjoyning without any settled minister to instruct them.'[90] The city of Bath fared no better for a while, after the rector of the Abbey, James Masters, had been ejected by the Committee for Plundered Ministers on 19th September 1645 'for joining the royal forces, fleeing to Bristol and staying there during the siege after Bath was taken, preaching much against Parliament'. The Corporation experienced considerable difficulty in finding suitable replacements. Two new ministers, Cothrington and Oliver, disappeared without trace after being kept out of the rectory by Masters' wife; and their successors, Joseph Bowden and Thomas Creese, remained only for a short time before moving on to other parishes. Indeed, it was not until 2nd May 1648 that parliament, showing concern that the city of Bath had been 'for a long time destitute of a faithful pastor', confirmed the appointment of George Long and Matthew Randall. Long, approved by the Assembly of Divines and recommended as 'a learned, orthodox and godly divine', remained there as minister until the Restoration in 1660, when he was replaced by James Masters.[91]

Why was it so difficult to fill the vacancies and to recruit men of the right puritan commitment in North-East Somerset? Parliament itself did little to relieve the crisis which had been clearly identified in letters written from Somerset in 1645 and 1646 (see above). 'Where are the men that must do the work?' was the heartfelt cry. According to W D Shaw, parliament only nominated two puritan clergy for appointments outside the city of Bath - Thomas Creese to Combehay (17th February 1647) and Richard Fairclough to Mells (24th September 1647).[92] There is some indication that stipends were too low to attract newcomers into the area - a situation which had also been experienced in Wells. There, however, after a petition to the House of Lords which bemoaned the 'sad condition they were reduced unto for want of the due preaching of God's word amongst them', parliament provided two minsters with a joint salary of £300 per annum from sequestered church lands. When the generosity of this settlement was queried in the Commons, 'it was alledged that unless they had good allowance, other places would outvy Wells and get them away'.[93] The parishes of North-East Somerset were in no position to compete on equal terms with places like Wells unaided. Margaret Stieg has shown firstly that, whereas the average value of Somerset benefices in 1668 was £58 16s 0d, the average value of livings in the north-eastern part of the county was only £39 16s 0d; and secondly, that although contemporary sources indicate that £30 per annum was an acceptable figure for a seventeenth century Somerset parson, 46 of the 359 parishes in Somerset offered stipends below that level - including ten from the north-eastern sector. In general, the value of livings in Somerset parishes had risen by more than the cost of inflation during the period 1635-1668, but those 'that increased less than average cluster around Bath and form a band across the Mendips towards Frome'. This is attributed in part to the decline of the woollen industry in those districts.[94]

The other reason, of course, for the under-funding of local parishes was the system of lay impropriation of tithes, which seriously reduced the amount of income available for the minister in many churches. In Corston, for instance, the great tithes of corn, hay and wool had previously been impropriated by the patron (the Bishop), leaving the vicarage endowed only with the small tithes, which were worth £20 per annum. A similar situation prevailed in Wellow, where the great tithes (valued at £160 per annum) belonged to Joseph Langdon, leaving just £30 per annum for the vicar. The curate of Dundry fared a little better with £30 13s 4d available from the small tithes and two-thirds of the great tithes.[95] Other benefices with low annual values in 1668 included Langridge (£20), North Stoke (£20), Charlcombe (£12), Bathford (£10), Bathampton (£20), Walcot (£20), Freshford (£20) and Woolverton (£20).[96] Furthermore, the Rector of Bath Abbey had only been receiving a stipend of £10 per annum in 1631, although this was often supplemented by fees for sermons.[97] It was hardly surprising, therefore, that the correspondent from Somerset in 1646 should speculate expectantly on the talk in London about 'getting maintenance for them'. The idea of augmenting the livings of puritan ministers had first been mooted in October 1641 through the Bill for the Better Maintenance of Ministers. However, the Commonwealth authorities never managed to implement a systematic policy over augmentations. Those parishes which received attention tended to be either large towns, or market towns lacking a preaching ministry, or places where a delinquent royalist controlled the tithes.[98]

The Committee for Plundered Ministers had initially been given the responsibility for putting the system into operation, partly through money raised from the sale of the lands of Bishops, Deans and Chapters and partly through the sequestration of tithe holdings from convicted royalists. As early as March 1643, Sir Edward Hungerford had informed his tenants of his warrant to receive on behalf of parliament the rents of papists, bishops, deans, chapters and prebendaries within his area.[99] Later, Sir Thomas Bridges was forced in December 1647 to settle £40 per annum 'for ever' on the church at Keynsham as part of his compensation for malignancy. However, apart from this one example, Shaw was only able to find two other parishes to benefit from augmentations during the period up to 1658 - Bath, where the minister now received £100 per annum (instead of the previous £10) and his assistant £50; and Midsomer Norton, where the minister received £20 per annum.[100] In addition to these instances, the Committee for Plundered Ministers ordered, on 14th April 1647, that a total of £50 should be made available from sequestered funds to support 'such ministers as this Committee shall approve' in the parish of Bathampton, a village of about 300 inhabitants, where the living was then worth only £10 per year - an indication of just why augmentations were necessary.[101] All this evidence goes to emphasise the fact that many livings were poor in value; that ministers were short in supply and that little real support had apparently been received from parliament in an attempt to improve the situation. It is not without significance that the benefices which could offer the highest stipends in the area were the ones that had attracted some of the most committed puritan clergy - Bath £100), Frome (£100), Beckington (£100), Mells (£100) and Priston (£80).[102] (see above, those signing the Attestation).

However, in spite of all these obstacles, a vigorous lead was being given by the puritan gentry of the area who were determined that the Presbyterian system, as established by parliament, should operate in Somerset. These were the very men who had succeeded in raising North-East Somerset for parliament in 1642. Although plans to reorganise the church met with little support in the country at large, the county committee of Somerset had responded favourably to the Speaker's request in 1646 to investigate the setting up of a Presbyterian system. Indeed, a working party, which had been formed under the direction of John Harington, Sir John Horner and William Prynne, submitted its report in March 1648. Harington himself refers in his diary to a meeting with Horner 'about the classis in Somersetshire' on 24th April 1647.[103] In their draft scheme, they proposed that the county should be made into one Province and 'divided into nine distinct classes' - at least when a sufficient number of suitable ministers became available. In the meantime, it was suggested that four classes should be established - the Bath and Wrington Classis, the Wells and Bruton Classis, the Ilchester and Ilminster Classis and the Taunton, Bridgwater and Dunster Classis. The Bath and Wrington Classis was to consist of one hundred and thirty-nine parishes, including all the parishes in the hundreds of Bathforum, Keynsham and Wellow and some of those in Kilmersdon and Frome. It would be under the control of a group of local ministers, including Joseph Bowden of Bath, Thomas Codrington of Keynsham, William Long of Priston and James Ashton of Kilmersdon, and a group of elders drawn from local congregations (see above). Outside the area of North-East Somerset, the list of elders included both John Pyne and his staunch ally, Henry Henley, while the list of ministers included John Baker, Pyne's own minister at Curry Mallet.[104] There was, therefore, much more common ground among local puritan gentry at the end of the war over the settlement of religion than over the settlement of constitutional issues. Although Pyne and the Pophams were 'Independent' in their politics, they were just as 'Presbyterian' in their religion as Horner, Ashe, Harington and Prynne. (See end of chapter for Glossary of terms used).

The setting up and partial implementation of a Presbyterian system for Somerset (there is evidence, for instance, that a number of ordinations were conducted within the scheme in the early 1650's) represented a considerable achievement.[105] One of only nine such schemes approved by parliament (the others being those of Cheshire, Essex, Lancashire, Middlesex, Shropshire, Suffolk, Surrey and London), it was a great tribute to the drive, determination and enthusiasm of the local gentry.[106] Although, as we have seen, they were supported actively by probably less than half of the parishes in North-East Somerset, such was the strength of their conviction and the power of their influence that they had been able not only to continue the cultural revolution and to draw the community into war, but now also to set up a Presbyterian system against the general trend in the country at large. Operating from their power-base in the hundred of Bathforum, William Prynne, Alexander Popham, John Harington and John Ashe - supported by Ashe's workforce along the Avon valley and the puritan majority in the Bath Corporation - proved an irresistable combination. The pulpits in all the key centres of population in the area were controlled by Presbyterian ministers - George Long at Bath, William Wright at Frome, James Ashton at Kilmersdon, Richard Fairclough at Mells, Thomas Ladde at Saltford and Thomas Creese at Combe Hay. Although, under adverse circumstances, the puritan elite proved itself unable to ensure that all the parishes toed the Presbyterian line, they nevertheless succeeded in conveying a lasting impression that this was indeed a puritan area. Anglicanism, 'shorn of its Laudian excesses', survived in a passive state almost unnoticed in perhaps up to 60 per cent of the parishes - at least until the Restoration, when a rapid reawakening was to occur.

Meanwhile, there were worrying indications locally that the Presbyterians were not likely to have matters all their own way. By 1646, observers were already noticing the profusion of sectarian preachers in Somerset. One of them remarked: 'We have numerous Sectaries, Anabaptists, Antinomians, Seekers and I know not what; all shows our dissolution to be neere'. In September of that year, a traveller to Bath commented: 'The most remarkable things in Towne are ye church and ye Bathes, and ye latter are ye most zealously frequented, though I think the Pulpitt to be ye hottest bathe in Towne; for it one day sweats Independency and Presbytery ye next, and that soe violently'. Shortly afterwards, Joseph Bowden launched a powerful attack on Independents in a sermon preached in Bath Abbey while he was still its minister.[107] With the occupation of London by the Army in August 1647 and the subsequent achievement of the principle of toleration, it became increasingly impossible to operate a Presbyterian system.

Local churches, therefore, muddled on for the next five unsettled years (1648-53), numbering a great variety of Anglicans, Presbyterians, Baptists and Independents among their clergy. The continued presence of regiments of the New Model Army in the vicinity ensured that sectarian activity continued unabated during the period 1646-1648. John Saltmarsh, the army chaplain, proclaimed during a sermon in Bath Abbey that 'as John Baptiste wore a leathern girdle, so the doctrine he preached was leathern doctrine'. Nevertheless, although there was at least one member of the council who was a Baptist (i.e. William Russell, who refused to swear the oath of allegiance in 1662 after the Restoration), there is no evidence that the Baptist movement took root in the city - nor that the formation of the Baptist Western Association in the 1650's had the same sort of impact locally as it did in Wells, Taunton and Bridgwater.[108]

Later still, during the Protectorate, the Quakers also made their appearance in the area - much to the consternation of many. There were disturbances in Bath Abbey in 1655 when Thomas Murford of Englishcombe 'being under a religious concern to publish the testimony of truth' was beaten up by the congregation and subsequently imprisoned. Other Quakers suffered a similar fate for uttering 'a Christian exhortation' to the priest and people inside their local churches - Christopher Holder and Robert Wastfield at Keynsham in 1655, Mary Hasel at Whitchurch in 1658 and Tobias Daniel at Keynsham, also in 1658. Nor was it any more acceptable to seek converts in the street. Katharine Evans of Englishcombe, for instance, was not only 'abused by the rude people at the instigation of the priest at Warminster and had her clothes torn off her back', but was also 'tied to a Whipping-post in the market' at Salisbury and whipped on the Mayor's instructions. The local Presbyterian elite did not hesitate to excite public opinion against this minority sect. According to Joseph Besse, therefore, Nicholas Jordan, Jane Murford,

John Evans and John Slade were 'assaulted and abused by the rabble' in the streets of Bath in 1658, as they were 'travelling quietly on the highway'. They were, allegedly, 'ordered by the Mayor to use them so, because they were Quakers'. Quakers also fell foul of the local clergy because of their refusal to pay tithes. William, Sergeant of Bathford, William Beakes of Backwell, James Pierce of Keynsham, Thomas Murford of Englishcombe, Julian Evans of Englishcombe (aged almost a hundred) and Thomas Hurd of Somerton were all imprisoned for their resistance to the 'antichristian oppression of tithes' - the latter on the suit of William Prynne. (109)

(vi) Prynne's Campaign for Moderation and Settlement, 1648 - 9

By 1648, William Prynne, much to the forefront in attempts to introduce a formal system of Presbyterianism in the area, was rapidly emerging as the leading political force in North-East Somerset and the only member of the local puritan elite capable of thwarting the more radical ambitions of Colonel John Pyne. His influence extended far and wide - to the Inns of Court through his work as a barrister, to the Commons through his recent election as member for Newport in Cornwall, to the inner circles of government through his membership of the Committee of Accounts, to political debate in all corners of the Kingdom through his prolific work as a pamphleteer and to the deliberations of Bath Corporation through his election as their Recorder. He had already challenged Pyne's faction over their improper use of the standing committee, their possible abuse of sequestration funds and the high-handed manner in which sequestration officials had harassed local people. He was now poised to launch a blistering attack on the most hated instrument of government both locally and nationally - the army.

The horrors of free quarter, requisitions and tax collection have already been described in Chapter Six. These continued unabated after the war with the movement of troops across the area to Ireland and the continuance of local garrisons. The outbreak of the second civil war in 1648 with tension-packed demonstrations in Bath (see above) gave the County Committee a further excuse to increase its forces. Alexander Popham was despatched from London at their request to raise a regiment of foot and a troop of horse, much to the disgust of local people, including Sir Edward Hungerford, who abruptly refused to house any garrison at Farleigh Castle, preferring instead 'to keep it himself from surprise'. The news that Pyne and Popham had further requested to make this militia permanent by means of a tax on all 'malignants and neuters' was greeted with uproar in the Commons. Not only would such a tax provide the Committee with a permanent force at its disposal, the word 'neuters' would 'reach to all the well-affected that are not of their crew, and indeed to almost all men of the county'. (110) In a statement to the Committee at Derby House, Pyne and Popham argued that the forces would be 'noe constant charge to ye countye'. Although the original troops raised .to secure Bath, 'that malignant city', were now on free quarter 'by necessity', they were supported by some 3000 other men under Popham's command who 'are not in constant pay, but at all meetings and musters receive some encouragement of a small sum of money from ye Committee which contents them'. These auxiliary forces consisted of 'many old souldyers that in this time of greatest hazard and perill came in voluntarily and freely to list under such officers as well liked them and are ready for service on an howers call'. They therefore urged retention of the militia as being both invaluable and inexpensive.

This proposition was, however, strongly opposed by four Somerset MP's, including John Harington and James Ashe. Their view that the forces should be 'disbanded forthwith' was based on three arguments; firstly, that 'att the time of the raysing .... it was pretended they would arme and serve at their owne charges'; secondly, they did not know of 'any necessitie of forces in the said countye'; thirdly, it would be far better (and more economical) to use a troop of Colonel Scroop's regiment of horse to quarter in two or three market towns - this would 'surely keepe ye country in quiet' without the expense of militia. (111) The Commons rejected Pyne's request.

Prynne now conducted a vigorous campaign against the army and in favour of a settlement with the King. Quite apart from his legal instinct which called for a return to the rule of law, Prynne had suffered personally from the terror of free quarter in the quiet of his own home at Swainswick. His book, *A Legal Vindication of the Liberties of England against Illegal Taxes,* published in 1649, contains a vitriolic attack on the army, including a graphic description of the day in May 1648 when thirty soldiers descended on his house. They were, he claimed, 'the rudest and deboistests in all kinds, that ever quartered since the warrs, and far worse than the worst of Goring's men, whereof some of them were the dreggs'. He continued:

> They climbed over my walls, forced my doors, beat my servants and workmen without any provocation, drew their swords upon me .... brake some of my windows, forced my strong-beer cellar door .... hollowed, roared, stamped, beat the tables with their swords and muskets like so many bedlams, swearing, cursing and blaspheming at every word; brake the tankards, bottles, cups, dishes wherein they fetched strong beer against the ground, abused my maid-servants, throwing beef and other good provisions at their heads, and casting it to the dogs, as no fit meat for soldiers, and the Heads and Conquerors of the Kingdom, as they called themselves .... They continued drinking and roaring before, at, and after supper, till most of them were mad-drunk, and some of them dead-drunk under the table. Then they must have 14 beds provided for them (for they would lie but two in a bed) and all their linen washed ....

Prynne suspected that the County Committee had singled him out for special treatment![112]

He now threw his weight tirelessly behind the leaders of the Presbyterian party in parliament. Denzil Holles and Sir Philip Stapleton had already outlined a programme in 1647 which would have secured a compromise settlement with the King, the abolition of the County Committees, the introduction of the presbyterian religion, the revival of old

The army visits the house of William Prynne for free quarter.

forms of local government - and the partial disbandment of the army (the remainder being despatched to Ireland). The army, stirred up by increasingly radical elements, retaliated by marching on London and excluded the 'Eleven Members' who had been most outspoken against them (6th August 1647). Prynne not only volunteered his services as one of the five lawyers appointed to defend the eleven on their impeachment, but also wrote a vigorous defence in his *Brief Justification of the Eleven Accused Members,* which was widely circulated. Once he had been elected as member for Newport in 1648, he was quick to join the fray in the House. After leading the attack against the Army's Remonstrance (lst November 1648), which he described as 'subversive of the law of the land' leading only to 'desolation and confusion',[113] he spoke for three hours in the debate on the King's answer to the Propositions, arguing in favour of the settlement proposed in the Newport Treaty (4th December 1648).[114] Two days later, the army purged parliament of its moderate majority of Presbyterian members.

'Mr Prynne', said Colonel Pride, 'you must not go into the House, but must go with me'. Prynne was one of forty-one members who were not only physically secluded from entering the House, but were also arrested. During his confinement, he almost certainly penned *A Solemn Protestation of the Imprisoned and Secluded Members,* in which he complained of 'the highest and most detestable force and breach of privilege and freedom ever offered to any Parliament of England'.[115] Then, shortly after his release on a writ of habeas corpus (10th January 1649), he published a *Vindication of the Imprisioned and Secluded Members of the House of Commons,* in which he again attacked the army with characteristic venom.[116]

In analysing Pryde's Purge and its consequences, David Underdown categorises the 471 MPs in the Long Parliament into five groups - the 'active revolutionaries' who committed themselves to the revolution while it was actually in progress during December and January; the 'conformists', who avoided commitment at the time, but accepted the *fait accompli* in February; the 'abstainers', who were not secluded, but showed their opposition by absenting themselves from parliament at least until the spring of 1649; those 'secluded members' who suffered in the Purge; and the 'hard core' of the Army's enemies who were both secluded and imprisoned.[117] It is interesting, therefore, to observe the stance taken by those leaders from North-East Somerset, who were in fact members of parliament at the time of the Purge in December 1648. William Prynne (MP for Newport) was quite clearly a 'hard core' enemy, a Presbyterian in religion and a member of the Presbyterian group in parliament. Alexander Popham (MP for Bath) who attended only on rare occasions between the Purge and the execution of the King, registered his dissent on 14th February[118] and is therefore classified as a 'conformist'. A Presbyterian in religion, he veered towards the Independent group in parliament. John Ashe (MP for Westbury), who was chairman of the Committee for Compounding, was surprisingly secluded in a secondary purge on 12th December. Although a Presbyterian in religion, he had originally been indentified with the war party in politics, before shifting his position later to the middle group in parliament. He took the dissent on 3rd February and was re-admitted to the House, thereby qualifying as a 'conformist'. James Ashe (MP for Bath) had voted against Pyne's proposal in 1648 to maintain regular forces in Somerset and, like his father, had supported the Eleven Members in 1647. Slightly more radical than his father, he nevertheless associated most frequently with the middle group in parliament and was not secluded in the Purge. He, too, should probably be classed as a 'conformist'. Edward Popham (MP for Minehead), a Presbyterian in religion, was closely linked with Pyne's radical faction on the County Committee and veered towards the Independent group in parliament. Like his brother, however, he should be ranked as a 'conformist' rather than a 'revolutionary'. John Harington (MP for Somerset) was a Presbyterian in religion who had given his support to the Eleven Members. He refused to be associated with any group or faction in parliament, left the House in protest after Pride's Purge and subsequently rejected all efforts to persuade him to return, even as late as 1652. He is therefore categorised as an 'abstainer'. [119]

By 1649, therefore, the puritan leadership in North-East Somerset, remained united in their religious beliefs sharing, as we have seen, a commitment to the presbyterian system. Politically, however, they had lost some of the common purpose that had united them on the outbreak war in 1642. Whereas Alexander and Edward Popham still retained much of the uncompromising outlook that had characterised their former membership of the war party, John and James Ashe had shifted their position into the middle ground of politics, finding it increasingly more difficult to associate with the likes of John Pyne. Although they had all conformed for the time being, neither the Pophams nor the Ashes could be regarded as true 'revolutionaries'. Of the six leaders under review, John Harington had clearly travelled the least and William Prynne the most from their political starting points seven years earlier. John Harington remained, as ever, true to himself and completely unshackled by the ties of group loyalties. William Prynne, whose commitment to the war had wavered long before its closure, was the only local member of the true peace party, pledged to strive for a compromise deal with the King. Nevertheless, the general consensus among the puritan leadership was undoubtedly veering towards moderation, if not at this stage towards healing and settlement - and Bath Corporation also reflected this view. Even Sir John Horner, who had been foremost in the resistance to the King's armies in North-East Somerset in both 1642 and 1645, had lost much of his revolutionary zeal by 1649. According to one later account of the family's activities, 'Sir John, like many other worthy gentlemen, had time to reflect upon their past proceedings, and bewail the calamities they had concurred upon their country. These must be his sentiments, for when the news of the King's murder was brought to Mells, and the Ringers set about ringing the bells, Sir John, old as he was, took a good oaken stick in his hand, and played it so well in the Belfrey that he stopped their music and rejoicing'.[120]

GLOSSARY OF TERMS (used in Chapters 7 and 8)

Augmentations: to counter the low salaries available to ministers in many churches (see below - Lay Impropriations of Tithes), parliament attempted to 'augment ' or increase their earnings through money raised from the sale of Bishops' lands and the confiscation of tithes held by convicted royalists.

Committee for Compounding: (see Goldsmiths' Hall Committee below)

Committee for Plundered Ministers: was set up in 1642 to relieve ministers plundered by the royalists and to consider the confiscation of the estates of royalist clergy; from 1643, it also dealt with clergy suspected of catholicism or scandalous living.

Composition: (see Goldsmiths' Hall Committee below).

Delinquent: the term was first used by parliament in September 1642 when it referred to the King's advisers and royalist supporters as 'delinquents, malignants and disaffected persons'. The term was increasingly used after the Second Civil War in 1648.

Directory of Worship: in January 1645, parliament passed an ordinance which abolished the Book of Common Prayer, replacing it with the Directory for the Public Worship of God, compiled by the Westminster Assembly (see below). This was the first step in the establishment of Presbyterianism.

Dissent: members of parliament who took 'The Dissent' made a declaration that they had dissented from or, if they had been present in the Commons at the time, the would have dissented from (or voted against) the decision taken by the Long Parliament on 5th December 1642 in favour of further negotiations with Charles I. It did not necessarily indicate their willingness to bring the King to trial, but rather their willingness to accept or conform with what had already happened.

Goldsmiths' Hall Committee (or Committee for Compounding): in March 1643, parliament ordered the sequestration or confiscation of the estates of all 'delinquents'; local committees organised this confiscation and management of royalist property. From September 1644, a committee under the chairmanship of John Ashe met at the Goldsmiths' Hall in London to arrange for royalists to 'compound' for the return of their estates (ie to pay a fine, which was normally one-tenth, one-sixth or one-third of the value of their estates, but could extend to two-thirds).

Impropriator: (see Lay Impropriation of Tithes below).

Independents: the collective name given to puritan sects (especially Baptists and Congregationalists). In religion, they believed in freedom of conscience and freedom of congregations to choose their own forms of worship; they opposed the organisation which Anglican Bishops and Presbyterians tried to impose. In politics, the Independents were usually identified with the 'war party', which stood for vigorous prosecution of the war and the defeat of the King; they were also responsible for Pride's Purge and the trial of Charles I. Their main strength was in the army.

Intruded Ministers: clergy who were put into churches as replacements for those clergy who had been ejected either for scandal or for supporting the royalist cause.

Lay Impropriation of Tithes: tithes (ie tax payments of one-tenth of income due to the church) had gradually been 'appropriated' or taken over by monasteries and bishops. After the dissolution of the monasteries in 1636-9, the tithes were often granted by the King to laymen who therefore became 'lay impropriators' or 'lay rectors'. These regarded the tithes as personal income and only paid a small fraction of the value in the form of salary to the vicar, who performed the religious duties in the church. The lay impropriator often kept the 'great tithes' of corn, hay and wool for himself, leaving only the 'small tithes' for the vicar.

Malignant: (see 'Delinquent' above)

Presbyterians: puritans who believed in church government by ministers and lay elders (or 'presbyters') elected by all who had taken the Covenant (see below); opposed therefore to rule by Bishops; wanted strict uniformity of beliefs and rules for worship on a national basis (cf the Independents, who believed that individual congregations should choose their own form of worship). In politics, they often identified with the 'peace party' which desired a settlement with the King after the end of the war. Conservative and opposed to social revolution, they were not in favour of religious toleration and were increasingly distrustful of the New Model Army.

Protectorate: established in December 1653; government to consist of a Protector, a Council of State and the House of Commons. From May 1657, a 'Second Chamber' was added and the Protector given the right to nominate his successor. The 1st Protectorate Parliament met in 1654, the 2nd between 1656 and 1658.

Recorder: a lawyer who was legal adviser to the Corporation; presided at some borough courts; administered oath of office to the Mayor; as a justice of the peace, sat at the Borough Court of Quarter Sessions.

Rector: a clergyman of a parish who performed the religious duties and enjoyed the tithes (ie they had not been appropriated by a lay rector - see Lay Impropriation of Tithes above). A vicar or 'substitute' was a clergyman appointed by a lay rector to perform the religious duties on his behalf at a salary (ie instead of the tithes).

Remonstance of the Army: presented by the Council of Army officers to parliament in November 1648, it demanded the removal of all Presbyterians and the trial of the King. It was rejected, thus speeding up Pride's Purge.

Rump: on 6th December 1648, Pride's Purge removed Presbyterians and their followers from the Commons, leaving a remnant of about 50 who were sympathetic to the Army; this Rump, which never exceeded 125, established a Commonwealth and, after the abolition of the monarchy, ruled the country until its removal by Cromwell in 1653.

Solemn League and Covenant: an alliance in 1643 between the English Parliament and the Scottish Covenanters (ie those pledged to resist the new Scottish Prayer Book in 1638); agreed to establish Presbyterianism (see above) in England and Ireland; all members of parliament and the army were obliged to 'take the Covenant' (or swear an oath to support it); this ruling was extended to everyone in 1644.

Westminster Assembly: in 1643, parliament established the 'Assembly of Learned and Godly Divines' to settle the government of the church according to the Solemn League and Covenant. Consisting of 120 puritan clergy and 30 laymen, it issued the Directory of Worship to replace the Prayer Book, the Confession of Faith and a plan for a Presbyterian system of church government.

8
Postscript, 1650-1662

Just over eleven years after the trial and execution of King Charles 1 (January 1649), Bath became the first city in England to proclaim Charles II King (12th May 1660) and the first to offer him a Loyal Address (4th June). John Biggs, the Mayor and a man who had favoured the parliamentarian cause throughout, described the local celebration in a letter to William Prynne, member for Bath in the newly-elected Convention Parliament:

> The Corporation being met at my House, my Self and the Aldermen being in Scarlet (the lowd Musick playing before us) we went about twelve a clock to the usual place of publishing Proclamations; where (after some pawse and proclamations for silence made) the Proclamation was read, which being done, all men waveing their hats or Swords over their Heads, cryed, GOD SAVE KING CHARLES, which was seconded by a volley of shot from 100 Musquetteers or young men raysed within our City for that purpose. By this time our Conduit began to run Clarett, and so continued running Clarett wyne for some few hours; In the meantime we, with the Gentry of our City, and divers Gentlemen of the Country (who came to joyne with us in this so happy and welcome solemnity) retyred into our Guildenhall, where with great Acclamations of Joy We spent several houres; during which time the Bells rung at every Church, and in the Evening great Bonfires were made: so that the whole Afternoon was spent in great Joy: all men testifying their obedience to their Lawfull Soveraign. [1]

What had brought about this remarkable transformation in attitude over the intervening years?

In the period immediately after the death of the King, the drift in attitude by the puritan gentry of North-East Somerset towards moderation and settlement continued. Initially, however, they were largely impotent in seeking to stamp their authority on the course of events in the county in the way that had been possible during the war. John Pyne's radical faction completely monopolised control of local government through their total domination of the Assessment Commission, the Commission of the Peace and the new Commonwealth Militia. Furthermore, the most outspoken critic of the radicals and their use of the army had been forcibly removed from the local scene. William Prynne was seized in July 1650 on orders from the Rump Parliament, imprisoned at Dunster Castle and subsequently transferred to Pendennis Castle in Cornwall where he remained until his release in February 1653.

But Pyne's days were numbered. The failure in 1653 of Barebones Parliament, whose radical reforms had seriously alarmed the majority of gentry, marked the end of the forward surge by militant revolutionaries. The Protectorate, which was established on 16th December 1653, was the first stage in a conservative reaction. In Somerset, Pyne's faction was gradually purged from local government commissions, which increasingly reverted to the control of old gentry families. In this new climate, which prevailed during the years of the Protectorate between 1654 and 1660, the puritan gentry of North-East

Somerset slowly began to resume their dominant role, making a number of vital contributions to the course of events. The families which had led the local rebellion in 1642 now became champions of the policies of moderation, which were eventually to lead to the Restoration of Charles II. Although several key figures were to die before that event took place (Sir Edward Hungerford in 1648, John Harington in 1654, Sir John Horner in 1659 and John Ashe in 1659), their sons carried on their work.

Even Alexander Popham, a former ally of John Pyne, became increasingly conservative in his attitude during the 1650's. When he arrived in July 1654 to take up his seat as member of Bath in the First Protectorate Parliament, he told Cromwell in the House that he came 'to do his country service, and not his Lordship'.[2] Later, in 1659, as he became increasingly disenchanted with the regime, he made secret contact with Edward Massey, one of Charles II's agents, in preparation for the moment when a restoration became possible. Subsequently, Popham was even suspected of complicity in Booth's attempted rising, subjected to a house search and summoned to appear before the Council of State.[3] Meanwhile, the drift back to normality and the traditional idea of monarchy had been further illustrated when John Ashe, former leader of the North Somerset rebellion, stood up in the House to propose that Cromwell 'take upon him the government according to the ancient constitution'.[4] Although Cromwell rejected the monarchy in name, he accepted the powers of Kingship including the right to appoint a 'Second House'. The nominations for this equivalent House of Lords included that of Alexander Popham - presumably as a ploy to silence his criticism in the Commons.

Events, however, had been moving rapidly on the national scene. The death of Oliver Cromwell in September 1658 had hastened the collapse of the Protectorate. First the Rump Parliament was recalled; then, the Long Parliament itself was re-instated, after the intervention of a Scottish army led by General Monck in February 1660. The moderate settlement with the monarchy, which had been the aim of William Prynne and the presbyterian party in 1648, could now be achieved. Bath Corporation, which was already firmly pledged to support these policies, now invited Prynne to become one of their two members in the Convention Parliament of 1660, along with Alexander Popham. Prynne not only accepted with readiness, even though he had been invited to stand in no fewer than nine constituencies, but also threw himself wholeheartedly into the work thay lay ahead, serving on 132 committees and making 90 speeches.[5] It was Prynne too who, on 4th June 1660, appeared personally before the King in the royal bedchamber, making a short speech on behalf of the City of Bath and delivering its Loyal Address 'into the royal hand'.[6]

This sudden outburst of loyalty to the crown in Bath was part and parcel of a national desire to return to normal government and established institutions. It did not, however, mean that Bath had surrendered its principles, its belief in parliamentary rights or its strong puritan faith. Indeed, all of these had been seemingly confirmed by the very election of Prynne and Popham as MPs for the city. These were men who could be trusted to see that the new King fulfilled the conditions on which he was restored. Bath was nevertheless relieved at the prospect of returning to her old ways. Political settlement was conducive to good trade and prosperity as a health resort. The return of the King at least gave the city the opportunity to heal its own local wounds. Ex-royalists were again permitted to live and work with their parliamentarian neighbours freely and without stigma. Henry Chapman, Samuel Wintle and Robert Sheppard were welcomed back onto the Council; James Masters returned as Rector (even though his successor, George Long, had wisely taken the precaution of signing the Loyal Address); William Prynne resumed his role as Recorder, receiving 20 votes against the 3 cast for James Ashe.[7]

The puritan gentry of North-East Somerset, therefore, had largely been reunited in a determination to frustrate any further threats to stability caused by radical sects in religion or by military radicals in local government. A legitimate monarchy, a free parliament, a moderate church policy and - above all - a restoration of the gentry themselves to their traditional authority within the country offered the most hopeful mixture for an acceptable agreement. A clear indication that healing and settlement had finally taken place was given in 1661 when two of the most ardent rebels from 1642, Alexander Popham and William Prynne, were elected to serve Bath in Charles II's Cavalier Parliament.[8] Prynne, as usual, was hyperactive. He was appointed to 396 committees over the course of seven sessions of parliament and was chairman of nineteen.[9] Although Popham, by contrast, only served on six committees, such was the extent of his rehabilitation that he even had the honour of entertaining the King at 'a costly dinner' at Littlecote in 1663.[10] Of those who had opposed their rebellion in the early years of the war, Sir Ralph Hopton had already died in exile (1652), but Sir Thomas Bridges was given the freedom of the city of Bath (11th November 1662).[11] The wheel of fortune probably completed its full cycle in 1669, when on the deaths of Prynne and Popham their places were taken by the sons of two men who had sat together as members of parliament for Bath in 1642 - Alexander Popham and William Bassett.[12]

Sadly, in spite of all this, the outward reconciliation of the local gentry in 1660 and 1661 gave a somewhat misleading picture of the situation as a whole. In the towns at least, hidden tensions were never far below the surface - and Bath was certainly no exception to this general rule. The old cavaliers were deeply suspicious of the new loyalty shown by the boroughs, feeling that their response to the events of 1660 was both hypocritical and devious. It was certainly true that old parliamentarians and presbyterians (like Matthew Clift's faction in Bath) remained the dominant force in municipal government immediately after the Restoration, in spite of the readmission of a number of previously ejected royalists. Time, however, was fast running out. In Bath itself, bitterness continued to fester as the old struggle for control of the city and its policies continued unabated. In the autumn of 1661, Henry Chapman and his followers on the city council joined forces with Sir Thomas Bridges, his old war-time associate, to attempt an extraordinary coup aimed at ending the grip on local power enjoyed by Clift's puritan group.

When writs were issued for the new elections of 1661, Chapman suspected (quite rightly) that the Corporation would again nominate Prynne and Popham as MPs for the city. Determined to prevent the return of these 'persons notorious enough for their actions in the late rebellions, and that still courte the populacy for their applause by their p'tended supporting of their libertyes', Bridges decided to offer himself for election together with Sir Charles Berkley. Unfortunately, the Mayor of Bath (John Ford) refused to show any interest in the claims of these self-appointed rival candidates. Not to be outdone, Bridges lodged a complaint against Ford before the Privy council, charging him with a history of various misdemeanours. His plan quite clearly was to get Ford dismissed by the Privy Council as Mayor and to secure, as his replacement, the appointment of Henry Chapman, 'a person whose loyalty is unquestionable not blemished by the least failing under his great sufferings'. It was his hope that Chapman would then be in a position to sway the Corporation in their election of the two MPs. The scheme failed dismally. When Ford appeared before the Privy Council in April, he was quickly able to refute the charges and secure his immediate acquittal, which allowed him time enough to return to Bath and organise the election. Prynne and Popham were returned to parliament by a majority of 21 votes to 7. Chapman and his faction stormed out the Council Chamber in protest.

At this point Chapman again revealed the bitterness with which he had previously been associated. Calling together his supporters, he now demanded that all the freemen of the city should be given the vote (which according to the Charter, was reserved for members of the Corporation only). Holding a spontaneous mock election, he declared that Bridges and Berkley had been duly voted (by what freemen he could assemble) as Members for Bath. His plot was foiled yet again, however, when the Commons on 16th May intervened by ruling that Prynne and Popham were nevertheless the rightful representatives.

But Bridges and Chapman were nothing if not persistent. In anger and desperation, they now pursued their schemes with almost lunatic frenzy. On 19th September, the opening day of the Quarter Sessions in Bath, they arranged for nine members of the Corporation to be arrested by the local militia and imprisoned some forty miles from the city. This was followed next day by the arrest of two more members. (Chapman, of course, had recently been re-instated as Captain of the Trained Bands as part of the general 'return to normal'). Prynne who, as Recorder, had just arrived to preside at the Quarter Sessions wrote an angrily-worded letter of complaint to the Privy Council. In it he listed the motives which lay behind these unjust and illegal arrests - 'to interrupt the quarter sessions of the citty this day, and the election of the Maior and all other officers for this citty on Monday next, for the yeare ensuing (wherein nine of them ought to have their voices), and to put an affront upon myself their newly elected and Sworne Recorder.' There was, indeed, more than a hint of a personal vendetta against Prynne. But the main object was clearly to gain control of the Corporation in the absence of some of its keenest puritan members (like Matthew Clift, John Biggs and John Parker).

Meanwhile, the election of the new Mayor proceeded with a depleted Council, which numbered twenty-one. During the debate, Chapman 'publiquely affronted and reviled with very uncivil language the said Mayor and Mr Prinn, Recorder of the said Citty'. On the question being put, 'who shall be Mayor of this Citty for ye yeare next ensuing', 8 votes were recorded for John Parker and 11 for Henry Chapman. A second vote resulted in 10 members supporting Parker and 11 supporting Chapman. The result of the election, amid uproar, was duly entered in the Minute Book in these works: 'Mr Henry Chapman is by the voyces present elected Mayor of this Citty Bath.' However, by the late evening, eight of those originally arrested had returned to the city. Hurrying to the Guildhall under the instructions of Prynne, they cast their votes for Parker and entered them accordingly in the Minute Book (the different ink is clearly visible). The statement recording Chapman's election as Mayor was then crossed out being substituted by the words 'Mr John Parker is Mayor elected for ye next yeare'.

In the meantime, true to his threat, Prynne had reported the matter to the Privy Council. When eventually it summoned all the parties to appear, it rebuked the city for its perpetual squabbles which were 'a bad example to other Corporations'; ruled in favour of John Parker who had been newly elected Mayor; and ordered that Henry Chapman should be dismissed as Captain of the Trained Bands. When Prynne's brother-in-law, George Clarke, was appointed to replace him, Chapman's defeat seemed almost complete. He was subsequently dismissed from both his position as Alderman and his place on the Council. [13]

This, however, was by no means the end of the story. Throughout the bitter controversy surrounding Henry Chapman and the 1661 elections, William Prynne had maintained that the chief objective of the cavalier gentry was to discredit the corporations in order 'to make way for their total purgation'. Events proved him right. The Corporation Act, which Prynne himself fiercely opposed in the Commons, became law in November 1661. It required all persons holding office to take the oath of allegiance and supremacy, to swear on oath of non-resistance to the King and to subscribe to the declaration removing the Solemn League and Covenant. In fact, the commissioners who were appointed by the King with powers to remove all those regarded as a threat to Church or State (even though they had taken the oaths) had almost limitless opportunity to remodel town government as they wished. Local cavalier gentry, many of whom became commissioners themselves, had finally gained their way.

On 27th October 1662, Bath Council took note of the fact that 'several persons are removed from their places in this Corporation' under the terms of the Corporation Act. Just over a fortnight earlier, on the tenth and eleventh of the same month, commissioners had visited the city to administer the oaths of allegiance and supremacy on the mayor, aldermen, councillors and officers of the corporation. The commissioners, who were composed of local cavalier gentry (Hugh Smyth, William Wyndham, John Warre, George Norton and George Stawell), noted that those present at the meeting 'did reddily take' the oaths - with the exception of William Russell, 'an Anabaptist', who refused and was in consequence disqualified from his place on the Council. Two failed to attend, however, and were also disqualified - namely, Recorder William Prynne ('a person disaffected to the peace and government of the Church') and Alderman Richard Druce (allegedly disaffected to both the Church and the State). Furthermore, of those who had taken the oaths, eleven were nevertheless considered, 'based upon just reasons shown', unfit to 'continue any longer in their respective places and trusts', bearing in mind 'the safety of the publick'. Those affected by this judgment were all close members of Matthew Clift's faction (including Clift himself) which had been involved in the election disputes of 1661. The men chosen by the commissioners to replace them in key positions on the Council were all members of Chapman's faction which had stormed out of the Council meeting in April 1661 in protest at the election of Popham and Prynne as members of parliament (see above).

In Bath, therefore, the Corporation Act had largely achieved in 1662 what Henry Chapman had striven unsuccessfuly to achieve one year earlier. Bearing in mind their public support for the Restoration and their willingness to take the oaths of allegiance and supremacy, there can be little doubt that Matthew Clift and his allies were perfectly willing to play their part in the healing and settlement process. It was not to be. Single-minded throughout, Henry Chapman, in alliance with the cavalier gentry, had never lost sight of his ambition to dominate the local council and thereby reverse the cultural revolution that had taken place. It is almost certain that the commissioners, in deciding that Clift and his faction were unfit to continue in office, based their verdict to a large extent on the 'just reason shown' to them in evidence presented chiefly by Chapman. Indeed, a letter of indictment survives from Chapman to two of the commissioners, Sir Hugh Smyth and Sir George Norton, written shortly after the expulsions as they awaited the back-lash. 'Ford, Clift, Collibee and Reeves', he wrote, 'were in Armes against his late Majestie: Boys and Brigges fled from their homes in 1643 when the Kings Army came to Bath and sheltered themselves in the Parliamentary Garrison at Bristoll; Druce, Parker and Atwood were carried away by the late Majestie in 1644 into Devon for indevoring what in them lay to starve the Kings Army, refusing to bake bread when required; Moor, Parker and Biggs were putt up into the Places of those turned out for their loyalty'.[14]

Matthew Clift and the twelve members of the group, who had fiercely resisted the pretensions of Henry Chapman in the disputed mayoral election of 1661 and at other times, were the real losers in the Restoration settlement. Whereas the local gentry, who had led the rebellion in 1642 (or their sons), had all been rehabilitated in the new regime, their lesser accomplices on the city council, the mercers and bakers, were the ones to have been sacrificed. For although Henry Chapman, who barely a year earlier had vigorously opposed William Prynne's nomination as member of parliament, describing him as 'a public enemy to the King and Kingdom, was willing to accept him now in that capacity, he was nevertheless unflinching in his determination to win the battle for local control.

The loss sustained by Matthew Clift symbolised for more than defeat in a bitter, local rivalry between strongly conflicting personalities. Defeat symbolised, in one respect, the defeat of the local puritan elite who had fought the war, at least in part, in order to impose their culture and their religion on a reprobate minority. The 'reprobates' had finally won. There would be no presbyterian system of religion, no guarantee that local affairs would in future be controlled by the godly. James Masters was back at the Abbey resplendent in surplice and vestments; Henry Chapman was back at the Guildhall resplendent at last in mayoral robes (1663). Chapman, in fact, turned out to be a remarkably inventive mayor, who devoted himself to the good of the community in a most business-like and efficient manner. Elected to that office also on a second occasion in 1672, he set about the task of promoting the City's healing waters by writing a book *Thermae Redivivae* (1673), and marketing its tourist attractions by placing the Corporation's first-ever advertisement in a London newspaper (*The Intelligencer,* 26th March 1664). In doing so, he helped to lay foundations for the golden days of Bath, half a century later, under the social leadership of Beau Nash. This was perhaps not quite what Matthew Clift and his friends had had in mind![15]

Extract from the Bath City Council Minute Book dated 23rd September 1661, the occasion of the vote to elect the new mayor. After the list of names present at a depleted meeting of the Council (ie without those 'kidnapped' earlier), the clerk has written: *Who shall be mayor of the citty for the yeare next comeing.* The voting shows 8 marks in favour of Alderman John Parker and 11 in favour of Alderman Henry Chapman in the first ballot. Then, after the strong vertical line, the voting in the second ballot shows 11 votes for Chapman and 10 votes for Parker with 8 additional votes for the latter cast later in a clearly different hand. Against the votes, the clerk first wrote *Mr Henry Chapman is by voyces p(re)sent elected Mayor of this Citty of Bath,* but later crossed it out and submitted above the lines *Mr John Parker is Mayor elected for the next yeere.*

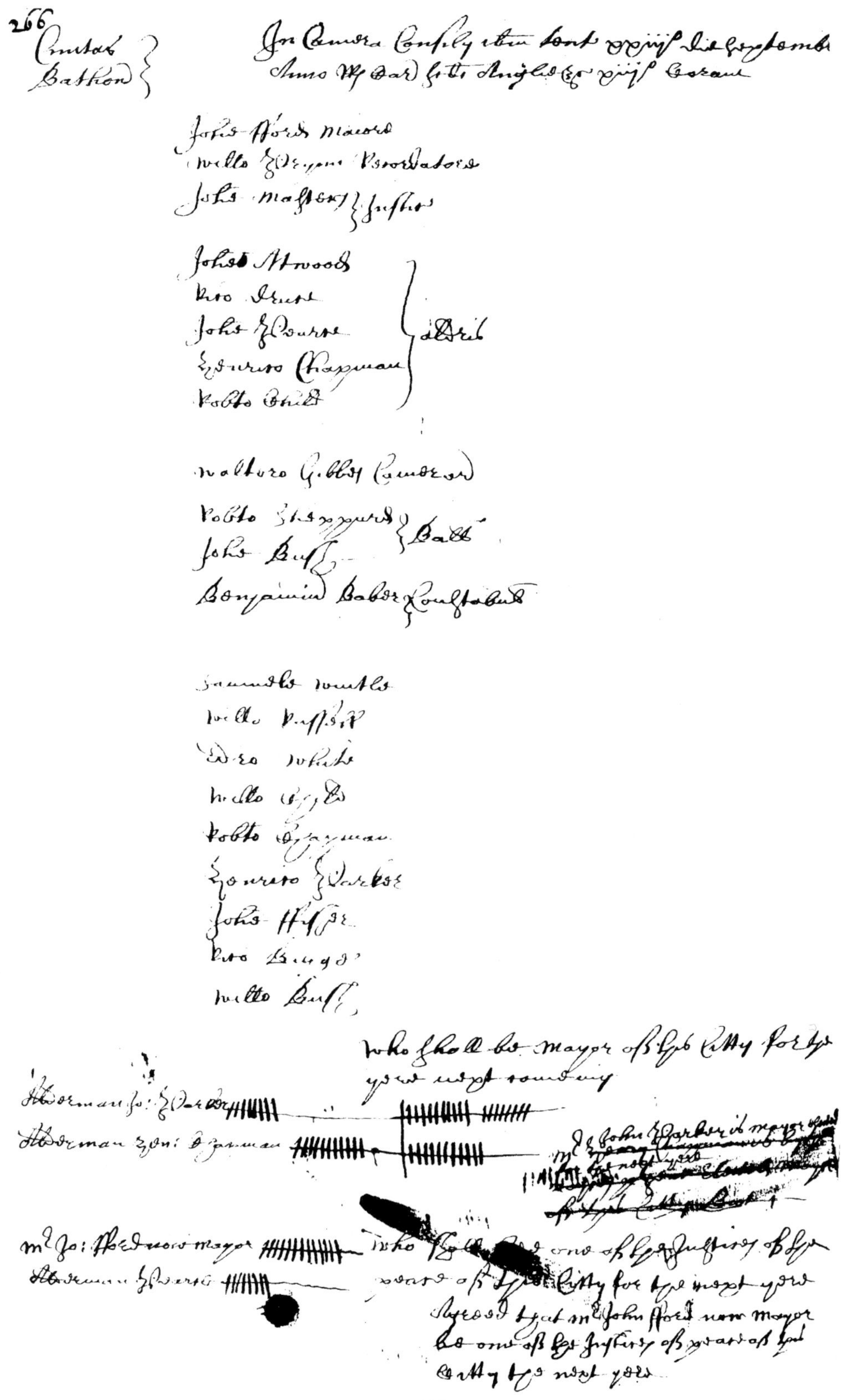

266 Civitas Bathon

In Camera Consilij ibm tent xxiiij° die Septembr Anno RR Car Anglie &c xviij° Coram

John fford Maior
Willo Prynne Recordatore
John Masters Justic

John Atwood
Rico Druce
John Parker
Henrico Chapman
Robto Child
Aldr

Waltero Gibbes Camerar

Robto Sheppard
John Bush
Ball

Benjamin Baker Constabular

Samuele Wintle
Willo Russell
Edro White
Willo Pyle
Robto Chapman
Henrico Parker
John Hilier
Rico Biggs
Willo Bush

who shall be Mayor of this Citty for the yeare next ensuing

Alderman Jo: Parker
Alderman Hen: Chapman

Mr John Parker is mayor … for the next yeare …

Mr Jo: fford now mayor
Alderman Pearse

who shall be one of the Justices of the peace of this Citty for the next yeare

Agreed that Mr John fford now mayor be one of the Justices of peace of this Citty the next yeare

ABBREVIATIONS

Bod.L	Bodleian Library
BL	British Library
BRO	Bath Record Office
BrRO	Bristol Record Office
CCSP	Calendar of Clarendon State Papers
CJ	Journals of the House of Commons.
CPCC	Calendar of the Proceedings of the Committee for Compounding.
CUL	Cambridge University Library.
CSPD	Calendar of the State Papers Domestic.
DNB	Dictionary of National Biography.
E.	British Library, Thomason Tracts.
EHR	English Historical Review.
HMC	Historical Manuscripts Commission.
LJ	Journals of the House of Lords.
PRO	Public Record Office.
SRO	Somerset County Record Office.
TRHS	Transactions of the Royal Historical Society
VCH	Victoria County History.
WRO	Wiltshire County Record Office.

References

1 THE COMMUNITY ON THE EVE OF WAR

(1) T G Barnes, *Somerset 1625-1640* (Oxford, 1961), pp 1-2.
(2) CSPD, 1644-5, p83 (Waller and Haselrig to Committee of Both Kingdoms, 30th October 1644).
(3) PRO, E179.256/16, Somerset Hearth, Tax Assessments, 1664-65 (Books 23-27).
(4) R Howell, *Newcastle-Upon-Tyne and the Puritan Revolution* (Oxford, 1967), pp 3-13.
(5) John T Evans, *17th Century Norwich* (Oxford, 1979) p6; Peter Clark and Paul Slack, *English Towns in Transition, 1500-1700* (Oxford, 1976), pp 21, 113-4; R Howell, *Newcastle-upon-Tyne and the Puritan Revolution,* pp 9-10.
(6) E H Bates-Harbin, *Quarter Sessions Records for the County of Somerset,* (Taunton, 1907-8), Vol 2, 1625-1639, p 290 (Wells, 1638, petition of the inhabitants of Walcot); SRO, The Survey of Walcot Manor, 1638-41, DD/BR/SB/N68(2).
(7) R Howell, Newcastle-Upon-Tyne and the Puritan Revolution, p9.
(8) Joseph Gilmore, The City of Bath, 1694 (map).
(9) CSPD, 1631-3, p213 (Justices of Peace for the County of Somerset to the Council, December 1631).
(10) BRO, The Survey of Bath, 1641.
(11) A similar population figure for 1680 is arrived at by Professor R S Neal in his book *Bath: A Social History,* 1680-1850 (London, 1981), p 44.
(12) P R James, *The Baths of Bath in the Sixteenth and Early Seventeenth Centuries* (Bath, 1938), pp 12-13.
(13) Peter Clark and Paul Slack, *English Towns in Transition,* 1500-1700, pp 1-10, 46, 83, 162; Philip Styles, *Studies in Seventeenth Century West Midlands History* (Kineton, 1978), p 213; John T Evans, *17th Century Norwich,* pp 4-5; Anthony Fletcher, *The Outbreak of the English Civil War* (London, 1981), p 393; Paul Slack, *Poverty and Politics in Salisbury,* 1597-1660 (in Peter Clark and Paul Slack, *Crisis and Order in English Towns, 1500-1700,* London, 1972) p 171; Roger Howell, *Newcastle-upon-Tyne and the Puritan Revolution,* pp 7-8.
(14) Thomas Venner, *The Baths of Bath* (London, 1628) p 1.
(15) John Leland, *The Itinerary of 1535-43* (edited by L T Smith, London, 1907).
(16) Peter Clark and Paul Slack, *English Towns in Transition,* 1500-1700, p 26.

(17) Henry Chapman, *Thermae Redivivae, The City of Bath Described* (London, 1673) p 1.
(18) BRO, Bath Chamberlain's Account, 1641-42.
(19) *The Diary of Samuel Pepys,* edited by John Warrington (London, 1953), p 247.
(20) BRO, Bath Chamberlain's Accounts, 1641-2.
(21) Rev John Collinson, *History of Somersetshire* (London, 1791), vol. 1, pp 29-33.
(22) BRO, Bath Chamberlain's Accounts, 1640.
(23) H Chapman, *Thermae Redivivae,* p 2.
(24) BRO, Bath Chamberlain's Accounts, 1639, 1641, 1643.
(25) BRO, Bath Chamberlain's Accounts, 1641, 1648.
(26) John Leland, *The Itinerary of 1535-43,* p 2
(27) John Collinson, *History of Somersetshire,* pp 29, 31, 54, 73.
(28) Shelagh Bond, *The Chamber Order Book of Worcester, 1602-1650,* (Worcester, 1974) pp 43-44; Peter Clark and Paul Slack, *English Towns in Transition, 1500-1700,* p 55; A M Johnson, *Politics in Chester during the Civil Wars and Interregnum,* 1650-62, (in Peter Clark and Paul Slack, *Crisis and Order in English Towns, 1500-1700,* London, 1972) p 127.
(29) *The Diary of Samuel Pepys,* p 246.
(30) BRO, Bath Chamberlain's Accounts, 1640.
(31) John K G Taylor, *The Civil Government of Gloucester, 1640-46* (in Transactions of the Bristol & Gloucestershire Archaeological Society, vol. LXVII, Gloucester, 1949) p 64.
(32) Shelagh Bond, *The Chamber Order Book of Worcester, 1602-50,* p
(33) A M Johnson, *Politics in Chester during the Civil Wars and the Interregnum,* 1640-62, p 209.
(34) Patrick McGrath, *Bristol and the Civil War,* (Bristol 1981) p 3.
(35) Roger Howell, *Newcastle-upon-Tyne and the Puritan Revolution,* pp 35-41.
(36) John T Evans, *17th Century Norwich,* pp 26-29; Peter Clark and Paul Slack, *English Towns in Transition, 1500-1700,* p 55.
(37) C G Parsloe, *The Corporation of Bedford, 1647-1664,* (in TRHS 4th series, vol. 29, 1947) p 154.
(38) John Collinson, *History of Somersetshire,* pp 22-25.
(39) BRO, Bath Council Book, No 2 November 5th 1649).
(40) BRO, Bath Chamberlain's Accounts, 1636.
(41) BRO, Bath Council Book, No 1 (February 15th, 1647)

(42) BRO, Bath Chamberlain's Accounts, 1640.
(43) BRO, Bath Chamberlain's Accounts, 1642-3.
(44) BRO, Bath Chamberlain's Accounts, 1641-2.
(45) BRO, Bath Chamberlain's Accounts, 1638, 1640.
(46) BRO, Bath Chamberlain's Accounts, 1636, 1639, 1640.
(47) T G Barnes, *Somerset, 1625-1640,* pp 107-116.
(48) BL, Add.Mss., 28,273, ff 105-118, Subsidy Assessments and other Memoranda by J Locke, 1623-1655.
(49) Patrick McGrath, *Bristol and the Civil War* (Bristol, 1981) p 7.
(50) E H Bates-Harbin, *Quarter Sessions Records for the County of Somerset,* Vol 1, 1607-1625, (Taunton 1907-8), pp 351, 355.
(51) BRO, Bath Chamberlain's Accounts, 1630.
(52) Thomas Fuller, *The History of the Worthies of England* (London 1662), p 21.
(53) BRO, Bath Council Book, No 1 (23rd May, 1632; 29th December, 1634); Bath Chamberlain's Accounts 1630, 1633, 1641.
(54) E H Bates-Harbin, *Quarter Sessions Records,* Vol 2, 1625-1639, p 13.
(55) BRO, Bath Chamberlain's Accounts, 1625-6.
(56) BRO, Bath Chamberlain's Accounts, 1625-6.
(57) Henry Chapman, *Thermae Redivivae: the City of Bath Described,* (London, 1673) p 4.
(58) John Collinson, *History of Somersetshire,* pp 42-43.
(59) BRO, Bath Chamberlain's Accounts, 1640.
(60) John Collinson, *History of Somersetshire,* p 44
(61) BRO, Bath Chamberlain's Accounts, 1640, 1641, 1643.
(62) John Collinson, *History of Somersetshire,* p 43.
(63) BRO, Bath Chamberlain's Accounts, 1642.
(64) BRO, Bath Chamberlain's Accounts, 1643.
(65) BRO, Bath Chamberlain's Accounts, 1643, 1649.
(66) BRO, Bath Council Book, No 1 (18th April, 1645).
(67) BRO, Bath Chamberlain's Accounts, 1638.
(68) BRO, Bath Chamberlain's Accounts, 1646.
(69) Peter Clark and Paul Slack, *English Towns in Transition, 1500-1700,* p 27.
(70) BRO, 1641 Survey, 60/1.
(71) BRO, Acc. No 59, Bundle 2 (Crook) No 1 (1656: George Long, Clerk, v Robert Fisher, Henry Chapman, Samuel Wintle and John Biggs, defendants).
(72) BRO, 1641 Survey 103/2. 210/1 (Numbers are page references in the Survey Book).
(73) BRO, Acc. No 59, Bundle 2 (Crook) No 1, Long v Fisher, 1656.
(74) BRO, 1641 Survey, 33, 59/2, 121/1.
(75) BRO, Acc. No 59, Bundle 2 (Crook) No 1, Long v Fisher, 1656.
(76) SRO, DD|Po|55, The Manor Survey of Farmborough, 1630;
SRO|BR|Sb|N68, Survey of Walcot Manor, 1638-41.
(77) R S Neale, *Bath: A Social History,* p 103.
(78) Peter Earle in *Stuart England,* edited by Blair Worden (Oxford, 1986) p 35.
(79) E H Bates-Harbin, *Quarter Sessions Records for the County of Somerset,* vol. 1, p 164 (Wells, 1616: petition of the inhabitants of Saltford), p 183

(Taunton 1616), p 341 (Wells, 1624: petition of the inhabitants of Widcombe); CSPD, 1619-23, p 391 (Letter of Mayor of Bath to Council, 12th May. 1622).
(80) SRO, Session Roll, 43 ii, f 166 (The humble petition of the vicar and other inhabitants of the parish of Frome Selwood, 13th August, 1622); E H Bates-Harbin, *Quarter Sessions Records for the County of Somerset,* vol 1, p 323 (petition of the inhabitants of Frome for some relief - Wells, 1623).
(81) PRO, SP 16.185.40 (Letter from Justices Horner, Hopton and Harington to the Council, 20th February 1631).
(82) PRO, SP 16.204.12 (Letter from Horner and Hopton to the Council (December, 1631).
(83) T G Barnes, *Somerset, 1625-1640,* pp 156-7.
(84) Buchanan Sharp, *In Contempt of All Authority,* (California, 1980) pp 6-7.
(85) CSPD, 1619-23, pp 392-3 (Letters to the council from the High Sheriff of Somerset, 14th May 1622; and from the Justices of Somerset, 15th May 1622).
(86) SRO, Session Roll, 64 ii, f 200 204 (examinations taken by Henry Ley, 2nd Earl of Marlborough, Custos Rotulorum, 1630).
(87) CSPD, 1629-31, p 403 (report on the rioters near Newbury, 6th December 1630).
(88) Buchanan Sharp, *Popular Protests in Seventeenth Century England* (in Barry Reay, Popular Culture in Seventeenth Century England, London, 1985) pp 276-7.
(89) John Leland, *The Itinerary of 1535-43,* vii, p 99.
(90) Acts of the Privy Council, N.S. xiv 93, 6th May 1580.
(91) CSPD, 1619-23, pp 291-93.
(92) J de L Mann, *The Cloth Industry in the West of England from 1640 to 1880* (Oxford 1971), pp xi-xii; Charles Wilson, *England's Apprenticeship,* 1603-1763, pp 69-75.
(93) WRO, Methuen Papers, 1742 (ff 1608, 2774, 1609, 2740, 2741) various conveyances, leases, etc.
(94) PRO, Privy Council Records, 1639, p 323.
(95) PRO, cl07/20, f. 22,45,72,92,100, The Groot Boeck (Cloth Purchasers' Book of the Ashe family firm in London, 1650-43); *Mercurius Aulicus,* 16th March 1643.
(96) PRO, cl07/20, f. 46,73,93,100; 23,58,63,115; 20,49,78,91,99,133 (The Groot Boeck, 1640-43).
(97) PRO, c107/20, f 107; WRO, Methuen Papers 1742.5918 (John Ashe's Will as remembered).
(98) CSPD, 1636-37 p 117 (Value of James Ashe's estate, 17th May 1637).
(99) J T Rutt (ed), *The Diary of Thomas Burton 1656-59,* (London, 1828), vol 1, p 127.
(100) Bod. L., Aubrey 2, f 62 (1686).
(101) CSPD, 1636-37, p 397 (Petition of John Ashe, James Haynes, etc., to the Council, August 1637).
(102) PRO, SP 16.345.5 (Petition of John Ashe of Freshford, Clothier, to the Privy Council, 1637).
(103) WRO, Methuen Papers, 1742 (ff 1622, 1617, 2942, 2856, 2846, 2899, 2931) - various leases and agreements.
(104) J de L Mann, *The Cloth Industry in the West of England,* p 94.
(105) BRO, The Survey of Bath, 1641; Furman Leases, 6/2. 47/1, 53/1, 37/2, 3/2.

(106) John Wood, *Essay Towards a Description of Bath* (London, 1745)

(107) Elizabeth Holland in *Citizens of Bath: Occupations in Bath in the Reign of James I* (Bath, 1988) pp 10-13, identified for 1625 a total of 20 weavers, 16 clothiers, 4 feltmakers, 6 tuckers and fullers, 1 cardmaker, 1 button maker, 1 hosier, 2 hatters, 8 mercers, 11 tailors and 1 merchant tailor.

(108) BRO, Leonard Coward's Bundle No 5: Mark Dallemore's Will, 1st January, 1647. This contains no reference to his clothmaking business, nor does the will of Peter Sherston, Bath clothier, dated 30th October, 1662 (SRO, DD\IX\SR 1 c/400 f51, The Holworth Collection of Wills, Vol. 1). No other wills or inventories of Bath clothiers have survived in either the BRO or the SRO; nor are any of them referred to in F Brown, *Abstracts of Somersetshire Wills,* 6 volumes (London 1887).

(109) PRO, SP16.282.81 (Letter of the Justices to the council, Bath, 24th January 1635).

(110) SRO, DD/BR/SB N/68(2) The Survey of Walcot Manor, 1638-41; BRO, The Survey of Bath, 1641; S Sydenham, *Bath City and Traders' Tokens during the 17th Century* (in Proceedings of the Bath Natural History and Antiquarian Field Club, vol X, 1905, pp 497-9).

(111) Thomas Venner, *The Baths of Bath* (London 1628), p 1.

(112) P Holland, *Camden's Britannia* (London, 1637), p 236.

(113) BRO, Bath Chamberlain's Accounts 1641, 1647, and Minute Book, No 1, 1642, 1645.

(114) Thomas Venner, *The Baths of Bath,* p 312.

(115) BRO, The Survey of Bath, 1641.

(116) Thomas Venner, *The Baths of Bath,* p 311.

(117) S Sydenham, *Bath City & Traders' Tokens,* pp 443-525.

(118) BRO, Bath Council Book No 1 (23rd May 1632).

(119) BRO, The Survey of Bath, 1641.

(120) Elizabeth Holland, *Citizens of Bath,* pp 13-20; BRO, Furman Title Deed, 3/1, The Inventory of Thomas Chapman; PRO, E179.256/16, Somerset Hearth Tax Assessments, 1664-65.

(121) Peter Clark and Paul Slack, *English Towns in Transition, 1500-1700,* pp 33-36.

(122) CSPD, 1634-5, p 146 (13th July 1634).

(123) PRO, E179.256/16, Somerset Hearth tax, 1664-5.

(124) SRO, Popham MSS, 32/1, (Hunstrete Audit, 1649-50).

(125) Historical Manuscripts Commission, Report xii, (London 1891) App. i, p 71.

(126) SRO, Popham MSS, DD/PO/12 (leases of coalmines).

(127) BRO, 1641 Survey, 210/1; Bath Chamberlain's Accounts, 1641, 1658.

(128) E H Bates-Harbin, *Quarter Sessions Records for the County of Somerset,* vol 2, p 203 (petition of the inhabitants of Brislington Wells 1634).

2 LEADERSHIP AND THE SEEDS OF WAR

(1) T G Barnes, Somerset 1625-1640: *A County's Government during the Personal Rule* (London, 1961) pp 11-12.

(2) *D N B;* M F Keeler, *The Long Parliament, 1640-11* (New York, 1954), pp 310-311; S W Bates-Harbin, *Members of Parliament for the County of Somerset* (Taunton, 1939), p 167; John Aubrey, *Brief Lives,* edited by O L Dick, (London, 1950), Vol 2., pp 159-60; *Journal of Sir Simonds D'Ewes,* edited by Wallace Notestein (Yale, 1923) p 52n.

(3) *D N B:* M F Keeler, *The Long Parliament, 1640-41,* p 310; S W Bates-Harbin, *Members of Parliament for the County of Somerset,* pp 167-169; D L Dick, *Brief Lives,* pp 159-60; J H Bettey (ed.), *Calendar of Correspondence of the Smyth Family of Ashton Court, 1548-1642* (Bristol Record Society, 1982).

(4) Margaret F Stieg (editor), *The Diary of John Harington, MP, 1646-53* (London, 1977) pp 1-12; S W Bates-Harbin, *Members of Parliament for the County of Somerset,* p 152

(5) PRO, SP 16.432(33-34), 10th November 1639.

(6) *D N B;* F T R Edgar, *Sir Ralph Hopton: The King's Man in the West, 1642-1652* (Oxford 1968), pp 1-17; M F Keeler, *The Long Parliament, 1640-41,* p 122; S W Bates-Harbin, *Members of Parliament for the County of Somerset,* pp 147-9; W Notestein, ed, *Journal of Simonds D Ewes,* p 91.

(7) *D N B;* F T R Edgar, *Sir Ralph Hopton,* pp 17-26; M F Keeler, *The Long Parliament, 1640-41,* p 222; S W Bates-Harbin, *Members of Parliament for the County of Somerset,* pp 147-9; W Notestein, ed, *Journal of Sir Simonds D'Ewes,* p 56; T G Barnes, *Somerset, 1625-40,* pp 35-6; F P Verney & M M Verney (editors), *Memoirs of the Verney Family during the Seventeenth Century,* (London, 1925) pp 220, 386.

(8) *D N B;* M F Keeler, *The Long Parliament 1640-41,* pp 225-6; W Notestein, *Journal of Sir Simonds D'Ewes,* pp 52n, 160, 162-3, 452n.

(9) M F Keeler, *The Long Parliament, 1640-41,* pp 100-101; CSPD, 1636-7, p 80 (8th May 1637 Letter from William Bassett to the Council); J Rushworth, *Historical Recollections of Private Passages of State* (London 1701), Vol 3, p 912.

(10) Rev John Collinson, *The History and Antiquities of the County of Somerset,* Vol. 2 (London, 1791), p 406; PRO, SP23.178 (282-292), Committee for Compounding, Sir Thomas Bridges.

(11) CUL, Western MSS, Add.89.fll0 (Mr John Ashe's Petition, 17th July 1646); M F Keeler, *The Long Parliament, 1640-41,* pp 91-2; S W Bates-Harbin, *Members of Parliament for the County of Somerset,* pp 158-9; PRO, SP 16.68(82), Refusers of the Loan, June 1627; SP 16.68(265), The Testimony of John Ashe ... against William Laud, 22nd January 1643.

(12) *D N B;* S R Gardiner (editor), *Documents relating to the Proceedings against William Prynne* (London 1877), p xxii; R E M Peach, *The Annals of the Parish of Swainswick* (Bath, 1892), pp 32-39.

(13) PRO, SP.16.255(39), Petition of 25 Justices for Somerset, 1633 (n.d.).

(14) BRO, Bath Council Book, No 1 (1638, 1643), Bath Chamberlain's Accounts, 1638-1643. Ages for individuals in this section are calculated from entries in the registers for baptisms and burials for the parishes of St Peter and St Paul, St James and St Michael (BRO).Occupations are taken from

leases in Furman's Repertory, the 1641 Survey and the Chamberlain's Accounts (all BRO).

(15) For a full account of the squabbles in 1661 and 1662, see John Wroughton *Puritanism and Traditionalism: Cultural and Political Division in Bath, 1620-1662* (in Bath History, Vol. 4, 1992, pp 52-70).

(16) BRO, 1641 Survey, 7/1. 9/1; great help in identifying occupations and properties has been gained from Marta Inskip's *Index of 17th Century Leases* (unpublished).

(17) BRO, Bath Chamberlain's Accounts, 1640, 1643.

(18) PRO, E179. 172/404, Subsidy, Bath, 17 Car 1 (1641).

(19) BRO, Bath Chamberlain's Accounts, 1640-43.

(20) BRO, 1641 Survey, 164/1, 121/1, 59/1, 33/1.

(21) BRO, Bath Council Book No 1 (1643-46), No 2 (1652).

(22) BRO, 1641 Survey, 63/1, 84/2, 85/1.

(23) BRO, 1641 Survey, 47/1, 48/2, 52/2, 54/1, 70/3.

(24) SRO, DD/BR/SB N/68(2), Walcot Manor Survey, 1641.

(25) BRO, Bath Chamberlain's Accounts (1641-43).

(26) BRO, Furman Leases, F.407; 1641 Survey 148/1.

(27) BRO, 1641 Survey, 60/1, Long v Fisher 1656 (Acc. No 59, Bundle 2, Crook, No 1).

(28) BRO, 1641 Survey, 55/1, 74/1, 74/2, 103/1, 142/1, 177/1; Bath Chamberlain's Accounts, 1639; Bath Council Book No 1, 1626, 1635.

(29) BRO, 1641 Survey 103/2; Furman Leases, F287; Bath Council Book, No 1, 1628, 1638; Long v Fisher, 1656.

(30) BRO, 1641 Survey, 105/2; Bath Council Book, No 1, 1636-39.

(31) BRO, 1641 Survey, 175/2; Long v Fisher, 1656, Bath Chamberlain's Accounts, 1640, 1641.

(32) BRO, 1641 Survey, 114/1; Bath Chamberlain's Accounts, 1639.

(33) BRO, Furman Leases, F294.

(34) BRO, Bath Council Book No 1, 23rd May 1632; Bath Chamberlain's Accounts, 1647, 1651; 1641 Survey, 67/2.

(35) BRO, 1641 Survey, 19/1; Bath Council Book, No 1, 15th December 1645.

(36) BRO, 1641 Survey, 98/1; Bath Council Book No 1, 1642.

(37) BRO, 1641 Survey, 116/2, 181/2.

(38) BRO, 1641 Survey, 14/1, 95/2, 115/2, 116/1; SRO, Walcot Manor Survey, 1641.

(39) BRO, Bath Chamberlain's Accounts, 1637, 1642, 1646, 1650.

(40) BRO, 1641 Survey, 73/2, 96/1, 159/1; Bath Council Book, No 1, 1639, 1641.

(41) BRO, Bath Council Book, No 1, 26th June 1648.

(42) BRO, 1641 Survey, 87/1.

(43) BRO, Bath Chamberlain's Accounts, 1643.

(44) BRO, 1641 Survey, 91/3.

(45) BRO, 1641 Survey, 178/1; Bath Chamberlain's Accounts, 1646.

(46) BRO, 1641 Survey, 72/2; Bath Council Book, No 1, 9th February 1646; No 2, 1st May 1654; 31st March 1656.

(47) BRO, Furman Leases, F.340; Bath Chamberlain's Accounts, 1656, 1657, 1661.

(18) PRO, E179. 172/404, Subsidy, Bath 17 Car 1 (1641); BRO, Bath Council Book, No 1, October 1643.

(49) In Norwich, by comparison, the average age of the pro-parliamentarians was 54 (John T Evans, *Seventeenth Century Norwich*, p 142).

(50) For the inter-relationship of Council members, I am indebted to two local works - Elizabeth Holland: *The Descent of the Chapman Mayors of Bath of the Seventeenth Century* (Bath 1989) and Marta Inskip: *Index of 17th Century Leases* (unpublished). Symbols used in the text: P = Clift's faction; R = Chapman's faction; M = moderate group.

(51) John T Evans, *Seventeenth Century Norwich*, pp 30-31, 142.

(52) W Page (ed.), *VCH, Somerset,* Vol 2 (London, 1911), pp 258-9.

(53) CSPD, 1635, p 495.

(54) BRO, Bath Chamberlain's Accounts, 1635-6.

(55) CSPD, 1636-7, p 446.

(56) CSPD, 1637, p 532.

(57) BRO, Bath Chamberlain's Accounts 1637.

(58) CSPD, 1637, p 402.

(59) CSPD, 1638-9, p 45.

(60) BRO, Bath Chamberlain's Accounts, 1640.

(61) CSPD, 1638-9, p 513.

(62) BRO, Bath Chamberlain's Accounts, 1640.

(63) CSPD, 1640, pp 220-1.

(64) BRO, Bath Chamberlain's Accounts, 1640.

(65) PRO, E.179.172.142, Subsidy 17 Car 1 (1641); BL, Add.MSS, 45, 367, fl28, Notes on Poll Money, 26th August 1641.

(66) CSPD, 1637-8, p 551.

(67) SRO, DIDICa 194, Comperta 1615 (presentments from the Archdeaconry of Bath).

(68) David Underdown, *Revel, Riot and Rebellion,* pp 77-9.

(69) BRO, Bath Council Book No 1 (3rd October, l9th December, 1631); Bath Chamberlain's Accounts, 1630-43.

(70) Shelagh Bond, *The Chamber Order Book of Worcester, 1602-1650,* p 45; J R Chanter and Thomas Wainwright, *Reprint of the Barnstaple Records,* Vol 1, p 201; H Stocks, ed, *Records of the Borough of Leicester, 1603-1688,* p 272.

(71) *Notes and Queries for Somerset and Dorset,* Vol 24, (ed. G W Saunders, and J Fowler, Sherborne, 1946) p 136.

(72) Margaret Stieg, *Laud's Laboratory: The Diocese of Bath and Wells in the Early Seventeenth Century* (Lewisberg, 1982), p 282.

(73) SRO, DIDICa 319, Camperta, 1638.

(74) Margaret Stieg, *Laud's Laboratory,* p 290.

(75) D Neal, *History of the Puritans,* Vol 1, (London 1732) p 587; *VCH Somerset,* Vol 2, (London 1911) p 42.

(76) BRO, Bath Council Book No 1 (30th September, 1633; 29th December 1645); Bath Chamberlain's Accounts, 1627-42.

(77) John T Evans, *Seventeenth Century Norwich,* pp 102-4.

(78) Shelagh Bond, *The Chamber Order Book of Worcester, 1602-1650,* pp

(79) Peter Clark and Paul Slack, *English Towns in Transition, 1500-1700,* p 151.

(80) An analysis of the *actual* strength and distribution of puritanism within the area in the 1640's and 1650's will be given in Chapter Seven.

(81) E H Bates-Harbin, *Quarter Sessions Records,* Vol 1, p 7.

(82) HMC, 3rd Report, *Calendar of Phelips' MSS,* p 286, (correspondence between Phelips and Charles I regarding Church Ales, 1632-3); Thomas G Barnes, *County Politics and a Puritan Cause Celebre: Somerset Churchales, 1633* (TRHS 5th Series, Vol 9, 1959), pp 103-122.

(83) SRO, DlDlCa 194, Comperta 1615 (presentments from the Archdeaconry of Bath).

(84) John Latimer, *The Annals of Bristol in the Seventeenth Century,* p 101.

(85) E Calamy, *The Nonconformists' Memorial,* Vol 3, (ed. Samuel Palmer, London, 1775) p 123.

(86) SRO, DlDlCd 71. 81, Depositions, 1631-4, 1635 (Fabian v Payton, Weeke and Horte); David Underdown, *Revel, Riot and Reform,* pp 67-8, 86-8.

(87) E H Bates-Harbin, ed, *Quarter Sessions Records for the County of Somerset,* Vol 3, 1646-1660, pp 2&5, 302, 324; CSPD, 1652-3, p 301, Council of State Proceedings; BRO, Bath Council Book No 2 (7th April 1634); SRO, DlDlCa 319, 330, Chapter Act Book, 1638-9, 1639.

(88) PRO, SP 16.375/84 (statement of the Beckington Churchwardens regarding their reasons for refusing to remove the communion table, 1634).

(89) *VCH Somerset,* Vol 2, p 44.

(90) Margaret Stieg, *Laud's Laboratory,* pp 297-306; PRO, SP 16.499.85, The Testimony of John Ashe, 22nd January 1643.

(91) David Underdown, *Revel, Riot and Rebellion,* pp 47-48, 53.

(92) E H Bates-Harbin, *Quarter Sessions Records,* Vol 1, pp 199-200.

(93) CSPD, 1619-23, p 501 (Mayor of Bath to the Council, 26th February 1623).

(94) E H Bates-Harbin, *Quarter Sessions Records,* Vol 2 pp 138-9, 144.

(95) E H Bates-Harbin, *Quarter Sessions Records,* Vol 2, p 269.

(96) BRO Bath Chamberlain's Accounts, 1582, 1617, 1618, 1624, 1628.

(97) E H Bates-Harbin, *Quarter Sessions Records,* Vol 1, p 250; Vol 2, p 109; BRO, Bath Council Book No 1 (7th April 1634).

(98) E H Bates-Harbin, *Quarter Sessions Records,* Vol 2, p 116.

(99) BRO, Bath Council Book No 2 (1st October, 1649).

(100) BRO, Bath Council Book, No 1 (31st December, 1632; 28th December, 1635).

(101) SRO, DlDlCa 194, Comperta 1615 (presentments from the Archdeaconry of Bath).

(102) BRO, Bath Chamberlain's Accounts 1603.

(103) E H Bates-Harbin, *Quarter Sessions Records,* Vol 1, p 7.

(104) CSPD, 1637-38, p 551 (The High Sheriff to the Council, 8th May, 1623).

(105) BRO, Bath Chamberlain's Accounts, 1602-1642.

(106) BRO, Bath Chamberlain's Accounts, 1569, 1578, 1589, 1612, 1616.

(107) Robert Alexander, (ed), *Record of Early English Drama: Bath,* (Toronto, forthcoming).

(108) BRO, Bath Chamberlain's Accounts, 1630, 1634, 1643-5.

(109) William Prynne, *Canterburies Doome,* p 92.

(110) Margaret Stieg, *Laud's Laboratory,* pp 297-306.

(111) David Underdown, *Revel, Riot and Rebellion,* pp 181-2.

(112) BRO, Bath Chamberlain's Accounts, 1644.

(113) E H Bates-Harbin (ed), *Quarter Sessions Records for the Count of Somerset,* Vol 1, pp 199-200; CSPD, 1619-23, p 501.

(114) CSPD, 1619-23, p374 (Mayor of Bath to the Council, 11th April 1622, Bath); *Acts of Privy Council* (N.S. ed. Dasent), 1620-23, p 123.

(115) J A Williams, *Post Reformation Catholicism in Bath,* Vol 1 (London 1975), pp 22-39; PRO, E.351-415 (Accounts of Receiver of Recusants' Forfeitures, 1627-39); SRO, Series A, No. 335a (Archdeacon's Presentations).

3 FOR KING OR PARLIAMENT?

(1) E Green: *On the Civil War in Somerset,* Somerset Archaeological and Natural History Society, Vol 14, (Taunton 1867) p 50.

(2) B L, E.155(16), *The Humble Petition of the Knights, Gentry and Freeholders of the County of Somerset,* July 1642.

(2) John Oldmixon: *History of England during the reigns of the Royal House of Stuart,* (London; 1730) p 208

(4) BL, E.109(24), Lord Hertford to the Queen, 11th July 1642, Beverley.

(5) C E H Chadwyck Healey (ed): *Bellum Civile,* Somerset Record Society, Vol. 18, (Taunton, 1902) p 1 (Sir Ralph Hopton's narrative).

(6) LJ, V, p226.

(7) BRO, Bath Chamberlain's Accounts, 1642.

(8) CSPD, 1641-43, p 361, (Petition of the Grand Jury for Somerset to the King, 25th July 1642).

(9) Hopton's narrative in Healey, *Bellum Civile,* p 2.

(10) Hopton's narrative in Healey, *Bellum Civile,* p 2.

(11) Hopton's narrative in Healey, *Bellum Civile,* p 3

(12) B L E.109 (24) *A letter from the Committee in Somersetshire,* 1st August 1642.

(13) Hopton's account in Healey, *Bellum Civile,* pp 3-5; Ashe's Account in BL, E.109(24) *A Letter from the Committee in Somersetshire.*

(14) Hopton's narrative in Healey, *Bellum Civile,* p 5.

(15) BL, E.109(24) *A Letter from the Committee in Somersetshire.*

(16) BL, E.111(7), *A Relation of all the Proceedings in Somersetshire and Bristoll,* 11th August 1642.

(17) BL, E.111(5), *A Perfect Relation of the proceedings of the Cavaleers that were in Walls. A Letter from the Committee in Summersetshire,* 7th August 1642.

(18) Hopton's narrative in Healey, *Bellum Civile,* pp 7-8.

(19) BL, E111(5), A Perfect Relation ... (Ashe's narrative).

(20) Healey, *Bellum Civile,* p 10 (Hopton's narrative).

(21) Healey, *Bellum Civile,* p 9 (Hopton's narrative).

(22) BL, E.111(4), *Joyful News from Wells in Somersetshire,* 12th August 1642.

(23) CSPD, 1641-43, p 370 (Petition of the Constables of the several hundreds of Somerset to Sir Robert Foster, Justice of Assize, 12th August, 1642).

(24) BL, 669.f6(62), *True Newes from Somersetshire,* 6th August 1642.

(25) BL, 669.f6(62), *True Newes from Somersetshire,* 6th August 1642.

(26) John Latimer, *The Annals of Bristol in the Seventeenth Century,* pp 156-160.

(27) BrRO, Common Council Book, No 4, 1642-49, ff 1, 2, 5, 11-16, 18, 19, 21; John Latimer, *The Annals of Bristol,* pp 160-4; Patrick McGrath, *Bristol and the Civil War* (Bristol 1981), pp 3, 10-12.

(28) Brian Manning, *The English People and the English Revolution,* pp 166-79; 196-213.

(29) Earl of Clarendon, *History of the Great Rebellion,* (Oxford, 1888), Vol II, p 296.

(30) Margaret F Stieg, *The Diary of John Harington, 1646-53,* (Somerset Record Society, Vol 74, 1977).

(31) BL, E111(5), *A Perfect Relation ...* (Ashe's narrative); Healey, *Bellum Civile,* p 7 (Hopton's narrative).

(32) Historical Manuscripts Commission, 5th Report, Part 1, Appendix p 44.

(33) Healey, *Bellum Civile,* p 2.

(34) E Green, *On the Civil War in Somerset,* p 69; the letter, forwarded to parliament, is published in BL, E.112(13).

(35) PRO, SP 23.107(809), SP 23.111(657), Committee for Compounding (papers relating to the petitions of Sir Christopher Neville and Richard Prater).

(36) PRO, SP 23.192(463), SP 23.180(24), SP 23.110(56), SP 23.204(663), SP 23.73(831), Committee for Compounding (papers relating to the petitions of Valentine Powell, Robert Leversage, Edward Paston, Robert Fisher and George Chapman).

(37) PRO, SP.23.73(844), SP.23.117(331), SP.23.204(701), SP.23.240(583,679,651,721), Committee for Compounding (papers relating to the petitions of Henry Chapman, Philip Sherwood, Thomas Gibbs and Maximilian Macie).).

(38) BL, E.1088(7), *Letter from Dr Charlatan.*

(39) E Green, *On the Civil War in Somerset,* p 57.

(40) BRO, Bath Chamberlain's Accounts and Minute Books, 1642-6.

(41) BL, E.111(5), *A Perfect Relation ...*; BL, 111(4), *Joyfull News from Wells ....*

(42) David Underdown, *Revel, Riot and Rebellion,* pp 168-170.

(43) BL, E111(5) *A Perfect Relation*

(44) Bod.L., Clarendon MSS, 22.75; Captain Henry Archbowlle to Colonel N Fiennes, Malmesbury, 6th June 1643.

(45) Clive Holmes, *The Eastern Association in the English Civil War,* pp 34-9.

(46) Anthony Fletcher, *The Outbreak of the Civil War,* pp 348-52.

(47) Derek Hirst, *The Representative of the People?* (Cambridge, 1975), pp 114-5, 192-3.

(48) J H Plumb, *The Growth of the Electorate in England from 1600 to 1715* (in Past and Present, No 45, November 1969), pp 91-2, 104.

(49) Brian Manning, *The English People and the English Revolution,* p 180.

(50) David Underdown, *Revel, Riot and Rebellion,* p 173.

(51) BL, E111(5) *A Perfect Relation*

(52) PRO, SP 28.175, Assessments, Somerset (Keynsham Hundred).

(53) David Underdown, *Revel, Riot and Rebellion,* p 173.

(54) BL, E.112(13) *Joyfull Newes from Wells ... A second Letter sent from John Ashe, Esq., to the Honorable William Lenthall, Esq., Speaker of the House of Commons in Parliament.*

(55) BL, Add.MSS, 28,273, ff 105-118, Subsidy Assessments and other Memoranda by J Locke, 1623-1655; PRO, SP 28.175 - Assessments, Somerset, Keynsham Hundred (Farmborough).

(56) BL, E.111(5), *A Perfect Relation ...*

(57) LJ, Vol V, p 133.

(58) BRO, Bath Chamberlain's Accounts, 1642.

(59) PRO, SP 16.345.5 (Petition of John Ashe of Freshford, Clothier, to the Privy Council, 1637).

(60) CUL, Western MSS, add.89.fllO, John Ashe's Petition, 1646.

(61) John K G Taylor, *The Civil Government of Gloucester,* 1640-6, pp 67-82.

(62) W T Baker, ed, *Records of the Borough of Nottingham,* Vol 5, 1625-1702, pp 207-9.

(63) Clive Holmes, *The Eastern Association in the English Civil War,* pp 39-40, 51-2.

(64) BL, Harleian MSS 2135, f50, Letter from James, Lord Strange to Mr Richard Brereton and Mr Hugh Wilbraham, 6th September 1642.

(65) Anthony Fletcher, *The Outbreak of the English Civil War* pp 393-4

(66) David Underdown, *Revel, Riot and Rebellion,* p 174.

(67) BL, 669,f6(62), *True Newes from Somersetshire;* BL, E.109(34), *A True and Sad Relation of divers passages in Somersetshire.*

(68) BL, E.155(16), *The Humble Petition of the Knights, Gentry and Freeholders of the County of Somerset,* July 1642.

(69) Clarendon, *History of the Great Rebellion,* Vol VI, p 4.

(70) BL, E109(24) *A Letter from the Committee in Somersetshire...*

(71) Healey, *Bellum Civile,* p 3.

(72) Clarendon, *History of the Great Rebellion,* Vol VI, p 4.

(73) Historical Manuscripts Commission, 5th Report, Pt 1, Appendix, p 44.

(74) David Underdown, *The Problem of Popular Allegiance in the English Civil War,* (in TRHS, 5th Series, Vol 31, 1981) pp 69-71.

(75) Clive Holmes, *The Eastern Association in the English Civil War* pp 33, 42.

(76) Philip Styles, *Studies in Seventeenth Century West Midlands History,* p 221.

(77) H Stocks, ed, *Records of the Borough of Leicester,* 1603-1688, pp 320-1.

(78) John Latimer, *The Annals of Bristol in the Seventeenth Century,* pp 156-7, 163.
(79) John Corbet, *An Historicall Relation of the Military Government of Gloucester,* pp 23-24.
(80) Anthony Fletcher, *The Outbreak of the English Civil War,* pp 3824.
(81) Ronald Hutton, *The Royalist War Effort,* 1642-1646, pp 7-14.
(82) Anthony Fletcher, *The Outbreak of the English Civil War,* p 405.
83) Ronald Hutton, *The Royalist War* Effort, p 20.
(84) Ronald Hutton, *Clarendon's History of the Rebellion,* in EHR, 1982, pp 70-73.
(85) CSPD, 1641-43. p 361 (Petition of the Grand Jury for Somerset to the King, 25th July 1642).
(86) LJ, Vol V, p 226.
(87) BL, E.109(24), *A Letter from the Committee in Somersetshire...*
(88) PRO, SP 28.175, Assessments, Somerset (Keynsham Hundred).
(89) BL, E.112(13), *A Second Letter sent from John Ashe, Esq ...*
(90) PRO, SP 23.208(520), Committee for Compounding (papers relating to the petition of William Bassett, 16th April 1646).
(91) BL, E111(5), *A Perfect Relation...*
(92) The emotional response of the people of North-East Somerset to the situation in 1642 is indicative of deep-seated religious beliefs. An analysis of the *actual* strength and distribution of puritanism within the area - and of the survival of Anglicanism - can be found in Chapter Seven.
(93) BL, E.111(5), *A Perfect Relation...*
(94) PRO, SP 28.175, Assessments, Somerset (Keynsham Hundred).
(95) John Vicars, *Jehovah-Jirah, God in the Mount,* (1644) p 134.
(96) BL, E.109(34), *A True Relation of divers passages in Somerset between the Country and the Cavaliers concerning the Militia and the Commission of Array,* 5th August 1642.
(97) BL, E.441, The Perfect Weekly Account, No 9, 3rd-10th May 1648
(98) William Prynne, Canterburies Doome, (London, 1646) pp 147-8.
(99) CSPD, 1636-37, pp 393-4 (Petition of John Ashe, Freshford, clothier, to the Council, 27th January 1637).
(100) Margaret Stieg, ed, *The Diary of John Harington, MP,* p 27ff.
(101) Brian Manning, *The English People and the English Revolution,* pp 163-5, 244-54.
(102) Anthony Fletcher, *The Outbreak of the English Civil War,* pp 397-9, 405.
(103) John T Evans, *Seventeenth-Century Norwich* pp 102-104, 148-9.

4 THE BATTLE OF LANSDOWN AND THE FALL OF BATH, 1643

(1) John Adair, *Roundhead General: A Military Biography of Sir William Waller,* (London, 1960), p 58.
(2) BL, *Speciall Passages,* 18th-25th April 1643.
(3) BL, *Mercurius Aulicus,* 28th April, 1643.
(4) BL, *The Kingdome's Weekly Intelligencer,* 21st-28th March, 1643.
(5) CCSP, Vol 1, No 1683, Colonel Alexander Popham to Colonel Nathaniel Fiennes, 22nd May 1643.
(6) BL, *A Perfect Diurnal,* 22nd-29th May, 1643
(7) CCSP, Vol 1, No 1683.
(8) CCSP, Vol 1, No 1701, Anthony Nicoll to Nathaniel Fiennes, 7th June 1643.
(9) CCSP, Vol 1, No 1705, Edward Cooke to Nathaniel Fiennes, 24th June, 1643.
(10) BL, E64(12), *A Relation Made in the House of Commons by Colonel Nathaniel Fiennes,* p 13.
(11) ibid, pp 17-21.
(12) ibid, p 25.
(13) ibid, pp 26-27.
(14) According to Richard Atkyns, each army consisted 'of about 6,000 horse and foot'. (Peter Young and Norman Tucker, eds, *Richard Atkins and John Bwyn,* (London, 1967), p 17.
(15) C E H Chadwyck Healey (ed), *Bellum Civile* (Somerset Record Society, Vol 18, Taunton, 1902), p 51.
(16) Bod. L, Tanner MSS, No 62, f.128.
(17) CSPD, 1645-47, p 455.
(18) Bod. L, Tanner MSS, No 62, f.128.
(19) BL, *Speciall Passages,* 2nd-9th May, 1643.
(20) HMC, Portland MSS, Vol 1, p 172; Cook's letter to the Speaker, 3rd June, 1643.
(21) CCSP, Vol 1, No 1701, Nichol's letter to Fiennes, 7th June, 1643.
(22) BL, E64 (12), A Relation Made in the House of Commons.
(23) BL, A Perfect Diurnall, 22nd-19th May, 1643.
(24) BL, E64(12), *A Relation Made in the House of Commons.*
(25) PRO, SP28.147, Accounts of Col. John Fiennes.
(26) Bod. L, Clarendon MSS, 22, f.45.
(27) PRO, SP 28.147, Accounts of Col. John Fiennes.
(28) F T R Edgar, Sir Ralph Hopton: *The King's Man in the West, 1642-1652* (Oxford, 1968), p 94.
(29) BL, E57(11), *Mercurius Aulicus,* 16th June, 1643.
(30) BL, E57(11), *Mercurius Aulicus,* 16th June 1643.
(31) BL, E 60(12), *A True Relation of the Great and Glorious Victory obtained by Sr Wm Waller.*
(32) Quoted by Edgar in *Sir Ralph Hopton,* p 99.
(33) Healey, (ed), *Bellum Civile,* p 52 - Hopton's narrative.
(34) John Vicars, *Jehovah-Jirah, God in the Mount* (London, 1644), p 377.
(35) Healey (ed), *Bellum Civile,* p 52 - Hopton's narrative.
(36) Healey (ed), *Bellum Civile,* p 52 - Hopton's narrative.
(37) Healey (ed), *Bellum Civile,* p 53 - Hopton's narrative.
(38) John Vicars, *Jehovah Jireh,* p 377.
(39) Healey (ed), *Bellum Civile,* p 53 - Hopton's narrative.
(40) Healey (ed), *Bellum Civile,* p 94 - Colonel Slingsby's Relation of the Battle of Lansdown.
(41) John Vicars, *Jehovah Jireh,* p 377.
(42) BL, E60(12), *A True Relation....*
(43) Healey (ed), *Bellum Civile,* pp 94-5 - Slingsby's account.

(44) John Vicars, *Jehovah Jireh,* p 378.
(45) BL, E60(12), *A True Revelation....*
(46) Healey (ed), *Bellum Civile,* p 95 - Slingsby's account.
(47) John Vicars, *Jehovah Jireh,* p 378.
(48) Healey (ed), *Bellum Civile,* p 95 - Slingsby's account
(49) BL, E59(25), *A Copie of a Letter sent from the Mayor of Bristoll unto a Gentleman.*
(50) Healey (ed), *Bellum Civile,* p 54 - Hopton's account.
(51) Healey (ed), *Bellum Civile,* p 95 - Slingsby's account.
(52) John Vicars, *Jehovah Jireh,* p 378.
(53) John Vicars, *Jehovah Jireh,* p 379.
(54) Young & Tucker (eds), *Richard Atkyns & John Gwyn,* p 19 - Atkyns' account.
(55) Healey (ed), *Bellum Civile,* p 96 - Slingsby's account.
(56) BL, E59(25), *A Copie of a Letter ....*
(57) Healey (ed), *Bellum Civile,* p 96 - Slingsby's account.
(58) John Vicars, *Jehovah Jireh,* p 380.
(59) Young & Tucker (eds), *Richard Atkyns & John Gwyn,* p 20 - Atkyns' account.
(60) Healey (ed), *Bellum Civile,* p 96 - Slingsby's account.
(61) Young & Tucker (eds), *Richard Atkyns & John Gwyn,* p 21 - Atkyns' account.
(62) Healey (ed), *Bellum Civile,* p 55 - Hopton's account.
(63) Young & Tucker (eds), *Richard Atkyns & John Gwyn,* p 20 - Atkyns' account.
(64) BL, E249, *A Perfect Diurnall,* 10th-17th July 1643.
(65) John Vicars, *Jehovah Jireh,* p 380.
(66) BL, E249, *A Perfect Diurnall,* 10th-17th July, 1643.
(67) BL, E59(25), A Copie of a Letter ....
(68) BL, E60 (12), A True Relation ....
(69) BL, E249, A Perfect Diurnall, 10th-17th July 1643.
(70) BL, Speciall Passages, 12th-19th July, 1643.
(71) BL, E60(18) Mercurius Aulicus, 8th July, 1643.
(72) PRO, SP 28.175, Assessments, Somerset (Keynsham Hundred).
(73) BL, E.60(12), *A True Relation of the Great and Glorious Victory ... obtained by Sir William Waller, July 14th 1643.*
(74) Clarendon; *A History of the Great Rebellion* Vol III, pp 89,94-5.
(75) Healey (ed), *Bellum Civile,* p 27 - Atkyns' account.
(76) BL, E64(12), *A Relation made in the House of Commons.*

5 THE COMMUNITY UNDER ROYALIST CONTROL 1643-45

(1) David Underdown, *Revel, Riot and Reform,* p 164.
(2) *Archaeologica,* Vol 14, (London, 1803) pp 121-8.
(3) BRO, Bath Council Book, No 1, (18th March, 1644).
(4) BRO, Bath Council Book, No 1, (18th March, 1644).
(5) BRO, Bath Chamberlain's Accounts, 1643-5.
(6) BRO, Bath Council Book, No 1, (13th May 1644; 6th August 1646).
(7) CJ, Vol III, p 505.
(8) LJ, Vol VI, p 612.
(9) BL, *Mercurius Civicus,* 11th-17th July, 1644.
(10) CSPD, 1644, p 335.
(11) CSPD, 1644, p 351.
(12) CSPD, 1644, p 474.
(13) CSPD, 1644-5, p 83.
(14) BL, *A Perfect Diurnall,* 24th-31st March, 1645.
(15) BL, *Perfect Occurrences,* 27th March, 1645.
(16) BL, Sloane MS, 1519, f.66, Waller's letter, 23rd March, 1645.
(17) Joshua Sprigg, *Anglia Redivivae: England's Recovery* (London, 1647), pp 75-6.
(18) BL, *A Full Relation of the Taking of Bath by Sir Thomas Fairfax, 1645,* p 2.
(19) BL, *The Proceedings of the Army under the Command of Sir Thos Fairfax, 24th-31st July, 1645.*
(20) ibid.
(21) BL, *A further Relation of the Taking of Bath, 1645.*
(22) Joshua Sprigg, *Anglia Redivivae,* p 76.
(23) BL, *A Full Relation of the Taking of Bath 1645,* p 3
(24) BL, *A Full Relation of the Taking of Bath* pp 3-4.
(25) ibid., pp 3-4
(26) ibid., pp 5-6.
(27) BL, E292(12), *The Proceedings of the Army ... 24th-31st July, 1645.*
(28) Joshua Sprigg, *Anglia Redivivae,* pp 76-7.
(29) ibid., p 77.
(30) Sir Hardress Waller, cousin to Sir William.
(31) BL, E297(14), *The Proceedings of the Army under the Command of Sir Thos. Fairfax, lst-7th August, 1645.*
(32) BL, *The Moderate Intelligencer,* 31st July-7th August, 1645.
(33) BL, E294(22), *The True Informer,* 2nd August, 1645.
(34) BL, *Mercurius Britanicus,* 28th July-4th August, 1645.
(35) BL, E295(98), *The Parliament's Post,* 29th July-5th August, 1645.
(36) Robert Bell (ed), *Memorials of the Civil War,* Vol 1, (London, 1849) p 244.
(37) LJ, VII p 484.
(38) John Morrill, *The Revolt of the Provinces* (London, 1976), pp 98.106.
(39) Ronald Hutton, *The Royalist War Effort, 1642-1646* (London 1982) , pp 159-172.
(40) David Underdown, *Somerset in the Civil War and Interregnum,* (Newton Abbott, 1973) pp 98-9, 107.
(41) BL, E.301(4), *Letter from Rupert to the Clubmen, 15th July 1645.*
(42) BL, E.294(22), *The True Informer,* 2nd August 1645.
(43) BL, E.294(11), *The Parliament's Post,* 23rd-29th July 1645; E.294(20), *The Scottish Dove,* 25th July-lst August 1645.
(44) Bod.L., MSS Tanner, 60.584, *Letter from Ashe dated 20th March.*
(45) BL, E.297(30), *The Kingdom's Weekly Intelligencer,* 26th August 2nd September 1645.

(46) BL, E.300(20), *The Moderate Intelligencer 28,* 4th-11th September 1645; E.301(2), *The Scottish Dove 99,* 6th-12th September 1645; E.301(4), *Mr Peters Report from Bristol;* E.301.7, *The True Informer 21,* 13th September 1645; E.300(9) *The Parliament's Post,* 2nd-9th September 1645; E.300(19), *Mercurius Civicus 120,* 4th-11th September 1645.

(47) Joshua Sprigg, *Anglia Redivivae: England's Recovery,* pp 84, 101, 110.

(48) BL, E.297(14), *The Proceedings of the Army under the Command of Sir Thomas Fairfax,* 1st-7th August 1645.

(49) PRO, SP 28.175, Assessments, Somerset (Bathforum and Keynsham Hundreds).

(50) BL, E.298(7), *Mercurius Civicus,* 119, 28th August-4th September 1645.

(51) BL, E.292, *The Kingdom's Weekly Intelligencer,* 8th-15th July 1645.

(52) David Underdown, *Somerset in the Civil War and Interregnum,* p 107.

(53) BL, E.300(20), *The Moderate Intelligencer,* 28, 4th-llth September 1645.

(54) David Underdown, *Somerset in the Civil War and Interregnum,* pp 155,177.

6 THE IMPACT OF WAR ON THE LOCAL COMMUNITY, 1642-46

(1) Rev H Harington, *Nugae Antiquae* (London, 1779), Vol 2, pp 280-87.

(2) John Morrill, *The Revolt of the Provinces,* (London, 1976) p 84.

(3) David Underdown, *Somerset in the Civil War and Interregnum* (Newton Abbot, 1973), p 141.

(4) PRO, SP28.242 - Subcommittee Accounts (Somerset).

(5) PRO, SP28.175 - Assessments, Somerset (Keynsham Hundred).

(6) Edward Hyde, Earl of Clarendon, *History of the Great Rebellion and Civil War in England,* edited by W Dunn Macray (Oxford, 1888), vol 4, p 354.

(7) PRO, E179.404, Subsidy (Bath), 17 Car.1; SP28.175 - Assessments, Somerset (Wellow Hundred).

(8) PRO, E179.256.16(23) Somerset Hearth Tax, 1664-6.

(9) PRO, SP28.175 - Assessments, Somerset (Wellow Hundred).

(10) Earl of Clarendon, *History of the Great Rebellion,* Vol 5, pp 336-37.

(11) PRO, SP28.175 - Assessments, Somerset (Keynsham Hundred).

(12) PRO, SP28.175 - Assessments, Somerset (Keynsham Hundred); John Latimer, *The Annals of Bristol in the Seventeenth Century* (Bristol, 1900) pp 190-95.

(13) David Underdown, *Somerset in the Civil War and Interregnum,* p 46.

(14) LJ, Vol VI, 1643-44, pp 164-70.

(15) PRO, SP28.175 - Assessments, Somerset (Keynsham Hundred). This compared with a payment by the village of £11 9s 4d in December 1641 towards the subsidy for the relief of the Army in the North (BL, Add.MSS, 28,273, Subsidy Assessments and other Memoranda by J Locke, 1623-1655).

(16) PRO, SP28.175 - Assessments, Somerset (Wellow Hundred).

(17) Bod. L., Clarendon MSS, 22.85, (Letter of John Ashe to Nathaniel Fiennes, Bath, 1st June, 1643); 22.71 (Letter of John Ashe to Nathaniel Fiennes, Freshford, 5th June, 1643).

(18) PRO, SP28.175 - Account of Col. William Strode, 1642-1643, given to Mr John Ashe; Bod. L., Clarendon MSS, 22.44, Colonel John Fiennes to Colonel Nathaniel Fiennes, Bath, 26th May 1643.

(19) PRO, SP28.175 - Assessments, Somerset (Wellow Hundred).

(20) *Archaeologia,* (London 1803), vol 14, pp 121-28.

(21) CSPD, 1644-45, p 511 (Richard March to Sir Edward Nicholas; Bristol, 22nd May 1645).

(22) BRO, Bath Council Book, No 1 (18th March, 1644).

(23) CSPD, 1644-45, p 511.

(24) BL, E.61, *Mercurius Civicus,* llth-17th July 1644.

(25) Philip Styles, *Studies in Seventeenth Century West Midlands History,* p 227; Shelagh Bond, *The Chamber Order Book of Worcester, 1602-1650,* p 38.

(26) W T Baker, ed., *Records of the Borough of Nottingham,* vol 5, 1625-1702 (Nottingham, 1900) pp 210-12, 219.

(27) H Stocks, ed., *Records of the Borough of Leicester, 1603-1688,* (Cambridge, 1923), pp 314, 317-9, 325.

(28) Donald Pennington, *The War and The People,* (in John Morrill, ed., Reactions to the English Civil War, London, 1982) p 129.

(29) BL, Add.MSS, 46.367, f 128, Notes on Poll Money, 26th August 1641.

(30) BL, Add.MSS, 28,273, ff 84-5, 89-101, Subsidy Assessments and other Memoranda by J Locke, 1623-1655.

(31) BL, Add.MSS, 28,273, ff 89-101, Subsidy Assessments and other Memoranda by J Locke, 1623-1655; PRO, SP28.175, Assessments, Somerset (Keynsham Hundred, Farmborough).

(32) PRO, SP28.175, Assessments, Somerset (Wellow); SP28.242, Subcommittee Accounts (Wellow), E179.172.142, Subsidy 17 Car 1 (1641).

(33) Ann Hughes, *Politics Society and Civil War in Warwickshire, 1620-1660* (Cambridge, 1987) p 262.

(34) John Morrill, *Revolt of the Provinces,* p 125.

(35) PRO, SP28.242 - Subcommittee Accounts (Wellow).

(36) John Morrill, *Mutiny and Discontent in English Provincial Armies, 1645-1647* (in Past and Present, No 56, 1972) pp 51-2.

(37) Ronald Hutton, *The Royalist War Effort, 1642-1646* (London, 1982) p 96.

(38) John K G Taylor, *The Civil Government of Gloucester, 1640-6,* pp 85-6.

(39) PRO, SP28.175, Assessments, Somerset (Keynsham and Wellow Hundreds).

(40) PRO, SP28.175, Assessments, Somerset (Wellow Hundred).

(41) PRO, SP28.175, Assessments, Somerset (Wellow Hundred).

(42) PRO, SP28.175, Assessments, Somerset (Wellow Hundred).

(43) PRO, SP28.175, Assessments, Somerset (Keynsham, Hundred).

(44) CSPD, 1644-45, p 83 (Letter from Waller and Haselrig to the Committee of Both Kingdoms, 30th October 1644).

(45) PRO, SP28.175, Assessments, Somerset (Keynsham and Wellow Hundreds).

(46) Rev E H Bates-Harbin, *Quarter Sessions Records for the County of Somerset,* vol 2, p 245 (licences to maltsters, badgers, etc., Wells, 1636).

(47) PRO, SP28.175, Assessments, Somerset (Wellow Hundred).

(48) BRO, Bath Chamberlain's Accounts, 1645-47.

(49) PRO, SP28.175, Assessments, Somerset (Wellow Hundred).

(50) PRO, SP28.175, Assessments, Somerset (Wellow Hundred).

(51) CSPD, 1645-47, pp 331-32 (Committee of Two Kingdoms to Maj. Gen. Skippon, 3rd February 1646).

(52) BRO, Bath Council Book, No 1 (9th February, 1646).

(53) Rev H Harington, *Nugae Antiquae,* vol 2, pp 179-87

(54) CSPD, 1645-47, p 439 (Committee of Two Kingdoms to Mayor and Aldermen of Bath, 29th May 1646).

(55) PRO, SP28.175 - Assessments, Somerset (Wellow Hundred).

(56) BL, E.102, *Special Passages,* 9th-16th May 1643.

(57) PRO, SP28.175 - Assessments, Somerset (Wellow and Keynsham Hundreds).

(58) PRO, SP28.175 - Assessments, Somerset (Wellow Hundred).

(59) Ronald Hutton, *The Royalist War Effort, 1642-1646,* pp 97-104; Donald Pennington, *The War and the People,* pp 115-124; John Morrill, *Mutiny and Discontent in English Provincial Armies,* 1645-1647, pp 52, 63; PRO, SP28.161, Assessments, Lancashire.

(60) BRO, Bath Chamberlain's Accounts, 1642, 1646.

(61) John Latimer, *The Annals of Bristol in the Seventeenth Century* (Bristol, 1900), pp 190-95.

(62) John K G Taylor, *The Civil Government of Gloucester, 1640-46,* pp 93, 110, 113.

(63) Roger Howell, *Neutralism, Conservatism and Political Alignment in the English Revolution: The Case of the Towns, 1642-9* (in John Morrill, ed., *Reactions to the English Civil War, 1642-1649,* London, 1982), p 79.

(64) Shelagh Bond, *The Chamber Order Book of Worcester, 1602-1650,* p 17.

(65) BRO, Bath Council Book, No 1, 1643-1646.

(66) BRO, Bath Council Book No 1, (29th April 1644).

(67) BL, E.256, *Perfect Occurrences,* (13th-20th September 1644).

(68) BRO, Bath Council Book No 1 (18th April 1645).

(69) BL, Harleian MSS, 2135 f 35, Letter from Sr Wm Legge, Governor, to Mr Randle Holme, the Mayor of Chester, 24th August 1644.

(70) BRO, Bath Chamberlain's Accounts, 1637-43.

(71) John K G Taylor, *The Civil Government of Gloucester, 1640-46,* pp 103-109.

(72) Philip Styles, *Studies in Seventeenth Century West Midlands History,* p 233; Shelagh Bond, *The Chamber Order Book of Worcester 1602-1650,* pp 38, 361, 362, 381, 391.

(73) BRO, Bath Chamberlain's Accounts, 1643-46.

(74) Peter Clark and Paul Slack, *English Towns in Transition, 15001700,* pp 60, 147.

(75) BRO, Bath Chamberlain's Accounts, 1637-1646.

(76) *The Arraignment and Tryal of the late Rev Mr Thomas Rosewell for High Treason* (London, 1718).

(77) Philip Styles, *Studies in Seventeenth Century West Midlands History,* pp 241-3.

(78) BRO, Bath Chamberlain's Accounts, (1637-1646).

(79) John K G Taylor, *The Civil Government of Gloucester,* 1640-46, p 113.

(80) Shelagh Bond, *The Chamber Order Book of Worcester, 1602-1650,* pp 38, 68; Philip Styles, *Studies in Seventeenth Century West Midlands History,* pp 218,233; BRO, Bath Chamberlain's Accounts, 1637-1646.

(81) BRO, Bath Chamberlain's Accounts. 1639-41.

(82) BRO, Bath Chamberlain's Accounts, 1642-43.

(83) BRO, Bath Chamberlain's Accounts, 1642-43.

(84) John K G Taylor, *The Civil Government of Gloucester,* pp 72-6.

(85) BRO, Bath Chamberlain's Accounts, 1643-45.

(86) BRO, Bath Council Book No 1, (1644 passim; 18th April 1645).

(87) BRO, Bath Council Book No 2, (29th March 1652).

(88) *Somerset Assize Orders, 1640-1659,* edited by J S Cockburn (Frome, 1971), p 15 (Taunton Assizes, 22nd March 1647).

(89) BRO, Bath Chamberlain's Accounts. 1643.

(90) H Stocks, ed, *Records of the Borough of Leicester, 1603-1688,* pp 335-50.

(91) John K G Taylor, *The Civil Government of Gloucester,* p 96.

(92) Shelagh Bond, *The Chamber Order Book of Worcester,* p 366.

(93) Philip Styles, *The City of Worcester during the Civil Wars,* pp 223-4, 233.

(94) Peter Clark and Paul Slack, *English Towns in Transition,* p 147.

(95) Bod. L., Rawlings D.945(34), A Letter to Mr Wm Sandcroft from Ch. Paman, 29th September 1646.

(96) John Oldmixon, *History of England during the reigns of the Royal House of Stuart* (London, 1730), pp 208-12.

(97) BRO, Bath Chamberlain's Accounts, 1644.

(98) CSPD, vol 1, nos 1832, 1836.

(99) CSPD, 1644, p 12.

(100) BL, E.61, *Mercurius Civicus,* 11th-17th July 1644.

(101) BL, E.69, *Mercurius Civicus,* 21st-28th September 1643.

(102) CSPD, 1644-45, p 493 (Sir John Culpepper to George Lord Digby; Bristol, 16th May 1645).

(103) BRO, Bath Chamberlain's Accounts, 1646-49.

(104) Peter Clark and Paul Slack *English Towns in Transition,* pp 8990.
(105) BL, E.69, *Mercurius Civicus,* 21st-28th September 1643.
(106) *Mercurius Aulicus,* 16th March 1643.
(107) LJ., vol V, 1642-43, p 670; C.J., vol III, 1642-43, p 17.
(108) PRO, C107/20, The Cloth Books of James Ashe.
(109) CUL, Western MSS, add.89, f 110 (Mr John Ashe's petition - read 17th July 1646).
(110) PRO, SP016.345.5 (petition of John Ashe to the Privy Council 1637)
(111) CUL, Western MSS, add. 89, f 110, Mr John Ashe's Petition.
(112) WRO, Methuen Papers, 1742.5918 (John Ashe's Will as remembered by Richard Singer and Edward Martin).
(113) Ian Roy, *England Turned Germany? The Aftermath of the Civil War in its European Context,* pp 138-40.
(114) Philip Styles, *Studies in Seventeenth Century West Midlands History,* p 232.
(115) John Latimer, *The Annals of Bristol in the Seventeenth Century,* pp 190-5; Ronald Hutton, *The Royalist War Effort, 1642-1646;* Bod.L., MS Eng Hist, c 53 f 73, The Letter Book of Sir Samuel Luke.
(116) BL, Harleian MSS, 2135 ff 53,54, The Lord Byron to Mr Holme, 3rd and 5th October 1645.
(117) PRO, C107/17 and 20 (The Cloth Books of James Ashe 1640-43).
(118) BRO, Council Book No 2 (22nd September 1662).
(119) BRO, Council Book No 2 (22nd September 1662).
(120) Ronald Hutton, *The Royalist War Effort, 1642-1646,* pp 60, 76.
(121) John Latimer, *The Annals of Bristol in The Seventeenth Century,* p 190.
(122) Donald Pennington, *The War and The People,* (in John Morrill, ed, *Reactions to the English Civil War, 1642-1649,* London, 1982), pp 126-7.
(123) PRO, SP28.131 (Part 1), August 1642, Account of Divers necessary provisions, materialls and instruments ...
(124) Somerset Record Office, DD/BR/SB/ N68(2), The Survey of Walcot, 1638-41; DD/PO/ 55, The Farmborough Manor Survey, 1630.
(125) John Wroughton, *An English Community at War, 1642-1646* (in History Review, No 10, September 1991, pp 12-16). For a fuller analysis of the cost of the war to the village of Farmborough, see John Wroughton, *The Community of Bath and North-East Somerset and the Great Civil War* (unpublished PhD thesis for the University of Bristol, 1990) pp 125-135.

7 THE COMMUNITY IN THE AFTERMATH OF War 1645-50.

(1) BRO, Bath Chamberlain's Accounts, 1645-7.
(2) BRO, Bath Chamberlain's Accounts, 1645-7.
(3) BRO, Bath Council Book No 1, (2nd September, 1646).
(4) BRO, Bath Council Book No 2, (28th October 1650).
(5) Rev Richard Warner, *History of Bath* (Bath, 1801), p 200.
(6) Rev Richard Warner, *History of Bath,* p 203.
(7) BRO, Bath Chamberlain's Accounts, 1648.
(8) Richard Warner, *History of Bath,* pp 202-3.
(9) BRO, Bath Chamberlain's Accounts, 1648.
(10) BRO, Bath Council Book No 1 (4th October, 1647).
(11) Richard Warner, *History of Bath,* pp 202-3.
(12) BRO, Bath Chamberlain's Accounts, 1645-7.
(13) PRO, SP28.175, Assessments (Somerset).
(14) CSPD, 1645-7, pp 300, 305.
(15) ibid.
(16) BRO, Bath Council Book, No 1, 1646.
(17) CSPD, 1645-7, p 439.
(18) BRO, Bath Chamberlain's Accounts, 1646-7.
(19) ibid.
(20) ibid.
(21) BL, Egerton MSS,m 2978, ff 151-152, List of those indicted for treason by the King, 1644-6.
(22) Bod L, Nalson Papers 14, MS Dep C 167, f 309: Orders of the Council of War, 23rd and 30th July 1646.
(23) PRO, SP28.214, Committee of Accounts.
(24) C H Firth and R S Rait, *Acts and Ordinances of the Interregnum* (London, 1911), Vol I, p 460.
(25) The power struggle on the committee and Pyne's dominance within the county are well described by David Underdown in *Somerset in the Civil War and Interregnum* (Newton Abbot, 1973), pp 124-128, 138, 143, 147-150, 152-167.
(26) Margaret Stieg, *The Diary of John Harington, MP, 1646-53,* pp 78, 27.
(27) David Underdown, *Somerset in the Civil War and Interregnum,* pp 118-20.
(28) David Underdown, *Pride's Purge* (Oxford 1971), pp 36-37.
(29) Bod L, Nalson Papers 5, MS Dep C156, f 101: Protest at the election of George Horner and John Harington, 2nd December 1645.
(30) Bod L, Tanner MSS 59.353, Somerset Committee to William Lenthall, 20th June 1646.
(31) Margaret Stieg, *The Diary of John Harington, MP, 1646-53,* p 22.
(32) C J., Vol 4, pp 565-6; BL, E.319(17), *The Scottish Dove,* 119, 21st-29th January 1646; HMC, *Report on the Manuscripts of the Duke of Portland,* Vol 1, pp 318-9.
(33) Rev H Harington, *Nugae Antiquae* (London 1779), Vol 2, pp 248-9. (34) BRO, Bath Council Book No 1, 8th December 1645.
(35) BRO, Bath Council Book No 1, 8th September 1646; 27th September 1647; 25th September 1648; October 1649.
(36) PRO, SP 28, Committee of Accounts; SP23, Committee for Compounding; see also Bod L., Tanner MSS, 58.667/687, The Answer of the Committee to Mr Prinne, 25th March 1648 and 59, 353, The Committee to William Lenthall, 20th June 1646.
(37) BRO, Bath Council Book No 1, 1645, 1646, 1647, 1648, 1649.
(38) BL, E.441, *The Perfect Weekly Account* No 9, 3rd-10th May 1648.

(39) Bod L., Tanner MSS, 58.667/687, William Prynne to the Standing Committee for the County of Somerset, 15th January 1648, and The Answer of the Committee, 25th March 1648.
(40) For a fuller account of Pyne's control, see John Wroughton, *The Community of Bath and North-East Somerset and the Great Civil War* (unpublished PhD thesis for the University of Bristol, 1990), pp 289293.
(41) HMC, *Report on the Manuscripts of the Most Honorable The Marquis of Bath* (London, 1968), Vol 4, p 279, Jane Rose to Mrs Norwood, 29th August 1646.
(42) Bod L., Tanner MSS, 58.667/687, William Prynne to The Standing Committee for the County of Somerset, 15th January 1648.
(43) BRO, Bath Council Book No 1, 13th December 1647.
(44) PRO, SP 23.178 (282-292), Committee for Compounding, Sir Thomas Bridges, November 1645.
(45) BRO, Bath Council Book, No 1, 26th August 1646; Bath Chamberlain's Accounts, 1647.
(46) PRO, E179.256, Somerset Hearth Tax, 1664-5.
(47) PRO, SP 23.73(844-848), Committee for Compounding, Henry Chapman, April 1646.
(48) PRO, SP 23.73 (831-832), Committee for Compounding, George Chapman, June 1646.
(49) PRO, SP 23.195 (821-829), Committee for Compounding, Richard Gay, June 1646.
(50) PRO, SP 23.117 (331-341), Committee for Compounding, Philip Sherwood, January 1646.
(51) CPCC, Vol 2, p 1812.
(52) PRO, SP 23.208 (509-525), Committee for Compounding, Sir William Bassett, April 1646.
(53) PRO, SP 23.204 (663-671), Committee for Compounding, Robert Fisher, February 1647.
(54) PRO, SP 23.204 (701-719), Committee for Compounding, Thomas Gibbs, February 1647.
(55) BRO, Bath Council Book No 1, September 1647.
(56) BRO, Bath Chamberlain's Accounts, 1648, 1653, 1655, 1661; Bath Council Book No 1, 1652-53.
(57) BRO, Bath Council Book, No 1, 27th September 1647.
(58) LJ, Vol IX, p 430.
(59) BRO, Bath Council Book, No 1, 13th December 1647.
(60) Quoted by Nicholas Marlowe, *West Country Boroughs, 1640-1662*, pp 123, 144.
(61) A M Johnson, *Politics in Chester during the Civil Wars and Interregnum, 1640-62*, pp 229-230.
(62) John K G Taylor, *The Civil Government of Gloucester, 1640-6*, pp 110-111.
(63) Roger Howell, *Neutralism, Conservatism and Political Alignment in the English Revolution: The Case of the Towns, 1642-9* pp 81, 83-5.
(64) Philip Styles, *Studies in Seventeenth Century West Midlands History*, p 231.
(65) BL, E.441., *The Moderate Intelligencer*, 17th April-4th May, 1648.
(66) BRO, Bath Chamberlain's Accounts, 1648.
(67) BL, E.441, *The Perfect Weekly Account*, 9, 3rd-10th May 1648.
(68) W D Shaw, *History of the English Church, 1640-1660* (London 1900), Vol 2, pp 6-8.

(69) Margaret Stieg, *Laud's Laboratory: the Diocese of Bath and Wells in the Early Seventeenth Century*, (Lewisberg, 1982), pp 325-39.
(70) A G Matthews, *Walker Revised* (Oxford 1948). The numbers in square brackets indicate the page numbers of the relevant entries. See also W D Shaw, *A History of the English Church during the Civil Wars and under the Commonwealth, 1640-1660* (London, 1900), vol 2, p 295.
(71) Margaret Stieg, *Laud's Laboratory*, pp 325-39.
(72) I M Green, *The Persecution of 'scandalous' and 'malignant' parish clergy during the English Civil War* (in EHR, vol 94, 1979) pp 522, 525.
(73) G E Aylmer, *Collective Mentalities in Mid Seventeenth Century England: IV Cross Current, Neutrals, Trimmers and Others* (in TRHS, 5th Series, vol 39, London 1989, p 16).
(74) A G Matthews, *Calamy Revised* (Oxford, 1934). The numbers in square brackets indicate the page numbers of the relevant entries.
(75) Margaret Stieg, *The Parochial Clergy in the Diocese of Bath and Wells, 1625-1685* (unpublished PhD thesis for the University of California, 1970) pp 108-122; A G Matthews, Calamy Revised, p xxii.
(76) G E Aylmer, *Collective Mentalities*, p 16.
(77) BL, E.456(26), *The Attestation of the Ministers of the County of Somerset, 9th August 1648*.
(78) Ann Hughes, *Politics, Society and Civil War in Warwickshire, 1620-1660*, (Cambridge, 1987), p 309.
(79) Margaret Stieg, *The Diary of John Harington, MP, 1646-53*, (Taunton, 1977), p 27ff.
(80) BL, E.430(16), *The County of Somerset divided into severall classes for the present settling of the Presbyterial Government, 4th March 1648*.
(81) I M Green, *The Persecution of 'scandalous' and 'malignant' parish clergy during the English Civil War*, p 518.
(82) John Morrill, *The Church in England, 1642-9* (in John Morrill, ed, *Reactions to the English Civil War, 1642-1649*, London, 1982), pp 90-91, 100, 104-8.
(83) David Underdown, *Revel, Riot and Rebellion*, p 255.
(84) HMC, 13th Report, Appendix Part 1, *The Manuscripts of His Grace the Duke of Portland* (London, 1891), Vol 1, pp 126-7, 310; Colonel Martin Pynder to William Lenthall, 2nd August 1645 and 13th November 1645.
(85) Bod L., Tanner MSS, 58,667/687, William Prynne to The Standing Committee for the County of Somerset, 15th January 1648.
(86) A G Matthews, *Calamy Revised*, p 327.
(87) BL, E.441, *The Moderate Intelligencer*, 17th April-4th May, 1648.
(88) John Morrill, *The Church in England 1642-9*, pp 111-2.
(89) BL, E.346(10), *The Scottish Dove*, 144, 22nd-31st July 1646.
(90) Bod L., Tanner MSS, 58,667/687, William Prynne to the Standing Committee, 15th January 1648.
(91) A G Matthew, *Walker Revised*, p 314; LJ, Vol X, p 240; BRO, Bath Council Book No 1, 4th December 1646.

(92) W D Shaw, *A History of the English Church,* Vol 2, pp 337, 345.
(93) Quoted by N Marlowe, *West Country Boroughs, 1640-1662,* p 216.
(94) Margaret Stieg, *The Parochial Clergy in the Diocese of Bath and Wells, 1625-1685,* pp 57-60, 108-122.
(95) BL, Harleian MSS, 6826 f 1, Value of the Somerset Livings (n.d.).
(96) Margaret Stieg, *The Parochial Clergy in the Diocese of Bath and Wells, 1625-1685,* pp 108-122.
(97) BRO, Bath Council Book No 1, 3rd October and l9th December 1631.
(98) Margaret Stieg, *The Parochial Clergy in the Diocese of Bath and Wells, 1625-1685,* p 58.
(99) Bod L., Clarendon MSS, 22.17, Notice by Sir Edward Hungerford, 29th March 1643.
(100) W D Shaw, *A History of the English Church,* Vol 2, pp 491, 499, 504, 540, 541, 562, 592.
(101) PRO, SP 22.1, f 356, Committee for Plundered Ministers - Order Book, 1645-47, (14th April 1647).
(102) Margaret Stieg, *The Parochial Clergy in the Diocese of Bath and Wells, 1625-1685,* pp 108-122.
(103) Margaret Stieg, ed., *The Diary of John Harington, MP, 1646-53,* p 27; W D Shaw, *History of the English Church, 1640-1660,* Vol 2, pp 413-21.
(104) BL, E.430(16), *The County of Somerset divided into severall classes for the present settling of the Presbyterial Government, 4th March 1648.*
(105) Nicholas Marlowe, *West Country Boroughs 1640-1662,* p 220.
(106) John Morrill, *The Church in England, 1642-9,* p 97.
(107) BL, E.346(10), *The Scottish Dove* 144, 22nd-31st July 1646, Letter from Somerset; Bod.L., Rawlings, MSS, D.945(34), Paman to .Sancroft, 29th September 1646.
(108) Nicholas Marlowe, *West Country Boroughs 1640-1662,* pp 223, 232-3.
(109) Joseph Besse, *A Collection of the Suffering of the People called Quakers,* Vol 1 (London, 1753), pp 216-222.
(110) *CSPD,* 1648-9, pp 159, 210, 297; CJ, Vol V, pp 569-70, 656.
(111) Bod L, Nalson Papers 15, MS Dep C 168, f 251, Statement by the County Committee to the Committee at Derby House; f 254, opposition by the four Members of Parliament, (1648).
(112) W Prynne, *A Legall Vindication of the Liberties of England against Illegal Taxes.* (London, 1649), pp 24-26.
(113) Bulstrode Whitelock, *Memorials of the English Affairs* (Oxford, 1853), Vol 2, p 457; CJ, Vol VI, p 81; *The Parliamentary or Constitutional History of England* (London, 1761-3), Vol 18, pp 238-9.
(114) BL, E.476(5), *The Moderate,* No 22, 5th-12th December 1648.
(115) BL, E.669 (13,55), *A Solemn Protestation of the Imprisoned and Secluded Members, 12th December 1648.*
(116) BL, E.539(5), *Vindication of the Imprisoned and Secluded Members of the House of Commons, 23rd January 1649.* For a detailed account of the Purge and its immediate sequel see David Underdown, *Pride's Purge* (Oxford, 1971) pp 139-172.
(117) David Underdown, *Pride's Purge,* pp 210-211.
(118) Dissenters made a declaration that they had dissented or, if they had been present, they *would* have dissented from the vote passed on 5th December in favour of further negotiations with Charles I. It did not necessarily indicate their willingness to bring the King to trial.
(119) David Underdown, *Pride's Purge,* pp 366-390.
(120) Horner MSS, Memoirs of the Family of Horner of Mells (by 'A.B.', c.l740), quoted in Rev. F W Cleveron, *History of Mells* (Frome, 1974).

8 POSTSCRIPT, 1650-1662

(1) William Prynne, *Brevia Parliamentaria Rediviva,* p 333.
(2) HMC, *Buccleuch & Queensbury,* Vol 1, p311; James Mountagn to Lord Mountagn, 10th January 1655.
(3) *CSPD,* 1659-60, pp 50,53,68, President Whitelock to Colonel Okey, 29th July 1659; Proceedings of the Council of State, 30th July 1659; President Whitelock to Colonel Okey, 2nd August 1659; David Underdown, *Royalist Conspiracy in England 1659-1660* (New Haven, 1960), pp 117, 192, 218, 224, 242, 261, 284.
(4) J R Rutt (ed), *Diary of Thomas Burton,* (London, 1828), Vol 1, pp 362-3.
(5) B D Henning, *The History of Parliament: The House of Commons 1660-1693,* Pt 3, (London, 1983), pp 195, 295-6.
(6) E W Kirby, *William Prynne: A Study in Puritanism,* pp 136, 147.
(7) BRO, Bath Council Book No 2, 29th June 1660; 27th August 1661.
(8) BRO, Bath Council Book No 2, 12th April 1661.
(9) B D Henning, *The History of Parliament: The House of Commons 1660-1690,* Pt 3, pp 263, 296-8; S W Bates-Harbin, *Members of Parliament for the County of Somerset,* p 169.
(10) S W Bates-Harbin, *Members of Parliament for the County of Somerset,* p 169.
(11) BRO, Bath Council Book No 2, 11th November 1662.
(12) BRO, Bath Council Book No 2, 15th November 1669; 27th November 1669.
(13) BRO, Bath Council Book No 2, 23rd September 1661; and 27th September 1661, Articles exhibited against Capt. Henry Chapman; William Prynne, *Brevia Parliamentaria Rediviva,* pp 346-7; PRO, PC2.55, Privy Council Register (3rd October 1660-30th May 1662), f.385 - Complaint against Sir Hugh Smith and Sir Thomas Bridges, 27th September 1661; f.419A - the Council's judgment, 25th October 1661; R E M Peach, *The Annals of the Parish of Swainswick,* pp 43-4; Nicholas Marlowe, *West Country Boroughs, 1640-1662,* pp 269-70; William M Lamont, *Marginal Prynne, 1600-1669,* pp 237-8. For a fuller account of this episode in 1661, see John Wroughton, *Puritanism and Traditionalism: Cultural and Political Division in Bath, 1620-1662* (in Bath History, Vol 4, 1992, pp 52-70).
(14) BrRO, AC|02|12, Smyth of Ashton Court MSS, Restoration of Bath to Sir Hugh Smyth and Sir George Norton (n.d.).
(15) A fuller account of the implementation of the Corporation Act is given in John Wroughton, *The Community of Bath and North-East Somerset and the Great Civil War* (unpublished PhD thesis for the University of Bristol, 1990).

BIBLIOGRAPHY
PRIMARY SOURCES

1 UNPUBLISHED MANUSCRIPTS

Bath Record Office
Bath Council Books, No 1 (15th September 1631-22nd August 1649)
No 2 (24th September 1649-26th December 1684)
Bath Chamberlain's Accounts, 1569-1662.
Freemen's Estate, 118, 119.
Long v Fisher, 1656, Acc. No 59, Bundle 2 (Crook) No 1.
The Furman Leases in Furman's Repertory.
The Survey of Bath, 1641.
The Will of Mark Dallemore, 1647

Bodleian Library
Aubrey 2, f62
Clarendon MSS, 22, 23, 28, Sir Edward Hyde's Recollections
Carte MSS, vol 7, The Marquis of Ormonde's Papers
MSS Eng Hist C 53, The Letter Book of Sir Samuel Luke
Firth MSS C6, Transcripts of Prince Rupert's Papers
Nalson Papers 5, 14, 15
Rawlinson MSS,   B239, Purchasers of Bishops' Lands
D.945(34), Charles Paman's Letter Book.
Tanner MSS, 58-52, The Lenthall Papers.

Bristol Record Office
Common Council Book No 4, 1642-1649
Smyth of Ashton Court MSS,   AC/02/10
AC/02/12

British Library
Additional MSS:
28272 : Subsidy Assessments etc by J Locke, 1623-1655
22619 : Norfolk Committee Papers
46373B : Harington Papers
4367,f128 : Notes on the Poll Money, 1641
Egerton MSS:
2978, ff151-2 : List of those indicted for treason, 1644-5
Harleian MSS:
6826, f1 : Value of Somerset livings
4606 : Survey of the Manors of Chewton, Keynsham, and
Queen Charleton, 1667
Sloan MSS: 1519

Cambridge University Library
Western MSS, add.89, f110 : Mr John Ashe's Petition, 1646

Public Record Office
SP 16 : State Papers Domestic, Charles I.
SP 18 : State Papers Domestic, Interregnum.
SP 20 : Papers of Committee for the Sequestration of Delinquents' Estates:
vol 1, March 1643-November 1645
vol 2, November 1645-November 1646
vol 3, December 1646-November 1647
SP 22 : Papers of the Committee for Plundered Ministers: vol l, Order Book, 1645-47
SP 23 : Papers of the Committee of Compounding.
SP 28 : Commonwealth Exchequer Papers - County Committee.
vol 147 : accounts relating to Somerset
vol 175 : assessments relating to Somerset
vol 242 : subcommittee accounts for Somerset

SP 29 : State Papers Domestic, Charles II.
C 107/17,20 : Chancery - Masters Exhibits: Master Senior -
   The Cloth Books of James Ashe
E 179 : Exchequer Papers - Somerset Subsidy, 1641; Somerset Hearth Tax, 1664-5
E 351-415 : Accounts of Receiver of Recusants' Forfeitures 1627-39
PC 2 : Privy Council Register, 3rd October 1660-30th May 1662

Somerset County Record Office

Churchwardens' Accounts :	D/P/ba ja 4/1/1, St James's Church, Bath 1654-1770
	D/P/ber 4/1/1, Berkley, 1659-1737
	D/P/mls 4/1/2, Mells, 1658-1736
	D/P/swk 4/1/1, Swainswick, 1631-1712
Diocesan Court Records:	D/D/Ca 319, Chapter Act Book, 1638-9
	D/D/Ca 330, Chapter Act Book, 1639
	D/D/Ca 194, Comperta 1615.
	D/D/Ca 319, Comperta 1638.
	D/D/Cd 71, 81, Depositions, 1631-45,1635.
	Series A, No.335a, Archdeacons'
	Presentations.
The Popham Papers:	DD/BR/SB/N68(2), The Survey of Walcot, 1638-41
	DD/PO/55, The Farmborough Manor Survey, 1630.
	32/1, The Hunstrete Audit, 1649-50.
	DD/PO/12, Leases of Coalmines.
Session Rolls:	1622 - The Humble Petition of the Vicar of Frome Selwood

Wiltshire County Record Office

The Methuen/Corsham Papers, ref: 1742 - John Ashe's will as remembered; conveyances, leases, agreements

2 PRINTED SOURCES AND UNPUBLISHED MATERIAL

Archaeologia, Vol XIV, London, 1803.
Bates-Harbin,Rev. E H (ed.): *Quarter Sessions Records for the County of Somerset,*Taunton,1907-8.
Bell, Robert (ed.): *Memorials of the Civil War: Comprising the Correspondence of the Fairfax Family,* 2 vols, London, 1849.
Bettey, J H (ed.): *Calendar of the Correspondence of the Smyth Family of Ashton Court, 1548-1642,* Bristol, 1982.
Birch, T (ed): *A Collection of State Papers of John Thurloe,* Vol VII, London, 1742.
Calendar of the Proceedings of the Committee for Compounding, 1643-60, 5 vols, London, 1889-92.
Calendar of State Papers, Domestic Series, 1619-62, 40 vols, London, 1858-93.
Cockburn, J S (ed.): *Somerset Assize Orders, 1640-1659,* Frome, 1971.
Dasent, A I (ed.): *Acts of the Privy Council, 1620-23.*
Dick, O L (ed.): *John Aubrey - Brief Lives,* London 1950.
Fuller, Thomas: *The History of the Worthies of England, 1662.*
Firth, C H & Rait, R S (eds.): *Acts and Ordinances of the Interregnum,* Vol 1, London, 1911.
Gardiner,S R (ed.): *Documents Relating to the Proceedings against William Prynne,*London, 1877.
Green, E: *Bibliotheca Somersetensis,* Taunton, 1902.
Healey, C E H Chadwyck (ed.): *Bellum Civile,* Somerset Record Society, Vol. 18,Taunton, 1902.
Historical Manuscripts Commission, Reports:
Third Report	:	Calendar of Phelips' MSS.
Fifth Report	:	Part l.
Twelfth Report	:	Appendix 1.
Thirteenth Report	:	Manuscripts of the Duke of Portland, Vol.l.
Fifteenth Report	:	Manuscripts of the Marquis of Bath, Vol.4.
Holland, Elizabeth: *The Survey of Old Bath* (unpublished).
Holland, P: *Camden's Britannica,* London, 1637.
Holworthy R: *Somerset Hearth Tax, 1664-65,* London 1916.
Inskip, Marta: *Map of 17th Century Bath*
Inskip, Marta: *Index of 17th Century Leases* (unpublished)
James, P R: *Documents of the City of Bath* (unpublished).

Journals of the House of Commons, Vols II-VII.

Journals of the House of Lords, Vols IV-X.

Macray, W D(ed.): Clarendon, Edward Hyde, Earl of - *The History of the Rebellion and Civil War in England,* 6 vols Oxford, 1888.

Manco, Jean: *Transcription of the Bath Survey Book, 1641,* Bath 1986.

Notestein, Wallace (ed.):*The Journal of Sir Simonds D'Ewes,*Yale,1923.

Peach, R E M: *The Annals of the Parish of Swainswick,* Bath, 1892.

Prynne, William: *A Legall Vindication of the Liberties of England Against Illegal Taxes,* 1649.

Prynne, William: *Brevia Parliamentaria Rediviva,* 1664.

Prynne, William: *The Republicans and Others Spurious Good Old Cause,* 1659.

Prynne, William: *Brief Justification of the Eleven Accused Members,1648.*

Prynne, William: *A Solemn Protestation of the Imprisoned and Secluded Members,* 1648.

Prynne, William: *Vindication of the Imprisoned and Secluded Members, of the House of Commons,* 1649.

Prynne,William: *True and Perfect Narrative of what was done the 7 and 9 of this instant,* May 1659.

Prynne, William: *Canterburies Doome: Or the first part of a compleat History of the Commitment, Charge, Tryall, Condemnation Execution of William Laud, late Archbishop of Canterbury,* 1646.

Rosewell: *The Arraignment and Tryal of the late Rev. Mr Thomas Rosewell for High Treason.*

Rushworth, J: *Historical Recollections of Private Passage of State,* London, 1701.

Rutt, J T (ed.): *The Diary of Thomas Burton, 1656-59,* Vol 1, London, 1828.

Saunders, G W & Fowler, J (eds.): *Notes and Queries for Somerset and Dorset,* Vol 24, Sherborne, 1946.

Shickle, Rev. C W: *Transcription of the Bath Chamberlain's Accounts.*

Smith, L T (ed.): *John Leland: The Itinerary of 1535-43,* London 1907.

Sprigg, Joshua: *Anglia Redivivae: England's Recovery,* London, 1647.

The Parliamentary or Constitutional History of England, Vol 18, London, 1761-3.

Vicars, John: *Jehovah-Jirah, God in the Mount: or England's Parliamentarie Chronicle,* 1644.

Venner, Thomas: *The Baths of Bath,* 1628.

Verney, F P & Verney, M M (eds.). *Memoirs of the Verney Family during the Seventeenth Century,* London, 1925.

Warrington, John (ed.): *The Diary of Samuel Pepys,* London, 1953.

Whitelocke, Bulstrode: *Memorials of the English Affairs from the beginning of the reign of Charles the First to the happy Restoration of King Charles the Second,* 4 vols, Oxford; 1853

Wood, John: *Essay Towards a Description of Bath,* London, 1745.

Young, Peter & Tucker, Norman (eds): *Richard Atkyns and John Gwyn,* London, 1967.

3 NEWSBOOKS AND PAMPHLETS

All these newspapers and pamphlets are to be found in the Thomason Collection in the British Library. The references in the footnotes are taken from G Fortescue's *Catalogue of the Pamphlets, Newspapers and Manuscripts relatinq to the Civil War, the Commonwealth, and Restoration, collected by George Thomason*, 2 vols, London, 1908.

(i) Newsbooks

A Perfect Diurnall:	22nd-29th May, 1643.
	10th-17th July, 1643.
Mercurius Britanicus:	28th July-4th August, 1645.
Mercurius Aulicus :	16th March, 1643.
Mercurius Civicus :	28th April, 1643
	8th July 1643.
	16th June 1643.
	21st-28th September 1643.
	11th-17th July, 1644.
	28th August-4th September 1645
	4th-11th September 1645.
Mercurius Politicus:	27th June-11th July 1650.
Perfect Occurences :	13th-20th September, 1644.
The Kingdom's Weekly Intelligencer:	21st-28th March, 1643
	26th August-2nd September 1645
The Moderate :	5th-12th December, 1648.
	23rd-30th January, 1649.
The Moderate Intelligencer:	31st July-7th August, 1645.
	4th-11th September, 1645.
	17th April-4th May, 1648.
The Parliament's Post :	23rd-29th July, 1645.
	29th July-5th August 1645.
	2nd-9th September, 1645.
The Perfect Weekly Account:	3rd-10th May, 1648.
The Scottish Dove :	25th July-1st August, 1645.
	6th-12th September, 1645.
	21st-29th January, 1646.
	22nd-31st July, 1646.
Special Passages:	2nd-9th May, 1643.
	12th-19th July,1643.
The True Informer :	2nd August, 1645.
	13th September, 1645.

(ii) Pamphlets (in chronological order)

The Humble Petition of the Knights, Gentry, and Freeholders of the County of
Somerset, July 1642.

A Letter from the Committee in Somersetshire, 1st August, 1642.

A True Relation of divers passages in Somerset between the Country and the
Cavaliers concerning the Militia and the Commission of Array, 5th August, 1642.

True Newes from Somersetshire, 6th August, 1642.

A Perfect Relation of the Proceedings of the Caveleers that were in Wells. A Letter
from the Committee in Summersetshire, 7th August, 1642.

A Relation of all the Proceedings in Somersetshire and Bristoll, 11th August, 1642.

Joyful News from Wells in Somersetshire, 12th August 1642.

Joyful Newes from Wells .... A Second Letter sent from John Ashe Esq., to the
Honorable William Lenthall, Esq., Speaker of the House of Commons in
Parliament.

A Relation Made in the House of Commons by Col. Nathaniel Fiennes, 1643.

A Copie of a Letter sent from the Maior of Bristoll to a Gentleman, 1643

A True Relation of the Great and Glorious Victory .... obtained by Sir William Waller,
July 14th, 1643.

A letter from Rupert to the Clubmen, 15th July, 1645.

The Proceedings of the Army under the command of Sir Thos. Fairfax, 24th-31st July,
1645.

The Proceedings of the Army under the command of Sir Thomas Fairfax, 1st-7th
August, 1645.

A Full Relation of the Taking of Bath, 1645.

A Further Relation of the Taking of Bath, 1645.

The County of Somerset divided into severall classes for the present settling of the
Presbyterial Government, 4th March, 1648.

The Attestation of the Ministers of the County of Somerset, 9th August, 1648.

A Solemn Protestation of the Imprisoned and Secluded Members, 12th December,
1648.

Vindication of the Imprisoned and Secluded Members of the House of Commons,
23rd January, 1649.

A Narrative of the Proceedings of the Commissioners appointed by O Cromwell for
ejecting Scandalous and Ignorant Ministers, 1660.

SECONDARY WORKS

Adair, John: *Roundhead General: A Military Biography of Sir William Waller,* London, 1969.

Alexander, Robert(ed.): *Records of Early English Drama: Bath,* Toronto (forthcoming).

Andriette, Eugene: *Devon and Exeter in the Civil War,* Newton Abbot, 1971.

Aylmer, G E: *Collective Mentalities in Mid Seventeenth-Century England: IV CrossCurrents : Neutrals, Trimmers and Others* (in TRHS, 5th Series, Vol 39,1989).

Baker, W T, (ed): *Records of the Borough of Nottingham,* vol 5, 1625-1702, Nottingham, 1900.

Barnes, G: *County Politics and a Puritan Cause Celebre: Somerset Churchales, 1633,* TRHS 5th Series, Vol 9, 1959.

Barnes, T G : *Somerset, 1625-1640,* Oxford, 1961.

Barry, Jonathan: *Popular Culture in Seventeenth-Century Bristol* (in Reay, Barry: *Popular Culture in Seventeenth-Century England,* London, 1985).

Bates-Harbin, S W: *Members of Parliament for the County of Somerset,* Taunton, 1939.

Besse, Joseph: *A Collection of the Suffering of the People called Quakers,* Vol 1, London, 1753.

Bond, Shelagh, (ed.): *The Chamber Order Book of Worcester, 1602-1650,* Worcester, 1974.

Box, J: *The Merchant Taylors of Bath,* 1666-1878.

Calamy, Edmund: *The Nonconformists' Memorials,* ed. Samuel Palmer, London, 1775.

Chanter, J R and
   Wainwright, Thomas: *Reprint of the Barnstaple Records, vol 1, Barnstaple, 1900.*

Chapman, Henry: *Thermae Redivivae, The City of Bath Described,* London, 1673.

Clark, Peter and
   Slack, Paul: *English Towns in Transition, 1500-1700,* Oxford, 1976.

Cleveron, Rev. F W: *History of Mells,* Frome, 1974.

Coate, Mary: *Cornwall in the Great Civil War and Interregnum, 1642-60,* Oxford, 1933.

Coleman, D C: *Industry in Tudor and Stuart England,* London, 1975.

Collinson, Rev. John: *The History of Somersetshire* Vols 1 & 2, London 1791.

Corbet, John: *An Historical Relation of the Military Government of Gloucester,* London, 1645 (in *Bibliotheca Gloucestrensis,* Gloucester, 1825).

Edgar, F T R : *Sir Ralph Hopton: The King's Man in the West, 1642-1652,* Oxford, 1968.

Evans, John T: *Seventeenth Century Norwich: Politics, Religion and Government, 1620-1690,* Oxford, 1979.

Everitt, Alan: *The County Community* (in E W Ives, ed, *The English Revolution, 1600-1660,* London, 1968).

Everitt, Alan: *The County of Kent and the Great Rebellion, 1640-60,* Leicester, 1966.

Everitt, Alan: *The Local Community and the Great Rebellion,* London, 1969.

Fletcher, Anthony: *The Outbreak of the English Civil War,* London, 1981.

Fletcher, Anthony and
   Stevenson, John(eds): *Order and Disorder in Early Modern England,* Cambridge, 1985.

Gardiner, S R: *History of the Great Civil War, 1642-49,* 4 vols, London, 1894.

Green, E: *On the Civil War in Somerset* (in Somerset Archaeological and Natural History Society Journal, Vol 14, 1867).

Green, I M: *The Persecution of 'Scandalous' and 'Malignant' Parish Clergy during the English Civil War* (in EHR, vol 34, 1979).

Harington, Rev. H: *Nugae Antiquae,* Vols 1 & 2, 1779.

Henning, B D: *History of Parliament: House of Commons 1660-90.* Part 3, London 1983.

Hirst, Derek: *The Representative of the People?,* Cambridge, 1975.

Holland, Elizabeth: *Citizens of Bath - Occupations in Bath in the Reign of James I,* Bath, 1988

Holland, Elizabeth:	*The Descent of the Chapman Mayors of Bath of the Seventeenth Century,* Bath, 1989.
Holmes, Clive:	*The Eastern Association in the English Civil Civil War,* Cambridge, 1974.
Howell, Roger:	*Neutralism, Conservatism and Political Alignment in the English Revolution: The Case of the Towns, 1642-9* (in John Morrill, ed, *Reactions to the English Civil War, 1642-1649,* (London 1982.)
Howell, Roger:	*Newcastle-upon-Tyne and the Puritan Revolution,* Oxford, 1967.
Hughes, Ann:	*Politics, Society and Civil War in Warwickshire, 1620-1660,* Cambridge, 1987.
Hughes, Ann:	*Militancy and Localism: Warwickshire Politics and Westminster Politics, 1643-1647* (in TRHS, 5th Series, vol 3, 1981).
Hutton, Ronald:	*The Royalist War Effort, 1642-1646,* London, 1982.
Hutton, Ronald:	*The Restoration,* Oxford, 1985.
Hutton, Ronald:	*The Royalist War Effort* (in John Morrill, ed, Reactions to the English Civil War,1642-1649, London, 1982.
Hutton, Ronald:	*Clarendon's History of the Rebellion* (in EHR, 1982).
Ingram, Martin:	*Religious, Communities and Moral Discipline in the Late Sixteenth- and Early Seventeenth-Century England* (in *Religion and Society in Early Modern Europe,* ed. K Von Greertz, London, 1985).
Ingram, Martin:	*Church Courts, Sex and Marriage in England, 1570-1640,* Cambridge 1987.
Ingram, Martin:	*Ridings, Rough Music and the Reform of Popular Culture in Early Modern England* (in Past and Present, No 105, 1984).
Ingram, Martin:	*The Reform of Popular Culture? Sex and Marriage in Early Modern England* (in Reay, Barry: *Popular Culture in Seventeenth-Century England,* London, 1985).
James, P R:	*The Incorporation of the City of Bath: its origins and workings* (unpublished PhD thesis for University of London), 2 volumes.
James P R:	*The Baths of Bath in the 16th and early 17th Centuries,* Bath, 1938.
Johnson, A M:	*Politics in Chester during the Civil Wars and the Interregnum, 1640-62* (in Peter Clark and Paul Slack, *Crisis and Order in English Towns, 1500-1700,* London 1972) .
Keeler, M F:	*The Long Parliament, 1640-41,* New York, l954.
Kerridge, Eric:	*Textile Manufactures in Early Modern England*, Manchester, 1985.
Kirby, E W:	William Prynne: *A Study in Puritanism,* Cambridge Massachusetts, 1931.
Lamont, W A:	*Marginal Prynne, 1660-1669,* Toronto, 1963.
Latimer, John:	*The Annals of Bristol in the Seventeenth Century,* Bristol, l900.
Mann, J de L:	*The Cloth Industry in the West of England from 1640 to 1880;* Oxford, 1971.
Manning, Brian:	*The English People and the English Revolution* London, 1976 .
Marlowe, Nicholas:	*West Country Boroughs, 1640-1662* (unpublished PhD thesis for Cambridge University, 1986).
Matthew, A G:	*Calamy Revised,* Oxford, 1934.
Matthew, A G:	*Walker Revlsed,* Oxford, 1948.
McGrath, Patrick:	*Bristol and the Civil War,* Bristol, 1981.
Morrill, John:	*Mutiny and Discontent in English Provincial Armies, 1645-1647* (in Past and Present, No 56, 1972).
Morrill, John:	*The Ecology of Allegiance in the English Revolution* (in Journal of British Studies Vol 26, No 4, October 1987)
Morrill, John:	*The Church in England, 1642-9* (in John Morrill, ed, *Reactions to the Civil War, 1642-1649,* London, 1982).
Morrill, John (ed.):	*Reactions to the English Civil War 1642-1649,* London, 1982.
Morrill, John:	*The Revolt of the Provinces, 1630-1650,* London, 1976.
Neal, D:	*History of the Puritans or Protestant Nonconformlsts, 1577-1688,* 4 vols, London, 1732-8.

Neale, R S:	*Bath: A Social History, 1680-1850,* London, 1981.
Oldmixon, John:	*History of England during the Reigns of the Royal House of Stuart,* London, 1730.
Page, W (ed.):	*Victoria County History of Somerset,* 2 vols, London, 1911.
Parsloe, C G:	*The Corporation of Bedford, 1647-1664* (in TRHS, 4th Series, Vol 29, 1947).
Pennington, Donald:	*The War and the People* (in John Morrill, ed, *Reactions to the English Civil War, 1642-1649,* London, 1982).
Phelphs, Rev.W:	*History of the Antiquities of Somersetshire,* 4 vols, London, 1836.
Plumb, J H:	*The Growth of the Electorate in England from 1600 to 1715* (in Past and Present, No 4, November 1969).
Ramsay, G D:	*The Wiltshire Woollen Industry in the 16th and 17th Centuries,* London 1985.
Reay, Barry:	*Popular Culture in Seventeenth-Century England,* London, 1985.
Roy, Ian:	*England Turned Germany? The Aftermath of the Civil War in its European Context* (in TRHS 5th Series, vol 28, 1978).
Sharp, Buchanan:	*Popular Protest in Seventeenth-Century England* (in Reay, Barry: *Popular Culture in Seventeenth-Century England,* London, 1985).
Sharp, Buchanan:	*In Contempt of all Authority: Rural Artisans and Riot in the West of England 1586-1660,* California, 1980.
Shaw, William A:	*A History of the English Church, 1640-1660* vol 2, London, 1900.
Slack, Paul:	*Poverty and Politics in Salisbury, 1597-1666* (in Peter Clark and Paul Slack, *Crisis and Order in English Towns, 1500-1700,* London, 1972)
Spufford, M:	*Puritanism and Social Control?* (in Fletcher, Anthony and Stevenson, John, eds: *Order and Disorder in Early Modern England,* Cambridge, 1985).
Stieg, Margaret:	*The Parochial Clergy in the Diocese of Bath and Wells, 1625-1685* (unpublished PhD thesis University of California, 1970).
Stieg, Margaret:	*Laud's Laboratory: The Dioceses of Bath and Wells in the Early Seventeenth Century,* Lewisburg, 1982.
Stieg, Margaret:	*The Diary of John Harington, MP, 1646-53,* Somerset Record Society, Vol. 74, 1977.
Stocks, H:	*Records of the Borough of Leicester, 1603-1688,* Cambridge, 1923.
Styles, Philip:	*Studies in Seventeenth Century West Midlands History,* Kineton, 1978.
Sydenham, S:	*Bath City and Traders' Tokens during the 17th Century* (in 'Proceedings of the Bath Natural History and Antiquarian Field Club, Vol X, 1905).
Taylor, John K G:	*The Civil Government of Gloucester, 1640-6* (in Transactions of the Bristol and Gloucestershire Archaeological Society, vol LXVII, 1949).
Underdown, David:	*The Problem of Popular Allegiance in the English Civil War* (in TRHS, 5th Series, vol 31, 1981).
Underdown, David	*The Chalk and the Cheese: Contrasts among the English Clubmen* (in Past and Present, No 15, November 1979).
Underdown, David:	*What was the English Revolution?* (in History Today, March 1984).
Underdown, David:	*Pride's Purge,* Oxford, 1971.
Underdown, David:	*Revel, Riot and Rebellion, 1603-1660,* Oxford, 1985.
Underdown, David:	*Royalist Conspiracy in England, 1649-1660,* New Haven, 1960.
Underdown, David:	*Somerset in the Civil War and Interregnum,* Newton Abbot, 1973.
Warner, Rev. Richard:	*The History of Bath,* Bath, 1801.
Williams, J A:	*Post Reformation Catholicism in Bath,* Vol 1, Catholic Record Society, 1975.
Wilson, Charles:	*England's Apprenticeship, 1603-1763,* London, 1965.
Wood, A C:	*Nottinghamshire in the Civil War,* Oxford, 1937.
Worden, Blair:	*Stuart England,* Oxford, 1986.
Worden, Blair:	*The Rump Parliament,* Cambridge, 1972.
Wrightson, Keith:	*English Society,* 1580-1680, London, 1982.

Wrightson, K and
Levine, D: *Poverty and Piety in an English Village: Terling, 1525-1700,* Toronto, 1980.

Wroughton, John: *An English Community at War, 1642-1646* (in History Review, No. 10, September 1991).

Wroughton, John: *Puritanism and Traditionalsim: Cultural and Political Division in Bath, 1620 - 1662* (in Bath History, Vol 4, 1992, ed. Trevor Fawcett).

Wroughton, John: *The Community of Bath and North-East Somerset and the Great Civil War* (unpublished PhD thesis for the University of Bristol, 1990).

Index